The Origins of Israel, 1882–1948

SOURCES IN MODERN JEWISH HISTORY

Series Editor

David Sorkin

The Origins of
Israel

1882–1948

A Documentary History

Edited by

ERAN KAPLAN

and

DEREK J. PENSLAR

The University of Wisconsin Press

The University of Wisconsin Press
1930 Monroe Street, 3rd Floor
Madison, Wisconsin 53711-2059
uwpress.wisc.edu

3 Henrietta Street
London WC2E 8LU, England
eurospanbookstore.com

Printed in the United States of America

Library of Congress Cataloging-in-Publication Data
The origins of Israel, 1882–1948: a documentary history /
edited by Eran Kaplan and Derek J. Penslar.
p.   cm.—(Sources in modern Jewish history /
David Sorkin, series editor)
Includes bibliographical references.
ISBN 978-0-299-28494-7 (pbk.: alk. paper)
ISBN 978-0-299-28493-0 (e-book)
1. Jews—Palestine—History—19th century—Sources.
2. Jews—Palestine—History—20th century—Sources.
3. Palestine—History—1799–1917—Sources.
4. Palestine—History—1917–1948—Sources.
5. Israel—History—Sources.
6. Israel—History—Declaration of Independence, 1948—Sources.
7. Zionism—Palestine—History—Sources.
I. Kaplan, Eran.   II. Penslar, Derek Jonathan.
III. Sorkin, David.   IV. Series: Sources in modern Jewish history.
DS125.075 2011
956.94′04—dc23
2011018955

Contents

Contents

Acknowledgments

The editors are grateful to David Sorkin, editor of the Sources in Modern Jewish History series for the University of Wisconsin Press. Marganit Weinberger-Rotman translated most of the Hebrew texts. Erin Hochman and Denis Kozlov provided translations from German and Russian, respectively. Special thanks are due to Hillel Gruenberg and Alexander Kaye, who located, translated, and annotated documents 22 and 27.

The staffs of the Central Zionist Archive, the Municipal Archives of Tel Aviv-Yafo, the Lavon Institute for Labour Research, the Center for Jewish History, the National and Hebrew University Library, Harvard's Widener Library, and the New York Public Library extended the editors every courtesy. Publishers and other copyright holders who graciously provided permissions to use images, maps, and previously published texts are acknowledged where these materials appear throughout the volume. Portions of the book's introductory sections were adapted from Derek Penslar's chapter in *The Illustrated History of the Jewish People*, edited by Nicholas de Lange (Toronto: Key Porter Books, 1997).

The editors' undergraduates at Princeton, Toronto, Harvard, and Columbia had the opportunity to read these documents as the volume was taking form, and we were gratified by their positive response. Josh and Talia Penslar transcribed documents, and Yonatan, Maya, and Tal Kaplan provided moral support.

This book is dedicated to the memory of Eran Kaplan's grandparents, Tova and Gutman Rabinovich and Ida and Julius Kaplan, and of Derek's mentor, Richard A. Webster.

ERAN KAPLAN, Princeton
DEREK PENSLAR, Toronto

The Origins of Israel, 1882–1948

Introduction

This reader provides a documentary history of the Yishuv, Palestine's Jewish community, from the beginnings of Zionist settlement in 1882 to Israel's establishment in 1948. It brings to the English-speaking world many sources that were previously unpublished or available only in Hebrew or other foreign languages. And it is different from other document collections or textbooks on the history of Zionism in its focus on Palestine rather than the Diaspora, and on social, economic, and cultural history as opposed to Zionist thought, high politics, and diplomacy.[1] Political and military affairs receive due attention within a broader framework of the construction of a new Jewish society in the Land of Israel. This book offers a holistic history of the process by which a small enclave of Orthodox Jews, numbering some 25,000 in 1880, was transformed within sixty-five years into a secular proto-state with well-developed political, military, and economic institutions, a vigorous Hebrew culture, and around 600,000 inhabitants.

The reader complements the recently reissued volume *Israel in the Middle East*, a documentary history focusing mainly on Israel since 1948.[2] This important work has a section on the pre-1948 period, but the documents are mostly related to diplomatic history or the origins of the Arab–Israeli conflict. Documents on these topics are also available on the Internet from the Israeli Foreign Ministry and many educational institutions and advocacy groups. Here, however, we have a different purview: to trace the Yishuv's internal development, the interplay between politics and culture, immigration and economics, ideology and material reality.

The Origins of Israel, 1882–1948 seeks to be innovative in other ways as well. Many of the documents were penned by leaders of the Zionist labor movement, which was the hegemonic political and cultural force during the Yishuv's formative decades. Appropriate attention is paid as well to Revisionism and other forms of right-wing Zionism, which, no less than Labor, strove to transform the old Diaspora Jew into a New Hebrew. The views of Orthodox Zionists and ultra-Orthodox, anti-Zionists, bourgeois urban intellectuals and artists, and apolitical functionaries are offered, thus mitigating the common tendency to identify the Yishuv with Labor Zionism *tout court*. Where possible, we have recovered voices of ordinary Jews, far from elite circles: factory workers and shopkeepers, pioneer farm wives and women workers. When we have dealt with subjects more familiar to the English reader, such as the origins of the Arab–Israeli conflict, we have included archival documents often cited in scholarly literature but never reproduced in full. When read in their entirety, such documents emerge as products of a time of crisis that demanded decisive action, yet whose consequences were unforeseeable. Taken together, the documents in this reader convey the ferment, energy, and anxiety that permeated the Zionist project from its inception to Israel's creation and beyond.

Each document is preceded by introductory material that provides background and biographical information. After the document, notes identify foreign language terms, historical personages and events, and references to works from the Jewish literary canon. Although the notes in the documents refer to relevant information elsewhere in the volume, each document is self-standing, and the book does not need to be read in any fixed order. That said, the book's sections correspond to certain overarching themes and chronological periods in the history of the Yishuv in its transition from foothold to state.

Section I covers the period from the beginning of Zionist colonization in the 1880s up to World War I. Sections II, III, and IV cover different aspects of the Yishuv over the two decades between the world wars. Section II traces social, economic, and political development; section III focuses on the invention and dissemination of a new Hebrew culture; and section IV deals with Jewish–Arab conflict. Sections V and VI deal with two related yet separate subjects: World War II and the Holocaust on the one hand, and on the other, the diplomatic and military struggle for Jewish statehood from 1945 until 1948.

It is the editors' intent for this book to be used as a classroom resource that might accompany a textbook or stand alone. As a stand-alone source, a documentary history can be more challenging than a textbook but also more rewarding. It does not provide a smooth and coherent narrative of the past but rather presents the reader with the sources upon which historical narratives are based. Textbooks present mediated history; documents offer immediate access to the past. Although many of the sources in this book have been translated from other languages, and some have been edited for style or abridged, they convey the mood of their era, the sense of what it was like to actually be in the

Palestine of many decades past. Unmediated confrontation with the past, however, can bring with it a sense of distance and strangeness, for as L. P. Hartley memorably wrote, "The past is a foreign country; they do things differently there."[3] At times, readers of this book will indeed feel as if they are treading on foreign soil, not only because the documents were produced thousands of miles away but also because of massive changes over time in how people construct social reality and communicate, in what they feel and how they feel it.

This much would be true for any collection of historical documents. In the case of the Zionist project, however, the pedagogic value of documents is especially great, as is the potential of these documents to stimulate complicated feelings among readers. There is probably no part of the world more closely observed and fiercely contested than Palestine. (Even its name is controversial; here we use "Palestine" in a value-neutral sense, as a territory not a polity.) It is central to the Jewish, Christian, and Muslim civilizations that claim more than half the world's population. Ancient historical memories have powerful contemporary applications. In the Jewish tradition, the territory is called "the Land of Israel" (*Eretz Yisrael*). According to the Hebrew Bible the land was promised by God to the descendants of the patriarch Jacob, who after a struggle with a divine being took on the name "Israel" (literally, "wrestled with God"). Christianity inherited the notion of Palestine as a Holy Land (*terra sancta*) whose sanctity was enhanced and rendered specifically Christian through Jesus' life and death on its soil. From its beginnings, Islam sanctified Jerusalem, and in particular the site of the ancient Jewish temples, to which, according to the Muslim tradition, the Prophet Mohammed undertook a miraculous night journey from Mecca and then to heaven (the *isra* and *miraj*). By the Middle Ages, Islam had developed a notion of Palestine as a whole as a sacred land, though not as central as the sacred cities of Mecca and Medina or, for Shi'ites, the holy cities of central Iraq.

In modern times, in the Middle East Palestine took on new meaning as an object of Western colonialism. From the mid-nineteenth century, Palestine became a site of large-scale Christian pilgrimage from the West, and the European Great Powers exerted diplomatic influence over Palestine by establishing consulates and protecting the interests of the land's Christian inhabitants (and at times its Jewish ones). The end of the First World War brought with it direct British rule over Palestine in the form of a mandate from the League of Nations. Throughout this period and after Israel's establishment in 1948, Israel was perceived throughout the Middle East as an outpost of Western colonialism because most of its population originated in Europe, and the Zionist movement fostered close relations with the West. Israel is viewed in this light throughout much of the world in our own day.

On top of all these factors, Israel is a Jewish state and thus a target for the complex, highly charged feelings that many people harbor toward Judaism and Jews. Israel's founding shortly after the Holocaust links the two historical events in popular imagination. (In fact, although the Holocaust deeply affected the Yishuv, it did not inexorably lead to Israel's creation, as shown in sections V and VI.) In many Western countries, Israel's triumphs and misdeeds alike provide fuel for working through guilt over having taken part in the genocide or standing on the sidelines while it happened. Also in the West, Jews are prominent in journalism, the arts, and academia, and Israel is often of great concern to them, although Jewish views on Israel range enormously from strident support to harsh condemnation.

Israel is thus at the center of an array of vectors, with multiple, often un-related points of origin but a common point of arrival. As a result the Arab–Israeli conflict receives exhaustive journalistic coverage throughout the globe and is consistently at the forefront of the international community's diplomatic agenda. In turn, students may bring to the study of modern Israel powerful pre-assumptions formed by public discourse about Israel and representations of the conflict in the media, and particularly from the Internet, which abounds with inflammatory and self-righteous rhetoric from all sides. What's more, some students feel personally engaged in Israel affairs: as Jews (who may or may not consider themselves Zionists, and who define Zionism in myriad ways); as Muslims, Arabs, or Christians; as peace activists and internationalists; or as champions of pluralism and liberalism in the Middle East.

The volume of debate about Israel can be deafening, but the debate often lacks substance. Rather than rely on sound bites and indirect information, students must have access to original sources, documents that are substantial, not fragmentary, and that are neither selected nor abridged to further a par-ticular political agenda. The purpose of a collection of documents about Israel is to give students the opportunity to read and make judgments for themselves about a matter of world-historical significance. As mentioned earlier, there is already an excellent collection of documents on post-1948 Israel; there is also a collection on the Arab–Israeli conflict from its beginnings to the present.[4] There is no understanding the conflict, however, without an appreciation of the ideas, sensibilities, and practices that characterized the founding generations of the state of Israel. Besides, there is little pedagogical value in presenting the history of complex societies solely through the lens of the disputes between them. Few students of modern Egypt or Syria would expect to understand these countries by reading only about their wars with Israel.

True, Israel is different from its neighbors in that it was established by immigrants within an indigenous population. In this sense Israel is similar to the settler–colonial societies of the New World, Australia, and South Africa, where encounters and conflicts between immigrants and natives indelibly stamped the newly formed societies. Many of the documents in this volume testify to multiple layers of contact between Jews and Arabs as the Yishuv inched its way to statehood. On this issue, as on all others, the documents represent the past as their authors perceived it. Despite widely differing places of origin, social class, and perspectives on politics and religion, the authors wrote from a Zionist position that took for granted the Jewish right to a national home within the Land of Israel. The Zionists' views on Palestine's Arab majority were framed in terms of this overarching concept. Yet until the early 1940s, the Zionist Organization did not officially call for Jewish statehood, and those who did favor Jewish sovereignty argued continuously about its nature and purview.

On one level, the documents in this volume speak directly to the present, as they depict the origins of many of contemporary Israel's political and social institutions. Yet no less often the documents are rooted in a bygone era, the foreign country to which we alluded earlier. The documents date back to the turn of the nineteenth century, when political and social ideologies played a more central role in people's lives than they do in most Western countries today. Zionism is a variety of nationalism, a belief that people are linked by descent and common culture into nations that deserve autonomy, if not full-fledged political sovereignty. For many decades Zionism was bound up with socialism, international workers' movements, and various forms of revolutionary radicalism. These ideologies were particularly powerful among the young Jewish immigrants, mostly from eastern Europe, who created the Yishuv's dominant political institutions. These Labor Zionists clashed, at times violently, with Revisionist Zionists, whose intellectual origins lay in right-wing nationalist movements in eastern Europe during the interwar period. There was a substantial minority of Orthodox, religious Zionists, some of whom also had socialist views, and a block of anti-Zionist, ultra-Orthodox Jews who, under pressure from Zionist challenges to their authority, created modern forms of political organization to defend their anti-modern way of life. We thus appreciate that the Yishuv was rent by factionalism and that political disputes filtered into the nooks and crannies of everyday life.

No less foreign to many readers was the Zionist passion for linguistic revival and the direct association between the invention of a new Hebrew culture and

the psychic transformation of the Jewish people. In our own time, language
tends to be seen in an instrumental fashion, as a means of communication and
little more, but such was not the case in most of the world until the recent past.
How one spoke or wrote revealed, and determined, his or her social position,
and the beauty of one's inner soul was identified with the grace of one's powers
of expression. Nationalists throughout the world labored to transform peasant
vernaculars into literary languages, while Zionists strove to do the opposite, to
render the Hebrew of the Bible, rabbinic literature, and the modern Jewish
Enlightenment (Haskalah) into a lively spoken tongue. As with language and
literature, so too did the fine arts play a central role in European sensibility of
the early 1900s, a role today paralleled perhaps only by popular music in youth
culture. Yet whereas the Hebrew language clearly set Jews apart from others
and was thus a prime element of Zionism, Zionists had to struggle to place a
nationally Jewish stamp on other forms of culture such as art and music. Cultural
politics of any form were just as serious, and just as divisive, as struggles for
power within the leadership of the Yishuv.

At the heart of the endless controversies about Israel's establishment is a
question of strength versus weakness. Some see the Zionist movement as a well-
organized machine that shrewdly forged alliances with Western powers, built
up powerful, autonomous institutions, and assembled a finely honed military
force whose defeat of the Palestinians, and then the Arab states, in 1948 was as
inevitable as it was tragic. Others dwell on the Yishuv's minuscule size vis-à-vis
the Arab world, vulnerability to attack, and lack of a regular army and military
equipment. For some supporters of Israel, the country's defeat of the Arab armies
arrayed against it in 1948 was nothing short of miraculous. The documents in this
volume should dispel mystical, romanticized, or exaggerated notions of Jewish
strength and weakness alike. The Yishuv had strong political leadership yet
became mired in internal strife, benefited from international Jewish organizations
and British rule but came into conflict with both, and by 1948 was in a position
to fight for statehood but could not predetermine the outcome.

Zionism before 1948 was characterized by numerous and conflicting ideological certainties. Its leaders' public statements rang of authority, confidence,
and clarity, yet their tactics were more likely than not to be improvised and, on
occasion, desperate. Today, more than sixty years after Israel's founding, it can
be difficult to access that moment of contingency, when the Yishuv was gradually
accumulating strength but was not yet a viable state, and assertions of Zionist
power often ran aground of material reality. This era's events account for
Israel's creation; its memories inform Israeli society to this day.

NOTES

1. For the history of Zionist thought, the classic source book is Arthur Hertzberg, *The Zionist Idea*, originally published in 1959 and still in print.

2. Itamar Rabinovich and Jehuda Reinharz, *Israel in the Middle East: Documents and Readings on Society, Politics and Foreign Relations, Pre-1948 to the Present*, 2nd ed. (Lebanon, NH: Brandeis University Press, 2008).

3. L. P. Hartley, *The Go-Between* (London: Hamish Hamilton, 1953), 9.

4. Walter Laqueur and Barry Rubin, *The Israel–Arab Reader: A Documentary History of the Middle East Conflict*, 6th ed. (New York: Penguin, 2001). There are also two mixed-format textbooks that include documentary sources: Ian Bickerton and Carla Klausner, *A Concise History of the Arab–Israeli Conflict*, 4th ed. (Upper Saddle River, NJ: Prentice-Hall, 2005); Charles Smith, *Palestine and the Arab–Israeli Conflict: A History with Documents*, 7th ed. (New York: St. Martin's, 2009).

SECTION I

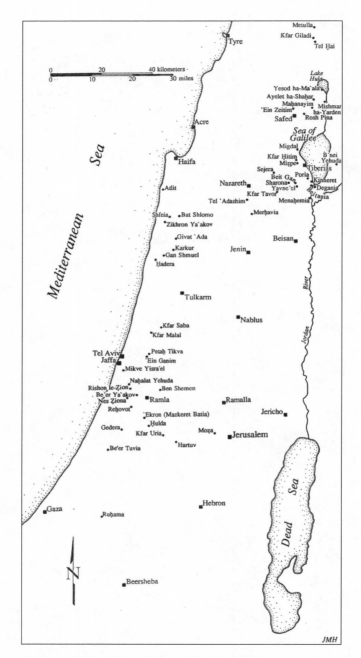

The Yishuv in 1914 (reprinted from Derek Penslar, *Zionism and Technocracy: The Engineering of Jewish Settlement in Palestine, 1870–1918* [Bloomington: Indiana University Press, 1991])

THE ROOTS OF
THE "NEW YISHUV"

In the nineteenth century, Palestine was part of the Ottoman Empire and was divided into administrative districts governed from Jerusalem and Beirut. In 1880 there were some 25,000 Jews and 450,000 Arabs in the area equivalent to today's Israel, West Bank, and Gaza Strip. Two-thirds of the Jews lived in Jerusalem; most of the rest were divided among three other ancient Jewish holy cities: Safed, Tiberias, and Hebron. About half of Palestine's Jews were Sephardim, whose ancestors had immigrated centuries before. The other half were Ashkenazim, immigrants from eastern and central Europe, who had begun to arrive at the end of the 1700s. The Ashkenazim were deeply traditional, and religious motives drove some of them to move to the Land of Israel. But for most, grinding poverty played at least as great a role in the decision to move. Palestinian Jewry, then, was both deeply Orthodox and wretchedly poor. It depended on charity from abroad and engaged primarily in the study of sacred texts rather than a paying livelihood.

In the mid-1800s west European Jews began to sponsor philanthropic projects to render Palestine's Jews more productive and independent. Modern Jewish schools and hospitals were founded in Jerusalem, and in 1870 the Paris-based Alliance Israélite Universelle established an agricultural school near Jaffa. By and large, the Jews were wary of these philanthropic ventures. But there was interest in building new neighborhoods in Jerusalem to relieve crowding in the walled Old City's Jewish quarter. (The most famous of these, Meah She'arim, was established in 1873.) A handful of Jerusalem Jews went much further, arguing that Jews should work the soil in order to be economically independent and to fulfill long-neglected biblical commandments tied to agricultural practices. They founded the settlement of Petakh-Tikvah ("Gateway of Hope") near Jaffa in 1878.

At first, Petakh-Tikvah failed, but the ideals behind its founding gained popularity in eastern Europe in the early 1880s. In 1881 anti-Jewish riots, known as pogroms, shook southwestern Russia, home to millions of Jews. Although few Jews were killed, the violence, combined with other forms of persecution as well as the poverty that afflicted many east European Jews, led to mass Jewish emigration, with a half-million Jews moving to the United States between 1882 and 1903. Some Jewish intellectuals and activists, primarily in Russia and Romania, saw the crisis as an opportunity to develop a full-blown Jewish nationalism and advocated immigration to Palestine. About 30,000 Jews made that move during the 1880s and 1890s, thus doubling the size of Palestine's Jewish community, which came to be called the *Yishuv*, or "settlement." (The term remained in use until Israel's establishment in 1948.) The immigration to Palestine was far smaller than that to the United States because of the relative economic backwardness of the land and the many restrictions that the Ottoman authorities placed on settlement by foreigners. Thus, many of the 30,000 who did come to Palestine were idealists of one sort or another— devout Orthodox Jews or, for the first time in history, avowed nationalists determined to create a flourishing Jewish community in the Land of Israel. The word "Zionism" would be invented only around 1890, but many of the immigrants were affiliated with societies called Hovevei Tsion (Lovers of Zion), which had a total membership of about 15,000 throughout Europe in the 1880s. There were, however, immigrants as well who were not Zionists but who had chosen Palestine over the New World for pragmatic reasons—a shorter and cheaper trip, better weather, and, depending on the case, family or social connections and employment prospects.

Jewish immigrants to Palestine in the early twentieth century retroactively called the immigration of the 1880s and 1890s the First Aliyah, literally "ascent," the term used in the Bible to describe the uphill journey from the Palestinian lowlands to Jerusalem, and by extension from the Diaspora to the Land of Israel. In another act of anachronistic taxonomy, after the turn of the century Zionists posited a clear break between Palestine's pre-1882 Jewish community and what came after, calling the former the "Old Yishuv" and the latter the "New Yishuv," the main difference being that the New Yishuv was allegedly Zionist whereas the Old Yishuv was not. In fact, many of the immigrants of the First Aliyah were Orthodox and not Zionist. Even those who were Zionists were usually religiously observant. Their self-image was different, however, from that of the Orthodox Jews who dominated the Yishuv. Rather than being a static community of pilgrim-scholars, depending on foreign charity or eking out a livelihood to support its spiritual labor of Torah study, the Zionists saw themselves as an avant-garde, preparing the way for future waves of immigration and laying the foundations for a revived Hebrew culture.

Four-fifths of the members of the First Aliyah settled in Palestine's cities, particularly Jaffa. The other fifth settled on the land and tried to earn a living through agriculture. These rural pioneers were by and large middle-class, middle-aged men and women, many with young children. In their demographic structure and social outlook, these settlers reflected the Lovers of Zion organizations, from whose ranks many of them came. Among this largely bourgeois community of early Zionists there was an important exception, the Biluim, a group of several hundred youths from the city of Kharkhiv in

Ukraine. The Biluim were dyed-in-the-wool socialists as well as nationalists. A few score Biluim came to Palestine to work as agricultural laborers but were plagued by inexperience and illness. The older Jewish settlers, who tried to become independent farmers, rarely did better. In Europe, the Lovers of Zion bought land for the first settlements, but the organizations, like the settlers on the land, lacked the money or expertise to make the settlements into going concerns. The settlements would have perished had they not been rescued by Baron Edmond de Rothschild (1845–1934), a scion of the Paris branch of the great banking family.

Rothschild was the sort of Jewish philanthropist who was not overtly Zionist but was deeply committed to improved circumstances for the Jews and the revival of Israel. Under his supervision (and that of the Jewish Colonization Association, to which he entrusted his Palestinian operations in 1900), the agricultural settlements flourished, but they were dependent upon Arab labor. This was so partly because there was not a stable and capable Jewish labor force in the land at the time. Also, the Jewish colonists frequently preferred Arab over Jewish labor because Jews demanded a higher wage and better working conditions.

The Lovers of Zion in Europe, and the First Aliyah in Palestine, were devoted to the cause of Jewish settlement but lacked political vision and organizational skills. The crisis in European Zionism was largely overcome by the spectacular rise to prominence of Theodor Herzl (1860–1904), a Viennese attorney and playwright who embraced Zionism in the mid-1890s. Herzl founded the Zionist Organization (ZO), presided over its annual congresses, and traveled widely, attempting to win support from Europe's Great Powers for what the ZO's Basel Program called "a home for the Jewish people in Palestine secured by public law." Herzl transformed Zionism into a popular mass movement, but he did little to promote the growth of the Yishuv, preferring to wait until diplomatic conditions favored mass immigration.

New approaches to Jewish settlement came from within a second wave of Jewish migration to Palestine. This wave was part of a far larger global Jewish migration than that of the 1880s. Pogroms, social upheaval during the years surrounding the Russian Revolution of 1905, and destitution drove more than 1.5 million Jews out of eastern Europe between 1904 and 1914. Thirty-five thousand of these, over four-fifths of them male, went to Palestine, yet only a fraction stayed in the country for more than a few years due to the difficulty of finding employment and establishing a stable life. In large measure, this Second Aliyah was similar to the First: a mix of traditionally pious Jews and middle-class Zionists who flocked to the Yishuv's cities and fostered their modernization. (In 1909, a group of bourgeois Zionists founded a new suburb of Jaffa that would become the city of Tel Aviv.) Truly exceptional about the Second Aliyah was a cluster of some two thousand to three thousand young people steeped in Russian revolutionary and Zionist ideology. This core of the Second Aliyah included many future leaders of the

Yishuv and state of Israel, including David Ben-Gurion (1886–1973), Berl Katznelson (1887–1944), and Yizhak Ben-Zvi (1884–1963). The accomplishments of this core of pioneers are all the more remarkable when one considers their youth—most were still adolescents upon arrival in Palestine.

These pioneers considered their move to Palestine to be a dual revolution, against both their own background and the gentile world. They had mainly grown up Orthodox and Yiddish speaking, but they identified Orthodoxy with passivity and Yiddish with moral disfigurement. Thus they became aggressively secular, struggled to speak Hebrew and, beginning a practice that would flourish in Israel until recently, Hebraicized their names. (Ben-Gurion had been Grin; and Ben-Zvi had been Shimshelevich.) After abandoning Jewish observance, some of the pioneers had become involved in Russian revolutionary movements, which promised to overthrow the oppressive tsarist regime and put an end to class and ethnic conflict. But anti-Semitism in the Russian Left and its failures to effect substantive change drove the pioneers to Zionism and Palestine.

The pioneers may have rejected eastern Europe, but they brought its political ideologies and operating methods with them. They immediately went to work founding political "parties," small groups of at most a few hundred members. The first party, Ha-Po'el Ha-Tsa'ir (the Young Worker), denied any connections with Marxism, but it was none-theless revolutionary in its call for the conquest of the labor market by Jews and the establishment throughout the Yishuv of a vigorous Jewish working class. A second party, Po'alei Tsion (Workers of Zion), was the Palestinian branch of an international federation of socialist-Zionist societies. The Workers of Zion adhered to a Marxist view that the Jewish state would emerge out of a class conflict between capitalists and prole-tarian laborers in the Yishuv. The party believed its mission was to organize the Yishuv's working class and prepare it for an eventual socialist revolution. This way of thinking appealed to some of the pioneers, who wished to see themselves as part of a process of international revolution and not parochially focused on Jewish liberation alone.

Eastern European political ideologies also help account for one of the Second Aliyah's greatest achievements, the agricultural collective settlement first known as a kvutzah and then later as a kibbutz. The pioneers who worked in the First Aliyah colonies had often lived communally. Communal living was a child of necessity, given the workers' desperate poverty. But the pioneers' hostility to private property, and their willingness to sacrifice what little they had for the common good, strengthened the commitment to communal living. This ideal was extended in 1908, when a group of pioneers coaxed the manager of the colony Sejera, in the Jezreel Valley, to let them farm a tract of land collectively for a year. The next year, the experiment was tried again, this time on land bought by the ZO's Jewish National Fund and located on the southern tip of the sea of Galilee. Named Deganiah, this kvutzah, or collective, flourished, and it became a model for other collectives founded in years to come.

The collectives were valuable to the Zionist workers' parties because they hired only Jewish laborers. In a pure market economy, Jewish labor could never compete against that of Arabs, but the collectives operated along socialist lines and on land owned by the ZO. The pioneers' aim of creating a Jewish national home and the imperative to create a functional Jewish working class led them to demand a separation of Jews and Arabs.

The Arab presence also stimulated the pioneers to develop military capabilities. Attacks on Jewish property by Arab marauders were common. Even without the Arabs, some of the impassioned Zionist youth would have been attracted by the idea of wielding force, because as revolutionaries they had come to believe that no political movement could be without a military arm, and as Jews they longed to overcome centuries of perceptions of Jews as weak, cowardly, and unfit for battle—perceptions that Jews had at times internalized. Some of the pioneers had taken part in Jewish self-defense during pogroms in Russia. The pioneers assumed that attacks on Jewish property were motivated by anti-Semitism of the type that Jews had suffered in Europe. Determined not to let the Yishuv suffer the humiliations heaped upon Diaspora Jewry, a handful of workers in Jaffa established in 1907 a secret military society, Bar-Giora. Two years later, members of Bar-Giora founded the Yishuv's first paramilitary body, Ha-Shomer (the Guard), to defend the Jewish colonies, first in the Galilee and then throughout the Yishuv.

By 1914 there were some 85,000 Jews in Palestine. The pioneers of the Second Aliyah had introduced political, economic, and military structures that would continue to develop throughout the interwar period. They had won support from the ZO to purchase land and inventory for agricultural settlement. These achievements, however impressive, were sorely strained during the First World War, when Palestine became part of the greater Middle Eastern theater of war. All of Palestine's population suffered, as the Ottoman rulers conscripted men and plundered the country for provisions and materiel. A British naval blockade throttled exports of food and other necessities. Jews, most of whom were not Ottoman nationals, were singled out for expulsion. By the end of the war, the Yishuv's population had plunged to some 55,000. In no way could the Yishuv be considered a viable economic or political unit. At this point, then, the Zionist project was still very much an experiment, a hypothesis and not a proof.

In this section, documents 1 through 4 present the founding of the first Zionist settlements and their relations with the rabbis of the "Old Yishuv," Baron Rothschild in France, and the Lovers of Zion in Russia. Documents 5 and 6 depict the highly politicized worldview of the youthful pioneers of the Second Aliyah, and documents 7 through 9 demonstrate some practical applications of their political programs. Documents 10 and 11 throw light on changes and continuities in women's roles in the settlements of the First and Second Aliyot. Document 12 emphasizes the centrality of the city of Jaffa in the New Yishuv of this entire period.

Letter of Complaint to the Settlers of Rishon Le-Tsion (1883)

BARON EDMOND DE ROTHSCHILD

Rishon Le-Tsion, some eight miles southeast of Jaffa, was the first of eleven agricultural colonies established by members of the First Aliyah, the first wave of modern Zionist settlement between 1882 and 1891. These colonies were the first attempts by European Jews to create in Palestine self-sufficient settlements that would not be dependent on funds from outside the country. Many of the older Jewish residents of Palestine, who resided in the country's older communities such as Jerusalem, Safed, Hebron, and Tiberias, had relied to a large extent for their existence on *haluka* (distribution) funds that were collected among Jewish communities abroad—the Zionist pioneers sought to create a new ethos whereby Jews engaged in manual labor, thus controlling their own social and ultimately political destiny. However, plagued by disease, lacking fresh water and infrastructure, and inexperienced with agriculture, the settlers soon turned in desperation to Europe for financial assistance. Nine of the colonies, including Rishon Le-Tsion, came under the control of Baron Edmond de Rothschild, who established a strict administrative regime over them in return for his considerable largesse. Upset about the loss of their freedom of action and association, the settlers of Rishon Le-Tsion rebelled twice against the baron's administration—once in 1883 and again in 1887. The

Source: Central Zionist Archive, Jerusalem: J41/72. Reproduced in *Sefer ha-Aliyah ha-Rishonah*, ed. Mordechai Eliav (Jerusalem: Yad Ben-Zvi, 1981), 65–66. Used with permission. Translated by Marganit Weinberger-Rotman.

first rebellion, directed against the colony's supervisor and agronomist, prompted the settlers to petition the baron in the belief that he was not aware of his employees' behavior and, if informed, would take the settlers' side. As this letter shows, Rothschild emphatically did not. In the end, the administrative staff was transferred elsewhere, but a new administrator and agronomist took their place. The document explores the gap between the idealistic vision of the members of the First Aliyah of creating a new society of Jewish farmers and the reality on the ground in Palestine that made realizing their ideals more challenging than they had anticipated before settling in Palestine.

Settlers of Rishon Le-Tsion:

I am writing to you personally because I am displeased and angry with you. You are the kind of Jews whom God deemed unworthy to enter the Holy Land and whom He left to die in the desert. You are not worthy of my munificence. If you do not mend your ways and if you do not satisfy me completely very shortly, you will no longer exist for me, and I shall transfer my benefaction to others, of whom there is no shortage. When you first settled in the Land of Israel, you were hunger-stricken and forsaken; you turned to me and asked for a 55,000 franc loan, to help make your settlement a success. I have since spent a much greater sum.[1] But you are ingrates; instead of being grateful for what I have done for you, you demand more, based on promises that nobody ever gave you. The only responsibilities are those you undertook and which you now renege on, because you are not working. You asked me for a well, and a well was dug, despite the enormous difficulties involved, and still you are not pleased and are asking for more. You claim to be settlers but, in fact, you are nothing but panhandlers, because you don't work and gain respect. You have the gall to take my donations and divide them among yourselves.

I sent a horticultural expert (*jardinier*) to assist you.[2] Instead of being grateful, you find faults and complain about him. He wrote to me about this, and I am writing you in response. I resolved once before to abandon you, but you pleaded with me to renew my support and I relented. But this is my last warning to you. I agree to continue supporting you, but I promise nothing. I will act as I see fit, and I will decide what you deserve to receive. But don't you dare put forward any claim because, if you do, you'll get even less from me. Listen to me well, and bear in mind: I want to support workers, not beggars. If you don't work properly, I will abandon you. You must obey my representatives to the letter. Those who do not obey them will not get my support and will be evicted from the houses I built, to be replaced by others more worthy of my generosity. You must follow the jardinier's instructions precisely, because he is the only one who can lead you to a respectable, self-supporting existence. God helps those who work, not those who beg. Remember, if I am not satisfied, I will withdraw my support, which will bring ruin and catastrophe upon you.

As for you Bilium,[3] know that Mr. Hirsch[4] is an excellent man who has your interest at heart and who tries to intercede on your behalf. I informed him that I am ready to help those who are truly willing to work and who have proven their worthiness by their conduct, diligence, and dedication to work. Only those who completely fulfill my criteria can hope to receive land and houses.

NOTES

1. Rothschild's total investments in Palestine would amount to some forty million francs (eight million dollars then), which is equivalent to at least 200 million dollars today.

2. Justin Dugourd, a Christian who had worked in Egypt and Algeria. Rothschild insisted on bringing to the colonies agronomists with expertise in Mediterranean agriculture. They strove to blend subsistence cereal farming with the cultivation of wine grapes, citrus and other orchard crops, and mulberry trees for the breeding of silkworms.

3. The Biluim were members of Bilu, a radical Zionist group based in Kharkiv. They are historically significant for their commitment to socialist as well as nationalist principles, but they were not a major force in the First Aliyah. The group's numbers in Palestine did not exceed fifty. Unskilled and penniless, they worked as day laborers at Rishon Le-Tsion and elsewhere until they established the independent, and ultimately successful, colony of Gedera.

4. Samuel Hirsch, the colony's supervisor.

2

Dispensation for the Sabbatical Year (1888)

The *Shemitah*, or Jewish sabbatical year, is prescribed in the Torah. Every seventh year the soil of the Land of Israel is to lie fallow, Jews who have been sold into servitude are to be set free, and debts are to be canceled. By the Second Temple period, the second provision was no longer an issue, and the third had been circumvented by a rabbinical enactment. In Talmudic times the first provision, refraining from tilling and harvesting the fields, was modified in various ways, but when Zionist settlement began it was still considered to be legally binding. Worried that the prohibition threatened the very existence of the fledgling colonies, Baron Rothschild and the Hovevei Tsion—Lovers of Zion, the name of several organizations that were formed in eastern Europe in the early 1880s to promote and support Jewish immigration to Palestine, chiefly for the purpose of establishing new agricultural communities—turned for assistance to Rabbi Yitzhak Elkhanan Spector (1817–96), chief rabbi of Kovno, Lithuania, and one of the most eminent Ashkenazic rabbis of his generation. In keeping with the tradition of respecting local rabbinic authority, Spector turned to rabbis in Jerusalem. These rabbis, representative of the "Old Yishuv"—the Orthodox, pre- and non-Zionist Jewish community of Palestine that took form over the century before the onset of the First Aliyah—rejected the Zionists' pleas for leniency. Not wishing to openly flout their authority, Spector turned to the Orthodox-Zionist Rabbi Shmuel Mohilewer (1824–98), the first president of Hovevei Tsion, who met in Warsaw with the other two of the signers of this document;

Source: *Ha-Melitz* 1889, No. 58, 19 Adar 5649. Reproduced in *Sefer ha-Aliyah ha-Rishonah*, ed. Mordechai Eliav (Jerusalem: Yad Ben-Zvi, 1981), 2:151–52. Used with permission. Translated by Marganit Weinberger-Rotman.

they worked out an agreement by which the three would collectively issue a dispensation from the provisions of the sabbatical year subject to strict rabbinic supervision and other limitations. There were Jews who decried the dispensation as too lenient or too stringent, but it served as a model for many years to come. The document reveals the unique challenges that the new Zionist pioneers faced in their attempt to upend centuries of Jewish practices by trying to return to the ancestral Jewish homeland and to a perceived Jewish golden age when Jews resided in their own land and controlled their historical destiny. Yet the Zionist pioneers sought to set a modern course for Jews that would "normalize" the Jewish condition, by creating a society of productive laborers (as opposed to the abnormality—from a Zionist perspective—of the Jewish condition in the Diaspora where Jews as members of a closed religious community were seen primarily as unproductive men of capital and trade or as scholars).

The coming year (1889) is a Shemitah Year according to the reckoning of Maimonides' calculations and according to tradition.[1] With God's blessing, several villages, known as "colonies" (*koloniyot*), have been established of late by Jews who till the land and earn a livelihood from fields and vineyards. If we prohibit them from plowing the soil and tending the vines, we may lay waste the land and, God forbid, bring about the destruction of the colonies; several hundred souls may perish from famine. Therefore, in order to save souls and save the settlements in Israel, to rescue bodies as well as property, we have issued a dispensation for this year (1889) to allow the sale this summer of fields and vineyards and everything pertaining to agricultural work to Gentiles, provided that when the Shemitah is over, we give them back their deposit as well as a sum of _____, their profit, and they are obligated to give us back the fields, the vineyards and all the rest.

The text of this promissory note will be written by the Jerusalem Rabbinical Court, and it will be subject to their approval. Thus, when they sell the land according to this promissory note, it will be permitted to cultivate the fields and the vineyards. It should be understood that those colonists who have the means to hire foreign workers must not do any forbidden work during the sabbatical year; the poor, who cannot afford to hire Gentiles, should do the work themselves, but only with the permission of the court in Jerusalem, which they must consult regarding which types of work are permitted and which are forbidden.[2] All this refers only to the year 1889, not to Shemitah years to come, which will require new dispensations. And perhaps the Almighty, in his infinite mercy, will grant us success and prosperity so we do not require a dispensation and the Shemitah will be observed as prescribed by Jewish law.

All the details of the above-mentioned dispensation have been approved by us according to the laws of the Holy Torah, spelled out at length in other documents. We have also secured the approval of the esteemed and renowned Rabbi Yitzhak Elhanan, head of the Rabbinical Court of Kovno.

May God hasten our redemption so we can observe all the commandments regarding the Land of Israel as prescribed by Jewish law.

We hereby sign on this on Friday, the twenty-ninth day of the month of *Shevat*, 5648 [11 February 1888] in Warsaw.

Yisrael Yehoshua Trunk, Kotna[3]

Shmuel Mohilewer, Bialistok

Shmuel Zangwill, Warsaw[4]

NOTES

1. Rabbi Moses ben Maimon (1135–1204) was the most influential Jewish jurist and philosopher of the Middle Ages.

2. While the rabbis of the Old Ashkenazic Yishuv prohibited any labor whatsoever, the Sephardic chief rabbi and his religious court supported the dispensation.

3. Polish rabbi and activist in the Hovevei Tsion.

4. Head of the yeshivah and Rabbinical Court of Warsaw.

3

The Rothschild Administration (1890)

MORDECHAI BEN HILLEL HA-KOHEN

Mordechai Ben Hillel Ha-Kohen (1856–1936) was a writer, journalist, member of Hovevei Tsion, and founder of the League of Hebrew Writers. In late 1889, Ha-Kohen visited Palestine and wrote a series of newspaper articles about his trip. This piece criticizes the administrative system established by Baron Rothschild and again reveals the fundamental gap between the pioneering aspiration of the Zionist settlers and the harsh conditions on the ground in Palestine.

The charitable deeds of Baron de Rothschild in the Land of Israel are truly legendary; since our early history we have not seen such generosity, that a man would spend millions to carry out an idea, and a controversial one at that!

There is no doubt that the assistance the Baron provides to the farmers improves the conditions of the colonies (*moshavot*) considerably. The support, which comes as a monthly allowance, guarantees the farmers a steady income, providing them with a firm foundation and assurance against common and uncommon adversity. They have a benefactor who takes care of their needs;

Source: *Ha-Melitz* 1890, no. 13. Reproduced in *Sefer ha-Aliyah ha-Rishonah*, ed. Mordechai Eliav (Jerusalem: Yad Ben-Zvi, 1981), 182–84. Used with permission. Translated by Marganit Weinberger-Rotman.

when phyloxera[1] attacks their vineyards; when their children want teachers and schools; when they need water for drinking and irrigation. He supplies them with doctors and pharmacies stocked with the best drugs, and with synagogues, rabbis, and all their religious needs. There is no doubt that the Baron's administrators teach the farmers obedience and respect for authority, inuring them to orderliness, organization, and good manners, as there are many habits and behaviors that our brothers had better free themselves of. Let's face it, there are many practices and customs in their countries of origin that we'd rather not see transplanted to Israel. The Baron's bureaucrats teach the farmers good citizenship and the notion that the individual is part of the community; they instill a sense of nationhood and belonging to the land— something that the farmers' forefathers never experienced. The bureaucrats are authoritative and overbearing; they are the decision makers, and they demand obedience of the settlers. If it were not for the administration, chaos and lawlessness might have reigned. But now there is authority and the farmers must, willy-nilly, submit to it.

This may be a good thing, but there is no absolute good in the world. I have just enumerated some of the good aspects of the Baron's help. But "this rose has a thorn."[2] The disadvantage is that the farmer is no longer dependent on the rains and the soil, on the sweat of his brow, and on God's blessing for his sustenance. This, to me, is a great evil, and it pains me deeply. In my travels, I have seen fields that lie fallow, even though it is planting season and other farmers do plow their land. Why is this farmer not tilling his field, I asked my companion, and his answer was that this farmer was using his horses to carry bricks for the construction of the Jaffa–Nablus railway, because the management of the railway pays well. Another farmer did not go there himself but hired an Arab and sent him with his horses to work on the railway. A third farmer had not prepared his plowshare yet, and a fourth had been ailing since planting season began, even though we saw him in the synagogue yesterday. These are all excuses we used to give to the rabbi when he asked, "Why did you not come to *heder* [religious school] yesterday?" There was some truth in those excuses then, too, but the rabbi accused us of being lazy and idle, and he was right. . . .

There are many among the Baron's farmers who are lazy and who shirk physical work. This laziness stems not only from the financial help and from the conviction that even if they don't work the fields their income is guaranteed, but from a deeper reason, which perhaps absolves them to some extent. The reason, in my opinion, is the system the Baron's administrators have been using since the settlers of Rishon Le-Tsion rebelled and drove the officials out of the colony.[3] It is now obligatory for all the recipients of the Baron's charity to sign a contract saying that their lands belong to the Baron and that they are considered day-workers who have no claim to the property. Consequently, many farmers consider themselves strangers on their own land, are not sure of their position, and thus fear for their future. They are demoralized and look for ways to put away money for a rainy day. They supplement their income by means other than agriculture because, once the harvest is done, the crops go to the administrator's storage, not to the farmer's own granary and winery. According to the prevailing system, the farmer receives a monetary allowance that covers his living expenses, seeds for planting, and fodder for the cattle and is, therefore, obligated to bring all the harvest to the Baron's stores.

The unhealthy situation I have just painted is not immediately obvious because the colonies look attractive and everything seems to be in place. But if you have a keen eye and can find the key to a farmer's heart, you'll realize that I am not maligning the settlers, that what I describe is the bitter truth and it is indeed deplorable. . . .

We should also worry about the next generation: Will they be the farmers we would like them to be? The Baron decreed, besides Hebrew and Arabic, that they should also be proficient in French, so "they could read scientific books about agriculture." Since the fathers were not simple farmers but rather owners of small estates, who can guarantee that the sons won't reject strenuous physical work that is inappropriate for educated people whose inspiration comes from Paris?

There is no doubt that the Baron's intentions are all good and honorable, and that all his great and exemplary deeds stem from one source—enormous love and devotion to the noble idea that the Baron has fostered and to which he has built a magnificent palace. But we must all look at the colonies as an experiment whose results are not yet known; every experiment is fraught with errors, foolishness, and unintentional outcomes.

NOTES

1. An aphid-like insect that destroyed vines throughout the world in the late nineteenth century.
2. A reference to Song of Songs 2:2.
3. In the wake of the second revolt of 1887; for information on the first revolt, see document 1.

4

Truth from Eretz Yisrael (1891)

AHAD HA-AM

Ahad ha-Am (Asher Ginzberg, 1856–1927) published "Truth from Eretz Yisrael" as a series of articles in the Hebrew daily newspaper *Ha-Melitz* (St. Petersburg) in 1891.

His first important publication, the article "This Is Not the Way," had appeared only two years earlier in the same newspaper and established him as a severe critic of the prevailing mode of settlement during the first decade of Zionist (or proto-Zionist) activity. In his view, the "Return to Zion" that began in 1882 was premature, disorganized, and inadequately conceived.

Despite his previous criticism, Ahad ha-Am professed, in a letter sent soon after arriving in Jaffa, that "I live in the hope that . . . I will find an answer to all my doubts." In fact, 1891 was considered a moment of renewed hopes for settlement of Palestine; the Ottoman Empire had relaxed its entry restrictions just as new pressures in Russia had created masses of potential new immigrants, and a wave of newcomers had already begun. But given Ahad ha-Am's predictions, and the perhaps inevitable chaos accompanying any sudden mass movement of people, his hopes of finding matters to his liking were doomed to disappointment.

"I know full well," Ahad ha-Am admitted in passing, "that my words here will infuriate many against me." They certainly did. *Ha-Melitz* printed numerous attacks on his article, some from close associates in the movement. The controversy did abate after

Source: Abridged from Alan Dowty, "Much Ado about Little: Ahad ha-Am's 'Truth from Eretz Yisrael,' Zionism, and the Arabs," *Israel Studies* 5, no. 2 (2000): 161–78. Used with permission from Indiana University Press. Dowty translated the text and added notes and a lengthy introduction, parts of which are reproduced here.

a while, only to be stoked again by a similar series of articles following Ahad ha-Am's second trip to "the colonies" in 1893. The result of the first article, however, was to isolate Ahad ha-Am within the movement at a time when he was emerging as, potentially, its natural leader; the cost of "Truth" may have been the loss of any chance to implement his own ideas from a pinnacle of power.

Ahad ha-Am's own solution to the problems he outlined in "Truth from Eretz Yisrael" was to turn to Jews in Western nations to provide the leadership, organizational skills, and wherewithal lacking in eastern European Jewry. The immediate impact of this proposal was slight; within a few years the idea was realized, with a vengeance, in the emergence of Theodor Herzl and the founding of the Zionist Organization. Needless to say this was not what Ahad ha-Am had in mind, and by this time he had formulated his conception of a "spiritual center" for qualified immigrants after extensive preparation, as an alternative to political Zionism in the Herzlian mode. The publication of "Truth from Eretz Yisrael" was thus an important landmark in the evolution of Ahad ha-Am's simultaneous position both as Zionism's most prominent ideologue and its most important internal critic.

Most references to the article today, however, do not relate either to its importance to Zionist ideology or to Ahad ha-Am's own thinking and career. Its most frequently quoted passages are those dealing with the Arab issue. In large part, this is because it stands as the first, and for some time as the only, serious commentary with at least a glimmer of recognition that relations with the Arab population would be one of Zionism's most severe tests. Ahad ha-Am's warning in 1891 appears as evidence that, while Zionists of the First Aliyah may not have focused on the issue, they were at least aware of it. On the other hand, the article's stern condemnation of the settler's mistreatment of Arabs is often cited as confirmation and admonition by anti-Zionist writers and publicists.

In view of its landmark status on both sides, it is indeed startling to discover that, apart from a few incidental references, only two paragraphs in "Truth from Eretz Yisrael" actually address the issue of relations with the non-Jewish population there. The truth about "Truth" is that the Arab issue was not a major concern nor was it a major focus of those who attacked the article. In his response to his critics, Ahad ha-Am does not mention the Arabs. Nor did he again mention the issue in his second "Truth from Eretz Yisrael," which followed his second trip there in 1893. Nor did he return to the subject in any depth until after another trip in 1911, when the impact of Arab nationalism was evident to all.

To be sure, in 1891 Ahad ha-Am did see beyond what others saw. He saw the Arabs not simply as passive objects of manipulation by others but as actors with their own desires and aims ("From abroad we are accustomed to believing that the Arabs are all desert savages, like donkeys, who neither see nor understand what goes on around them. But this is a big mistake."). He recognized a collective dimension to Arab identity; their hostility to foreign intrusion was not simply a matter of local or isolated frictions but was potentially part of a general pattern of resistance that Zionism would one day face. He also never claimed that Palestine was "an abandoned land" (*eretz azuva*), a phrase that occurs with regularity elsewhere in Zionist writings of the period, sometimes even from those living in the clearly non-abandoned land.

In other respects, however, Ahad ha-Am's response to the presence of Arabs in Palestine did not depart significantly from the received wisdom. As the in-house monitor of the movement, he naturally targeted the empty optimism and fantasies that characterized much of early Zionism and took upon himself the role of forcing attention to the unpleasant realities and imponderable problems that others tried to ignore. In his list of obstacles and hardships that were being ignored, the Arabs were simply another item to be ticked off, and not the main one at that. The Arabs come *after* the problem of land scarcity and *before* the problem of the Turkish government. They were an active rather than a passive force but still basically an obstacle to be overcome rather than an opposed party that Zionism had to either accommodate or else mobilize to defeat by force.

In other words, for Ahad ha-Am, the Arabs, while possessing a collective interest that others did not see, still did not constitute a *political* problem. Ahad ha-Am thus subscribed in the end to the basic assumption about "the Arab problem" that differentiated this earlier period from the later era that began, roughly, with the Second Aliyah (1904–14) and the 1908 Young Turks' revolt (which brought Arab nationalism to the fore). Stated baldly, this assumption was: no solution is needed apart from success in the Zionist enterprise itself. This being the case, there was no need to analyze the issue apart from the established Zionist program, nor to offer specific proposals or compromises of one kind or another directed toward dealing with the roots of Arab hostility, nor (if compromise is impossible) to mobilize as required for a decision by force of arms. Thus, while his talent for puncturing balloons led to recognition of a larger problem than others saw, even Ahad ha-Am did not see its real dimensions. His essay is, in essence, the exception that proves the rule.

To Eretz Yisrael or to America? This question, which in its time gave birth to an entire polemical literature, has stirred almost no one in recent years. This is because the better people in both camps have, over time, had to make certain admissions. Those singing the praises of Eretz Yisrael admitted to their opponents that it could not, at present, absorb the mass of people moving from their countries of birth, especially merchants and craftsmen looking for an *immediate* source of sustenance who do not have the energy to prepare everything required for working the land and waiting for the fruit of their labor. And the other camp was also compelled to admit that America could not gather together in one place a huge mass of the children of Israel and establish them on the soil for the purpose of founding a *Hebrew center*. The true answer, therefore, is: to America *and* to Eretz Yisrael, the economic side of the Jewish question needs to be answered in America, while the idealistic side—the need to create a fixed center for ourselves by settling a large mass of our brethren in one place on the basis of working the land, so that both Israel and its enemies will know that there is one place under the heavens, even if it is too small for all the nation, where a Jew can raise his head like any other person, earning his bread from the land, by the sweat of his brow, and creating his own national spirit—if this need has any hope of being fulfilled, it is only in Eretz Yisrael.

And if so, if settlement of Eretz Yisrael is not an answer to the question of "what will we eat?" for each and every person, but instead to the question of the life of the whole community, then it follows that those going to America do so by their own decision and on their own responsibility, while the settlement of Eretz Yisrael is a matter for the people as a whole. Every step needs to be measured and carried out with sober and considered judgment, under the direction of the nation's statesmen and leaders, in order that all actions be directed to one end and that individuals do not, in their private actions, upset the applecart. But in order to appreciate even more the absolute need for unified and orderly action, we need to examine the current situation in Eretz Yisrael in relation to our own goal and to the stumbling blocks in our path.

From abroad, we are accustomed to believe that Eretz Yisrael is presently almost totally desolate, an uncultivated desert, and that anyone wishing to buy land there can come and buy all he wants. But in truth it is not so. In the entire land, it is hard to find tillable land that is not already tilled; only sandy fields or stony hills, suitable at best for planting trees or vines and, even that, after considerable work and expense in clearing and preparing them—only these remain unworked, because the Arabs do not like to exert themselves today for a distant future. And thus it is not possible to find good land for sale every day. Not the peasants alone, but the owners of large properties as well, do not easily part with good land that has no drawbacks. Many of our people who came to buy land have been in Eretz Yisrael for months, and have toured its length and width, without finding what they seek.

From abroad we are accustomed to believing that the Arabs are all desert savages, like donkeys, who neither see nor understand what goes on around them. But this is a big mistake. The Arab, like all children of Shem,[1] has a sharp intellect and is very cunning. The cities of Syria and Eretz Yisrael are full of Arab merchants who also know how to exploit the public and to proceed furtively with all those with whom they deal, exactly as in Europe. The Arabs, and especially those in the cities, understand our deeds and our desires in Eretz Yisrael, but they keep quiet and pretend not to understand, since they do not see our present activities as a threat to their future. Therefore they try to exploit us as well, to extract some benefits from the new visitors as long as they can. Yet they mock us in their hearts. The farmers are happy to have a new Hebrew colony founded in their midst since they receive a good wage for their labor and get wealthier from year to year, as experience shows; and the owners of large properties are also happy with us, since we pay them a huge price—more than they dreamed possible—for stony and sandy land. However, if the time comes when the life of our people in Eretz Yisrael develops to the point of encroaching upon the native population, they will not easily yield their place.

From abroad, we are accustomed to believing that the Turkish government is so feeble and so disordered that it will pay no attention to what happens in Eretz Yisrael, and that, thanks to its love of lucre, we can have our way there, and even more so if we have the protection of the European representatives. But in this we are also grievously mistaken. *"Baksheesh"* is indeed a potent force in Turkey that even state officials do not resist. But at the same time, we must realize that the top ministers are also patriots and great devotees to their own religion and government, and, in questions that involve the honor of either of these, they do their duty faithfully and no amount of money will change that; and in such cases, the intervention of consuls will sometimes cause more harm than good, as I have it from reliable sources.

In addition, we must remember that traces of modern culture have already appeared here and there in Eretz Yisrael. The Jaffa–Jerusalem railroad will soon be completed, and there is a report that a government permit has already been issued for a more substantial line from Haifa to Damascus. The blasts of the locomotive's whistle will undoubtedly bring great changes to the land and its inhabitants, and our work will be even harder than before. . . . And when we add to this the general obstacles, material and moral, that any mass immigration of people coming to settle in a new country encounter in their path—and even more when their intent is to change their entire way of life, to transform themselves from merchants into workers of the soil—then, if we truly and seriously seek to achieve our end in the land of our fathers, we will no longer be able to conceal from ourselves the fact that we are setting forth in a massive war and that such a war requires extensive preparations: it requires overall planning to delineate in advance all future actions, and it requires good weapons—not sword and spear, but a mighty will and total unity—and above all it requires skilled leaders, suitably trained, who will go before the populace, who will bring together and organize all the activities in accord with the requisites of the goal, and no one will defy them. Only under these conditions can we hope that, despite all the obstacles, the doable will be done and we will be well able to overcome,[2] because nothing can stand against the will and unity of an entire people.

The basic principle upon which all rests is thus not the *quantity* of our actions, but their *quality*, and from this viewpoint we must survey the current state of our affairs in Eretz Yisrael if we are not to deceive ourselves and those who believe in us. [. . .]

I know full well that my words here will infuriate many against me, but I consider it a sacred task to publish the truth: up to this very day we have no experience on which we can rely that can tell us what to expect from the new vineyards in Eretz Yisrael. All the colonies, old and new, are blindly following the agricultural experts sent by the Benefactor.[3] If Rishon Le-Tsion begins planting Bardello grapes, henceforth the entire nation plants Bardello, and if the planters in Rishon go back to Malbec grapes, it comes to pass that the entire nation gropes in the darkest corners for Malbec — without noticing that all of these French guests are only experiments on the sacred soil and that the result is yet uncertain. Moreover: despite the promises of the French specialists and despite the lies spread in the journals, *the wine did not turn out well in Rishon Le-Tsion last year and could not be sold in Europe.* To be sure it is possible, as the experts say, that this was due to various circumstantial causes and that we should not yet despair; but for all that, *so far there isn't a glimmer of anything beyond high hopes* — hopes that cannot remain in suspense forever. That is to say, it is possible that the new wine will not bring a good price in distant markets after costs of transport and custom duties, and then it will be sold in limited quantities, domestically and in the region, and if our brothers plant tens of thousands of vines at once, then where will all this flow of wine back up and what will be its price? If wealthy investors living abroad put only a part of their money in vineyards in Eretz Yisrael, and do not get fifty percent back, by their way of thinking it is not a tragedy. But those of modest means or the poor who have put all their money into working a small vineyard and have waited with bated breath for the jubilant day when every man shall sit under his vine and celebrate to the tune of the jangling silver that his wine will bring — if *they* have miscalculated, and the income of the vineyard is not even enough on which to live, then what will be with them and with the settling of Eretz Yisrael?

This view of the current planting of vineyards, and the danger posed to settlement built on such a foundation, is not mine alone, but is shared by most of those who know Eretz Yisrael. The more sensitive add that it is a bad moral commentary on our people if it aspires to make its land into liquor, to convert the holy earth into a vast field of intoxication—and perhaps such an "idealistic" claim also has a grain of truth. Be that as it may, there is no doubt that, if the movement sets out from a pure source and relies on credible information, then it would never take this form. All those who want to get rich and do not want to work would then seek their fortunes elsewhere, and only those of Israel who cherish the land and its cultivation for itself, and not for the sake of huge earnings, will come: people who are truly and simply fed up with a life of degradation and meaninglessness and will go to the land of their fathers in firm determination to leave behind their disreputable traits, the consequences of commerce, and to devote themselves with a whole heart to physical labor with spiritual repose. Such people would not put themselves at risk by entrusting their destiny, and that of Eretz Yisrael, to a conjecture that is not yet sufficiently examined, but would rather choose to buy cultivable fields and bring forth *bread from the earth* by the sweat of their brow, while at the same time they could plant vineyards in their spare time, gradually, without outside labor or huge costs. [. . .]

Whoever has not seen how land is now bought and sold in Eretz Yisrael has never seen a vile and vicious competition. All that goes on among the small shopkeepers and middlemen of the "Pale"[4] is justice and virtue compared to what currently goes on in Eretz Yisrael. When I arrived three months ago, there were only two companies of speculators (who buy land in order to sell it piecemeal), and already then we could see that speculation would become an obstacle to settlement. And behold it has come to pass! In only a short time, the speculators have been fruitful and multiplied at a frightening pace, and when I left Eretz Yisrael, I left behind *six* such companies, and undoubtedly they will continue to multiply, apart form the large camp of petty middlemen and agents, among them tailors and cobblers, who left their trade for this "commerce," and various swindlers among the *new immigrants*, some of whom, to their shame, bought land also for themselves and style themselves as "future colonists." All of them strive together and provoke each other and try to harm their fellow man at each step. And what methods they use! Any abomination, trick, or deceit is ritually pure in their eyes; by bribery they intercept letters and telegrams, they employ spies to slink around stealthily in order to uncover their rivals' activities and the dispositions of the buyers—and, all the while, profiteering wildly on the land while making Arab landowners wiser about what is going on. . . . When I arrived in Eretz Yisrael, some of our notable brethren there complained to me that one large parcel, with more than one hundred thousand dunams of good cultivable land, was for sale, but that the seller had decreed his price as twenty francs per dunam, and that it was "*unthinkable* to pay such an *appalling price*, because other sellers would hear and we would be buying trouble in the future." Three months have not yet passed, and one of the speculators bought the land at the "appalling" price, twenty francs per dunam, and even before he had confirmation of purchase others came along with an offer of *twenty-seven* francs. And when the owner saw this, he decided not to sell the property for the time being, hoping that the buyers' frenzy would go on growing by leaps and bounds. Another incident involved one of the emissaries of the societies, who had been trying for more than half a year to find a plot for purchase, and had several times concluded a deal; but, each time, speculators entered the picture and pushed up the price with their many wiles. [. . .]

And as witness to the lack of wisdom and order in all our deeds, here is one more spectacle, one that brings a blush of shame to my face every time. After a decade's work and the composition of thousands of articles and the travels of numerous learned wayfarers, we are still ignoramuses in all the questions related to settling the land, even in the basic matters where knowledge is essential. There is hardly any question on the work of field or vineyard in which you do not hear different and contradictory answers. For example, we ask the colonists: how many vines should be planted on a dunam of land? And you hear various responses beginning from 400 on down to 225. And the same thing with other questions. And likewise regarding the sowing of crops and the planting of various fruit trees, where everything is done according to rumor, mouth to mouth, and sometimes a single case, some stray word from the mouth of one of the "experts," becomes the foundation upon which all proceed to build, each following the other and also proclaiming to anyone who asks that it is an established truth borne out by experience. Is it good to leave land fallow every few years? There are those who say it is good and proper, and others who say it does harm. How many measures[5] will average land produce in an average year? The Arabs produce (according to rumor!) fivefold or sixfold. But there is no evidence for this—say others—because Arabs work inefficiently and their tools are ineffective, and they would produce much more if they farmed with European tools. Others claim, to the contrary, that local conditions are wrong for a European plow. Now everyone in Eretz Yisrael knows that many of the Germans,[6] and also the rich Arabs, use European tools, and this it would be simple to collect statistical information from different sources and to get a clear answer based on experience. And yet—no one knows. Have you, the reader, ever heard that almost all the houses in Eretz Yisrael are damp in rainy season and unhealthy, especially to those with respiratory ailments? You have never heard, even though you assiduously read all the news from there. But it is true. Moreover, according to expert builders with whom I spoke, this defect could be easily remedied by various means in the construction of the houses. Yet no one takes the trouble to investigate the matter. Also in regard to court cases over land purchases, where the need for information is felt on every side, we still grope like blind people in a fog, and we still do not have even one *reliable* person who can at least read Arabic fluently. And our Jewish brethren buy land for thousands and tens of thousands, without being able to check *clearly* whether the purchase deeds or building permits are properly written, and for this they are compelled to rely on rumors floating in the breeze. [. . .]

But before we become too astonished about the absence of knowledge in matters where we still lack experience, but which we could master from various sources, we should be yet more astonished that our people have not been able or willing to benefit from the experience we already have.

Some ten colonies have now been in existence for several years and not one of them can yet exist without support. The good news published in the journals, that in one of the colonies many stopped receiving aid this year, is a lie. In all my endeavor and entreaty, *I was not able to locate a single person living from the fruit of his land alone.* And why? In fact, is it in vain that the plower will plow and the sower will sow there, and his labor will yield nothing? God forbid! In Eretz Yisrael, as in all lands, he that tilleth his land shall be satisfied with bread,[7] and even in this year, though it was not a productive one, the traveler sees along the roads flourishing fields and grain-covered valleys. The Arabs sow and reap, the Germans sow and reap, only on us alone has the wrath gone forth.[8] But why?

The correct answer, to which all the more perceptive in Eretz Yisrael agree, is: because the first colonists brought with them a great idealism, and some of them a little or a lot of money, but they all lack the aptitudes and abilities for working the land, and are not capable of being simple farmers, of laboring, they and their households, a hard labor, and making do at the same time with the least possible. Not only the intellectuals, but also the ordinary folk among them are not overly fond of the work in the field that brings forth bread, and thus most of them in the end become simply vine growers, and we see them now sitting and waiting for their future profits, and because of future bounty they forget the present; they pay little attention to the garden behind their house, they do not raise livestock or poultry as they should, the Arabs bring them butter, eggs, and vegetables, and they buy everything at full price, and do not even always do the labor in their own vineyards themselves. To be sure there are exceptions, but these are all poor people with insufficient land. [. . .]

In recent years, a new immigrants' party has been born: the "Workers' Party," made up of people who have come to Eretz Yisrael to work for others as day laborers. With the encouragement of the "Executive Committee," they find work in one of the new colonies. They receive a good wage by local standards (1.5 francs per day), which enables them also to put something aside, and the administrators, who are honest men and true Lovers of Zion, treat them with kindness and mercy and try to better their condition as much as possible. Any worker of another nation in this situation would find no cause to complain overmuch about his fate, but not so the Hebrew worker in Eretz Yisrael. I specify "Eretz Yisrael," because from America we hear glad tidings also from the Hebrew workers: this one and that one found themselves work that furnishes a minimal living, yet they rejoice and advise their relatives to come too so that they too will find such joy there. But not so in Eretz Yisrael. Here those who look for bread and find it in exchange for their labor also think of themselves as sacrificing for the general welfare, and therefore feel justified in demanding recompense for this from the Jewish people. Many of them, with the passage of time, will despair of such work, which brings neither riches nor respect to its practitioners, and they will conclude that there is no future "higher purpose" in it, and they will become incensed with the community for which they are toiling, and the ungrateful community will neither pay them what they deserve nor buy them fields and vineyards, etc. Claims of this kind were published recently in one of the Jerusalem papers, and I heard from trusted colleagues in Eretz Yisrael, who know the workers very well, that this is not an isolated opinion but echoes the voices of many workers.

From this experience as well, we do not learn what we could learn, and there are those in Eretz Yisrael who are trying to increase the number of Jewish workers *artificially*, not from *natives of* Eretz Yisrael—which would be good and beneficial—but from abroad, in such a way that, in time, we may see a sight never seen before: the question of labor and capital before capital has managed to enjoy any return from labor.

But not this alone; in all things it is our custom to learn nothing from the past for the future. There is certainly one thing we could have learned from our *past and present* history: how careful we must be not to arouse the anger of other people against ourselves by reprehensible conduct. How much more, then, should we be careful in our conduct toward a foreign people among whom we live once again, to walk together in love and respect, and needless to say in justice and righteousness. And what do our brethren in Eretz Yisrael do? Quite the opposite! They were slaves in their land of exile, and they suddenly find themselves with unlimited freedom, the kind of wild freedom to be found only in a country like Turkey. This sudden change has engendered in them an impulse to despotism, as always happens when "a slave becomes a king,"[9] and behold they walk with the Arabs in hostility and cruelty, unjustly encroaching on them, shamefully beating them for no good reason, and even bragging about what they do, and there is no one to stand in the breach and call a halt to this dangerous and despicable impulse. To be sure our people are correct in saying that the Arab respects only those who demonstrate strength and courage, but this is relevant only when he feels his rival is acting justly; it is not the case if there is reason to think his rival's actions are oppressive and unjust. Then, even if he restrains himself and remains silent forever, the rage will remain in his heart and he is unrivaled in "taking vengeance and bearing a grudge."[10] [. . .]

So what do we do? To whom do we speak, to whom do we turn, who will go before us and who will hear our voice?

Israel's deliverance will not come from the favors of *individual* "benefactors," even though their righteousness is like the great mountains.[11] This, experience has already shown. We can also expect little from our brothers in Eastern Europe. Their material, moral, and political condition will not enable them to do great deeds, much less to take the lead. [. . .]

What remains therefore is to turn to our brothers in the West, especially in England, who have lately been very active on the issue of settlement in Eretz Yisrael. If there are really among these activists, as reported in the press, some outstanding figures who are natives of Eretz Yisrael, they might yet be able to make the crooked straight and put the whole issue into proper perspective. These people, who are accustomed to an ordered life and who know what modernity is, and who also have the necessary means, should found a large national company for the settlement of Eretz Yisrael. First they need to send there a commission of various experts, who will traverse the width and length of the land for a year or two and conduct experiments and collect accurate information on all the subjects relevant to settling and working the land. And after that it would try to buy any estate up for sale, doing this wisely and knowledgeably, with great caution and without hue and cry. The company would divide all its lands into two parts: land mostly for crop cultivation with a little plantation agriculture, and land entirely for plantation agriculture. On the former, colonies would be established at once, divided into plots sufficient to maintain one person and his household. The company would calculate the cost of each plot *with house, cowshed, and all the livestock and necessary tools*, all of this not extravagantly but on a *minimal* basis only, and then those plots with their improvements would be sold to those *without means* who are fit, according to their aptitudes and abilities, to be farmers in Eretz Yisrael. They would also receive reductions in their payments, as the company deems fit, simply for fulfilling the conditions put before them in advance regarding their way of life and their work. The company itself would work the land in the second category, employing Hebrew workers who have been tested and found worthy, and when each vineyard or orchard has been developed and is ready for sale, it would be sold to a member of the company, and the workers who worked it faithfully during these years would be settled on land in the first category, given a "plot" and all that goes with it, on condition that they live by recognized rules, and they would pay their debt little by little over a number of years.

In such a way we could acquire considerable land at an inexpensive price and without bringing on the Evil Eye; competition and speculation would be banished, because all those supporting various societies that promise them a vineyard in due time would prefer to participate in such a company and to buy a vineyard from it, also in due time, and thus there would no longer be a "buyer" for lands outside the company. Those who want to settle in Eretz Yisrael immediately as workers of the land would also find everything ready for them, and if they are truly capable of it, they will achieve their desire without huge expenses, and the destitute workers would also know that there is hope of recompense if they work conscientiously. And consequently, after ten or twenty years, we would find in Eretz Yisrael not a motley mixture of gold-diggers and indigent *exiles* who are good for nothing, but rather healthy, good, and honest people who love their work and live from the labor of their hands in peace and good order. People such as these would not stir up hatred from the country's populace at the first opportunity, as they would not provoke them and would not encroach upon them, and even if, in the course of time, jealousy might cause hatred, this is nothing. Because by that time our brothers would be able to secure their position in Eretz Yisrael by their large number, their extensive and rich holdings, their unity, and their exemplary way of life. [. . .]

NOTES

1. One of the sons of the biblical Noah; in Western civilization, often conceived as the ancestor of Middle Eastern peoples.

2. Num. 13:30.

3. Baron Edmond de Rothschild (see documents 1 and 2), whose support for the colonies was supposed to be anonymous so as not to antagonize the Ottoman authorities, was in fact widely known.

4. The Pale of Settlement, the region to which the vast majority of Russia's Jews were restricted from the early nineteenth century until 1917.

5. "Measures," *She'arim* in Hebrew, from Gen. 26:12: "Then Isaac sowed the land and received in the same year a hundred-fold (*me'ah she'arim*)."

6. A German Protestant sect, the Templers, began to establish agricultural colonies in Palestine in 1868. The Templers' successful farming techniques were much admired by the First Aliyah settlers.

7. Prov. 12:11.

8. Num. 17:11.

9. Prov. 30:22.

10. Lev. 19:18.

11. Ps. 36:7.

5

Outline for an Agenda (1906)

HA-PO'EL HA-TSA'IR

Ha-Po'el Ha-Tsa'ir (the Young Worker) was founded in 1905. The founders of Ha-Po'el Ha-Tsa'ir were inspired by Marxist and socialist schools in the West (especially in Austria) that questioned Marxist orthodoxy and the primacy of the notion of class struggle, and unlike other Zionist workers' parties of the period, they emphasized the role of conquering Hebrew labor and the revitalization of Hebrew culture. A. D. Gordon (1856–1922), a founder of Ha-Po'el Ha-Tsa'ir and one of the more colorful members of the Second Aliyah, became a fierce champion of Hebrew labor and the return of Jews to the land, while eschewing organized party (Marxist) structures. While the leaders of Ha-Po'el Ha-Tsa'ir championed the creation of communal agricultural settlements, they were not opposed to the idea of private property. Among the political leaders of Ha-Po'el Ha-Tsa'ir were Chaim Arlosoroff, Eliezer Kaplan, and Yoseph Shprintsak. Members of the movement were instrumental in the creation of the agricultural settlements of Degania (see document 7) and Nahalal, and in the creation of the Histadrut, the trade union federation (see document 18n2). In 1930, Ha-Po'el Ha-Tsa'ir joined Ahdut Ha-Avodah, the largest workers' party in the Yishuv to form Mapai (Mifleget Poalei Eretz Yisrael—the Palestine Workers Party). The document emphasizes the movement's commitment to the general principles of the Zionist movement (Jewish settlement in Palestine, the revival of Hebrew) while emphasizing the importance of labor and communal organizations in attaining those goals. Unlike other Zionist labor movements of that period (see document

Source: *Sefer ha-Aliyah ha-Sheniyah: Mekorot*, ed. Yehoshuah Kaniel (Jerusalem, 1998), 47–48. Used with permission. Translated by Marganit Weinberger-Rotman.

6), this founding document of Ha-Po'el Ha-Tsa'ir refrains from referring to class issues and emphasizes the need to cooperate with the various Zionist institutions.

General Principles:

1. One of the main purposes of the Zionist enterprise in Palestine is to take charge of economic, cultural, and political positions.
2. A necessary condition for economic control is the concentration of property and labor in Jewish hands.
3. The task of Ha-Po'el Ha-Tsa'ir in Palestine is to fulfill the Zionist mission in general and to ensure that labor is in Jewish hands.

The Tasks of Ha-Po'el Ha-Tsa'ir:

1. Protect the interests of Jewish workers in Palestine; increase their number, and improve their economic and mental condition.
2. Transfer work into the hands of Jewish laborers. Organize employment and analyze working conditions.
3. Assist in settlement activities of the Zionist movement by providing important data and information.
4. Ensure that local institutions and their activities are consistent with the goals and aspirations of the nation as a whole.
5. Raise the economic and cultural levels of the Jewish population in the country.
6. Make Hebrew the dominant language in the country.

Measures:

1. Establishment of communal kitchens, stores, lending and public assistance funds, laundries, and housing.
2. Creation of labor exchanges for the purpose of teaching professions, taxation, and introduction of new lines of production.
3. Development of small-scale business and handicrafts.
4. Sick and unemployment funds.
5. Establishment of libraries, evening classes, and organized trips and excursions.

6. Facilitation of immigration to Palestine.
7. Gathering and providing information about working conditions in the country.
8. Information and advertisement to encourage settlement in the land.
9. Maintaining continuous liaison with all the institutions involved with Jewish settlement in the country.[1]

NOTE

1. In addition to the Jewish National Fund (Keren Kayemet), which coordinated the Zionist Organization's land acquisition and settlement policy in Palestine, another organization involved in the Zionist settlement effort was the Society for the Support of Jewish Farmers and Artisans in Syria and Eretz Yisrael, more commonly known as the Odessa Committee. It was founded in 1890 by Leon Pinsker (1821–91) and was instrumental in establishing several agricultural settlements during the First Aliyah such as Hadera and Rehovot. The Odessa Committee closed in 1913.

6

Platform (1906) and Proposal for a Program (1907)

PO'ALEI TSION

Po'alei Tsion (Workers of Zion) was a Zionist-Socialist party. The party, inspired by the teachings of Ber Borochov (1881–1917), sought to synthesize Marxist notions of class struggle with Jewish nationalism. The party's founding congress took place in 1906 in the Ukrainian city of Poltava, and later that year the party's branch in Palestine was founded. The first document here is the party's Ramla platform, which was produced in Palestine—an indication that the party's centers of power soon shifted to Palestine. Among the leaders of the party in Palestine were David Ben-Gurion and Yitzhak Ben Zvi. After the First World War, Po'alei Tsion split into two factions. Po'alei Tsion Left adhered to a more rigid interpretation of Marxist and Bolshevik dogma and joined the Third International, the Comintern (it was allowed to operate in the Soviet Union until 1928). In Palestine, members of Po'alei Tsion Left created the Israeli Communist party. Those on the Right, who adopted a more social democratic outlook that emphasized the national aspects of the Zionist mission, joined forces in 1919 with the group of nonaffiliated labor Zionists to form Ahdut Ha-Avodah (the United Labor Party)—a party that would emerge in the 1920s as the dominant political force within the Zionist movement. This document

Source: *Sefer ha-Aliyah ha-Sheniyah: Mekorot*, ed. Yehoshuah Kaniel (Jerusalem, 1998), 48–51. Used with permission. Translated by Marganit Weinberger-Rotman.

consists of two texts: the "Platform for the Jewish Social-Democratic Workers Party in Palestine," composed in 1906, and the "Proposal for a Program," composed in 1907, which reflects the early Marxist nature of the Po'alei Tsion party. The two texts combined provide a materialist analysis of the social and economic conditions in Palestine at that time and calls for policies that promote workers' rights and interests.

A. Platform for the Jewish Social-Democratic Workers Party in Palestine (Po'alei Tsion)

1.

Human history is marked by national wars and class wars.

The methods used to produce basic necessary commodities and the natural and historical conditions of the production process have divided humanity into societies and classes.

Certain methods of production create privileges for the ruling classes, which result in class warfare between the rulers and the oppressed masses. The former wish to maintain and strengthen their privileged positions while the latter wish to revoke them.

Under certain conditions, when the means of production are no longer sufficient for the development of creative forces, the nation is impelled to seize a foreign economic base—territory—that creates resistance on the other side; thus war between nations ensues.

2.

An examination of social-economic life in Palestine confirms that it is governed by [a] feudal system. At the same time, there are signs of budding capitalism fueled by production forces imported into the country that revolutionize the existing order. The Jewish immigrants to the country play an important part in this process.

These signs of emerging capitalism are most evident in agriculture, which is governed by middle-size capital. In as much as it is possible to predict future developments, it seems that the middling capital will continue to prevail in the agricultural economy.

(A question remains: what kind of capital will develop in industry?)

3.

The capitalism developing in Palestine requires intelligent and energetic workers. Since local laborers are still inferior and in a poor state, the capitalist development of Palestine depends on the immigration of overseas laborers who are better qualified.

Capitalism, while it revolutionizes the feudal structure, slowly turns farmers into proletariat, as they find better investments for their labor force—only where labor intensity does not matter much.

4.

The reasons for the influx of large-scale capital into Palestine is a function of the nature of capitalism itself, which creates a surplus in the developed countries, forcing the capital to look for new investment in noncapitalist countries.

The reasons for the entry of middling capital are rooted in the fact that Jewish capital in general, and middling capital in particular, is driven out of countries of the Diaspora by national competition.

The reason why some Jewish emigration flows to Palestine is that large masses of Jews have been expelled from many areas of production and forced to emigrate. The Jewish immigration, which increases in proportion to capitalist expansion, must come to Palestine, because in highly developed countries there are too many barriers to its absorption.

B. Proposal for a Program

1. Maximal Program: The Jewish Socialist-Democratic Workers Party of Palestine (Po'alei Tsion) aims at concentrating the means of production and at building society on the foundations of socialism. The Party sees class struggle as the sole means of achieving these objectives, while the struggle itself depends on circumstances of time and place.

2. The national question: As for the Jewish question, the party aspires for national independence for the Jewish people in this land.

3. The question of aliyah: Convinced that emergence of a Jewish proletariat in Palestine depends on the productive forces that come here, the party will fight to eliminate all the obstacles that

stand in the way of Jewish immigration to Palestine and will demand that the Jewish agencies (Jewish Colonization Association, the Zionist Organization) create the proper institutions needed for the organization and administration of immigration.

4. The Zionist Congress: To further the interests of labor, the party will participate in the Zionist Congress as a separate delegation, distinct from the other parties in Palestine.

5. Jewish workers' movements in the Diaspora: Since conditions in the Diaspora cause masses of Jewish workers to emigrate to Palestine, and since conditions in Palestine have given rise to a working class, and seeing that Po'alei Tsion is the only workers' movement abroad to understand this historical process—the party will join its affiliates in the Diaspora regarding all shared concerns and interests.

6. The International Socialist Congress: In recognition of the shared interests of the Jewish worker and international workers, the party will participate in the International Socialist Congress.

7. Our urgent demands: A. Universal representation and the right to vote in all councils and administrative bodies in cities and villages. B. Free and open monitoring of all institutions financed by Jewish public funds in Palestine.

8. Trade unions: Since the economic situation of the workers might be better served by unions that comprise larger numbers of members, the party recognizes the need to organize the Jewish workers in Palestine in nonpartisan trade unions.

9. Philanthropy: The party is opposed to philanthropy as damaging to the morality of the Jewish population and a hindrance to the development of creative forces.

7

The Strike at Kinneret Farm (1911)

DAVID BEN-GURION

In 1908 Arthur Ruppin, the Zionist Executive's representative in Palestine, formed the Palestine Land Development Company (PLDC). One of the PLDC's first major endeavors was the creation of the Kinneret Farm in 1908 on the southern shore of the Sea of Galilee. Kinneret, which was intended to be a training farm for Zionist agricultural laborers, employed more than thirty Jewish workers. In 1909 the workers at the farm went on strike, calling for, among other things, greater political autonomy. In December, Ruppin and seven workers signed a contract for them to collectively work the nearby land of Um Juni, east of the Jordan. In October 1910, a different group of workers took on the task of collectively farming the settlement, which they called Degania. Degania would become known as the first kvutzah, the ancestor of the kibbutz. In 1911 workers at the Kinneret Farm again went on strike; the farm was eventually disbanded and replaced by a women's training farm.

In 1911 David Ben-Gurion (who had come to Palestine in 1906) was a member of Po'alei Tsion's central committee and served on the editorial board of *Ahdut*, the party's newspaper. In this article, Ben-Gurion recounts the short history of labor tensions on the Kinneret Farm and the broader tensions between the workers' movement and the Zionist bureaucracy, and between the pioneers in Palestine and Zionist executives in Europe. We also see in this document an early formulation by Ben-Gurion of a principle

Source: *Ha-Ahdut*, March 24, 1911. Reproduced in *Sefer ha-Aliyah ha-Sheniyah: Mekorot*, ed. Yehoshuah Kaniel (Jerusalem, 1998), 92–95. Used with permission. Translated by Marganit Weinberger-Rotman.

that would dominate his political thinking and practice in the years leading up to the creation of the state and in the early years of Israeli independence—the organic link between class and nation, the shared interests of the workers and broader national body (as opposed to more doctrinaire Marxist thinking that stressed the inherent tension between the interests of the workers and that of the rest of the national body or classes).

The bureaucracy is reverting to type.

We thought we were rid of this affliction—a bureaucracy that thrived during the days of the Baron's patronage but was almost done away with when JCA (Jewish Colonization Association) was instituted—but we were apparently wrong.[1] We now see a revival of the old bureaucracy system, under the name *Palästina-amt*,[2] which repeats the same mistakes of the old administrators; the vast experience, which has cost our settlements so dearly, is not enough to convince the new "colonizers" that you cannot build the Yishuv only through orders from outside, completely ignoring local public opinion. We now see a repetition of the old sins committed by imperious and malicious administrators who pay no heed to the demands and requests of the inhabitants. The affair in Kinneret is a case in point.

A certain "agronomist" was sent here . . . who spent his time doing what he does best, that is, drawing his weekly, monthly, or yearly salary.[3] A few years later, when the Palestine Land Development Company was set up, that "agronomist" was appointed director of the farm, which the company was to establish. Everyone in Palestine familiar with this "agronomist" knew that he was completely unsuitable for the job, both because of his ignorance and his personality. In addition, he was known for the bad relationship he had with the Jewish workers. In a general assembly of the executive board, the Palestinian members voiced their objection to his appointment but, as you know, in Cologne and in Berlin,[4] they don't listen to voices coming from Palestine. Thus, the project of building and managing the farm was entrusted to the hands of that "agronomist."

But the workers did not limit themselves to verbal protests. The workers of the Galilee, who were close to the site of the farm and who knew how important and necessary the new farm was for the Yishuv and for Jewish labor, being convinced that the facility could not thrive if that "agronomist" ran it—resolved to boycott the new farm for as long as the "agronomist" served as its head.

When the boycott was declared, the administrator went to Judea and there selected workers, motivating them with arguments about sacred work on a "national" farm and with glowing promises of fraternity and camaraderie between the "director"(which is how he referred to himself, rather than the derogatory "bureaucrat") and the workers. To our shame, about ten workers ignored the resolution of the Galilean workers and went to work under that bureaucrat. Naturally, those workers regretted their move as soon as they recognized the true nature of their boss. When their contract ended, after a year, they hastened to leave Kinneret; several left the farm even before. The "honeymoon" of brotherhood was soon over, and the bureaucrat's promises went up in smoke. There were conflicts and frictions between the workers and their director, and the turnover at the farm was considerable, because it was impossible to work under the "national" administrator. Thus, while the "non-national" JCA farm at Sejera[5] attracted the best workers in the Galilee, the "national" JNF farm at Kinneret[6] became anathema to Jewish laborers; no decent worker was willing to work there. The end was not surprising. For three years the bureaucrat maneuvered and schemed, sometimes cajoling and enticing workers, at others times firing the "rebels." He made empty promises and used ruses and subterfuges. The workers protested, staged several strikes, and more than once the directors of *Palästina-amt* were forced to come to Kinneret to mediate between labor and management. Eventually, the workers got fed up and, using the last resort at their disposal, they demanded that the Palestine office dismiss the "agronomist." It took three years of blunders, disputes, and all kinds of adventures for the administrators to finally heed the workers' complaints and accede to their demand. . . .

The bureaucracy is reverting to type. But times have changed, and so must bureaucrats, because circumstances have changed. Previous administrators dealt with farmers[7] whom they themselves supported and trained, whereas the new administrators must deal with workers who simply work for them; this small difference will eventually bring about a fundamental change in the entire administrative system and alter its character.

The farmer was dependent on the moshava for his subsistence, and the moshava, for its part, was dependent on the administration, which claimed credit for starting the whole settlement project. The farmer's property belonged to the administration, and so he had no choice but to obey the bureaucrats. The support and allowances they were receiving deprived the farmers of their freedom, independence, self-respect, and human value. People who were gradually becoming inured to subjugation, slavery, and obsequiousness cannot stand up to authoritarian administrators or rid themselves of their yoke.

Not so the workers. As our great Labor leader[8] said, the worker is doubly free: he is unencumbered by property and free from any [administrative] burdens. He is not beholden to the bureaucrats for favors and donations, and thus he is not under their sway or dependent on their opinion. Moreover, of all the social classes, he is the most independent, progressive, and active. Therefore, the worker will never surrender any of his rights as a member of the community in Palestine and as a worker.

How many times have we heard our "friends," and even those who purport to represent the workers from within the "true nationalistic" camp say that here in Palestine, the worker should sacrifice some of his class interests for the sake of national interests, and that class politics detracts from the general national enterprise and should, therefore, be curtailed.

But all those workers who have not been confused and besotted by "holy names" and empty, pompous phrases know that it is only deception and trickery. There is no contradiction between class politics and national politics. The workers need not compromise or give up one for the other. Of all the classes and sectors in our society, the workers are the only ones whose interests and needs are consistent with those of the interests and needs of the nation as a whole. The interests of the workers and the general national interests are one and the same; there is no discrepancy between them whatsoever.

NOTES

1. The JCA was founded by in 1891 by Baron Maurice de Hirsch to organize the emigration of Jews from Eastern Europe primarily to the New World (and after Hirsch's death in 1896 also to Palestine) by settling them in agricultural communities. Ben-Gurion here contrasts the JCA and its policies with those of Baron Edmond de Rothschild who took over many of the settlements of the First Aliyah.

2. Ben-Gurion is referring here to Arthur Ruppin's office in Palestine.

3. The agronomist was Yitzhak Berman who ran the farm from its inception until he was fired by Ruppin in 1911.

4. These were the sites of the Zionist Organization's executive offices.

5. In 1899, the JCA purchased land in the lower Galilee and founded the Sejera Farm, a training farm for agricultural workers. In 1902, several of the workers leased the land from the JCA and created a farming settlement. Ben-Gurion spent eighteen months in Sejera as a farm laborer.

6. The Kinneret Farm was built on land purchased by the Jewish National Fund (JNF).

7. Ben-Gurion is referring here to the settlers of the First Aliyah.

8. Karl Marx.

8

The Yemenite Immigrants and Their Absorption in the Settlements (1913)

SHMUEL YAVNIELI

Between 1881 and the start of the First World War, nearly 5,000 Jews came from Yemen to Palestine. Initially, the Yemenite immigrants settled in the land's old cities, but many of those who arrived in Palestine between 1906 and 1914 settled in the new agricultural colonies. Shmuel Yavnieli (1884–1961), a labor Zionist activist, was sent to Yemen in 1911 to recruit Jewish workers who might help the fledgling Jewish agricultural settlements in Palestine and allow them to not rely on Arab workers. While bringing the Yemenite workers to Palestine was a realization of the Zionist ideal of ingathering the exiles and the Labor Zionist goal of the conquest of labor, the reality on the ground proved to be more complex. There were growing tensions between the Yemenite workers and the predominantly Ashkenazi (and less observant) more veteran settlers in the colonies. The historian Yosef Gorny has described the attitude of the (Labor) Zionist leadership vis-à-vis the Yemenite workers as a case of constructive paternalism. In this article, published a year after Yavnieli concluded his mission to Yemen, he examines the absorption of the Yemeni workers in the colonies, and while he lists the many difficulties that the Yemenites faced in Palestine, he still recommends that an effort be made to bring more Jews

Source: *Sefer ha-Aliyah ha-Sheniyah: Mekorot*, ed. Yehoshuah Kaniel (Jerusalem, 1998), 175–79. Used with permission. Translated by Marganit Weinberger-Rotman.

from that part of the world, who were living under harsh conditions, to their ancestral homeland. Although in the wake of the rise of Nazism and after the creation of the state the idea of saving Jews by bringing them to Palestine/Israel was a staple of Zionist ideology, in the movement's early years there had been a tendency to encourage the immigration of Jews who seemed to be more fit to assume the mantle of Zionist pioneering and discourage the arrival of those who were deemed less physically, emotionally, or culturally fit. This document depicts this very contradiction at the heart of the Zionist idea, a contradiction that would manifest itself vigorously in the early years of Israeli independence, when the Zionist/Israeli establishment debated whether to bring Jews from Arab and Muslim countries to the Jewish State.

The Yemenite immigration has come to a halt. In the last year, between 250 and 300 Yemenite families settled in the moshavot [colonies]. The internal migration of Yemenites from moshava to moshava has also stopped. And no Jews return to Yemen either. Life has become more or less stable. One can look at the life of Yemenites in the moshavot and draw some conclusions.

A.

In Hadera, Petach-Tikva, and Rehovot, the Yemenites have all but taken over the spadework. In Rishon Le-Tsion some of them work in the wine cellar and others in the orange groves, rarely in the vineyards. Very few work for the farmers, and wagon driving they have not mastered at all. In Zikhron Ya'akov a few of them work in the orchards of JCA [Jewish Colonization Association] and some do occasional jobs in the moshava. They do not do any cultivation of field crops. In Yavniel, the JCA employs them in land measuring and other jobs. Some go to nearby Poriya to work, but very few are employed by the farmers. In the other moshavot in the Galilee, there are no Yemenites at all.

The newly arrived Yemenite comes from a place where he has never seen a plowshare, a horse used for plowing or a cart; he cannot easily adapt to the European methods of the local farmer. This requires physical adjustment, certain agility, and psychological adaptation, as well as a sense of responsibility. Agriculture and wagoneering require a more complex relationship (long-term as opposed to the more simple relationship with day laborers) between employer and laborer that includes: monthly work; tending to the farm animals (almost always entrusted to the laborer); yearly work, or five-year plan, involving harvest and threshing that are done on a contractual basis and, according to the custom of the land, are paid for in wheat, oil, etc. All these are forms of agreement between two sides that know each other well and have maintained a relationship over years. This does not exist between the Yemenite worker and the farmer. There is no mutual trust and everything is unstable and unpredictable, unlike the connection between the farmers and the Arabs, which have strengthened over the years and are not easily broken. There are financial deals between them and, sometimes, even bonds of friendship involving respect and also obsequiousness. The Yemenite cannot compete with the Arab who can show flattery while harboring hatred in his heart.

Thus, there are several reasons that prevent the Yemenite from entering agricultural work and wagoneering in the Galilee. You don't see new Yemenite immigrants or even older ones trying to approach a horse. There are Yemenites in Rehovot and Rishon Le-Tsion who have been in the moshava for four years and are still not used to working with horses.

But it does not mean that the Yemenite is incapable of working with horses or in the fields.

We see that the Yemenite has adapted to many jobs that require skill and energy. In Rishon Le-Tsion, many work in the wine cellar and operate machinery. In Jaffa and Hadera, they work in the cement and tile industry. Last year and this year, many have excelled in picking oranges. There are many outstanding and praiseworthy workers among the Yemenite agricultural laborers of Rishon Le-Tsion and Rehovot. In Zikhron Ya'akov, there is one (maybe two) who works with horses. We can see that they have a true desire to integrate into the moshavot, and that they wait impatiently to take possession of the houses that are being built for them, with their adjacent yards. In those moshavot where they already occupy lots, most of them cultivate those tracts with enthusiasm and skill. Some have bought cows, others raise chickens, and some (though very few) have bought donkeys.

And yet, when we examine the life of the Ashkenazi workers, we see that although a community of *fellahin* has grown in the country and continues to develop, no group of Jewish coachmen has formed among the farmers in Judea, and no Jewish sharecroppers among the farmers in the Galilee.

B.

While we rejoice at the revival of aliyah among the Jews of Yemen, we must also take care lest masses of hundreds and thousands immigrate here, more than the country is capable of supporting. At the same time, we should not aggravate our brothers and upset their lives, at a time when the nation is awakening and things are changing on a grand scale.

On the other hand, we need to double our efforts to help this part of our nation that is dwindling in exile and is so eager to come to the Land of Israel. We must facilitate their settlement here. History has presented us with a promissory note: twenty to thirty thousand Jews are ready to immigrate. We must redeem this note. If we don't—we are bankrupt!

Thus, if in the first year, all the energy was directed toward absorbing the Yemenites in the moshavot and providing them with temporary arrangements, this year we must accomplish much more. We must introduce Yemenites to field crops and cattle, so that they can find their right place in the moshavot, and in due time take part in the conquest of the land, when the time comes to distribute new parcels of land.

We have to mold the immigrants from Yemen, just like the ones from the north, and create a new type of Jew, one that tills the land and subsists on what he and his family grow.

The Yemenite, who is frugal and contents himself with little, and who has demonstrated that he is skillful and hardworking, should be able to make a decent living by working intensively on a small plot measuring a few dunams, with the help of advanced equipment, without depending on beasts of burden.

9

Founding Statement (1909)

HA-SHOMER

Ha-Shomer (the Guard), a Jewish defense organization, was founded in 1909 for the purpose of providing protection to Jewish settlements in Palestine rather than relying on Arab watchmen or foreign consulates. Ha-Shomer grew out of Bar Giora, a small, clandestine defense organization founded in 1907. Ha-Shomer was highly hierarchical and selective; by 1914 it had about forty members and around fifty candidates. Most of its members came from the ranks of the socialist Po'alei Tsion, and some members had been previously involved in Jewish self-defense efforts in eastern Europe. During the First World War, the Ottoman authorities exiled many of Ha-Shomer's members and executed several of them. In 1920 leaders of the Yishuv created the Haganah, a more comprehensive defense force, and Ha-Shomer was dissolved. In addition to its security responsibilities, members of Ha-Shomer established agricultural settlements in Palestine, including Tel Adashim and Kfar Gila'di.

This is Ha-Shomer's founding document, which was composed in April 1909; it lays out Ha-Shomer's main goals and its organizational structure. The creation of Ha-Shomer was one of the first responses to the brewing violence between Jews and Arabs in Palestine, though at that time most Jews did not see the conflict through a nationalist prism—as a political conflict between two national movements—nor did they assume that it would dominate social and political developments in the country. In

Source: "Tohnit ha-Shomer," in *Kovetz ha-Shomer* (Tel Aviv, 1937), 35. Reproduced in *Sefer ha-Aliyah ha-Sheniyah: Mekorot*, ed. Yehoshuah Keniel (Jerusalem, 1998), 370–71. Used with permission. Translated by Marganit Weinberger-Rotman.

fact, Arabs, against whom members of Ha-Shomer were supposed to guard the new settlements, are not mentioned in this document. What the document does emphasize, however, are notions of health, masculinity, and the development of militaristic values among the young pioneers—a manifestation of the idea of the negation of the Jewish diasporic ethos and the creation a new Jewish society that was based on such notions as strength, resolve, and self-reliance.

The Goal:

To cultivate a contingent of Jewish guards capable of carrying out the task of self- defense.

The Means:

1. To organize guards already operating in the moshavot (colonies).
2. To prepare the moshavot and the farms for the formation of self-defense units by creating the necessary conditions such as: purchase of gym equipment, horse-riding instruction, sports activities, the use of weapons, etc.
3. To improve and alleviate the economic conditions of the members by creating communal facilities and raising salaries.
4. To set up two funds: (a) Loans Fund, to enable members to purchase necessary equipment (such as horses, weapons, etc.). (b) Securities Fund, for the sums required as guarantees when the Association is contracted by a moshava to protect it.

The Organization:

1. The Shomer Association will be headed by a three-member committee overseeing all its interests. The committee will be elected by the members in a general assembly. [Note: the three members will appoint one of themselves as a representative to carry out negotiations with the outside world.][1]
2. The representative will enter negotiations with the committees of moshavot and farms regarding guard duties, etc.

3. All contracts will be written in the representative's name, and their content will apply to all the members of the association.

4. Any man, healthy in body and mind, who has served as a guard for at least six months, can apply for membership in the association.

5. New members must be approved by two-thirds of the vote. Note: When members suggest a candidate who may be of service to the association, they may submit his name to a vote, and he must be approved by two-thirds of the members.

6. Members are obligated to follow the orders of the committee, even when they deal with the members' personal interests.

7. When a member disobeys the committee's order, the committee has the power to punish him or to expel him from the association, on condition of approval by the majority of members.

NOTE

1. The three members were Israel Giladi, Mendel Portugali, and Ha-Shomer's leader Israel Shohat. Other notable leaders of Ha-Shomer were Yitzhak Ben Zvi, Alexander Zaid, Manya Shohat (the wife of Israel Shohat), and Eliyahu Golomb, who would become one of the leaders of the Haganah.

10

Letters from
an Anonymous Farm Wife
of the First Aliyah (1889)

About a fifth of the settlers of the First Aliyah established themselves as farmers in agricultural colonies. Most of the women in these settlements were farm wives, although some worked as teachers, midwives, and nurses for the Rothschild administration. A handful of women became in later years prominent public figures in the Yishuv, and some women of the First Aliyah wrote memoirs at an advanced age. But contemporary documentation of the lives of ordinary women is almost nil. Herein lies the significance of these letters. It is also worth paying attention to the traditional Jewish elements in the letters; they reveal that many members of the First Aliyah, while they were trying to upend important aspects of Jewish life (creating a self-sufficient society based on manual labor) in their daily lives, remained well within the Jewish tradition of their forebears.

We do not know the name of the author; her husband, Shlomo Kalman Kantor, was an engineer who moved to Palestine in 1886 and worked for Baron Rothschild. He and the author had three children, who are referred to in the text. The author wrote these letters in Yiddish and apparently did not intend them for publication, but apparently the recipient, the author's sister-in-law, passed them on to a Hebrew newspaper, *Ha-Melitz*, which published them in Hebrew translation.

Source: Ran Aaronsohn, "Through the Eyes of a Settler's Wife: Letters from the *Moshava*," in *Pioneers and Homemakers: Jewish Women in Pre-State Israel*, ed. Deborah S. Bernstein (Albany: State University of New York Press, 1992), 34–47. Used with permission.

Letter from the Wife of Kalman Kantor, Zikhron Yaakov, October/November 1889[1]

And we reached our place, on *Erev Shabbat* [Friday evening], after dark, and we entered the guesthouse. During *Shabbat*, I managed to look over the house that had been given to us. It was a walled house with three rooms and a cooking shed, as well as a large barn for the animals, but I didn't like it because it was outside of the town, in the new colony,[2] even though it was only a ten-minute walk to town; and the air wasn't very good there.

So I asked to get a house in town, and, fortunately, we found an available house of this sort in town, and it was given to us. The house is actually smaller than the first one, because it's missing one room, and it's at the edge of the colony, at the entrance to the town; but the air is very, very good there, because it overlooks the sea[3] and the area is inhabited by people.

Also, anything one desires that is sold in town is brought there by way of the end of the street, and as a result, we are the first to see the merchandise. The Arabs bring all sorts of things to sell: milk, eggs, chickens, wood, grapes, and different kinds of fruit.[4] And everything is sold cheaply: ten eggs for seven kopecks,[5] a chicken for thirty kopecks—and there are lots of these—a log [a liquid measure, about ten fluid ounces] of milk for 3.5 kopecks, et cetera.

So far we have nothing, because we have not yet gotten settled down completely, but if God pleases, we will see the time when we will have a lot of possessions. . . . It is absolutely true that after the *Pesach* [Passover] holiday, please God, the Baron will come to visit the colonies.[6] New houses will be built then, and we will be given another house, which will be larger than the one we now have.

And during the winter, we will be able to live comfortably even in the house in which we are living right now, because it also has a cooking shed and a large barn built of stones and plastered with mortar both inside and out, and only its windows are smaller than the windows in the house. Half of the barn we are keeping for the cow and the sheep and the horse, and the other half will be used for living purposes, if the house is too small. Many have already done this. Around the house we will make a garden. Our vineyard is far from the house, but it hardly makes a difference.

We won't be lacking for anything, even now. There is plenty of all the things that a person needs to keep alive. The Baron provides us with whatever is needed and required. We will be getting fifty-four francs a month, and E.[7] will also be getting thirty francs a month, and we are all living together, thank God, and we hope that with the proper attitude, our situation will improve in the near future. We don't have to pay fees for *shechita* [ritual slaughter of animals], nor do we have to pay for the synagogue, or tuition for schooling. The children are studying French, Arabic, and Hebrew in school, and they will be taught to sew with a sewing machine and all sorts of other handicrafts. There are four teachers at the school, and the children are taught dancing and singing as well. If, God forbid, someone gets sick—the doctor will treat him without charge, and medicines are also free and the midwife is available for those who need her without cost.[8] We have to pay bathhouse fees only.

After all this, I still yearn for Russia. The heat and the *khamsin* [the desert wind] are very difficult for people from Russia; in the winter it is raining, and this is the best time of the entire year, when we are able to live well. The winter season here is full of different types of vegetables and fruit that grow on trees. Twelve apples for seven kopecks, three liters of figs for seven kopecks, three liters of raisins for seven kopecks. For food, we serve compote and eat bread. It's possible to live well here if God grants health and strength!

When I came to town, the change in climate affected me badly, and on the fifth day after my arrival I got sick with malaria, God forbid, and I lay in bed for eight days. And even now I'm still weak and have little strength, but thanks to God, I have strength enough now to walk. D.[9] also got sick with malaria, and he too, thank God, recovered. Every foreigner who comes here from a faraway land has to drink from this cup, no one is spared. The change in climate has a bad effect. You mustn't drink water immediately after eating fruit that grow on trees, because it brings on the fever; also if someone drinks water while his body is still sweating—immediately the fever takes hold. You have to be very careful here.

We usually drink water here, mixed with wine or flavored syrup, or vinegar. The wine here is very cheap: ten kopecks a log. Spirits are also cheap: fifteen kopecks a bottle. The only thing that's expensive is beer, and it's warm and doesn't taste good. We have here geese, swans, turkeys, pigeons, and various other kinds of poultry—nothing is missing.

Our synagogue is very elegant; it's built like the synagogue for the neologics in K[10] but has even more paintings and decorations. The *parochet* [the curtain covering the ark] and the pulpit cloth are made out of red silk, finely made and embroidered with pure gold threads.

We also have a *hazzan* [a cantor] here, who conducts the choir on days of joy and happiness in our moshava [colony]. The Turkish governor came to visit last week in order to see the colony; he came accompanied by a large number of soldiers and army officials. He was honored greatly when he came, just like in Russia, when all the Jews would line the streets and greet him with songs and verse. A big banquet was made for him and his men, and they ate and drank and enjoyed their meal, and he left the colony very pleased.

My dear, beloved sister-in-law! Don't be angry with me because I have made you read such a long letter; when I write, I feel as if we're sitting face to face and talking, because I still haven't forgotten the tears you shed on the day we parted. Only God knows when we'll be able to see each other again. So, my deepest wish is that all of you not forget us and that you write frequently, and let us know how you are and whatever happens to all of you, so we will know that we still have relatives in the faraway land and won't start thinking that we were born amongst the stones of the field. Because my heart grieves mightily when I remember how we wandered so far away from our family nest, so the letters that you send us will be our only consolation. Write us as often as you can, just write.

We will be very careful to answer every single letter. Don't blame me for not writing until now. You'll understand that lately my heart wasn't into writing letters. In addition, I was sick—we shouldn't know from such problems again! I hope that in the near future I will be able to send you good letters and pleasant tidings.

I'm giving you regards from K.[11] Right now, with God's help, he is completely healthy; he doesn't know about this letter and will write you himself shortly. E. [Eliyahu] sends regards. He is quickly learning to speak French and Arabic as if they are his mother tongues; he's a fine young man—if God wishes, we will have a lot of *nachas* [pleasure], happiness, and pride from him. S.[12] and D. [David] give you warmest regards.

Letter from February 1890[13]

We've already forgotten all of the troubles and problems that I wrote about in my previous letter; because, thank God, our situation is improving as time goes by. We have already grown accustomed to our work and the conditions of life here, as if we grew up and were born here. We have, thank God, a good and pleasant life. Our house is full of God's blessings, and our table has everything that a rich woman in Vilna has—nothing is lacking.

Every day I bring home a basket of eggs laid by my own hens; in the morning we drink good, fat milk from my cows; we have chicken every day for our noon meal, while over there we would only have such luxuries on holidays. For supper, we drink tea and eat bread with delicious butter. We have never been as quiet and tranquil, without worries, as we are today, and I have never imagined a life that is better than the life we have today.

We planted all sorts of vegetables in our garden; we've been eating green onions for quite a while; we've been eating roasted vegetables and tender radishes all winter. By *Pesach* we will have, if God permits, new potatoes; and shortly the fruits will begin to ripen. We sowed wheat for eating all year round, as well as barley for our horses. We have a horse and wagon, which cost 200 SR,[14] for taking trips and traveling whenever we need or feel like going.

We also planted a vineyard and are happy to see its beauty and pleasantness. There is a wall of stones around the vineyard, so that the land is like a Garden of Eden laid out before us, while in the past it was wasted and desolate. We also have a grove of trees that provides wood for heating. We have to bring water and building stones by ourselves. Kalman performs all of these tasks with joy and happiness; and, may God be praised, he's very handy. Our garden has every sort of fruit tree, even apples and cherries; but most of the vineyard is planted with grape vines.

Now I'll describe our home: our house is the second house on the street when you enter the colony. It has three large rooms as well as a room for cooking. We also have a large stable for our horses, a large yard, and two large gardens. The whole valley surrounding us is covered with green—wheat, barley, and vineyards. Facing our house is the sea in all its splendor and glory; the scenery is beautiful and very uplifting.

The air is clean and healthy. Everyone out walking passes by our house, all of the things brought into the moshava for sale pass by our house, so I buy everything cheaply without having to weary my feet going to the market to buy what I need. I've already learned to speak Arabic quickly, because everything is brought to my home and all of the sellers are Arabs. I also have nice household utensils as well as curtains for the windows, because we live like in the cities: we have a bit of luxury, but not too much.

All of us women wear white kerchiefs covering our heads. On Shabbat I wear a nice kerchief, which cost me three SR, when I go to the synagogue. Our dresses are pretty and are sewn in the best of taste. Eventually Zikhron Yaakov will become a bustling place, but actually it's already become a town. Soon, they will build ducts in order to bring water to the houses of the colony, and pipes and stoppers will be in every house.[15] Shortly, they will begin to excavate a wine cellar here, and soon they will build a railroad from Jaffa to Jerusalem and a railroad yard will be built in Zikhron Yaakov.

Eventually, we hope that the face of the land will be renewed. In areas where jackals run, railroads will run full of passengers instead of desolate rocks—there will be hotels for tourists; in places where man does not set foot, people will work and engage in all sorts of handicrafts, day and night. My heart pounds inside to think of all of these pleasant hopes. If God has revived our precious land and turned the desolate desert into populated town, we pray that God will also turn all of the scorched and ravaged areas into homes for people, into vineyards and grapevines.

With all my heart, I wish that I could write you more, but I don't have enough time to write, because there is a lot of work to do today. In the morning, in the fifth hour, I must wake up in order to feed my household. Kalman goes to the field to do his work, along with ten Arab men; Eliyahu goes to work in the gardens all day; David and Bezalel go to school, where they learn Hebrew, French, Arabic, and how to read and write in all of these languages; and I am the only one who stays at home. Then I have to feed the hens, the geese and the ducks, the goats, the pigeons, and the horse. After finishing all of this, I can rest; and in the evening I have to give them food once again.

I've also divided up the housework according to the days of the week: on Sundays I bake bread, on Mondays I do the washing, on Tuesdays I prepare and ready the clothes that have been washed. Wednesdays are for sewing and mending torn clothes, and on Thursdays I bake challah and cakes for Shabbat — everything with pure olive oil; the price of a liter of the choicest olive oil is twelve kopecks, so that we use it almost in place of water. On Fridays I prepare everything and put up *cholent* [a slow-cooking stew of beans, potatoes, and meat] for Shabbat. Shabbat is a day of complete rest for us.

I will never lack work, and thank God, the household work is always on the increase. I wash the floors of the house by myself, and I clean all of the copper and bronze utensils every Friday until they shine; I even whitewash the walls of our house by myself. I also bought a sewing machine and I sew myself everything that I need. I have never known a better, more satisfying life than the one I am currently leading.

We live here in the shadow of the Baron, who feels the pain of his sons, may God be merciful on him, and we know no want. If a woman bears twins, then the Baron provides four SR a month for hiring a second wet nurse and will also send her a second bed — but I pray that God will save me from this excessive blessing. Indeed, I don't have enough time to write of all the good and merciful deeds done by the Baron for us. May God reward him and his administrators as they have rewarded us.

NOTES

1. The notes below are taken from Aaronsohn's annotations to the text. They have been abridged and modified. The date of the letter is not known. The date has been estimated according to the date the letter was sent from Vilna to *Ha-Melitz*, which published the letter on December 2, 1889.

2. It should read "the old colony" and refers to the eastern hill of Zamarin, a Hovevei Tsion agricultural settlement established in 1882 but which failed within the year. This site was called in Yiddish "olt Zamarin," as opposed to the "new colony", or "the town" of Zikhron Yaakov, which was established under Baron Rothschild's patronage in 1883. Zikhron Yaakov was to the west of Zamarin on a higher hill. It is not surprising that the family of Kalman Kantor, who was employed by the Rothschild administration, was first offered a house at Zamarin, as it became the neighborhood of the estate administrators.

3. Indeed, the breezes in the western hill of Zikhron Yaakov were much better than those at Zamarin, which was lower and toward the east. It is worth remembering that "good air," as meant by the settlers then, referred to air that was thought to be less prone to spreading malaria (literally, *mal-aria*, bad air). In those days, it was widely believed that malaria was spread through the air by poisonous emanations (miasmas) originating in stagnant water. The parasite that causes malaria was discovered in 1880, but a firm link between the anopheles mosquito and the transmission of the parasite was established only in 1898.

4. The need to purchase basic foodstuffs from Arabs of the area was a result of the type of farming characteristic of Zikhron Yaakov and the other moshavot. Their farms were based on growing cash crops (commercial agriculture) rather than the staples necessary for home consumption (subsistence farming). As a result, the Jewish settlers were dependent on Arabs, as described here and elsewhere. This dependency was the subject of a great deal of criticism. Notwithstanding this state of affairs, many of the farmers' wives supplied some of their household requirements from small vegetable gardens that they grew in their yards, as the author herself eventually did.

5. The kopeck was a Russian coin worth very little (one-hundredth of a ruble). At that time, it was equal to about six Turkish grush, or about three-hundredths of a French franc, which was the common currency in the moshavot.

6. The reference is to Baron Rothschild, who did not actually visit Palestine until 1894.

7. Her son Eliyahu, who completed his studies that year at the Workers' School at Zikhron Yaakov, began working for the Rothschild administration at the basic wage paid to starting workers (thirty francs a month). This was in addition to the monetary support received by each family from the Baron, which was distributed according to family size.

8. All of these communal services, which were provided at no cost to the settlers, were budgeted by the Baron and administered by his officials.

9. Her son David, who was then a pupil in the elementary school of the moshava.

10. K means Kovno, Lithuania. "Neologics" refers to the moderately progressive Neolog movement in nineteenth-century Central European Judaism. The author is probably referring here to the placement of the *bima* (pulpit) near the *aron kodesh* (the holy ark containing the Torah scrolls) on the back wall, as opposed to the center of the synagogue. (The Neolog practice made the interior of the synagogue more closely resemble a church.) The author is perhaps referring as well to the synagogue's many paintings and its luxurious interior decoration. The location of the choir, mentioned below, also belonged to the new customs, which were introduced into the religious and cultural life of the moshava by the Baron's administrators. These innovations angered the traditionalist settlers.

11. Her husband, Kalman.

12. The third son of the author was usually called by his middle name, Betzalel. Perhaps he had another name, which began with the letter "S."

13. The date on the letter reads February 1. This is almost definitely according to the Julian calendar, which was the accepted calendar in eastern Europe at the time; in other words, February 28, according to the Gregorian calendar that we use today.

14. SR refers to silver rubles, Russian coins, then worth approximately 2.5 French francs or about fifteen Turkish grush.

15. "Ducts" refers to a system of pipes; "stoppers" refers to faucets. Running water was supplied to the houses of Zikhron Yaakov only in the middle of the 1890s. Until then, the settlers brought water from a public faucet in barrels, which they loaded onto wagons. The faucet was located next to the colony's reservoir, which was built in 1891.

Pioneer Women of the Second Aliyah

The Plough Woman consists of memoirs composed between 1915 and 1928. It was originally published in Yiddish in 1931 and then in various English editions. Compared with document 10, these memoirs demonstrate the difference in political consciousness, ideology, and everyday experience between women of the First and Second Aliyot. The Second Aliyah's core of youthful, politically committed immigrants included women dedicated to establishing themselves as laborers and leaders, as equals to their male counterparts. Their dual struggle as Zionists and feminists was a trying one, as their strivings for equality in a pioneering society that championed images of strength and masculinity encountered considerable resistance from their male comrades. Moreover, once they began to have children, maternal and revolutionary-egalitarian drives clashed, leading to the search for new forms of child-rearing.

Batya Brenner[1]
(Kibbutz Ein Harod)

I

Two days I waited for my sister Hemdah to take me down to the workers' club [in Jaffa]. But she never had the time. And at last I decided to go there alone.

Source: *The Plough Woman: Records of the Pioneer Women of Palestine —A Critical Edition*, ed. Mark A. Raider and Miriam B. Raider-Roth (Lebanon, N.H.: Brandeis University Press, 2002), 47–61, 156–61. Used with permission of University Press of New England.

A group of workers stood outside the building. As I drew up, not knowing a soul there, they looked me over curiously, and began to talk about me in friendly mockery.

"Who's this? Pretty, isn't she?"

"And doesn't she know it! Look at the way she holds her head."

I went up boldly and answered, "Suppose I am pretty? What's wrong with that?"

Two young fellows stood apart, looking more impudent than the others. One of them called out, "We can see from your clothes that you aren't a worker." I answered in the same tone: "What have my clothes got to do with it? Here—is this the hand of a worker?"

There was a shout of laughter, and voices:

"That's a worker's hand. Big and hefty. Say, how old are you?"

I answered, "I have a friend and she's married."

"And what about you?"

"If you'll be nice boys, I'll marry, too."

At this point my nerve broke down. I blushed and began to stammer. This was my introduction to the club.

When I went inside I felt a strange chill of disappointment. The whitewash was peeling from the walls. The tables were small, without covers. At one table sat some workers drinking soup. The waiter came up to one of them, and said sharply, "Listen, you! You've taken two plates of soup and given me only one ticket. Where's the second?"

This was beyond me. What were tickets needed for? Didn't they just put the soup on the table and let people eat whatever they wanted?

Someone explained to me: "Every plate has to be paid for separately. You don't think a kitchen can be conducted without some sort of account, do you?"

"But I didn't think you've got to check up on each man, how much he eats."

No, no, this was not what I had expected, and I felt a depression coming over me.

The two laughing boys who had been standing outside came up to me.

"Well, how do you like our club?" And without waiting for an answer one of them added, "I suppose you expected a great big hall, with lots of gold-framed pictures on the wall."

I answered frankly: "I didn't quite expect gold frames. Only I thought the place would be simple in another kind of way."

"Well, what way?"

"I did expect a big room. And I also expected big long tables. I don't like little tables; it's too much like a saloon. A big table is homier and friendlier—it draws people together. And why can't you have a white tablecloth on the tables? And why can't you have pictures of the first *halutzim* [pioneers] on the walls, the first tillers of the soil?"

"Why, of all things, the pioneers on the soil?"

I answered: "Because we Jews have plenty of city workers everywhere, and there's nothing new in that."

"And what else did you expect?"

"You could have had a few flowerpots in the corners. And if you want to know something more—I thought the food would be handed out by girls in white pinafores."

"Why don't you come into the club and fix things the way you want?"

"I don't want to work in the kitchen. I want to join a kvutzah.[2] I want to learn to work."

"They won't take you into a kvutzah. The kvutzot aren't for young [women] like you. Besides, you can't speak Hebrew.[3] Forget the kvutzah—it's just a dream."

"It's not a dream," I answered proudly. "My brother has friends in a kvutzah, and they'll take me in."

"You have a brother here?"

"Yes, and a sister too."

"Well, well. And who are they?"

"You know them, I think. Their names are Ezra and Hemdah."

"What? Hemdah is your sister? You don't look a bit like her. Listen, if your brother vouches for you, they may let you in. But you might as well know that's just pull."

"No it isn't. My brother is known over there, and he says they can use me. And I hope to start work soon."

"But what do you want a kvutzah for?" they started again. "Why don't you join us? We need a girl in the kitchen right now."

"No, I'm going to wait. I want to go to a kvutzah if I can."

When I went out of the club that evening the two [young men] went out after me, and for a little while I caught part of their conversation. . . . They were wondering whether I would ever become a real worker.

II

Two long weeks passed, and no answer came from the kvutzah. I grew uneasy and wondered at the reason. Was it true that it was all a matter of pull? Were they ashamed to answer "No" just because my brother had applied for me? . . .

What was going to happen with me? Would I have to work in the club after all? . . .

[Batya then hears from her brother that there is a place for her in a kvutzah—in the kitchen and that she must depart the next day.]

"Kitchen?" I stammered. "I don't know how to cook. What am I going to do there?"

But this was no time to turn back. I did not sleep that night. At five in the morning I was already up. My sister heard me, and she asked me, "What are you getting up so early for?"

"I want to pack my things over," I said. "I'm ashamed to land there with all this baggage—like a bride getting ready for her wedding. I want to leave out my holiday clothes, and I want to take just a little underwear with me."

"Wait," my sister said. "Don't close up that basket till I've been to the village. I want to give you some money to pack in, just in case."

"In case of what?" I added, "Do you think I'm going to keep money tied up over there, in the kvutzah? You're just making fun of me—I suppose you think I don't know what a kvutzah is. I know there's no such thing as "yours" and "mine" in a kvutzah."

"Well, well," said my sister ironically. "Even in a kvutzah they have 'mine' and 'not-mine.' But I know there is no use arguing with you."

Very hastily, I prepared my basket. Then I made a separate bundle of my bedding. My sister watched in astonishment.

"What are you making two separate bundles for?"

"I want to see whether I can carry them myself to the station."

"But listen," my sister said, patiently, "I've ordered a porter to come to the house."

"All right," I said. "He'll carry the basket and I'll carry the bundle. I'm not going to follow him with nothing in my hands, like a countess."

III

In the train, a woman came up to me and said: "I saw a Jewish child, so I had to come and speak to you. There are only Arabs on the train. Where are you going?"

I wiped away the tears quickly and said: "To a kvutzah."

"A kvutzah? What is that?"

"It's a kind of group," I said, "where everyone works like everyone else, and they all live together."

"What do you mean, 'they all live together'?"

"Well, they all eat in one kitchen, and they all work together."

"Eating and working together—does that mean living together?"

I began to see that neither this woman nor I knew clearly what a kvutzah was.

"And why must you go and work?" she asked me. "Your parents aren't dead, God forbid?"

"No."

The woman was silent awhile. Then she began again: "You don't look like an ordinary girl to me. I suppose you've been to school. Why can't you be a teacher, or a nurse?"

"I want to work."

"You want to work? Good luck to you. I suppose you're from Russia. My daughter in Jaffa told me that Jews are coming from Russia these days and building themselves houses on the sands. Some of them have nice clothes, but won't wear them; instead of hats they wear *kefiyas* [Arab headdresses] and they work on the land. Good luck to them, too. Maybe they'll put an end to the famine."

I remembered now the day I left home, and my mother's parting words: "God be with you, my child. Work! But you are only a child. Don't take on more than you can carry, and don't despise what the world says."

I had always listened to my mother, but I could not understand what those words meant: "Don't despise what the world says." The world says many things. The world says that money is important. If I had taken along what Hemdah wanted to give me, I would not have to worry now. If there was no one at the station to meet me, I could continue with this woman as far as Jerusalem, and there I could write my brother Ezra to come and fetch me. But what would I do now, without a *piastre* [4] in my pocket?

Just before my station, the conductor comes around and takes my ticket from me. My heart begins to beat fast. I try to behave calmly. I straighten out my two braids and smooth out my belt. As the train rolls in, I lean out of the window. The long stretch is as empty as a wilderness. Finally I see a little *shtibl* [small house] under some eucalyptus trees. Near the shtibl is a group of Arabs, and when I look closely I see among them a tall, dark boy wearing a white shirt and carrying a whip in his hand.

When the train stops, the tall boy with the whip is already at my window. I shout: "Is there a Jew here?"

"Are you Amunah?"

"Yes."

"My name's Avraham. I'm a *haver* [member] in the kvutzah, and I was sent down to meet you. Let me take your things."

"Not all of them, please."

"Why, what's the matter? You'll get dirty and you'll tear your dress. Here, you hold my whip. I'll take the basket, then I'll come back for the bundle."

"Please, I'll carry the bundle".

The [young man] laughed out loud and stopped arguing with me. Basket and bundle were packed into the middle of the cart. He examined the arrangement thoughtfully, and said: "Well, that won't upset." It was a real task to climb into the cart, for my dress was too tight. He watched me with great solicitude and felt guilty when something ripped.

We hardly spoke along the journey. All his attention was given to the driving. He watched every stone, every rut, and managed the mules with the utmost care. Before every bump he warned me anxiously to hold tight.

IV

When we crawled into the yard, not a soul was visible. Avraham called out: "Before long it'll be easier to steal things here by day than by night. At night we have the guard, but during the day there's no one around." Then he added, half solicitously, half sarcastically: "I suppose that Shahar, the *shomer Yisrael* [guardian of Israel], is sitting all the time at Hasidah's bedside."

Then he turned to me, and his face beamed: "And we didn't upset the cart!"

I went into the house with a beating heart. The first to meet us was Shahar himself. He stood there, book in hand, and said in amazement: "When did you get here? I didn't hear the creaking of the cart." Then he introduced himself. "My name's Shahar, one of the haverim in the kvutzah." He looked at me out of watery, colorless eyes, and added: "I suppose you're tired. That road would tire out anybody."

"No," I answered, "In fact, I enjoyed the ride."

"Enjoyed it?" he repeated. He turned to Avraham. "And didn't the cart upset?"

Avraham seemed hurt. "You talk as if I did nothing but upset carts. You're a first-class *shomer*, I must say. Here we come riding into the yard and you don't even hear us."

Angrily Shahar answered, "No, I didn't hear you. I had to change the compress for Hasidah, and I sat with her a while."

"All right, then," Avraham said. "But now will you tell me where the grain measure is? I don't know when you fellows will learn to leave it where it ought to be. I've got to feed the mules. Will you look after that, Shahar? I'm the cook today, and I've got to get supper ready."

"I can't. I've got to be near Hasidah." And then Avraham told me to follow him, so that Hasidah could have a look at me. When we got into the room, he asked the [woman] who was lying down whether she wanted the cold compress changed. Then he added: "Here's the new *haverah*" [female member].

Hasidah opened her eyes and, without greeting, she said, "Oh, she's too young, too young. Have you been long in Jaffa?"

"Two weeks," I answered.

"Then why didn't you cut your braids off? They'll be ruined here, anyway."

"Why should I cut them off?" I asked, startled. "My sister has even longer ones, and she manages all right."

"Your sister doesn't work in the field," she answered. "If you want to work, you'll have to cut those braids off."

"Of course I want to work. I'll cut my braids off, if I have to."

"And look at your dress. It's ripped. That isn't the kind of dress to come to work in."

"That's nothing," I said, wretchedly. "I've got other dresses."

She made a motion for Shahar to change the compress, and then she closed her eyes. I went away from this reception with my heart in my shoes. "I'll go to Avraham," I thought. "I feel better near him."

I found him in the kitchen. "Come in," he said cheerfully. "You'll see what kind of a cook I am. Can you cook?"

"No."

"Doesn't matter. I'll teach you. I'll teach you Hebrew, too."

"Honest?"

"Can you ride a horse?"

"No. I've never been on one."

"You'll learn that, too. We'll go out riding in the fields."

"Can I help you to get supper ready?"

"No, it's all right. I'll be through soon. If you like, you can clean the lamp glass. It hasn't been wiped since Hasidah fell sick."

He gave me a rag, and I, not noticing there was a button in the holder, smashed the glass.

Avraham started. "Hey, what's that? What are we going to do now?"

I didn't know the extent of the catastrophe, but I guessed from his tone. I remained standing in a sort of paralysis.

After an awful silence, he began to console me. "Oh, well, we'll get another one tomorrow. But you don't know what a lamp chimney means in a village like this. We've had to sit in the dark for a whole week, sometimes, before we could lay our hands on one of those treasures. Without one you can't do a thing nights—not even read the newspaper."

In the evening they began to return from the fields. The first man in was Aharon, and his first words were, "Well, is the new girl here?"

"Yes."

"Why is it dark? Why don't you light the lamp?"

"Can't. The new girl's already broken the glass."

"She has? That's not so good. Tell me, is she pretty at least?"

"Oh, be quiet. I don't know."

Aharon dashed off, and came back in a moment with the stable lantern, and set it on the table. He looked me over, and then said with a smile, to Avraham, "You've nothing to be angry about."

Somebody else came in, grumbling: "What's the idea of taking the lantern out of the stable? I nearly knocked one of my eyes out."

"Don't get excited. I took it. I wanted to see our new haverah, and there's no lamp. So I took the lantern."

"Was it worthwhile, at least?"

"I didn't get a good look, but I guess it was."

V

In the morning, Avraham remained behind to show me my work. The first thing he asked me was whether I could cut onions into small pieces. When I said I could, he went for two barrels of water, and in the meantime told me to keep an eye on the oil, which was standing over the fire. I was to take it off as soon as it had warmed up, but I was to be very careful about it because if the oil became too hot the onions would burn when thrown in. He went out, and I remained alone in the kitchen. I was eager to do my best, but in taking off the oil I slopped half of it on the floor. A feeling of despair came over me. In the evening, my great skill was the subject of wide discussion. They asked Avraham whether he would go on teaching me how to cook. He answered angrily: "What makes you all so impatient? Were you born workers? Did you find it so easy to learn?"

The next day things went more smoothly. I peeled onions. I washed the breadbox. I did everything according to Avraham's instructions and he was happy. "They'll have nothing to grumble about today. Now put the milk on the stove, and for God's sake, watch it closely, and don't let it run over. I've got to get more water, or there'll be no tea for dinner."

I stand watching the milk closely, waiting for the first sign of the rise. And suddenly I hear Hasidah's voice: "Amunah, bring me a glass of water. I don't feel well." I run in, give her water, straighten out the cushions, and ask anxiously: "Is that better?" But suddenly she makes a face, and asks abruptly: "Did you leave the milk on the stove? What's the matter with you?" I dash back. Too late! The milk is running down the sides of the pot, and streaming onto the floor. My heart dies in me. What's going to happen now? How will they be able to eat the gruel? They'll be hungry—and all on my account. But what could I do? Shouldn't I have given the sick woman a glass of water?

When Avraham came in, he turned pale. "Again?" he said.

In an instant, he had fixed everything, added coals, and thrown salt on the stove.

"If you'd at least thrown salt on. The smoke is terrible."

"Thrown salt on what?"

"On the stove, so as to keep the smoke down. I forgot to tell you. I didn't expect this to happen."

He put water on for tea and went into Hasidah's room.

I wiped the milk off the floor and began to sweep the room. A cry came from Hasidah: "Shut that door. I'm choking with the dust and smoke."

Avraham came in: "Why don't you sprinkle water on the floor before sweeping? You're not like a girl at all. . . . Don't you even know how to sweep?"

"I know how to sweep. I didn't want to use water because you've got to bring it such a distance, and perhaps all of it is needed. And I was frightened to ask you because you looked so angry before."

"Don't you think I ought to be?"

VI

That evening, I was again the subject of discussion. Again they asked Avraham: "Well, are you still going to teach her?"

Avraham lost his temper: "Why do you pick on me? Am I responsible? Did I bring her here?"

Shahar added: "I talked with Hasidah. She said we ought to take her out of the kitchen—we can't stand all that damage. Anyway, she can do some washing. Since Hasidah fell sick, no washing's been done, and we haven't a clean thing to put on for work."

I am asked if I can wash clothes. Sure! I am filled with joy: here's something I can do, at last.

When I got up early next morning, there were already two barrels of water at hand, brought by Arvaham. He showed me the three stones that served as a stove and the heap of thorns for fuel. Following Avraham's advice, I poured a lot of washing soda into the hot water, and rubbed the clothes well. But when I got to the dark clothes, I couldn't rub any more, because there was no more skin on my hands. I could neither wash the clothes nor wring them out. Miserable, ashamed, humiliated at my helplessness, I began to cry. It was the first time in my life that things were going against me. And when Avraham came up, I showed him my hands.

He smiled. "You're a real worker," he said, "there's no getting away from that. Leave the clothes in the boiler, with water. You'll finish tomorrow."

I took down the wash, which was dry by now, and went into Hasidah's room. The village nurse was there. As I came in, I heard her say:

"Now that you've got a new girl, things will be easier for you."

"She's not much of a help," Hasidah said. "We've made an unlucky choice. She wants to work, but she doesn't know how. And she's too childish for a kvutzah."

The nurse asked me to sew two towels together and make a compress.

"I can't," I said. "My hands are all raw, and I can't straighten my fingers out."

"Let me see. How did you get them that way?"

"From the wash."

There was a frightened look on her face. "Don't let any water come on your hands for the next few days."

"How can I do that? There's a tubful of laundry outside."

Hasidah smiled. "That's my help. There's something queer about her. The first thing she told me was that she has a lot of clothes, and her sister has even longer braids than she."

And after a pause she added: "It looks as though a long time will have to pass before we have the right kind of people coming to the country."

VII

Those three days without work were misery. Meanwhile, Hasidah got up from her bed, and with her about the house things improved, and the mood improved, too. We had to do the baking now. Hasidah said: "If your hands get better, I'll give you the kneading to do." I would work under her direction, and she would attend to the cooking, because sowing time had come and Avraham could no longer remain at home. Mornings there was a lively feeling of work in the air, and everyone was up with the dawn.

"Amunah, today you'll do the kneading. Are your hands all right?"

I answered resolutely, "Yes." I put a white kerchief round my head and took a new apron out of my basket, one that I had not yet worn in the country. I was preparing as if for a ritual.

"I'm ready, Hasidah." She looked me over. "White!" she exclaimed. "From head to foot, like a nurse at the operating table." And when she gave me flour and water and told me to start kneading, I was as excited as if I was undergoing rather than watching an operation. I kneaded away lustily. From time to time, the dough clung to my hands and was flecked with blood from my half-healed flesh. Without saying a word, I would detach the bloodstained pieces of dough and throw them on the floor. Hasidah called out to me: "Be careful no flies get into the bread."

When the dough was kneaded to her satisfaction, she said: "We've got to heat the oven now."

"I'm frightened. I know I'll spoil something."

"Don't be frightened. I'll watch."

Oh, how much certainty and confidence there was in that "I'll watch"! The bread came out beautifully.

And I thought to myself: Who of my old friends in the shtetl back home knows what real happiness is? Who of them has lived through such a joyous day?

Hasidah had magic in her fingers. Whatever she did came out right. By the time the men returned from the field, everything was ready.

They asked her anxiously how she felt. There was an atmosphere of solicitude and respect around her. The next morning, Aharon fell sick and there was no one to follow the plow with the seed. Avraham suggested that I be taken along. There was much laughter and yet, in the end, they had to take me because there was no one else. And so I was to go out on the fields! I had no idea of what I would have to do—but I was happy. The boys made room for me at the table, and called out: "Sit next to me, *fellah* [Arab tenant farmer] . . ." All day long, I went after the plough and dropped the seed. I did not get tired. Around me I heard voices: "Good work." In the evening, I returned on horseback, my hair falling loose over my shoulder. I did not care. I felt well. I was happy. On the porch stood the nurse, together with Hasidah. She had come to attend to Aharon. I rode up to the pair of them and sprang off my horse. I wanted to run to Hasidah, take her aside, pour out all my joy—but her cool look froze the words on my lips.

The nurse exclaimed: "What youth! What health!"

Hasidah answered: "Just a girl—like all the others. Out there, in the fields, among the boys, she becomes another person. And all the kitchen work falls on me again."

I hear her, and I understand her only too well. And I ask myself what this attitude of hers means. What am I to deduce from it? Have I any right to stay on here? She calls me "little girl," but I want to be a worker. I must make up my mind what to do.

That evening, I did not go in to dinner. And when they asked "Where's the fellah?" they were told, "in bed." "No wonder," they said, "after that long day in the sun." I did not close my eyes that night, and I could not decide on a course of action. It was impossible to return to Jaffa, to have them say, "Our little worker is back so soon?" And I could not stay on. I had heard enough to make me feel that I was not wanted.

VIII

Early the next morning, the train brought a welcome visitor, Kotik, the secretary. They clustered round him in the dining room, asking for the news, but the first thing he said was: "Where's that [new] haverah that just came here? I have a letter for her from her brother Ezra."

I took the letter and found myself turning pale. "If you want," Kotik said, "you can send an answer through me. I'm leaving for Jerusalem tomorrow."

Ezra wrote that he had been persuaded to go to Jerusalem, and he was not sorry at all. Things were going well with him and he had a nice room. If I wanted, I could come to him for a little time. Kotik, who was a good friend of his, would advance me the money for the fare. The letter was like the voice of a deliverer! I could leave the kvutzah without going back to Jaffa! I was saved!

When breakfast was over, I wend up to Kotik, and in a low, timid voice told him that Ezra had asked me to come to him, and that he, Kotik, might lend me the money.

"Why, certainly" he said, with a charming smile.

Then I added: "And, if you won't find it a burden, I'd like to travel together with you."

"Of course," he said, eagerly. "Ezra's little sister . . ."

The haverim looked at me in amazement. They began to ask me: "Are you really leaving? Why has your brother sent for you? When are you coming back?" I did not answer. Only Hasidah seemed to be satisfied.

"Well, what did I tell you? A child. Your fellah. She's been here a few days and she's off to Jerusalem." And suddenly she became very serious. "Pity she went into the fields yesterday. My room hasn't been cleaned once since I was sick."

"There's still time," I said. "Kotik isn't going till twelve o'clock tomorrow. And if there's no other work for me, I'll start on your room at once."

Hasidah's face lit up. "Will you really? Let's carry the things out, and I'll prepare whitewash for you. And if you'll whitewash the room for me, I'll have something to remember you by."

"What do you mean, 'remember her by'?" Avraham put in. "How long do you think she's going to stay in Jerusalem?"

But no one answered him, and Avraham turned away depressed. I threw myself into the work, and in it almost forgot my hurt and my anger. I did my best to make a straight line of whitewash, to keep it from sprinkling the windows and running down on the floor. When the whitewashing was done I washed all the floors, and in the evening I helped Hasidah carry the things back into her room. Hasidah looked thoughtful. "How clean it is!" Then after a pause, she added: "Suppose you did come back, after all. It wasn't so bad here, was it?"

When the haverim returned, they talked in low tones about me. I learned afterwards that they felt guilty. They had not treated me as they should have done. They wanted to persuade me to stay. Or perhaps Hasidah could persuade me to come back after a short stay in Jerusalem.

And sure enough, in the morning, Hasidah said to me: "I forgot to ask you when you're coming back. We were so busy all yesterday that we hadn't time to talk it over."

"I'm not coming back," I said, shortly.

"But why? Do you find the work too hard? Never mind that. Come back. You're too young, I know, but I'll teach you everything, and you'll like it here. And listen, Amunah, I've got a half pound saved up. I've been thinking a long time of buying myself a pretty dress, and now you're going to Jerusalem, perhaps you'll buy the material for me. You're a good judge, I'll leave it to you."

She went over to her basket and began to rummage in it. From underneath the books she dragged out a brown dress, a heritage of her half-forgotten student days in Russia. But to her horror she found that the mice had eaten away the pocket and the half pound with it. But I had no sympathy for her at that moment, for this was my revenge. She had kept money of her own in the kvutzah! How was such a thing possible?

IX

Kotik knocked at my door. "Young lady, it's time to start out. We can't have the wagon today, it's needed for the sowing. We'll have to make the station on foot. Get ready."

All the way to Jerusalem, Kotik did his best to keep me cheerful. He did not care that I could not speak Hebrew. He spoke Yiddish and Russian to me. But

I hardly answered a word. I was thinking how I would face my brother Ezra, and what I would say to him.

We knocked a long time at my brother's door, and finally he came out. "I didn't hear you. I was writing letters. Oh, Amunah, so you came! You're not sick, are you? I suppose you came just to see Jerusalem."

I was silent. I felt the tears gathering in my eyes, but my brother's "nice" room was so small that I could not turn away from him.

That day, we hardly spoke. The next morning, when Ezra had gone out, I sat at the table to write. I did not notice the passing of the time, and it seemed I had scarcely begun before Ezra was back for the noon-day meal.

"Are you writing mother?" he asked.

"No, I'm writing you," I answered. "Every time I want to tell you what happened, I feel like crying. So I'll tell it to you on paper instead." And I handed him what I had written.

He looked through it earnestly, and then he said: "Promise me you won't write any more. Writing makes people old. It throws a shadow over their lives. And you're only a young [woman]. Don't go in for such things. It's better for you to learn how to bake bread and milk a cow. That's a lot more important in Eretz Israel."[5]

Eva Tabenkin
(Kibbutz Ein Harod)[6]

Group Upbringing and the Child

It was before our marriages that we, the first haverot in the kvutzot, decided in advance that our children would be brought up in the group; not because we considered it a necessity of our life in the kvutzah, but because we regarded it as a high ideal. Later, having become mothers, we still clung to this view.

We were proud and happy in the first trials of our strength and faith, in Dagania, Kineret, and Tel Adas.[7] Calmly, and in full consciousness of what we were doing, we chose the ablest of our haverot for the task, and were prepared to entrust our children to her care while we went about our own work. Those first years exacted heavy sacrifices from us—of all the trials we underwent in the country and in the kvutzah, this was the hardest and the most important. It will always remain so, for with every mother the old story begins anew.

Now, after these ten years of experience let us make an accounting and let us choose one standard of evaluation—the physical and mental development and well-being of the child.

It has become clear to us that for school children the richest and most harmonious form of upbringing is the children's home as it exists in our midst—not an isolated little world, but a children's community integrated with our own, growing with us, nourished with the spirit of our soil, lovingly cared for and watched over not only by the parents, but by the kvutzah as a whole.

We have never thought of finding a substitute for parental love. We only wanted to add to it the love of the community, so that the child might never feel that when it steps out of its own home it is among strangers, needing protection. How much the first mothers in the kvutzot suffered because of the false idea that parents must actually be alienated from their children! But, as the number of children and of parents grows among us, the old errors die out.

Even in the kvutzah the child without parents suffers, though it is known and felt in the children's home—from the comrade in charge down to the youngest one—that such a child must be treated with more tenderness than any other. Externally that child lacks nothing.

But watch an orphan closely! See him waiting eagerly for someone to come to him specially, and you will understand the pain which loneliness means even in the group form of upbringing.

For there are no bounds to the love that a child must have, so that its warmth may serve it through all the heavy afterlife. And these children of ours, who will certainly inherit some of our burdens, do not look forward to an easy life.

Love and compassion alone can give us the strength needed to stand constant guard over the lives of our children, to listen with utmost patience to their needs and demands, to understand them without speech as long as they cannot speak for themselves.

And because among the comrades in charge, the nurses and educators, there are "many who are called, few who are chosen," difficulties must arise between them and the parents. We must bear in mind that the mother instinct of itself makes the mother a "chosen one" in respect to her child.

But this deep mother instinct no longer suffices to fill our lives, as it once sufficed for our mothers. I do not know whether it is good that this should be so, but so it is. The child does not, by itself, satisfy our life needs, does not answer all the demands that we make of ourselves.

And I also know that there is no road leading back to the one-time mother and one-time wife. Each of us women must now tread her own path, and even the child cannot hold us back. And if one of us should become weary, and should want to turn back—she will find it impossible. Those of us who still carry in their hearts the beautiful idyll of the past, lose it when they have the chance to observe closely what has become of family life in the cities today. . . .

And this consciousness that there is no road back, makes the road before us all the harder. And yet . . .

The hardest time in the life of the child, the period that calls for the maximum care and worry in the mother, is in the first three years. And when, a few days after the birth, the mother must relinquish her child into other hands and cannot herself tend to all its needs, her sufferings begin. For all these little cares and attentions are so important. The newborn child changes from day to day, and the progress is observed in all of these trifles, when the child is being bathed, when it wakes from sleep, when it smiles for the first time, and when the first glimmer of consciousness lightens in its eyes—in every movement, in every note of its voice, it reveals itself anew.

And in the baby house, even when it is developed to the highest point, no one will wait for these little events with the same eagerness and tenderness as a mother does. But, on the other hand, it is impossible to estimate the significance of the help that the baby house gives the mother when, ignorant, helpless, and weak, she leaves the hospital after her confinement. It is seldom that a young mother in Eretz Israel can fall back on a family with generations of tradition and experience to help her in her new role. What substitute has this young mother? The book of instructions? Not every woman has the time and the opportunity to read books; besides which, do we not know how much help there is in a book when we have to face realities—with a crying baby in our arms? Only those who have seen for themselves what the lonely working-class mother must suffer, in the towns, or in the *moshav ovdim*,[8] when her first child is born, can estimate the worth of the baby house for mother and child, can appreciate the value of its accumulated experience.

The baby house does not grope blindly through its problems, as even the educated and able mother often must. Under the direction of the children-doctors and the devoted nurses they go forward with certain steps. But we are worried constantly by one thought: How can we bring into the life of the child that is being cared for in the home the bright glance and the loving smile of the mother—for which even the tiniest creature instinctively longs?

It will be observed that when we compare the condition of the children in the kvutzah with that of other working-class children in Palestine and elsewhere, or even with the condition of the children of other classes, we are perhaps demanding too much of the group method of upbringing. But we cannot forget what was in our minds when we approached the whole problem at the beginning—what ideals and wishes we had regarding life in Palestine generally and our own lives in particular. For it is only as part of a high cultural life that the group upbringing of children has meaning, and only in the larger setting of a general ideal will we find the strength to continue seeking, through this form, a loftier and finer life for ourselves and for our children.

NOTES

1. Sister of the famous Hebrew writer Yosef Haim Brenner, Batya employs pseudonyms for herself and her siblings. This is a self-consciously literary piece, with fictionalized dialogue and a clear narrative strategy, but it does illustrate the yearnings and travails of pioneer Zionist women of the time.

2. Small agricultural settlements based on collective landholding and a common wage.

3. This fictionalized dialogue is taking place in Yiddish or Russian.

4. The piaster was another name for the kurus, 1/100 of the Turkish lira.

5. In the memoir's final section, Batya travels to Jerusalem and yearns to return to the countryside. She writes an account of her time on the kvutzah, only to tear it up when her brother Ezra critiques it. Although eager to emancipate herself from her brother, Batya essentially accepts his suggestion that she devote her life to labor, not writing. Ezra secures her a place in a Zionist training farm, and she goes off, determined to become a successful worker.

6. Eva Stashevsky Tabenkin (1889–1947) was born in Warsaw and became an activist in Po'alei Tsion as a youth. Possessed of higher education as well as a powerful political consciousness, Stashevsky immigrated to Palestine in 1912 and worked as a laborer in several Jewish agricultural settlements. She was a founder of the first kibbutz, Ein Harod, in 1921. (A kibbutz is larger than a kvutzah and combines agriculture with light industry.) Stashevsky married Yitzhak Tabenkin, a leader in the United Kibbutz movement, and was herself a leader in kibbutz education.

7. A part of Kinneret land became the first kvutzah, Dagania, in 1910. The lands in and around Kinneret became a cradle for Labor Zionism, as most of the movement's leaders worked there at some point. (See document 8) The lands of Tel Adas were purchased in 1913, and members of the Zionist militia Ha-Shomer established a camp there. In 1923, a moshav was founded on the site.

8. A form of agricultural settlement that combines elements of the moshav and the kibbutz.

12

Jaffa Changes Its Face (1907)

ZE'EV SMILANSKY

Ze'ev Smilansky (1873–1944) was a writer, journalist, and farmer. Born in the Ukraine, he first came to Palestine in 1891 and settled permanently in the country the following decade; he spent most of his time in Rehoboth, where he owned and operated a small farm. Smilansky wrote for several publications in Palestine and abroad, especially on economic and business-related themes. Smilansky was the nephew of the noted Hebrew writer Moshe Smilansky and the father of the important Israeli writer S. Yizhar (the pen name of Yizhar Smilansky). In this article, written in 1907, Ze'ev Smilansky examines the impact of Jewish immigration on the city of Jaffa. Smilansky extols what he sees as the overwhelmingly positive influence of the Jews on Jaffa, especially the way they modernized life in the city.

Jaffa, one of the oldest cities in Palestine, witnessed substantial growth in the second half of the nineteenth century, which transformed it from a marginal, dilapidated port city into a thriving and cosmopolitan commercial hub. The city's Jewish population also grew substantially in the latter part of the nineteenth century and the beginning of the twentieth century. In 1890 the city's overall population was 16,000 of which 2,700 were Jews. In 1907 the city's population was 40,000, including 8,000 Jews who lived in Jaffa's old center as well as in new Jewish neighborhoods (Neveh Tsedek, Neveh Shalom), which were founded in the late 1880s. These developments would lead to the

Source: Ze'ev Smilansky, "Ha-Yishuv ha-Ivry be-Yafo," *Ha-Omer* 1 (1907): 16–19, 35–36. Reproduced in *Sefer ha-Aliyah ha-Sheniyah: Mekorot*, ed. Yehoshuah Kaniel (Jerusalem, 1998), 238–41. Used with permission. Translated by Marganit Weinberger-Rotman.

establishment of the neighborhood of Ahuzat Bayit in 1909, the kernel of the future Tel Aviv—a city designed to incorporate many of the urban characteristics that Smilansky describes in the this document (on the development of Tel Aviv see document 20).

In this document Smilansky equates modernization and development with Western values and customs—a common theme among other early Zionist writers and thinkers such as Theodor Herzl and Max Nordau. And, as Herzl had done in his utopian novel *Altneuland*, here Smilansky describes how (from an early Zionist perspective) the development of the Jewish community in Palestine would improve the living conditions of the non-Jewish residents of the country as well.

We must emphasize the impact Jews are having on the town of Jaffa. Those who knew Jaffa in the past can testify that the town owes a lot to the Jews; its appearance has changed dramatically over the last few decades. Jewish immigrants have infused it with new life, and their presence is felt everywhere, especially in the northern part. Interestingly, the Jews, who were the last to settle in Jaffa, are the ones who have left the greatest impression. They did not only infuse new life in it, expanding trade and commerce, but they also introduced new industry and manufacturing. . . . In some respects, they gave the town a new direction altogether. The Germans and the Greeks preceded the Jews in Jaffa,[1] but they did not have much effect on the inhabitants or on the character of the town. These days, you find European furniture in many homes here, and "patriarchal"[2] garments are giving way to European styles.

Ten years ago you did not see the inhabitants wearing shirts with starched collars; there was not even one laundry in town. Now there are three laundries owned by Jews, providing the population, including Muslims, with washing, starching, and ironing services. The younger generation, in particular, has adopted the European style of dressing. Previously, you could hardly spot a carriage on the streets of Jaffa; today, many elegant carriages, decked out in the European and American style, rumble through the streets of Jaffa. Nowhere are they more plentiful than in the northern section, where the German colonies and the central station are located. On Saturdays and on Jewish holidays, when you walk along the storefronts in the marketplace, you notice, unlike weekdays, that they are closed. Life is much less hectic in Jaffa when the main shops are closed. The fellahin from neighboring villages also refrain from bringing their crops into town on those days. On the other hand, if you go to the beach in the late afternoon, especially in summer, you'll see thousands of our people, of all ages, walking along the shore. Not only Jews crowd the beaches on Saturday evenings, but people of all religions.

Ashkenazi Jews have had an influence on other Jewish communities as well. Not long ago, Sephardic and even Western women would dress like Arab women. Now they have removed the veil and walk about baring their faces. Many of them have discarded Arab dress for European garments. Female pioneers were the trailblazers in this respect, followed by our sisters from Middle Eastern countries. As for young Sephardic girls, if it weren't for their tanned complexion and dark eyes, you wouldn't be able to distinguish between them and the Ashkenazi immigrants; in dress and hairstyle they look the same.

The growth and development of Jaffa, particularly of the Jewish community, are due to the town's particular advantages, compared to other towns in Palestine. Jaffa is more conducive to trade and commerce, and it offers opportunities for gainful employment. Its greatest merit, apart from the fact that it lies along the Mediterranean and has a harbor, is its proximity to Jerusalem, the most populous town in Palestine. All the commerce coming into Jerusalem goes through Jaffa. Similarly, the thousands of immigrants coming to the country must go through Jaffa. Jaffa is also close to other towns: Nablus, Bethlehem, Hebron, Ramleh, and Lod, which also use Jaffa as a center for transporting, buying, and selling goods. All this has contributed significantly to Jaffa's prosperity. The new Jewish colonies, many of which are situated around the town, have also played an important part in its development. Those moshavot have infused new life into Jaffa, and many of the millions that went into the establishment and development of the moshavot ended up in the hands of Jaffa residents; even non-Jews have benefited from this munificence, and many among them have improved their standard of living as a result. Nature, too, has been kind to Jaffa, blessing it with an abundance of citrus groves. The climate and the soil of Jaffa are conducive to the cultivation of oranges, and Jaffa oranges have an excellent reputation around the world. New tracts of land around town are now turned into orchards. All the empty spaces near Jaffa are now covered with orange groves.

NOTES

1. Smilansky refers here to Greek merchants who settled in Jaffa in the mid-nineteenth century, and to the Templers, members of a German Protestant sect who arrived in Palestine in 1868 and established a colony near Jaffa in 1869.

2. Smilansky alludes here to Middle Eastern garb.

SECTION II

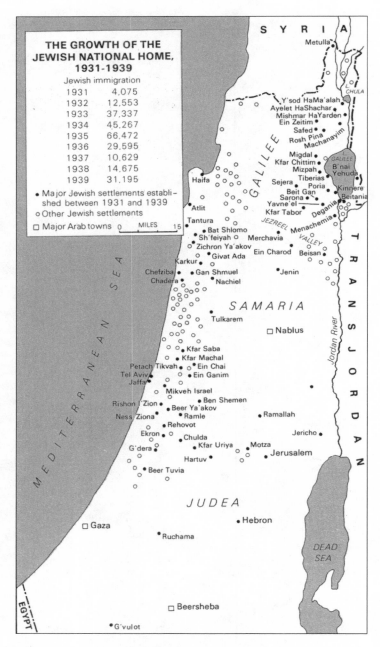

THE GROWTH OF THE JEWISH NATIONAL HOME, 1931-1939

Jewish immigration

Year	Number
1931	4,075
1932	12,553
1933	37,337
1934	45,267
1935	66,472
1936	29,595
1937	10,629
1938	14,675
1939	31,195

● Major Jewish settlements established between 1931 and 1939
○ Other Jewish settlements
□ Major Arab towns

0   MILES   15

SYRIA

Metulla

L. CHULA

Y'sod HaMa'alah
Ayelet HaShachar
Mishmar HaYarden
Ein Zeitim
Safed
Rosh Pina
Machanayim
Migdal
Kfar Chittim
Mizpah
Tiberias
Sejera
Poria
Beit Gan
Sarona
Yavne'el
Kfar Tabor
Degania
Menachemia

GALILEE
B'nai Yehuda
Kinnere
Beitania
JEZREEL
VALLEY

Haifa

Atlit

Tantura

Bat Shlomo
Sh'feiyah
Merchavia
Zichron Ya'akov
Givat Ada
Ein Charod
Beisan

Karkur

Chefziba
Gan Shmuel
Chadera
Nachiel

Jenin

SAMARIA

Tulkarem

□ Nablus

Kfar Saba
Kfar Machal
Ein Chai
Petach Tikvah
Ein Ganim
Tel Aviv
Jaffa

Mikveh Israel
Ben Shemen
Rishon l'Zion
Beer Ya'akov
Ness Ziona
Ramle
Rehovot
Ekron
Chulda
G'dera
Kfar Uriya
Motza
Hartuv
Jerusalem

Ramallah

Jericho

Jordan River

TRANSJORDAN

Beer Tuvia

JUDEA

□ Gaza

Hebron

Ruchama

DEAD SEA

MEDITERRANEAN SEA

□ Beersheba

EGYPT

● G'vulot

The Yishuv in 1939 (reprinted from Howard Sachar, *A History of Israel: From the Rise of Zionism to Our Time* [New York: Knopf, 2000])

BUILDING THE JEWISH
NATIONAL HOME

The Zionist enterprise succeeded as a result of the efforts of three separate but intertwined actors: the New Yishuv, Diaspora Jewry, and the United Kingdom. Between 1914 and 1918, while the Yishuv endured the privations of war, Zionism's fate was determined by an alliance between a handful of Zionist leaders and high officials of the British government. Chaim Weizmann (1874–1952), a Zionist activist and chemist, enjoyed access to the British political elite thanks in part to his wartime discoveries in the formulation of explosives. In 1917 Weizmann and his colleagues in the English Zionist Federation successfully negotiated a declaration of British support for "the establishment in Palestine of a national home for the Jewish people."

As part of the general Allied campaign against the Turks, and Britain's desire to hold Palestine in the postwar division of the Ottoman Empire, the British army invaded Palestine in October 1917. By Hanukkah, Jerusalem had been taken, and the entire land was under British control by September of the following year. Several thousand Jews from North America, Britain, and the Yishuv served in Palestine during the war, organized into three battalions and known collectively as the Jewish Legion. The Legion was the brainchild of three Zionist activists—Joseph Trumpeldor, Vladimir Jabotinsky, and Pinchas Rutenberg—who believed that a Jewish unit fighting for the entente would gain international support for Zionism in the postwar restructuring of the Middle East. But they were wrong: the Legion was disbanded, its members sent home, and the fate of postwar Palestine was determined not by Zionists but by the Allied powers and the League of Nations.

Palestine remained under British military administration until 1920 when, at the San Remo conference, the Allied powers formally divided former Ottoman territories between France and Britain, with the former receiving Lebanon and Syria and the latter Palestine and Iraq. The Allies and the newly formed League of Nations spoke of these dependencies as "mandates," that is, charges on the Great Powers, who were obliged to guide them toward eventual political independence.

The Zionists, seeking to maximize the economic capacity of their national home, envisioned a Palestine that would include the fertile land east of the Jordan River and the sources of the Jordan in southern Lebanon and the Golan Heights. The British, on the other hand, did not need to reach so far north in order to fulfill the strategic goal of protecting Egypt and the Suez Canal. Also, policymakers in London did not want to clash with French interests in Syria. As to the territory east of the Jordan River, although the British Mandate in Palestine included what is today's kingdom of Jordan, from the beginning it had a special status. During the war, much of this territory had come under the control of military forces loyal to Husayn, a British ally and the emir of the Hejaz, an area of western Arabia that included the holy cities of Mecca and Medina. In 1921 the Transjordanian territory was closed to Jewish settlement, and the British formally offered it to Husayn's son Abdullah. In 1923 Transjordan was pronounced an autonomous entity.

In July 1920, British military rule in Palestine was replaced by civilian colonial control. The first high commissioner for Palestine was Sir Herbert Samuel, a Jew and committed Zionist. Samuel opened the doors to Jewish immigration, which jumped from 1,800 in 1919 to more than 8,000 in 1920 and 1921. But the surge of Jews into Palestine, occurring at the same time as the overthrow by French forces of an independent Arab kingdom in Damascus, enraged Palestinian Arabs. In May 1921, rioting in Jaffa and nearby Jewish colonies killed dozens of Jews. The British government reacted by affirming the 1917 Balfour Declaration while denying that Palestine was to become an entirely Jewish land. They also tied Jewish immigration to the economic capacity of the land to absorb it. This policy actually pleased the Zionists, as the Yishuv was too small to absorb large numbers of immigrants, and the Zionist Organization did not have the resources to make work for them. Selective Jewish immigration thus served Zionist as well as British interests.

The mandate benefited the Zionists in other ways as well. Jews in Palestine were better educated and more likely to speak English than Arabs, so they had more access to the colonial government. For example, the Zionist Norman Bentwich served as Palestine's attorney general between 1920 and 1931. Because the Arabs refused to sit with Zionists on a joint Jewish–Palestinian Legislative Council, the British encouraged each entity to set up its own semi-autonomous governing bodies, and the Zionists' higher levels of political and organizational expertise were evident. The British also built up Palestine's infrastructure: its railroads, roads, communication lines, and first deepwater port in Haifa. They did this to promote effective military administration, not for the benefit of the Jews or Arabs. Yet the Yishuv depended heavily on British public works projects for employment (in, for example, Haifa's harbor and petroleum refineries). And the Yishuv's exports were fostered by Palestine's integration into the British colonial empire.

The British also worked against Zionist interests by denying Zionists access to state-owned land, as in the Beisan Valley, where the British wanted to create a class of independent Arab farmers. Until the late 1930s, though, the British allowed a nearly constant stream of Jewish immigration despite strenuous Arab opposition and tolerated most Jewish land purchases. Thus the British allowed the Zionists to gain a toehold in the country, but it would require vast amounts of labor and money to turn that toehold into a polity. Unlike other modern national movements, which seek independence for a native people resisting imperial or colonial rule, Zionism required the buildup of a critical mass of Jews in Palestine and the construction of a national economy before independence could even be considered. Other national movements, including that of the Palestinians, featured a peasantry that held the land, sustained itself, and provided food and a labor force for cities. The Zionists, however, had no agricultural class and set out to invent one among one of the world's most urbanized peoples. In short, the Zionist Yishuv had to create the preconditions for its own existence. And to meet that challenge it relied upon diaspora Jewry.

In 1920 Chaim Weizmann was elected president of the ZO, and he held that position for most of the time up to 1946. His two major responsibilities were maintaining good relations with Britain and raising funds for the Yishuv. (Thus the ZO's Executive had branches in London and Jerusalem.) The British Mandate had called upon world Jewry to create a "Jewish Agency" to promote the development of the Jewish national home. At first, the ZO was designated as this agency, but Weizmann envisioned a vast increase in the agency's resources and scope if it could include wealthy non-Zionist Jews, particularly in the United States, which was now home to the world's largest and most prosperous Jewish community. In principle, it should not have been difficult to win the support of non-Zionists for the building of the Yishuv, for, as we saw in section I, there was a tradition of Jewish philanthropists going back to Edmond de Rothschild, who cared about the well-being of the Yishuv but did not subscribe to the central Zionist belief in a separate Jewish nationality. The problem was a practical one: American Jewish leaders, whether Zionists like Supreme Court Justice Louis Brandeis or non-Zionists like the financier Felix Warburg, saw the ZO as a business corporation that should attract as much private investment as possible and use public funds only for unambiguously nonprofit undertakings like education. They wanted strict accountability and the placement of experts, not politicians, in positions of authority. Weizmann and his allies, however, saw the ZO as a government, its officers as politicians, and its funds as a national treasury. In 1929 Weizmann finally won the allegiance of the American non-Zionists. Although the ZO remained a separate entity, a new Jewish Agency, representing both the ZO and the non-Zionists, set up executive offices in London and Jerusalem.

Contrary to the Americans' expectations, the Jewish Agency, and in particular its Jerusalem Executive, quickly took on the trappings of a government. This was largely the doing of the Yishuv's workers' movement, which was driven by unshakable political ambition and became the leading political force in the Jewish national home. From the outset, representatives of the Yishuv's workers' movement sat on the Jewish Agency Jerusalem Executive, and when David Ben-Gurion became chair of that body in 1935, he effectively became the prime minister of a Zionist provisional government. By that time, workers' parties commanded the support of some 40 percent of the Yishuv electorate, and they dominated the Yishuv's representative National Assembly and that assembly's executive, the National Council.

Labor Zionism's rise to dominance in the Yishuv was the result of two forces: the molding of socialist ideology into a form compatible with Zionist ideals and the construction of a formidable political machine. The former enabled the latter. Already by 1914 the Po'alei Tsion party had begun to lose its Marxist tinge. The Yishuv's working class was so frail, and the challenges of building a nation so great, that socialist Zionists could not afford to take a purely adversarial stance toward the ZO and the Yishuv's bourgeoisie. In a land as poor as Palestine, capital was not the worker's enemy, as Marxists thought it was in industrialized countries, but rather the only hope for a livelihood. What's more, for those hardy few pioneer laborers who had immigrated to Palestine and successfully made a stand there, Zionism meant far more than a small component in an international socialist revolution. The Bolshevik Revolution (1917) entranced many Po'alei Tsion not for its impact on the world so much as the lessons it taught about how hegemony could be attained in Palestine.

Thus in 1919 Ben-Gurion pushed the Po'alei Tsion into dissolution by melding the party with a group of independent activists to form a new party, Ahdut Ha-Avodah (Unity of Labor). Most of the leaders of the new party, including Berl Katznelson and Yitzhak Tabenkin, came from the independents. The party's name reflected wishful thinking, however, as it encountered stiff resistance from within the Yishuv's labor movement. Ha-Po'el Ha-Tsa'ir, the more romantic and purely nationalist of the two prewar parties, remained suspicious of Ahdut Ha-Avodah because of its continuing lip service to class struggle. And a surge of support for a more solidly Marxist approach came from thousands of socialist youth who arrived with Zionism's Third Aliyah (1919–23).

Many of these young people took part in what they called Gedud Ha-Avodah (the Labor Brigade), a mobile and revolutionary community of workers. The brigade's collectivist spirit manifested itself in communes among the road builders and urban laborers, as well as the creation in 1924 of a new form of communal settlement, the kibbutz, which was much larger and economically more varied than the prewar kvutzah. In time, the Labor Brigade collapsed, a victim of exhaustion, rivalry with Ahdut Ha-Avodah, and the ideological factionalism that is so common on both extremes of the political spectrum.

Like Marxism, the agrarian orientation of the early pioneers was subject to compromise. During the 1920s, two-thirds of the members of the Zionist labor parties and trade unions were urban workers. The kibbutzim quickly became an enclave within the labor movement, with their own interests and champions, competing for scarce resources with the urban workers and their party bosses. One political party, the far-leftist Ha-Shomer Ha-Tsa'ir (Young Guard), did commit itself entirely to the kibbutz ideal, but this case was exceptional.

Although true unity within Labor Zionism remained unattainable, the movement consolidated itself into a formidable political force with the creation in 1930 of Mapai (an acronym for the Land of Israel Workers' Party). This party melded Ha-Po'el Ha-Tsa'ir and Ahdut Ha-Avodah. The result was a complete renunciation of the concept of class struggle. Ben-Gurion acknowledged that the Yishuv depended on private capital. (More than three-fourths of capital imports during the mandate period came from private sources.) At the same time, Ben-Gurion argued, the labor movement had an obligation and unique ability to lead the nation toward independence, and he favored a strong public sector as a guiding and regulating economic force. The centralization of power, economic and political, was an essential vehicle for the realization of Zionist aims.

In this spirit, Ben-Gurion favored expansion of the Histadrut, a national trade union that had been founded in 1920. There was widespread support in the Zionist labor movement for such a union, but opinions differed as to its relationship with the political parties. Staunch Marxists from the Third Aliyah wanted a clear separation between a party whose chief function was to plot revolution and a trade union, which had the more humble task of improving the workers' present circumstances. But Ben-Gurion, as secretary of both Mapai and the Histadrut, sought to meld the two and to extend the union's purview from representing employees to being its own employer and producer. Thus the Histadrut founded a bank (Bank Ha-Po'alim), a construction company (Solel Boneh), and a variety of other enterprises.

Although young pioneers streamed into Palestine throughout the 1920s and 1930s, the bulk of Jewish immigrants were what the British authorities called "capitalists," that is, middle-class Jews possessed of at least modest means. Between 1924 and 1939, some 300,000 Jewish immigrants reached Palestine. During the 1920s, immigrants of what is called the Fourth Aliyah (1924–29) came mainly from Poland, whose three million Jews encountered severe economic instability and discrimination in the interwar era. The United States' adoption in 1924 of extremely low quotas for immigrants from eastern Europe enhanced Palestine's appeal for people who had not previously been committed Zionists. The general deterioration of Jewish life throughout central and east Europe during the 1930s, coupled with the Nazi rise to power in 1933, accounts for the massive influx of the Fifth Aliyah (1929–39).

Whereas the Second (1904–14) and Third (1919–23) Aliyot gave the Yishuv its political leadership and laid out the framework for its public sector, the Fourth and Fifth Aliyot created a vibrant private sector. As in the previous waves of immigration, approximately three-fourths of the newcomers settled in urban areas. Tel Aviv's population, not even 4,000 in 1921, was 135,000 in 1935. By that same year, Jerusalem had close to 70,000 Jews, and Haifa 40,000. Those immigrants who chose the countryside expanded both the network of collective settlements and the capitalist plantation colonies, which made handsome profits through the export of citrus fruits. Thanks to private investment, industrial development quickened; the number of Jewish industrial workers increased sixfold between 1921 and 1936.

The newcomers were pioneers in the professions as well as business. Approximately one-fourth of the Fifth Aliyah came from Germany, and these immigrants possessed a high level of education and professional expertise. The German Jews included physicians, lawyers, economists, scientists, and scholars of all sorts. German Jews figured prominently in the teaching staff of the Yishuv's high schools and even more so in the Hebrew University of Jerusalem, founded in 1925.

Many of the middle-class immigrants associated with two political parties known as General Zionists. These parties defended the interests of commerce and industry but were often willing to serve in coalition with the labor parties in Yishuv government and the ZO. Other middle-class Jews were attracted to the Revisionist Party, the Palestinian offshoot of Vladimir Jabotinsky's World Union of Revisionist Zionists, which was founded in 1925. The main feature of Revisionist Zionism was a maximalist political program calling upon Britain to oversee the rapid creation of a Jewish commonwealth in all of Palestine (including Transjordan). But Revisionism also preached hostility to Labor Zionism and to socialism in general, which it presented as stifling to individual enterprise and creativity. Whereas the Labor Zionists wanted to transform Jews into proletarian slaves, argued Jabotinsky, Revisionists glorified the Jews as heroic entrepreneurs. Jabotinsky accused Labor Zionism of fomenting class conflict, to which he counterpoised the ideal of a national unity transcending class interest.

During the early 1930s, Revisionist Zionism was highly popular among Jews in Europe, particularly Poland. It spoke to the psychological needs of Jews fearful of anti-Semitism and frustrated by the slow pace of Zionist nation-building. The Revisionists were not as popular in the Yishuv, where Labor had a strong a grip on power and the middle-class parties failed to organize effectively. Nonetheless, the Revisionist youth group, Betar, mobilized sizable numbers to protest the Histadrut's monopoly over employment and collective bargaining. Violent clashes erupted between Histadrut members and Betar strikebreakers in workplaces and spilled out into the streets. In these altercations, Labor and Revisionist forces alike displayed considerable brutality and condoned the use of force. All the major European political movements that influenced interwar Zionism—Bolshevism, Fascism, and eastern European authoritarianism—considered violence to be the continuation of politics by other means.

The ideologies of both Labor and Revisionist Zionism were secular, reflecting the nonreligious character of most of the Third, Fourth, and Fifth Aliyot, which overwhelmed the anti-Zionist, ultra-Orthodox Jews of the Old Yishuv. The ultra-Orthodox looked upon the secular, Zionist, and quasi-socialist New Yishuv with suspicion, even contempt. They saw Zionism as an act of idolatry because it strove to create a Jewish national home through human action alone, prior to the coming of a divinely appointed messiah. Most of the Yishuv's ultra-Orthodox Jews were organized in a political party called Agudat Yisra'el, which was part of an international Orthodox federation that had been founded in 1912. Immediately after the war, the ultra-Orthodox agreed to take part in elections for the Yishuv's National Assembly. Constituting half the Yishuv's population at that time, the ultra-Orthodox counted on winning control over the assembly. But a disappointing electoral performance, followed by waves of secular immigration in the 1920s, caused Agudat Yisra'el to secede from the Yishuv's political structure and thus function as a separate body. The party was hostile to not only secular Zionists but also the 10–15 percent of the Jewish immigrants who were both Orthodox and Zionist.

Unlike the ultra-Orthodox, religious Zionists believed that Zionism was a rescue operation in which all Jews had to join forces. The religious Zionists' political party, the Mizrahi, had an offshoot that embraced Labor Zionist social values, cooperated with the Histadrut, and founded religious kibbutzim. Religious Zionists felt they had a mission to infuse the Yishuv with Torah values and prepare the way for a state, one administered— to the greatest extent possible—according to Jewish law. The most dynamic exponent of this view was Abraham Isaac Kook, who in 1921 was appointed the first chief Ashkenazi rabbi of Palestine. Kook believed that the Zionist movement represented the beginning of a process of divine redemption and that secular Zionists were God's unwitting vehicles for the realization of his plan.

The first two documents in this section (13 and 14) present the views of two of the Zionist movement's most prominent settlement experts on what sort of immigrant and what type of settlement would be optimal in creating a class of Jewish agriculturalists in Palestine. Document 15 is a famous poem that embodies the romantic ethos of Labor Zionist rural settlement, and document 16 demonstrates the vitality of Labor Zionism in striving to penetrate all economic sectors. Documents 17 through 19 depict the situation in Palestine's cities from the point of view of young Labor Zionists who struggled to find employment and implement revolutionary ideologies of class struggle. In documents 20 and 21 we encounter more positive, centrist, and middle-class evaluations of the New Yishuv's cities. The middle-class General Zionists are presented in document 22, the radical anti-socialist ideology of Revisionist Zionism follows in documents 23 and 24, and examples of strife between Revisionist and Labor Zionists over economic issues are provided in documents 25 and 26. The section concludes with two documents that present the worldviews of religious Zionism and anti-Zionist ultra-Orthodoxy, respectively.

13

The Selection of the Fittest (1919)

ARTHUR RUPPIN

Arthur Ruppin (1876–1943) was the chief planner of Zionist settlement from 1908 until the mid-1920s. Raised and educated in Germany, Ruppin brought to the Zionist movement expertise in political economy, demography, and sociology, which he had acquired as a student and while working in the Berlin Office for Jewish Statistics. In 1907, Ruppin toured Palestine at the behest of the Zionist Organization, and a year later he moved to Jaffa, where he directed the ZO's Palestine Office. Ruppin promoted Zionist land purchases, cooperative agricultural settlement in various forms, the founding of Tel Aviv, and the development of Jewish holdings in Haifa. From 1926 until his death, Ruppin lectured on the sociology of the Jews at the Hebrew University of Jerusalem and wrote numerous books on this subject. He also wrote extensively on Zionist agricultural settlement.

This essay, published just after World War I and at the beginning of the Third Aliyah, or wave of Zionist immigration (1919–23), reveals the influences of early twentieth-century social and racial thought on Ruppin's attitudes toward Zionist immigration. On the one hand, Ruppin's concerns were purely practical: given the enormous challenges facing the Zionist project, it was essential that Jewish immigrants be either young and vigorous people capable of rigorous manual labor, or well-to-do, middle-class tradesmen and professionals who could foster the growth of the Yishuv economy. On the other hand, Ruppin had a quasi-biological view of humanity as a substance that needed to be molded by political elites and mobilized in a struggle for national survival. Moreover,

Source: Originally published in *Der Jude* (1919), translated in *Three Decades of Palestine: Speeches and Papers on the Upbuilding of the Jewish National Home* (Jerusalem: Shocken, 1936), 66–72, 78–80.

this document was one of earliest articulations of a Zionist immigration policy, when the emphasis was not on drawing the Jewish masses to Palestine but rather on attracting those who can potentially make the greatest contribution to the fledgling new Yishuv (on early Zionist immigration policy, see also document 8 on the absorption of Yemenite Jews in the Yishuv).

1. The Importance of Selection

One of the most important problems connected with our Palestinian colonization work of the future is the choice of the human material,[1] for it is on the proper solution of this problem that the entire structure of the Jewish community in Palestine will essentially depend. Hitherto this problem has received practically no attention either in theory or in practice. In the matter of theory we devoted ourselves extensively to the question of the economic, legal, and social structure of the Jewish society, which we were erecting in Palestine, but in this we proceeded very much like a physicist who makes his calculation on motion without taking into account the pressure of the atmosphere. We assumed that all we needed to do was find a good social structure, proclaim it by fiat, and presto! it would be there; we seemed to forget that even the best of social structures become flesh and blood realities only by virtue of the individuals that fit into them, and that if the individuals who make up the society do not, in their education, occupation, and character, belong to that structure, they will either alter its form or else reduce it to an empty shell. It had already become evident in the work which had been done in the past of the colonization of Palestine that the best theoretical counsels and preparations came to nothing if they were alien to the views and habits of the east European immigrants. Many of the proposals put forward by European scientists and experts for the improvement of Palestinian conditions would have been excellent if the immigrants had happened to be German peasants, but as applied to individuals who had brought along with them, besides the habits and customs and ways of thought of the Russian cities, the nervous and mental equipment of the town-dweller, they were simply absurd. We must at last learn that in Palestine too we shall achieve good results for the future only by basing ourselves on the realities of the present, i.e., on the actual ways of life of the immigrants, and by a slow development, which starts out from this reality. The higher the level of the immigrant, the more easily the objective can be reached. And the level will be raised if, by sifting our immigrants as far as possible, we shall help bring into the country such elements as by education, occupation, and character come closest to our ultimate aims.

In practice, as in theory, the choice of human material played no part in our plans. Every Jew who immigrated into Palestine was welcome; let him be old, sick, incapable of work, or even possessed of an anti-social character, public opinion in Palestine was not interested. It looked upon him as an addition to the numerically small settlement [the Yishuv], and that was considered enough.[2] Even those who had seen the ruin of the old settlements which, in the cities of Jerusalem, Hebron, Safed, and Tiberias subsisted, without working, on the slender gifts that came in from abroad, had nothing to say against a continued immigration of old people incapable of work; they seemed to think that this kind of immigration was at least better than no immigration at all. In brief, it was the cult of numbers, which overrode all considerations relating to the physical, occupational, and moral equipment of the immigrants.

If, in spite of this absence of critical sifting, we did not suffer too heavily in the composition of the Jewish population, and did not face serious damage in our colonization, the circumstance must be attributed to three factors. In the first place, the immigrants who came to Palestine in order to live there by their work as artisans, businessmen, intellectuals, or agriculturists were spiritually divided from the old Yishuv by so deep a gulf that they remained completely uninfluenced by it. We had two population elements that lived side by side practically without contact. The faults of the old Yishuv, namely its unproductivity and its highly developed system of mendicancy, could not, because of this insulation, infect the new settlement.

The second reason was that in the new Yishuv there was a process of automatic sifting at work, which rejected the bad elements. This automatic sifting resulted from the fact that Palestine offered the Jewish immigrant from east Europe poorer prospects than did the other great immigration centers, like England and America. Those emigrants whose aim it was to make much money in a short time either did not go to Palestine at all, or, having tried it, left it soon. In the main only those remained behind who had some understanding of and love for the idealistic elements connected with Palestine as a land for Jewish settlement. This resulted in a selection in the direction of persons devoted more to the pursuit of an ideal than that of money. To this should be added the fact that Palestine, a land where little could be earned, was also a land unsuited for easy and comfortable living. It lacked the pleasures and amusements of other countries. Living in Palestine meant a kind of renunciation, which could be practiced for any length of time only by those who did not consider material pleasures and worldly amusements the aim and object of life. The consequence therefore was that only the serious elements among the immigrants remained in Palestine, the others were automatically rejected.

There was another direct factor. Before the war the Jewish settlement was so small that every individual in it saw himself not simply as a cipher, but rather as a spiritual potentiality, an important member of the community. As a result of the great interest manifested by world Jewry and the world Jewish press in this handful of Jews in Palestine, every individual conceived himself to be standing at the focus of public interest, his actions under the constant scrutiny of public opinion. And in fact public interest and public curiosity did penetrate deeply into the business and private life of the individual. The general effect was to increase the sense of private and public obligation.

Thus it came about that the composition of the new Yishuv in Palestine was, in spite of the absence of any conscious system of selection, generally satisfactory, and in some respects even extremely good. The communal spirit was admirably developed, and if instances were to be found of mentally confused individuals who for a short time managed to lead public opinion astray, or of others who used idealistic principles as the cover to their egotistic aims, these were nothing more than incidental cases, and the individuals in question could not achieve any lasting influence over public life. Here a healthy idealism ruled.

But the future will see the gradual disappearance of these factors, which made for an automatic selection. The better transportation system that has been introduced both in Palestine, and to and from the country during the war years, will lead to a rapid development of the economic life; it will become easier to earn money, life will become more comfortable, and finally, with the increase in numbers, the individual will no longer feel himself under the control of public opinion, but will, in anonymous obscurity, be able to act more or less as he pleases. There is some fear that Palestine, which lies at the back door of east Europe, can too easily become the hunting ground for many undesirable elements, some motivated by an unnatural idealism,[3] others by a mean egotism. The question is, what stand are we to take in the face of this danger? Shall we act as we have acted hitherto, i.e., welcome every comer and keep on trusting that on the whole the good elements will remain while the bad elements will leave? Shall we go on hailing every newcomer, without exception, as a welcome addition to our numbers? Or shall we pay more attention to quality than to quantity, and seek at the beginning of the process to bring into Palestine only such immigrants as, from the point of view of occupation, health, and character are most desirable for the Jewish community?

I believe that for the future we shall have to abandon the policy of *laisser aller*, which we have followed till now, and substitute for it a conscious and programmatic immigration policy. The aim of this policy must be to secure among the immigrants a maximum percentage of those persons who, by occupation, health, and character, are best fitted to serve the Jewish community in Palestine, and a minimum percentage of those who are unfitted.

2. Occupational Selection

We will begin with the question of occupation. Palestine needs all those who have a trade or occupation by the pursuit of which they can maintain themselves in the country without becoming public burdens and without taking away the livelihood of others in the same line. Palestine is a preponderantly agricultural country. The first need of the Jewish community, if it is to consolidate its position on a firm foundation, is an agricultural population. The second necessity is for artisans and workers. Merchants and members of the professions (teachers, doctors, etc.) come only third. Expressed in numbers, this means that an immigration of the right composition would contain at least 50 percent land workers,[4] at least 30 percent artisans and workers, and at most 10 percent each of merchants and members of the professions. Rentiers must find their place among the last two groups.

But it so happens that the composition of the Jewish population of East Europe, which will supply most of the immigrants, is pretty nearly the diametric opposite of what we are asking for; for in it merchants and members of the professions constitute the large majority, while those employed in agriculture are a tiny minority. This difference of composition can best be represented by the image of a pyramid. In east Europe the broad base of the pyramid is made up of merchants and professionals, the narrower middle section of artisans and workers, while only the small apex consists of agricultural workers. But what Palestine needs is a pyramid whose broad foundations are made up of agricultural workers, while the artisans and workers make up the middle, and the merchants and professionals constitute the narrow apex. If immigration is permitted to run its own course, there is every danger that, in accordance with the occupational composition of the Jewish population of east Europe, we shall have, among the immigrants into Palestine, far too many merchants and professionals and far too few agriculturists. We therefore need a restratification of the population for purposes of immigration. How can this be brought about?

I see the matter as follows. The first thing to do is to find those who follow a trade that we can use and direct them to the positions that can be found for them in Palestine. At the top of the list would be those east European Jews who have already worked in agriculture, vegetable-growing, and cattle-breeding, whether in Jewish colonies or as individuals. In particular, the Jewish colonies of southern Russia[5] could probably furnish us with several hundred, or even several thousand, families. Next we must turn to the artisans and workers, who are numerous enough among the Jews of Europe; they must be carefully tried out for Palestine, where they will find both a home market and export possibilities, as well as working conditions as good as those they have known in Europe. I believe it would be useless to attempt to develop in Palestine industries and crafts with which the Jews of Europe are not familiar. It would need a tremendous amount of work to train these Jews for new industries and crafts; and it is a great saving in time and money to arrange first for the introduction of occupations that are known to masses of Jews in Europe. It is a well-known fact that the immigrant masses of New York succeeded in getting an economic foothold as rapidly as they did because they brought with them the particular craft that they had practiced in Europe and developed it to a higher level in America.[6] In introducing these industries in Palestine, we must, however, see to it that the system is something better than the famous sweat-shop system of New York. I believe that the best way to face this problem is through workers' production cooperatives.

Given the small percentage of Jews engaged in agriculture, it is obvious that this group will not be able to furnish a large enough contingent of immigrants into Palestine. On the other hand it is absolutely essential to increase the number of Jews engaged in Palestinian agriculture, so that the agricultural training cadres may increase in volume. The position is not very different from that which obtains in the army: if there are large enough trained groups (cadres), it is possible to fit into them, year after year, a correspondingly large number of recruits, who thus receive their training. What is most important and most necessary is therefore the creation of these cadres. Unfortunately the number of agricultural centers and enterprises, which we have in Palestine in condition fit to absorb and train newcomers, is a very small one; and not more than 300 land workers could be assigned to them yearly. We must therefore direct our efforts to the enlargement of the cadres, for the education and training of the future Jewish land worker in Palestine itself has much more promise in it than the same education and training anywhere else. The young man who gets his training in Palestine not only learns what he needs to learn in the matter of agriculture as such (besides which it must be borne in mind that the Palestinian training is actually more detailed and more relevant) but he becomes familiar— while acclimatizing himself at the same time—with the manners and language of the country. Those persons who cannot become acclimated, or who are not fit for an agricultural life, generally leave the course early on. We may expect that of those who have passed through a training of several years—very few will be lost to the country later. As regards those who have received their agricultural training in Europe, the percentage of those who will remain in Palestine after they have tried the country is naturally much lower. In my opinion more than half of them will not find themselves suited to the country, that is to say, less than half the number of those we have trained will stay with us.

[. . .]

3. Physical Selection

It would of course be very fine if only strong and healthy persons would come to settle in Palestine, so that we would in this wise be assured of a strong and healthy succeeding generation. Unfortunately, this much desired objective cannot be carried out with this generalized simplicity, as the concepts "strong" and "healthy" are not particularly clear. Weak persons may in time become strong; for many professions physical strength and perfect health are much less important than mental and spiritual makeup; and, finally, the constitution of a person has, in many cases, nothing to do with the capacity to beget strong and healthy children. On these grounds we shall have to limit ourselves, in regard to the physical equipment of immigrants, to rejecting those individuals who are dangerous by virtue of some infectious disease (syphilis, advanced tuberculosis, etc.) or are likely to become public charges (the mentally deranged, epileptics, all those who are prevented by sickness from making a living). The elimination of such persons should be taken care of by the doctors of the Palestine Immigration Offices in the ports of sailing; but a second examination should take place in Palestine in the ports of arrival.

Another question may be touched on here that is not without importance: that is, whether it is possible to work for the keeping pure of the Jewish racial stock. Since it is our desire to develop in Palestine our Jewish side, it would naturally be desirable to have only "race" Jews[7] come to Palestine. But a direct influence on the process, via the selection of such immigrants as most closely approach the racial type, is not practically possible. On the whole, however, it is likely that the general type in Palestine will be more strongly Jewish than the general type in Europe, for it is to be expected that the more strongly Jewish types will be the ones who are most generally discriminated against in Europe, and it is they who will feel themselves most strongly drawn toward a Jewish community in Palestine.

4. Elimination of Anti-Social Types

It has become evident in the foregoing that we place the elimination of anti-social types from among the ranks of the immigrant groups at the very head of our list of problems. In Palestine the process of selection can issue from the further development of the economic life along the lines of the cooperative as the smallest economic unit. Persons who cannot find admittance into any cooperative will find themselves heavily handicapped from the outset, and will in many cases leave the country, particularly if there is a pressure of public opinion against cranks and anti-social types.

We may anticipate that, against the system of selection here advocated, the objection will be raised that entire groups can be anti-social, and that when twenty persons act in concert this is not necessarily a proof that they are of higher morality than an individual. But the objection is untenable. In general these groups, which will be mostly drawn from the mass of east European Jews, will reflect the moral standards of this mass. These moral standards are not anti-social. By far the great majority of east European Jews would make desirable immigrants. (Were it otherwise, all our efforts to construct a Jewish life in Palestine on a sound social basis would be wasted, for the transplantation into another country of masses of morally inferior persons does nothing to improve their moral standing, and a good social system imposed from without on a morally inferior population is either smashed or evaded.) It is only through an unfortunate chain of accidents, or through a purposive and conspiratorial organization of "outsiders" that we could have a morally inferior majority among a group of twenty to fifty persons obstructing selection in our sense.

It is also of capital importance that public opinion shall help us in this process of selection, in the countries where the groups are formed not less than in Palestine. The importance of a right selection must be appreciated and understood everywhere. And inasmuch as the morality of a group is—as mentioned above—a mirror of the morality of the general population, it may be hoped that as the general morality and the feeling of responsibility among the Jews of Palestine rise to higher levels, particularly through a return to agriculture, through the development of the school system, and of municipal self-management, the moral demands that the groups will make of their individual members will also rise. Much depends on making each group understand that any laxity in the admission of members reacts to its own hurt, for the member of an inferior type is like a social ulcer, and the economic progress of the group can be heavily hindered by the presence of such persons. The inclusion of members in an immigrant group must therefore follow the rule that every applicant must go through a six-month period of probation, during which he attends all the sessions of the group, takes part in the proceedings, and becomes well known to the other members. Since a good deal thus depends on the type of person composing the founding group, it will be the task of the local representatives of the Palestine Immigration Offices to see to it that individuals unfitted for such an enterprise should be prevented from undertaking it; they should on the other hand, encourage the formation of such founding groups as, in their opinion, will instill the right spirit into the completed body.

In Palestine there should be an effort to bring together the organizations and cooperatives of similar trades into larger, more general organizations, and particularly to bring about the organization of individual workers, artisans, etc. into groups. We believe that this cooperative concentration will result in a raising of professional standards and a strengthening of the sense of common responsibility.

NOTES

1. In the original German, *Menschenmaterial*; in Hebrew, *homer enoshi*. This was a common term in early twentieth-century Europe and gained currency throughout the Zionist movement.

2. Ruppin is referring to the period of the First and Second Aliyot.

3. Probably a reference to communist revolutionaries.

4. When Ruppin first wrote on this subject in 1907, he posited that fully 80 percent of the Yishuv's Jewish population should till the soil. Ruppin's strong preference for agriculture stemmed from romantic-idealist as well as pragmatic motivations.

5. Since the early nineteenth century, Jews had been allowed to settle as farmers in the southern portions of the Pale of Settlement. Their numbers reached some 40,000 by World War I.

6. Tailoring and related trades.

7. A vague concept uniting physical and psychological attributes, "racial" Jewishness connoted descent from Jewish parents, a self-conscious identification as a Jew, and a commitment to Jewish collective life in cultural, religious, or national forms. The term "race" as used by Ruppin is closer in meaning to our contemporary use of the term "ethnicity" rather than the way the term "race" was used later on in the twentieth century.

14

The Collective Agricultural Settlements in Palestine (1927)

YITZHAK WILKANSKY

Wilkansky (1880–1955) was raised in a Lithuanian shtetl and received an Orthodox rabbinical education before studying natural science, economics, and agronomy at universities in Switzerland and Germany. In 1908 Wilkansky moved to Palestine, where he was employed by Arthur Ruppin's Palestine Office as a farm manager. A member of the Labor Zionist political party Ha-Po'el Ha-Tsa'ir, Wilkansky was a vital link between the Zionist Organization's largely German and bourgeois senior leadership and the young east European pioneers of the Second Aliyah.

As this document shows, Wilkansky had a deep romantic streak. He loathed industry and capitalism, and he touted the collective (or "communist") kvutzah as a shining inspiration for the Zionist project as a whole. At the time he wrote the book from which this passage is taken, the Yishuv was suffering from an economic recession, and there was considerable opposition in the Zionist Organization to the kvutzot and their larger cousins, the kibbutzim, which combined agriculture with industry. Zionist leaders in the United States and western Europe thought that the collective settlements were inefficient and ideologically suspect. Thus Wilkansky passionately defended the collective as having a supreme, meta-economic value.

Source: Yitzhak Wilkansky (Isaac Elazari-Volcani), *The Communistic Settlements in the Jewish Colonization in Palestine* (Tel Aviv: The Palestine Economic Society, 1927; repr. Westport, Conn.: Hyperion, 1976), 18–23.

Ironically, Wilkansky's romantic individualism caused him to be more attracted to the smallholding cooperative agricultural settlement known as the *moshav ovdim* (worker's moshav). (The first experiments with this type of settlement were attempted before World War I, but the first truly successful moshav, Nahalal, was founded in 1921 under the guidance of another pioneer agronomist, Eliezer Joffe.) Wilkansky's use of the phrase "Robinson Crusoe islands" in a positive sense is very telling in this context. Marx used this phrase several times in his writings to debunk the attempts of liberal economists to draw conclusions from the experience of the individual to society as a whole: Wilkansky, as a member of the non-Marxist Ha-Po'el Ha-Tsa'ir, is more comfortable with smaller social units than perhaps the more doctrinaire socialists who thought in terms of the social body as a whole.

There are . . . three dominant features of the formation of the group settlements: (1) Sectarian idealism (2) occupational strategy (3) economical rationalism.

Degania[1] was the first communistic settlement in the country; and as it was the first, so it was the best in virtue of the harmony both of spirit and of action with which it was pervaded. This harmony was a wonderful thing for a body like a kvutzah, compounded of mutually conflicting elements and bearing the yoke of a self-imposed discipline at the bidding of a power really above and outside of itself, though seeming at the first glance to be within it.

No new theories have originated from Degania; and perhaps even those that will be written about it by others will not meet the approval of its inmates and will not fit in with their notions. In any case the impartial observer who seeks to get a true idea of the spirit of this group will not go far wrong if he says: we are here in the presence of a lofty idealism. The dominant purpose before which everything else here must give way is to preserve the soul in its purity; and the "economic laws" of which others stand in so much awe are here regarded as nothing but the outward material garment, the gross earthenware vessel that holds the precious wine.

The outlook of the isolated group is not essentially different from that of the individual who flees from society with the secret purpose of saving his soul— secret, because it is largely subconscious. The refined soul cannot stand the storms and buffetings of the everyday world. It cannot avert the storm; it is not willing to be swept away by it. What then does it do? It seeks to build itself a citadel of refuge, to encircle itself with fences and hedges. It feels an urgent necessity to shake itself free from many social duties, which are incumbent on every member of society, and to devote itself to "higher duties," which society tramples under foot. Artists, poets, and philosophers also seek solitude each in his own way, and in obedience to an inner impulse, endeavor to liberate themselves from many conventional duties that conflict with their desire for self-expression, and so to gain a freer field for their creative powers, which find expression also in directions that though unconventional are for the benefit of the mass. In the same way individuals who do not trust their own powers, or who fear that they may find themselves in situations against which the individual is powerless, seek for strength in a combination of forces. Some attain this end by adopting a hermit life, dwelling in caves and deserts, or between the walls of monasteries, where they look for the most complete escape from a world of sin. Others separate from society with its grades and class distinctions in order to avoid them and to escape from the dominant, the very justice of which is rooted in injustice. In an isolated group there is still a slight possibility of escaping from evil, as within its bounds each one can live his own life according to his own ideas and not be the slave of convention. These societies are not formed with the deliberate purpose of being a shining light to others, or to society. If they are genuine they set up an example automatically, without any preaching or propaganda. Like radium through a dark body, so their example will pierce through ignorance and prejudice.

Settlers of this type do not pretend to discover new ways and methods in the economic structure either of individual or national concern. It is not in order to increase production that they choose their peculiar way of life. It is true that the increase of the communal wealth is of great value for the purposes of the settlement, but each individual has only two hands and one brain, the capacity of which is limited; and he who grasps too much is in danger of holding nothing. The voice of common sense says: "Do not be over-pious even for the benefit of the community. Live your isolated life, in justice and uprightness, from the labor of your own hands, not like those who sanctify themselves in monasteries, and in appearance flee from the sins of society when in fact they are being supported from the sources of those same sins." But on the other hand, there is no obligation to increase the national wealth of the people if such increase conflicts in the slightest with the ethical purpose that is the very foundation of the whole existence of the group-settlements.

We see then the raison d'être and the justification for settlements of this type are essentially ethical, and they are not be assessed by economic standards. Let us grant that the breaking up of the communal large farm into individual farms would result in an increased yield from the soil, and a large production in all branches of the farm, as well as in a reduction of expenses and consequent increase in net profit. These balance-sheet advantages are not decisive reasons for changing the form of the farm. Of what benefit will this surplus be to the men who see the root of all social ills—envy, hatred, and competition in private property, who believe that so soon as a man draws bounds round his field, the evil inclination,[2] which leads men astray and sets nation against nation, finds its sustenance there, and that only through the elimination of such bounds can its domination be terminated. What is the use of the wealth gathered up by private enterprise if one year of war can destroy the accumulation of generations? And it is for the sake of private property that all wars are undertaken. There are some individuals who deliberately choose an easy and ill-paid profession that suits their taste in preference to a harder one that would bring them a higher return, but which would entail sacrifices of principle and compromises on their part. Would anyone think of saying to these persons: "It is better that you shall violate your conscience and dedicate your surplus powers to the good of the community in order to increase the communal wealth and to enlarge the boundaries of our settlements?" Matters of conscience like this cannot be regulated on a commercial basis. If communists are forced into styles of farming that they do not like, their capacities will be still further diminished, and the national wealth will be lessened proportionately. The national economy cannot dispense with any producer, whether he is a believer in the kvutzah or the moshav, since it is only through the living faith with each that he adds to the national assets. Without this burning fire of faith there is no creativeness or intensity or effort; and the fire burns differently in each individual. In most cases it can go on burning even when foreign elements are mixed with it, but with exceptional natures it burns only when it is in its purity. Then it is able to produce at least a little. Otherwise it is liable to go out, and its motive power vanishes. And it is impossible after shutting off steam to make the engine work.

[. . .]

The essential feature of these settlements is that they set out to swim against the current, and therefore the current itself, strong as it is, does not frighten them. The reforms they introduce in their private life are to them an end in themselves, and therefore the universal transformation of society, important as it is, is not a prevailing and decisive moment in their unusual efforts. The capitalist system is strong, and domineering, and it will not be diverted from its path by the sight of occasional "Robinson Crusoe islands" with the lessons they provide. Give to it what belongs to it. "Mad is the man of spirit"[3] who even in a sinful generation does not prevent his steps, and who, if he cannot turn the current as he desires, is not swept away by it, and does not bend his head before the prevailing winds. He lives in isolation, and he is prepared to sacrifice his life for his opinions, for without them he has nothing to live for. It is possible that these "Crusoe islands" will not stand before the irresistible march of the capitalist system, intolerant as it is of any rival power. It is possible to prove logically that without a world-revolution no isolated socialist experiments will ultimately succeed, and all the "Crusoe islands" will be swept away in the stormy sea of life. But all these arguments are wasted on our communists. It is no use to anticipate trouble, and a brief space of freedom is also good. A spirit of revolt is in the hearts of the members of these settlements, a spirit that has never known what it is to make compromises or concessions.

NOTES

1. See document 7.
2. *Yetser ha-ra*, in rabbinic Hebrew often descriptive as sexual urges, or more generally, impure thoughts and motives.
3. Hoseah 9:7.

15

Song of the Valley (1934)

NATHAN ALTERMAN

Nathan Alterman (1910–70) was the most eminent poet associated with the Zionist labor movement during the interwar period and the early years of the Israeli state. From 1934 Alterman had a weekly column in major Yishuv newspapers (first *Haaretz* and then the Histadrut's organ, *Davar*) in which he wrote about current affairs in verses that ranged from poignant to satirical. Alterman was also a serious poet who produced some of the most important work in modern Hebrew literature. On top of all this, Alterman wrote the lyrics for many Zionist folk songs that were created during the period of the British Mandate.

"The Song of the Valley" (*Shir Ha-Emek*) became one of the most popular and beloved of the Zionist folk songs from this era. (The music was written by Daniel Sambursky.) Accompanying the theme of redemptive physical labor is that of guarding, defending, and dying for the land. Allusions here to gunplay between Arabs and Jews ominously link the silence of the valley at nightfall with the silence of the grave, a reference to the "valley of the shadow of death" in Psalm 23. These lyrics are typical of a genre of Zionist poetry and song that glorified Jewish physical labor, which was perceived as bringing about the reclamation and redemption of the Land of Israel. The references to the land as "blessed and praised," redolent of the traditional Jewish liturgy, reveal the tension between Labor Zionism's overt secularism and its underlying religious, even messianic, dimension.

Source: http://www.shiron.net/artist?type=lyrics&lang=1&prfid=349&wrkid=2980. Accessed March 7, 2011. Translated by Derek J. Penslar.

Rest has come to the weary,
Comfort to the laborer.
Pale night spreads forth
Upon the fields of the Valley of Jezreel.[1]
Dew below and moon above
From Beit Alpha[2] to Nahahal.[3]

What, what, from night to night?
Silence in the Valley.
Sleep, Valley, land of glory.
We stand guard over you.

The sea of grain sways gently,
The tinkling song of the flock.
This is my land and its fields;
This is the Valley of Jezreel.

May my land be blessed and praised
From Beit Alpha to Nahalal.

Darkness upon Mount Gilboa,[4]
A horse gallops from shadow to shadow.
The sound of a cry flies upward
Upon the field of the Valley of Jezreel.

Who fired? And who fell there,
Between Beit Alpha and Nahalal?

What, what, from night to night?
Silence in the Valley.
Sleep, Valley, land of glory.
We stand guard over you.

NOTES

1. Located between the lower Galilee and the northern West Bank, this was a focal point of Labor Zionist agricultural settlement during the mandate period.

2. Kibbutz at the eastern edge of the Jezreel Valley, established in 1922.

3. Moshav in the western Jezreel Valley, established in 1921.

4. On the southeastern edge of the Jezreel Valley.

16

Going Down to the Sea (1937)

DAVID BEN-GURION

This essay provides a good example of the combination of boundless energy, extreme optimism, and dark trepidation that characterized David Ben-Gurion's thinking about the Zionist project and the directions it may take in the future. Writing as an organized Palestinian nationalist rebellion was shaking the land, Ben-Gurion emphasizes as a positive development the construction of a new port in Tel Aviv, but he is concerned about the ease with which the nascent Jewish national home can be blockaded by sea and contemporary Jewry's general estrangement from maritime pursuits. Thus in this document Zionist ideological yearnings to transform Jews into productive workers blend seamlessly with geo-political strategy.

Ben-Gurion's call was not heeded within his own Labor movement that at the time was all consumed with "conquering the land," with acquiring more and more land and developing new Jewish settlements in Palestine. British policies were restricting the ability of Jews to purchase land. His archrivals, however, the right-wing Revisionists (see documents 23, 24), valued seafaring in keeping with their militaristic and commercial–capitalist ideology. Indeed, the timing of this essay suggests that it was written in order to co-opt or compete with the Revisionists, who in the mid-1930s were providing naval training for Zionist youth in Riga and Civitavecchia. Ben-Gurion's vision of a vigorous Zionist merchant marine and commercial shipping fleet would be realized after 1948.

Source: *The Jewish Frontier* (1945), 274–79.

If I should be asked what event looms most important in the history of Palestinian colonization during 1936, I should unhesitatingly answer: neither the disturbances nor the riots, but the inauguration of the Tel Aviv port. I am convinced that a review of events, judged in historical perspective and unaffected by press bally-hoo, would reveal the real milestone in the past year to have been the creation of the Tel Aviv port. That innovation has indeed a permanent value, which promises to give a new turn to our political and resettlement program.

For the Tel Aviv harbor is a starting point that leads up to the much larger maritime question. We should never forget the all-important fact that Palestinian Jews constitute only a picayune percentage of the Jewish people scattered throughout the world. And yet (barring one or two clusters of Jews in Persian and Iraq) we have no way of maintaining connections with the rest of the Jewish world, save by means of the sea. And in turn, no Jews—except those living in Syria, Mesopotamia, Turkey, or Persia—can possibly reach us other than by boat. Now inasmuch as communication with the Diaspora plays a vital part in our work, our sea predicament creates a grave danger. Observe what happened during the riots. We suffered not only from the Arab "strike"[1] but from terrorist gangs, recruited not from local Arabs but in major part—if not numerically, at least from the point of view of their viciousness—made up of neighboring Syrians and Iraqi [sic] imported from bordering countries. These murderers had a direct land route for both entrance and egress. But Jews who arrive to create cannot come by land. They must take ship to enter Palestine. And yet, though sea communication is so all-important to us, Jews have no ships of their own. The many Jews in the Diaspora constitute an appreciable power and possess economic, financial, and in some cases even political influence. New York boasts an enormous Jewish population of two million, which can sometimes turn the tide in mayoral elections and which is no mean factor in determining the outcome of a hotly contested presidential campaign. It possesses financial power and controls many institutions and industries. But in one particular economic enterprise—that of the sea—Jews are complete outsiders. And yet the realm of the sea is neither an empty one nor an unpopulated desert of water. In its own way, indeed, it is an inhabited area, an immense economic resource, the main artery of communication for humanity. On this vast expanse we have staked out no holding. Jews conduct many businesses throughout the world. They own factories, banks, and corporations—but on the boundless sea teeming with transports, freighters, passenger vessels, fishing yawls, tourist and scout-boats, we cannot find even one Jewish launch. Of their own volition, Jews have excluded themselves from this potential economic activity. And this self-elimination has taken place despite overcrowding into various occupational fields, vain searching for new trades, and grasping for new means of livelihood.

Why have Jews neglected the mighty mart of the sea, which promises economic openings to thousands and tens of thousands of Diaspora families residing in coastal cities? Must Jewish workers in America, for example, devote themselves entirely to indoor shop work? Why should not some of them enter maritime occupations? The same holds true of Jewries in Holland, England, and similar lands. Why perpetuate a self-enclosed *terra firma* ghetto?

And can we afford to resign ourselves to this situation? We who have undertaken the great and arduous task of gathering together a dispersed people and of bringing it back to the land by sea—can we submit to having the sea locked in our very faces? Even under the best of political conditions—we could not risk continuing in this predicament. Certainly at the present time, when not one of us knows what the morrow holds in store for us, we dare not accept a self-imposed injunction that excludes us from the major part of the earth's surface and leaves us without an independent link between the concentration of Jews in Palestine and the Jewish dispersions in other parts of the world. Somehow we must win our rightful place in maritime economy, the main artery of world communication. Does such achievement lie beyond us?

A sound historical instinct led our movement to use as its point of departure the wish to return to the soil. Hence from the days of Bilu[2] to those of Hekhalutz,[3] we were all dominated by the desire to strike roots in the soil. Though we have achieved much in this direction, our agricultural conquest remains in its incipient stage still. And now, when we heed the call of the sea, we certainly do not aim to weaken or diminish our agricultural development. We do not propose to substitute seacraft for farming, nor do we urge self-dedication to the sea at the expense of agriculture. We intend only to include maritime activities in their proper place in our economic program. For clearly our future as a creative people and a militant labor movement is bound up with our sea strength no less than with our skill in working the soil. The time has come to expand our economic conquest and structure. We shall not budge one jot from our determination to inaugurate and develop more and more points of settlement on the land. But in addition to these land colonies, I foresee upon the sea highly promising, valuable elements of economic growth. Every Jewish sailing vessel will be both a "colony" and a source of strength. A Jewish boat means Jewish deckhands, sailors, and naval officers. Further, it implies not merely a Jewish boat, but a workers' boat, which, for me, is fully as much a labor settlement of economic, cultural, and political value as any rural or urban center. Indeed the very mobility—its moving at will—increases its importance and strength. This fluidity does not suggest shiftlessness but on the contrary indicates a flow of power and might.

At this time, above all, when we are forging the tools of self-defense and rallying all our physical and economic forces to ward off the terrible dangers that beset us, we must embark on the high seas and undertake the high duty of establishing a solid maritime economy. This we can do only if our movement rouses all its latent powers of conquest and recognizes its new noble mission— to conquer the sea with the same strength displayed in winning the *Emek*.[4] The very effort has its own validity—even apart from its significance to our difficult political position. Extension into maritime activities portends new economic possibilities and further opportunities for immigration, additional absorptive power, settlements, and generation of future strength. We must build up Jewish shipping, and as much as possible make it a proletarian Jewish marine. We need Jewish labor vessels not only for commerce and travel but also for broader reasons. First of all we must create a merchant marine: tens and hundreds of Jewish ships manned by Jewish workmen but under the tutelage of the Jewish labor movement—must sail the sea. These ships will drop anchor in the ports of Roumania [Romania] and Poland to embark thousands of pioneers. This is not beyond our attainment since we have at our disposal pioneer forces the like of which no other national movement perhaps has ever enjoyed. True, we are not familiar with nautical trades and maritime economy. None of us ever sailed before the mast. Yet how many Emek colonists farmed before they came there? There is no trade that we cannot learn to master. Without vital impetus, however, without throwing behind this endeavor, all our movement's enthusiasm (and by the movement we do not mean individuals or isolated groups, but the creative spirit of all Zionism), without this, I say, it will be impossible to attain our great goal. For we are land-bred and alien to the sea. As yet the lore of the waters is a closed book to us. But neither have we yet exploited all our hidden talents. We ignore the wide extent of our own complacency. The Histadrut[5] is an instrument with infinite capacity and resources that have not been exhausted, not by a long shot. In a short time we have erected numerous institutions, every one playing a specific role in our society. But each of our institutions has obligations beyond its own needs. In addition to its specific functions each bears a direct relationship and responsibility toward other elements in our movement. Once we view our going down to the sea as a matter of great historical moment— parallel to our own entrance into agriculture—the necessary strength will be found and the effort will be forthcoming. The Histadrut institutions represent great potential resources. Also we may draw on the strength of the entire Zionist movement, whose character, purpose, method, and will largely depend upon us. Just as we directed the Zionist movement toward the acquisition of national wealth, pioneering, agriculture—and we have not yet completed this difficult task that runs counter to traditional Diaspora psychology—so we must now orientate the Zionist movement toward a new goal and begin to muster will power and wherewithal for the great nautical project required of us.

Our entry into sea commerce presents this additional advantage: It neither involves conflict with Arab competition nor limits us within the confines of Palestine. The sea lies open, free, and almost without bourne. Not only the Mediterranean at our door but all "the seven seas" of the world, the gigantic expanse surrounding the six continents. Nothing hinders our having ships docking at all ports of Europe, the Americas, Asia, Africa, and Australia, just as nothing prevents the ships of all other nations from calling at our ports. Jewish boats will make Palestine known everywhere. By carrying the Jewish Palestinian flag to all corners of the earth, they will forge a new, living, heartening link between the Yishuv in the homeland and scattered Jewish communities every- where. Our boats shall bring tidings of Jewish labor and Jewish settlement to all dispersed Jewry, which may thus also be stimulated to engage in maritime work.

We may use the ocean to batter down the walls between Palestine and the Diaspora. We can build Jewish ships not only in Palestine but also in Latvia, Roumania, Holland, and England. Land settlement can be affected only in Palestine. But Jews may penetrate into the sea from any land. Our movement at all times aimed at synthesis, at bridging Palestine and the Diaspora, and the sea alone constitutes such a material bridge. American-Jewish workers can share only metaphorically in agricultural resettlement. But nothing can deter their actual participation, not only by financial contributions but by their own labor, in a Jewish proletarian maritime scheme. Jewish deckhands in England, America, and elsewhere may join the company of their sea-going, Palestinian, fellow workers. Just as we acquire and build ships here, our comrades in other Jewries may do the same in their respective countries. The maritime profession may thus form an economic framework including all branches of the Jewish people, all our workers and pioneers, wherever they may be.

NOTES

1. The Palestinian general strike that preceded the armed rebellion of 1936–39.
2. A Socialist-Zionist movement from the period of the First Aliyah. See document 113.

3. A Zionist youth organization, founded after World War I and centered in eastern and central Europe, devoted to the agricultural training of potential immigrants to Palestine.

4. The Jezreel Valley.

5. On the Histadrut, see document 18n2.

17

Labor Incidents in Palestine (1925)

W. ORMSBY GORE

This letter was composed by William Ormsby Gore (1885–1964), who at the time was the parliamentary undersecretary in the Colonial Office. During the First World War, Gore was stationed in Egypt, and he served as the British liaison officer with the 1918 Zionist Mission in Palestine. The letter was addressed to Arthur Henderson, MP (1863–1935), who in 1925 served as home secretary (he became foreign secretary in 1931). The letter provides an overview of labor disputes among the Jewish population in Palestine, based on a report by Lord Plumer (Herbert Charles Onslow Plumer, 1st Viscount Plumer, 1857–1932), the British High Commissioner in Palestine from 1925 to 1928. The letter indicates that in the mid-1920s the main cause of social unrest in Palestine was not the bourgeoning Arab–Jewish conflict but rather internal Jewish divisions that tended to stem from labor disputes.

Colonial Office, Downing Street, S.W. 1
October 5, 1925

Dear Henderson,

　　With further reference to your letter of the 18th September regarding certain labour incidents in Palestine, I find that we have just received a full report from Lord Plumer in reply to the despatch which we sent to him on this subject on the receipt of your earlier letter.

Source: Lavon Institute Archive, 4/36/4.

Lord Plumer reports that during July there occurred at Tel-Aviv a series of attempts by the local Council of the Jewish Labour Federation to interrupt work undertaken by private Jewish contractors who were employing non-Union Jewish labour. It was found that, in the course of this dispute contractors and workmen had been waylaid and beaten, and as a result two men, who were stated to have instigated and directed the policy of violence were brought before the President of the Jaffa District Court and, on the ground that they had been making speeches inciting to violence were ordered to produce bonds with surety of L.E. [Egyptian pounds] 100 each to be of good behaviour for six months. There was no question of imposing any condition that during that period they should take no part in industrial activities; all they were required to do was to give an undertaking not to break the ordinary law of the land. As they failed to produce the bonds they were committed to imprisonment for three months. Lord Plumer states that he was advised that the fact that acts of violence had been committed by strikers against persons who remained in employment afforded good ground for applying the Prevention of Crime Ordinance at Tel-Aviv. The legality of applying that Ordinance was, however, being tested by an application to the Eigh [sic] Court of Palestine which has been dismissed, the Governments view of the law being confirmed.

As regards the trouble at Haifa, Lord Plumer reports that on the 23rd of August a crowd, numbering about 200, composed of members of the Jewish Labour Federation who were on strike, and of their sympathizers, assembled to prevent workmen of the rival labour organization, which is known as the Labour Association of the Mizrahi Zionist Organization,[1] from continuing their work. Orders were given by the District Commandant of the Police that the crowd should disperse, but they refused and attacked the Police with stones. As a result thirty persons were arrested, of whom ten were identified as having thrown stones, ten others were identified as having obstructed the Police, and the remainder was released. The accused have been committed for trial. Lord Plumer also reports that he is advised that there was sufficient reason for applying the Ottoman Law of Illegal Assembly at Haifa on this date, as the strikers were acting in a disorderly manner which seriously threated [sic] the public peace.

The ten strikers at Haifa, to whom your previous letter particularly referred, were arrested on the 9th of August for molesting members of the Mizrahi Organisation while at work, and for trespassing upon private premises. They were sentenced to five days' imprisonment each by the Magistrate at Haifa, and while being conveyed to Acre Jail to serve their sentences they were linked together by a chain, in accordance with the Prison Regulations.

I trust that the information which I am able to give you will enable you to reply satisfactorily to your correspondent. I may say that, when forwarding the report, for which I have given you the substance, Lord Plumer stated that he wished to repudiate the suggestion that the Government of Palestine is hostile to the Organisation of Labour. He pointed out that there are certain special difficulties in Palestine, since the two rival Jewish Labour Unions are constantly in dispute on the questions affecting general labour principles, and morever [*sic*] there is between them a fundamental conflict of attitude due to the fact that the Mizrahi Organisation consists of the more religious elements. In addition, the attitude of organized Jewish labourers towards minority groups of Jewish workmen causes particular anxiety to the authorities in Palestine, since it is a possible disturbing factor in a counter where racial differences require the firm maintenance of Government authority.

It must also be remembered that most of the persons concerned in this disputes [*sic*] have entered Palestine comparatively recently from Eastern and Central Europe and are therefore very prone to settle their quarrels by serious violence. They have not got the tradition which we have in this country of settling matters in a goodtempered and friendly fashion, and the authorities are therefore bound to intervene much more in such disputes than they would here.

Yours sincerely,
Signed: W. Ormsby Gore
The Right Honourable
Arthur Henderson, M.P.

NOTE

1. The writer refers here to tensions between workers who were members of the Histadrut (see document 18n2), which was dominated by the secular, socialist Zionists and members affiliated with the Mizrahi movement, a national religious faction within the ZO that was formed in 1902 and sought to combine traditional Judaism with the political goals of the Zionist movement.

18

The Pechter Strike (1927)

ANONYMOUS JEWISH WORKERS

In 1927, the Palestine Electric Company began the construction of the Naharayim hydroelectric power plant at the intersection of the Yarmuk and Jordan rivers on the eastern bank of the Jordan. This was one of the largest civil projects in the history of the Yishuv, and it required extensive investment in infrastructure, including the construction of a special rail line and special train cars. The Pechter et Hoffman and Sons Company from Tel Aviv, an iron casting factory, built special train cars for the Naharayim project. Workers at the Pechter company went on strike, but they were pressured by the Yishuv's political leadership to return to work. In this document, a small faction of the Zionist Labor movement calls for continuing the strike and for the leadership of the Labor movement to stand behind the workers and not to represent the interests of their employers. The document reflects the growing social upheaval in the Yishuv at that period and the escalating tensions between the Zionist movement's commitment to social values and the interests of the workers, and its commitment to the overall strength and well-being of the Jewish community in Palestine, which was highly enhanced by grand projects such as the construction of the Naharayim power plant.

Source: Lavon Institute Archive, 4/36/5. Translated by Marganit Weinberger-Rotman.

Workers of the World Unite!

The Ruling Parties Betray Pechter Strikers!
Comrades!

By order of Pinchas Rutenberg of London,[1] the leaders of the ruling parties in the Histadrut[2] have ordered the 130 Pechter workers to end their strike. The strike, which lasted four weeks, had been declared by the workers and garnered the support of the entire working public. A few days into the strike, it became apparent that Pechter is the abject lackey of the industrialists, entrusted by them to lead the battle against the Laborers' Union, to deprive the workers of their class achievements. This explains his stubborn conduct in prosecuting this strike until the final capitulation of the protesters.

The workers had only one course of action: to expand and intensify the confrontation using all the means at their disposal. Workers in other factories and the public in general hoped for a successful outcome of this strike, because they knew that it would affect their own interests. But Ahdut Ha-Avodah [United Labor] and Ha-Po‘el Ha-Tsa’ir (the Young Worker),[3] who expected the strike to be over within two or three days and who planned to use it as a beacon to light their way to victory in the elections, were stunned when they saw how extensive and harsh it was, and how far it exceeded the parameters that they had set for it. It was then that they determined to put an end to the strike, by hook or by crook.

Thus, they limited the strikers to one demand: arbitration in the matter of the metalworkers' salaries.

The leaders agreed that all the other demands (raises, work in the chemistry department, seven working hours on Fridays, compensation for strike days, and sanitary conditions) would be consigned to later arbitration, but Pechter objected to this compromise, too.

The general working public was deliberately prevented from aiding and supporting the strikers. *Davar*,[4] instead of championing the strikers' cause, looked for ways to supply the employers with excuses. No money was collected on behalf of the protesters, except in Haifa, and the workers were left to starve. Eventually, the leaders gave in and entrusted the decision to a man of good sense and integrity, Mr. Pinchas Rutenberg.[5]

Workers!

A few days ago, without your consent, it was decided to put an end to the strike. Without consulting you, you were faced with a *fait accompli*.

This treachery is only the last in a series of perfidious acts taken by the

Party of the Workers, resulting from a conciliatory policy of national compromise and "peace and quiet in industry," which is done at the worker's expense.

Workers! You are facing a united front of Pechter-Rutenberg-Ben-Gurion. You must draw a lesson from this defeat and intensify your fight for your just demands, so that in the battles to come, you will prevail over your perfidious leaders and march to victory in your class warfare.

Down with the parties of national compromise! Stop the betrayal of the working class!

Long live the constant class struggle!

The "left-wing faction" in the Histadrut
Organizer: Gina P. Feingus

NOTES

1. Pinchas Rutenberg (1879–1942) founded the Palestine Electric Company. Born in the Ukraine, he received technical training in St. Petersburg. In Russia, he was involved in revolutionary activities, and after the failed revolution of 1905 he fled to Italy where he worked as a civil engineer. He came to Palestine in 1919 where, in addition to exploring opportunities for constructing hydro-electric power plants, he was involved in organizing Jewish self-defense units. The first power plant of the Palestine Electric Company was completed in October 1923 in Tel Aviv. It was diesel-powered and produced 300 megawatts. Naharayim was Rutenberg's most ambitious project, and he came to be associated with it in the public imagination. It was an important part of the massive infrastructure works that were a hallmark of the Zionist enterprise in Palestine. It is possible that he is referred to in this article as Pinchas Rutenberg of London because of his close ties to the British authorities in Palestine.

2. *Ha-Histadrut ha-Kalalit shel ha-Ovdim ha-Ivri'im be-Eretz Israel* (The General Federation of the Hebrew Workers in Palestine) was founded in 1920 in Haifa as a trade union of Jewish workers and included more than 4,000 members. Over time it became one of the major strongholds of the Zionist Labor movement. By 1927, under the leadership of David Ben-Gurion, the Histadrut had more than 22,000 members and by 1933 more than 33,000 members, which represented 75 percent of the Jewish workforce in Palestine at the time. The Histadrut was not a traditional labor union: it took control over companies and became the largest employer in the pre-state period; it operated a bank and provided its members with health services; and it took an active role in the Zionist settlement effort.

3. In 1919, the Po'alei Tsion party headed by David Ben-Gurion, the Organization of Agricultural Laborers and a group of unaffiliated activists associated with Berl Katznelson merged to form the United Labor Party. The party combined socialist and Zionist principles, but it shifted away from traditional Marxist ideas, while seeking to represent broader segments of the Yishuv. Members of Ha-Po'el Ha-Tsa'ir (see document 5) opposed such traditional socialist notions as class struggle, and they refused to join international socialist organizations.

4. *Davar* was the daily newspaper of the Histadrut. The newspaper was founded in 1925 by Berl Katznelson and Moshe Beilinson, and for the next seven decades (the newspaper was shut down in 1996) it was regarded as the all-but-official mouthpiece of the Labor movement.

5. The writers are clearly using irony in their description of Rutenberg.

19

The Labor Brigade (1926)

Gedud ha-Avodah ve-ha-Haganah al-shem Yosef Trumpeldor (the Joseph Trumpeldor Labor and Defense Brigade) operated in Palestine between 1920 and 1927. It was founded six months after Trumpeldor's death at Tel Hai (see document 38). The brigade set out to fulfill three pioneering missions: settlement, defense, and Hebrew labor. The conflation of militaristic titles and sense of hierarchy with civilian goals (labor, settlement) underscores the importance of the conquest of the land and of labor in early, socialist Zionist ideology. The brigade was divided into companies, and at its peak, in 1926, it had over 600 members. Throughout the brigade's seven-year history it counted more than 2,500 members. Members of the brigade created three kibbutzim: Ramat Rachel, Ein Harod-Tel Yoseph, and Kfar Gila'di (which was originally founded in 1916 but was deserted after the battle of Tel Hai). Some companies were situated in urban centers and built new neighborhoods there; others were involved in road construction. The brigade underwent some internal turmoil in its brief history. In 1923, at a time of economic stress in the Yishuv, the brigade's kibbutz Ein Harod-Tel Yoseph split up. In 1926 the Labor Brigade divided into Right and Left Brigades, with the leftist element developing a communist, anti-Zionist position. In 1927 some members of the Left Brigade, under the leadership of Menachem Elkind, moved to the Soviet Union, where they founded the Via Nova commune. Elkind and most of his comrades were killed during the Stalinist purges.

This document details the type of activities in which the Jerusalem Company of the brigade was engaged. It also reflects the type of financial and institutional difficulties that members of the brigade were facing, just a few months before it was disbanded.

Source: "*Gedud ha-Avodah ve-ha-Haganah al-shem Yosef Trumpeldor Jerusalem* to Members of the Zionist Executive, Jerusalem, the 8th of Sivan [May 21], 1926," Central Zionist Archive. Translated by Marganit Weinberger-Rotman.

The Joseph Trumpeldor Labor Brigade is facing a serious problem: the need for permanent facilities for its companies. At the moment, of all the urban locals, the one in Jerusalem requires our consideration most urgently. The Jerusalem local was set up in 1922, and its goal was to introduce Jews to stonecutting—a craft they had never practiced before.

Four years ago the Jerusalem branch consisted of forty members. Over time the number increased and with it came a transition from temporary to permanent jobs, which gave the group a permanent basis and contributed to a more stable life for its members. When the number of families and children grew, the local was able to train a large number of professionals in all the areas it managed to penetrate, which are:

1. Masonry. This was the first occupation that the Labor Brigade mastered. As building in and around Jerusalem expanded, the importance of masonry increased and it now includes stone-cutting, chiseling, and polishing. The Brigade has trained a cadre of members who know how to run an independent stonecutting business, who learned their trade at the Ratisbon Quarries, Givat-Shaul, and sites around town. The Brigade also introduced new techniques—carving rocks into sheets using power tools and motors, which has offered a decent workplace for female workers and has great potential for expansion.

2. Construction. The mason's local of the Laborers' Brigade has built many public and private buildings, including Hadassah Hospital and residential houses in Beit Hakerem, Rehavia, and Talpiyot.[1] There is also a group of plasterers and tile layers working with the masons.

3. Carpentry. The carpenter's shop set up by the Laborers Brigade is the only one currently operating in Jerusalem. It has gained a good reputation for quality and precision. The carpenters work mostly in construction, but also in furniture production. The workers are good professionals and their ambition is to expand the premises and introduce machinery capable of handling large-scale commissions.

4. Metalwork. The workshop (near Talpiyot) is also connected to the construction business (gates, doors, shutters, banisters, handrails, etc.) as well as performing turnery, lathing, and machine repairs. The workers in this unit work diligently and meticulously, under the management of our member Engineer Spitz.

In summing up four and a half years of work in Jerusalem, we state that the local has successfully established itself in the following professions: stonecutting, chiseling, polishing, construction, plastering, bricklaying, painting, carpentry, metalwork, and plumbing. Over time, transportation and plant nursery were also introduced. One important detail related to the absorption of (female) pioneers is the fact that women constitute 43 percent of the work force. This means that the local has to make a special effort to find them productive jobs, preferably self-employed, since the professions that the Jerusalem local engages in require physical strength and are not suitable for women. Lack of permanent accommodation is a serious problem, particularly considering the climate in Jerusalem and the harsh working conditions. The members are faced with the challenges of finding a position, settling in the city, and establishing their professional status. We would like to expedite the accommodation of 120 families in Jerusalem.

We are happy to report that we found understanding and consideration in our dealings with the board of directors of *Keren Kayemet* [the Jewish National Fund]; they overcame all the financial obstacles and granted us a piece of land near the city in a place most suitable for our purposes. It is conveniently close to town and to work places, water is obtainable from the government reservoirs, the land is of good quality, and it does not require much investment to develop since the terrain is flat; thus, construction expenses will be minimal.

The biggest challenge for us is putting up the buildings, which is urgent. The temporary quarters of the Jerusalem Brigade are ramshackle and crowded and prevent the members from conducting normal lives.

The governor of Jerusalem, Ronald Storrs,[2] has ordered us to dismantle the camp forthwith and vacate the premises. This order means social and economic disaster for our people. Our children, too, need houses to live in; we cannot leave them in the present oppressive conditions. Knowing the financial constraints of the Work Office, we are appealing directly to the Zionist Administration to hasten sending us help, so we can:

1. Take possession of the land and build the first units.
2. Create an auxiliary farm for the women so they can be self-supporting.
3. Create a permanent facility for the local and build apartment houses; education for the children and economic support.

Our most pressing problem is the governor's decree that we dismantle the camp by July tenth of this year. Until we establish our permanent housing, we must take possession of the land and build temporary accommodation, so we can gradually build the settlement.

For this purpose we need the sum of 3,000 pounds right away. We, therefore, appeal to you, imploring and demanding that you comply, to help us avert the disaster that awaits us in our present predicament. Please give us the required sum.

We are willing to supply all the details and explanations necessary for your decision.

Respectfully,
Signed: The Central Committee

NOTES

1. New Jewish neighborhoods in Western Jerusalem.

2. Ronald Storrs (1881–1955) was appointed the military governor of Jerusalem in 1917 and the civil governor of Jerusalem and Judea from 1921 to 1926. Most Zionist leaders were critical of Storrs and viewed him as either indifferent, or even hostile, toward the Zionist movement.

20

Tel Aviv (1933)

YITZHAK GRUENBAUM

Yitzhak Gruenbaum (1879–1970) was one of the leaders of the Zionist movement in Poland. He served in the Polish parliament, the Sejm, from 1919 to 1930. Gruenbaum was a staunch secularist and a bitter opponent of Agudat Yisra'el, the ultra-Orthodox party. In 1930, he lost his seat in the Sejm to Rabbi Aharon Levin, the Agudah leader from Warsaw. In late 1933, Gruenbaum immigrated to Palestine. He served as Israel's first minister of interior affairs in the provisional government that was formed in 1948.

In this article, written before Gruenbaum immigrated to Palestine, he describes his impressions of Tel Aviv, the first "Hebrew city," and the vitality of the burgeoning Jewish community in the Yishuv.

At the time of the First Aliyah and during the early years of the Second Aliyah, the Zionist pioneering efforts focused mainly on agricultural settlements. But as the Jewish community in Palestine expanded, urban development was crucial for the growth and viability of the Yishuv. In Zionist iconography, pioneering would continue to be associated with farming for decades, but the new urban centers of Tel Aviv and the port city of Haifa would become the Yishuv's economic backbone, and Tel Aviv would emerge as the country's cultural center as well.

Tel Aviv was founded in 1909 by a group of activists who sought to create modern, urban neighborhoods adjacent to the predominantly Arab city of Jaffa. The first neighborhood, Ahuzat Bayit, consisted of sixty families. By 1914 the population grew to more than 1,400 residents, and by 1915 it passed 2,000. After the establishment of

Source: *Yediot Iryat Tel Aviv*, vol. 7, April 1933. Translated by Marganit Weinberger-Rotman.

the British Mandate and the incorporation of different neighborhoods to the city, the population jumped to nearly 13,000 in 1922 and 34,000 by 1925, and in 1936 the city's population was 150,000. On May 15, 1948, Israel's Declaration of Independence took place in Tel Aviv, and the city served as the country's temporary capital until December 1949. In 2007, Tel Aviv's population was just over 380,000.

Renowned leader of Polish Jewry, Mr. Yitzhak Gruenbaum, recently visited Palestine and published accounts of his travels in the Warsaw newspaper *Haynt*. We hereby present a chapter from his impressions of Tel Aviv:

Tel Aviv is in the process of construction and expansion, which are being carried out at a hectic pace. New buildings and new streets are constantly added. The city changes its form and its character. It is in a state of flux; it's hard to determine its real nature. Houses and buildings have the air of still being constructed; no street is complete. Everything is percolating, seething, bubbling. We are witnessing an act of creation; we are assisting in the birth of a city, an entire world.

Around Tel Aviv, too, everything is humming with activity: building and planting, new settlements cropping up, old villages expanding and developing. Everywhere you look, you see spurts of creativity, the joy of labor, expanding horizons, new opportunities, and fresh beginnings.

A new world is unfolding and we are its instigators, with our capital, toil, know-how, and industry. In Tel Aviv, every enterprise is Jewish, from the simplest landscaping job to the most complex intellectual activity. It is 100 per cent Jewish: the mason, the bus driver, the street sweeper are all Jews. This is the source of the city's pride and joy, its originality, and its significance. In this respect, it is the most Jewish city in the world.

The Jews of Tel Aviv are visibly happy. The rest of the Jewish world is mired in worries, anger, and bitterness; here people seem content, even when they have worries. Living in Tel Aviv has restored confidence to Jewish hearts. In Europe (except perhaps in the west) Jews feel insecure, threatened, and disrespected. In Tel Aviv, they walk around proud and erect.

This is their city, built by their own flesh and blood, sweat, and toil. Here they all feel like first-class citizens, building and developing the country. No disturbances, no obstruction from the authorities can detract from this feeling.

Nowhere in the world do Jews have this feeling, not even in countries where they have attained high social status. In those countries, they tend to feel inferior and apprehensive. Alienation, hopelessness, rationalizations—such sentiments oppress the Jews even in countries where they live peacefully; while outwardly they exhibit security and self-assurance, inwardly their nerves are frayed and their minds are troubled. In the Diaspora, the Jew is forced to trust others; in Tel Aviv, as in the rest of Palestine, the Jew believes in himself, in his powers and talents, which are in evidence everywhere, surprising perhaps even himself. It used to be said of Jews in New York that they wonder at themselves, how far they got; in Tel Aviv, Jews are curious to see what else can this city that sprang from the sand offer them, what else can they create, invent, inspire. There, in America, Jews became arrogant and smug; in Tel Aviv people feel they are in the middle of a race, and they must redouble their efforts in order to reach the finish line.

Jews in Tel Aviv appear somehow more refined, self-assured, at peace. The passengers on a bus, as well as the driver (who also doubles as conductor) all seem relaxed, calm, polite, trusting.[1] You don't see pushing or screaming, even when the buses are full to capacity. When you see the same Jews on a bus in Warsaw they push and shove, grumble and squabble shamelessly.

The Jew in Tel Aviv is different, even on a street that looks like your typical Polish town, as if he is enveloped in bliss. It is obvious that the Jews in Tel Aviv are happy. Not a stupid, bovine kind of happiness, but contentment derived from a sense of confidence and self-assertion, from the satisfaction of creating a new world.

Ask a Jew in Tel Aviv how he's doing, and the answer is invariably, "Excellent, everything's wonderful." And this is not a phony answer, even when it contains a measure of exaggeration. It may be because he knows that eventually things will turn out okay in Tel Aviv, or perhaps because he knows that in Poland and in other countries, the situation is hopeless and there is no going back there. Who knows? He may not know the reason himself, and it does not really matter.

They used to say about Tel Aviv that it is no more than a summer resort built on sand, without any visible source of income, a mirage produced by a wretched people deluded and misled by fantasy and false hope. The first houses, built during the Third and Fourth Aliyot,[2] resembled castles and palaces; they were the fulfillment of every Jew's dream of not just leading an ordinary life here, but basking in the glory of the *Shechina*.[3] In contrast, the houses built here in the last few years look like practical, ordinary houses, pleasant, comfortable, suitable for regular working folks. Tel Aviv is gradually becoming a city of working people who lead gainful, fruitful lives. True, speculation and profiteering are still practiced here, but it does not overshadow the honest productive work that most people engage in. True, the capital amassed in the vaults of the banks here has not been used for pioneering enterprises; the bank is still very cautious and dares step only in well-trodden paths. Land and real estate speculation is rife, profiteering and black marketing, shady deals and dishonest competition are much in evidence, and it is clear that not much good can come of such activities. But this is not the true image of the city; it is merely the side effect of prosperous times. What really characterizes the city is the increase in industry. Typical in this respect is the middle class; small manufacturers and craftsmen with little capital who quite often lose their investments and learn the hard way. And the same is true of big industry, both long established and new. If only we could exert more influence on the capitalists and direct them as we direct labor, we could avert great disasters and prevent disappointments. But one thing is firmly anchored in Tel Aviv: work and productivity are the forces that determine the life and development of the city.

Tel Aviv is fast becoming a center, a meeting point for people and organizations coming to Palestine to settle. They converge on Tel Aviv, even though Haifa is very attractive and has good prospects, and Jerusalem is the hub of the government and the Zionist administration. Tel Aviv can hold its own and will not surrender its place. It has a certain mystique, a seductive power that no logical arguments and foreseeable dangers can dispel.

Where does this charisma of Tel Aviv come from? Is it its Jewishness? Possibly. Both Haifa and Jerusalem have mixed populations; Jews there rub shoulders with other nationals and get hurt in clashes and riots. In Tel Aviv, Jews feel at home, free to build and create. There is a sense of homeland here, autonomy and statehood. This is something we have yearned for and hungered after for many generations in exile, when we had to accommodate to others' wills and interests. Here, whether aware of it or not, we walk in the only Jewish city in the world, in the entrance hall to a free and independent homeland; this is the first act in the staging of the kingdom we have dreamed of and prayed for.

Tel Aviv is still a Babel of tongues: Russian is heard but only infrequently. What you mostly hear is Polish and, lately, German. But in Tel Aviv the dominant element is Polish-Jewish; thus, Yiddish is more prevalent than any other language, especially among craftsmen. But out of this hodgepodge of languages the sounds of Hebrew are coming through loud and clear, in the streets, on the buses, in shops, restaurants, and coffeehouses. And not only among children and youngsters. Hebrew is spreading and gaining control. The Jews are submitting to the dictate of one unifying language that will turn them into one body. We are here in the midst of an ongoing process of fusing various, sometimes distant, parts of the Jewish people.

So far this process does not seem to be painful. People divest themselves of the language and the culture they brought with them slowly, but without sadness. There is no knowing how long this process will take, especially if the influx of masses continues to come from the Diaspora.

As I walk along the streets of Tel Aviv, a thought sometimes strikes me: perhaps this is only a dream, a beautiful dream about a state, a dream borne out of the affliction and anguish of exilic life. Everything here looks like a fairy tale; the lovely houses, awash in sunlight, sometimes look like bewitched palaces.

But this is not a dream. This is reality, perhaps the most concrete reality in Jewish existence.

NOTES

1. The historian Anat Helman has shown that riding the bus in Tel Aviv at that time was in fact a loud, cramped, and in many cases an uncomfortable experience. See Anat Helman, "Taking the Bus in 1920s and 1930s Tel-Aviv," *Middle Eastern Studies* 42, no. 4 (2006): 625-40.

2. The third (1919-23) and fourth (1924-29) waves of Jewish immigration to Palestine.

3. In rabbinic Judaism, the divine spirit.

21

Tel Aviv as a Jewish City
(1939)

Tel Aviv, today Israel's largest metropolis, began in 1909 as a suburb of Jaffa (see also document 20). It was the eleventh Jewish neighborhood established in Jaffa since 1887; Tel Aviv's founders, however, wanted to establish something more than another Jewish neighborhood in a mostly Arab city. (On the eve of World War I, Jaffa's population was about 50,000, one-fifth of whom were Jews.) They yearned to establish what was known in Europe at the time as a "garden city," with wide and clean streets, attractive residences, public squares, and green spaces. Zionist activists also wanted to create a separate Jewish urban space removed from Arab Jaffa. In Zionist ideology, the modernity of Tel Aviv was inseparable from its Jewishness, just as the Arabness of Jaffa was thought to be linked with economic and cultural backwardness. (In fact, Jaffa underwent considerable modernization in the late nineteenth and early twentieth centuries, with some twenty new Muslim- and Christian-Arab neighborhoods built up outside the Old City since the mid-nineteenth century.)

Under British rule, Tel Aviv became an independent municipality, and rising tensions between Jews and Arabs caused many of Jaffa's Jewish neighborhoods to be annexed to Tel Aviv. By 1939 Tel Aviv was home to 160,000 residents, one-third of the Yishuv's population. It had a well-developed European high culture, which, intriguingly, the author implies is a sign of the city's Jewish character.

Source: B. M. Ediden, *Rebuilding Palestine* (New York: Behrman Jewish Book House, 1939), 164–67.

How Jewish Is Tel Aviv?

There is no mistaking Tel Aviv for anything but a thoroughly Jewish community from the names of its streets, written in Hebrew: Herzl Street, Bialik Street, Jeremiah Road, Rothschild Boulevard, Judah Halevi Street, Ahad ha-Am Avenue, Bar-Kochba Street. Walking through the Tel Aviv streets is like leafing through an album of Jewish history.

A Hebrew City

To ascertain whether Tel Aviv is truly a Jewish city from the language spoken one must listen to the children and youth rather than to the adults. Many of the adults, as yet, speak Yiddish, Polish, German, English, Arabic, and other languages. The children, however, all speak Hebrew at school, at home, and at play. In the schools, all the subjects, including arithmetic and science, are taught from Hebrew textbooks. Teachers and pupils speak only Hebrew.

Without a knowledge of Hebrew it is difficult to get along in Tel Aviv. The newspapers and magazines are in Hebrew. All lectures, meetings, and plays are in Hebrew. At meetings of the City Council and in the offices of the municipality only Hebrew is used. All official documents, records, and instructions are printed in Hebrew.

Rest and Joy

Further proof of Tel Aviv's Jewishness is the fact that the official rest days are the Jewish Sabbath and the Jewish holidays. All business and work cease on these days. Only a few restaurants and drug stores keep open. Some of the holidays are observed in new ways. Purim is celebrated with masquerade balls and entertainments and with a monster carnival and parade. (The carnival and parade have been discontinued these past several years, partly due to the sad condition of Jews in Germany and other countries.) On Hanukah the school children hold a parade, carrying torches and lighted candles and singing as they march. On *Hamishah Asar Bishevat*,[1] Palestine Arbor Day, trees are planted in the city proper and on the outskirts. On *Shavuot*,[2] *Bikkurim* or First Fruits are brought by the children to the *Keren Kayemet*.[3]

Devotion to Education

In the year 1931, when the population of Tel Aviv numbered only 45,000, there existed 100 schools with an enrolment of 13,000 pupils. In 1938, there were 25,000 pupils. Hebrew, of course, is the language of instruction. It should be remembered that Palestine has no compulsory education, and, also, that many Tel Aviv parents are required to pay tuition fees.[4] In spite of these two obstacles practically every child in Tel Aviv attends school.

Public Buildings

Several of Tel Aviv's public institutions are particularly beloved by the people. One is called *Ohel Shem*, the Tent of Shem,[5] which houses the *Oneg Shabbat*[6] founded by Bialik,[7] and is also used for afternoon and evening classes, for meetings, conventions, lectures, concerts, and plays.

Equally popular is the *Bet Am* or People's House, the municipal auditorium of Tel Aviv, where large mass meetings, concerts, and dramatic performances are held.

A third building is an ordinary one-story home. But in the eyes of Tel Avivians it is more sacred than the other two. It is Ahad ha-Am House, where the great Jewish thinker, Hebrew writer, and Zionist leader Ahad ha-Am lived out his last years. To honor his memory, his house was turned into a library for students and scholars.

The beautiful house where the great Bialik lived has also become a center for the use of writers, artists, and scholars. Bialik's study and books have been left intact. The other rooms are used for exhibits, lectures, and meetings. The garden surrounding the house, planted and cared for by Bialik himself, offers shade and rest to everyone.

On Rothschild Boulevard, right off Herzl Street, is located Tel Aviv's Art Museum. It was founded by Meir Diezengoff,[8] the man who is remembered as the "father" of Tel Aviv. The Museum contains a small but fine collection of Jewish and general paintings and sculptures.

North of the city, where the Yarkon River flows into the Mediterranean Sea, stand the permanent Fair buildings.[9] One of these buildings has been remodeled into a music hall where the Symphony Orchestra holds its concerts. It is known as the Hubermann Auditorium, in honor of the founder of the orchestra.

On a low hill in the center of the growing city, the new home of the famous Habima Theater is nearing completion. Near it several other public buildings are to be erected: the new City Hall, the Art Museum, and the Orchestral Hall. On the map of Tel Aviv these grounds are labeled "Civic Square."

Other Marks of Jewishness

Public servants, from mayor to street cleaners, are Jews. The municipal courts are not only presided over by Jewish judges but also guided by Jewish law. The plays presented by the famous Habimah and Ohel theaters deal with Jewish themes. Their best-known plays are "Jacob and Rachel," "The Dybbuk," and "Jeremiah." Plays of a general interest are also presented, of course. The newspapers, magazines, and books tell of specifically Jewish events, as well as of international events. . . .

NOTES

1. *Tu Bishevat*, the fifteenth day of the Hebrew month of Shevat (January–February), was determined by the rabbis of the Mishnah and Talmud to mark the new year for the determination of agricultural cycles and the paying of tithes on produce.

2. Literally meaning "weeks," a Jewish festival seven weeks after Passover. In rabbinic Judaism, the festival primarily observed the giving of the Torah to Moses on Mount Sinai. Zionism, reflecting the ideal of returning Jews to work the soil of their ancestral land, emphasized *Shavuot*'s earlier, biblical significance as a harvest festival.

3. The Jewish National Fund, a Zionist land purchase agency.

4. The British colonial administration offered limited social and educational services. The Yishuv had to provide many of these services on its own and muster the resources to do so.

5. In Genesis, Shem is one of Noah's three sons and the ancestor of Abraham.

6. A Friday-evening gathering in honor of the Sabbath.

7. Chaim Nahman Bialik (1873–1934) is considered Israel's national poet. Born in the Ukraine, he moved to Tel Aviv in 1924. His home in Tel Aviv became one of the city's cultural centers.

8. Dizengoff (1861–1936) was a founder and longtime mayor of Tel Aviv.

9. From the sixth international Levant Trade Fair of 1934. The fairground was built on the southern bank of the Yarkon River.

22

Platform for the 1931 Elections to the Representative Assembly (1931)

UNION OF UNITED GENERAL ZIONISTS

Originally, the name "General Zionist" was assigned to those members of the World Zionist Congress who did not officially belong to a specific faction such as the Labor, Revisionist, and Religious Zionist camps. The vast majority of General Zionists did not live in the Yishuv itself, so while their power within the Zionist Congress was considerable, their popularity in Palestine itself was much less so. Though General Zionists coalesced into an official bloc in the World Zionist Congress in the early 1920s, General Zionists in the Yishuv failed to unite and form a single faction, and were represented in the Representative Assembly, the legislative body of the Yishuv, by an assortment of "civic" parties. On the eve of the establishment of the Union of United General Zionists, General Zionists in the Yishuv were clearly split into two camps, with one leaning to the Right and the other to the Left. Most differences in opinion between the two camps regarded economic policy and the group's relation to and cooperation with the labor camp, as well as foreign policy to a lesser extent. As a faction in the political life of the Yishuv the General Zionists protested against the increasing partisan activity of Zionist groups within the Yishuv, as well as the distribution of social services according to party lines. The flag around which the group rallied was that of "national responsibility" and preference

Source: Lavon Institute V-411-3. Translated by Hillel Gruenberg.

for the general national interest over a specific class or ethnic interest, as well as a preference for "general" Zionism over Zionist ideologies compounded with socialism, militant territorial maximalism, and/or religious dogma. The majority of General Zionist supporters were middle-class professionals, small business owners, and independent farmers, craftsmen and artisans living in Tel Aviv and its suburbs, with some coming from Jerusalem as well. Soon after the 1931 elections there was a palpable rift among the General Zionists along the same lines as the party had been split before, with a right-leaning "civic" group and a left-leaning "progressive" faction. The two General Zionist factions came to be known as General Zionists A and B with their official names being Histadrut ha-Tziyonim ha-Klaliyim (Union of General Zionists) and Brit ha-Tziyonim ha-Klaliyim (Federation of General Zionists), respectively. Group A advanced an "above party" and collectivist (though nonsocialist) ideology, had its members join the Histadrut trade union, and tended to be conciliatory toward Labor Zionists. Group B was of a more markedly pro–middle class and pro–free market orientation and, in opposition to the Histadrut trade union, created its own federation of General Zionist workers.

In this trying time, as *'Am Yisrael* (people of Israel) fights for its right to rebuild its homeland in the land of its forefathers, the United General Zionists recognize their obligation to emphasize, more so than at any other time, the values that unite and bond the nation and not those that divide and separate it. We call to the Hebrew Yishuv in the land to marshal its forces in *Knesset-Yisrael*[1] through the elections to the Representative Assembly, to unite around this flag [of national unity]. In order to constitute a bloc in the Representative Assembly, whose task will be to bring together all the forces of Knesset-Yisrael toward productivity and construction on the basis of preference for the general national interest over all other class, partisan, and ethnic ambitions.

A.

The statutes of Knesset-Yisrael, with all their defects, can be used as a foundation for facilitating the organization of the Yishuv. It is incumbent upon the Representative Assembly to reform, improve, and adjust itself to our demands, so that the Yishuv may be firmly organized on the bases of obligation and self-determination in all areas of its life and its needs. Those regulations of the statutes that differentiate between the different religious and ethnic communities and lend legal legitimacy to the tendency towards divisiveness, the fruit of the exile, must be rescinded. The organization of the Yishuv must be singular and total, the organization of one nation on the basis of complete equality of duties and rights. By means of gradual and systematic work Knesset-Yisrael must reach a situation of a living and thriving organization operating according to its needs and those of its constituent institutions.

B.

Knesset-Yisrael in the Land of Israel is the kernel of the Hebrew nation; in its national, political and cultural renaissance it has returned to rebuild the national Hebrew home in the historical homeland of 'Am Yisrael. Accordingly, it must concern itself not just with the needs of the Yishuv as it stands today, but also for its growth, expansion, and development in the future.

Passionate pleas for and systematic cooperation towards Jewish immigration on a large scale from all communities and streams of our people, for the purpose of expansive settlement, development of industry as a basis for the immigration of the masses—all these are the fundamental tasks of Knesset-Yisrael.

These goals require organic cooperation between the administration of the Jewish Agency as the representative of the nation in all its diasporas and Knesset-Yisrael in the Land of Israel as the pioneer of the nation in the homeland, in such a way that Knesset-Yisrael will be a noticeable influence on all activities of the Jewish Agency and a deciding influence on issues directly affecting the life of the Jewish settlement in the land.

An important task, one that directly concerns Knesset-Yisrael, is the management of the relationship between us and our neighbors[2] in the land. This matter can and must be conducted on the basis of mutual aspirations for cooperative work for the benefit and development of the land, but only on the basis of full recognition of our historic right to build our national home in the Land of Israel and not on bases of obsequiousness and concessions like those proposed by leaders of Brit Shalom.[3]

Knesset-Yisrael needs to stand on guard, ensuring that that no change or weakness be imposed against the decision of the national council[4] [to fully cooperate with the British authorities], by way of absolute non-participation of the Hebrew Yishuv in the legislative council as advised by the [mandatory] government.

C.

With all recognition of the great value of our national funds and their large role in building up the land—the attraction of private capital and initiative to the land is a crucial necessity. In this matter there is a broad cushion provided to the labor sector by Knesset-Yisrael due to its influence on the institutions of the Jewish Agency.

Concern for productivity of the existing Yishuv is an important and central task of Knesset-Yisrael, by means of fulfilling our duties of organization, guidance, and initiative for the purpose of all types of settlement on the ground. [We must pursue] creation of industry and manufacturing on both a large and small scale, increasing cooperative activity in the Yishuv based on organization of Hebrew business owners, a fervent campaign on behalf of using products from the land, and a political struggle for an appropriate system of taxes and customs. The concentration, organization, and guidance of our economic forces in the land are a crucially needed condition to bring the existing settlement in the land to stand on its own authority from an economic perspective, and for the generation of a basis for new Jewish immigration on a wide scale.

The great principle of Hebrew labor, that the [mandatory] government has tried to suppress with the White Paper, is among the foundational principles of our national and economic construction. Knesset-Yisrael is obligated to impose this principle in the city and the village, in all branches of the market, and in our economic production. The generation of conditions ensuring the total realization of this principle and the facilitation of its penetration into all areas of our lives, for example: debt arbitration, councils for setting labor conditions, labor offices based on national authority—are among the central and primary tasks of Knesset-Yisrael.

D.

The Hebrew language that came to be resurrected in the Land of Israel and its recognition as an official language is the basis of the national life of our people that has returned to be reborn in the land of our forefathers. It is incumbent upon Knesset-Yisrael to guard its status from external threat, and to ensure its development and cultivation from within.

Educational and cultural work in all its aspects must hold a central and fundamental place in the work of Knesset-Yisrael. The value of such work in the land not only fulfills the need of the existing Yishuv, but also serves as a mechanism producing general national values, a source of new forces of national creation for all dispersed communities in exile, and is of interest to the entire people. Accordingly, such work must be done by Knesset-Yisrael in conjunction with the Jewish Agency in such a way that the influence of Knesset-Yisrael will be assured, and so that the general national characteristic of this work will not be minimized and its scope will not be diminished.

E.

Issues of [public] health within the Yishuv must acquire an important place in the activities of the organized Knesset-Yisrael. Responsibility for medical institutions must be gradually transferred to the authority of Knesset-Yisrael,[5] and the Jewish Agency must aid Knesset-Yisrael in provision of medical and sanitary supplies needed in the first stages of absorption and settlement of immigrants. Knesset-Yisrael must fight for the right of the Yishuv to supply basic supplies in the field of public health from the government treasury; it will fight for an appropriate allocation of funds for public health and for the full recognition of the health enterprises of value to the general public, which the government and municipalities must support.

F.

All branches of activity in the field of social aid, all works of charity and social justice in their various fields; systematic aid arranged for the unemployed, concern for orphans, for elderly people without a place of refuge, and for sick people lacking medical treatment, public kitchens, social work for mother and child— all these important issues are of a public character and concern. Such matters are currently neglected and are left to happenstance and anarchy; they are owed reinvigorated concern and organized activity. The responsibility for such activity falls with Knesset-Yisrael, and it is among the institution's most important obligations.

The United General Zionists demand and require that the many factions of the Yishuv and the non-partisan masses whose hearts are oriented to general-national construction fulfill their national obligation and to go to the elections for the Representative Assembly in the name of building and creation, in the name of the national constructive mission.

The Yishuv, with its broad divisions is required to unify its ranks and to organize its forces; it is required to build up its national organization, so that it will be prepared for this important task of the pioneering camp that passes before the people on the way to its rebirth and stands in honorable guard on the first lines of the front; the Yishuv must testify in front of the [Jewish] people and the world with total resoluteness that it is yet alive and that because of our national will, the will of rebuilding and revival, that we will not be broken and we will not be stopped.

All those whose heart is for the work of construction and creation, for national responsibility, that prefers the interests of the general public over the interests of classes and the ambitions of parties;

All those who feel a great responsibility, that the moment of trial has fallen upon the Yishuv, are the pioneers in the movement of the renaissance and redemption of the nation;

All those who have in their heart a spark of recognition of national obligation and responsibility;

All those whose hearts are free from the destructive work of demagoguery that does not care for means and does not foresee results;

All those that want to stand defiant, so that the Representative Assembly for Knesset-Yisrael will not turn into a platform for unimpeded partisan battle that would dissolve the Yishuv entirely and tear Knesset-Yisrael to shreds;

All those that do not want the supreme institution of the Yishuv to be like the tree "whose two limbs ate fire and in it it was consumed"—will listen to our calls, will walk together with us to build up our national organization on the political-national foundations of General Zionism and will vote for our list in the elections for the Representative Assembly.

Union of The United General Zionists

NOTES

1. Knesset-Yisrael was the general organization of the Yishuv under the British Mandate; Asefat Ha-Nivharim, or the Representative Assembly, was its legislative branch.

2. The Palestinian Arabs.

3. Brit Shalom, literally "the covenant of peace," was a group advocating the establishment of a binational Jewish–Arab state in Palestine in the late 1920s.

4. The National Council, or Va'ad Le'umi, was the chief governing body of the Yishuv.

5. Health care, as with other social services, was at this time generally provided on a partisan basis.

23

Thou Shalt Not Wear *Sha'atnez* (1929)

VLADIMIR JABOTINSKY

Vladimir (Ze'ev) Jabotinsky (1880–1940) was the founder and leader of the Revisionist Zionist movement, a writer, poet, essayist, and translator. During World War I, Jabotinsky and Joseph Trumpeldor were active in the establishment of Jewish units as part of the British Army; In 1920 the British authorities jailed Jabotinsky for his involvement in Jewish self-defense activity during riots in Jerusalem. After his release later that year, Jabotinsky left Palestine never to return on a permanent basis.

In 1921 Jabotinsky became a member of the Zionist Executive, but his positions on such issues as militarism and the movement's relationship with the British government eventually led to his resignation from the Zionist Executive in 1923. In 1925, in Paris, Jabotinsky established Ha-Tzohar, the Union of Zionist Revisionists. During the following decade, Jabotinsky and his movement were part of the Zionist Organization. By the mid-1930s, however, tensions between Jabotinsky and the Zionist establishment intensified, and in 1935 the Revisionists left the ZO and founded Ha-Tzah (an acronym for the New Zionist Organization).

In addition to his political activities, Jabotinsky also made considerable contributions to modern Hebrew culture. His poems, two novels (*Samson the Nazarene, The Five*), and especially his translations of such great poets as Dante, Poe, Verlaine, and Omar

Source: *Haynt*, January 18, 1929, in Ze'ev Jabotinsky, *Ketavim: ba-Derech la-Medinah* (Jerusalem, 1959), 69–76. Translated by Marganit Weinberger-Rotman.

Khayyam into Hebrew had a profound impact on the bourgeoning Jewish national language.

In this article Jabotinsky provides a theoretical and practical framework for one of his, and his movement's, core ideological principles: monism. Drawing on the biblical prohibition against wearing *sha'atnez*—fabric that contains wool and linen (Lev. 19:19, Deut. 22:11)—Jabotinsky argues that unlike Labor Zionism, which was committed both to the creation of a Jewish national home but also to universal social ideals (socialism), his movement was committed to only one ideal: the pursuit of political independence. This pursuit of a single ideal, according to Jabotinsky, is more attuned with human nature that is more comfortable with one motivating force. Jabotinsky often used biblical motifs to articulate ideological programs. He called his economic program to battle poverty "biblical socialism" (he used such biblical concepts as the jubilee year, in which all debts and obligations are canceled, to construct his plan) and he wrote a historical novel, *Samson the Nazarene*, that among other things celebrated the biblical judge's physical strength, a type of Jewish power, which Jabotinsky wanted young Zionists to embrace.

Sha'atnez is a fabric made of mingled threads, half linen and half wool. Scripture strictly forbids the wearing of such material. The reason for the ban is clear. In ancient times, world economy consisted of two basic categories: tilling the land and raising cattle. A primordial enmity existed between the two (witness the rivalry of Abel and Cain), because the shepherds needed large tracts of un-cultivated land for their flocks. The tiller of the soil wore linen, while the shepherd wore wool. Thus, it was immediately apparent who is who. But a person wearing clothes made of mingled materials could not be identified as either, and he might be an antagonist. Thus, the Torah considered *sha'atnez* non-kosher and banned it.

"Brit Trumpeldor"[1] is an attempt to do away with *sha'atnez* of the soul.

Since Zionism today is an abbreviated and watered-down version of itself, it cannot be the only reigning ideology among our young people. You cannot whip up enthusiasm in people for a worthless thing, for they will turn to other ideals. This is why young people become "leftists" and seek socialist revolution and other ways to right social wrongs. And they try to connect these aspirations to Zionism. The result of this mingling is that Zionism has become a shorter version of itself, a "conditional" Zionism; the rescue of the Jewish people is no longer a goal in itself; it is only a means, a channel, an instrument, or a way of teaching other nations' morality, etc. Hence, the Jewish "national home" should be built by other means, communist or proletarian or whatever you call them, without capitalism and without exploitation. All this is fine and dandy, but what if it turns out that it is unrealizable? It is already evident that this is not feasible in real life; the Land of Israel cannot be built without private capital and capital will not come in without the prospect of profit (which, according to Marxist theory, is always the result of "exploitation"). When the premise does not hold, the corollary does not follow: the "leftist" youth organizations are becoming way stations on the road away from Zionism. I doubt whether anyone except the party secretaries denies this fact.

This is how every ideological *sha'atnez* must end. When you seek to beautify and enhance an ideal, mixing it with other ideologies and aspirations, you're bound to conclude that the other aspiration is prettier, holier, and more universal. And thus, with regards to Zionism, it is logical and inevitable that new ideals seem more attractive, and thus youth (and the more honest and clear-minded among them will be the first to realize this) will determine to join other movements unconditionally, for it is absurd to hold on to two ideals.

Indeed, two ideals are absurd, just as holding on to two gods, two altars, two temples is inconceivable. I wish to offend no one, but a mind that can happily mingle two ideals is a defective one. A perfect soul is a monistic soul. Ideal, by its very nature, is a singular concept. There is no room for duality in it. If Zionism is the ideal, then there is no room for another independent ideal with equal rights next to it. You cannot enter a partnership or a "cartel" or any other combination with it. An ideal excludes all extraneous concepts, be they beautiful, pure, and sacred. It may very well be that socialism is indeed an attractive and pure concept—I personally do not subscribe to this view—but even if this is the case, it is irrelevant. When we were young and led a campaign against assimilation, we never doubted that the national values of other peoples had merit; those values that the assimilationists wanted to espouse were also noble and pure, perhaps even superior to ours, and yet we demanded allegiance to one set of principles only—the Jewish one. If abandoning foreign ideals is too hard, because one is truly enamored of those ideals, then this is the true test, which proves whether one's soul is whole or defective and inferior. Pure and perfect minds are dedicated to the service of the ideal and are ready for sacrifices.

The new movement that is slowly emerging now—Brit Trumpeldor—is distinguished by ideological monism. The majority of its members, if allowed to immigrate to Palestine, will work as salaried employees for a certain period. They are aware of it and are preparing themselves for the service. But, at the same time, they are also preparing for something else, and they know that their participation in the building project does not affect their soul. A person can work as a stonecutter, a teacher, an engineer, or a policeman—but he is first and foremost a pioneer, which is a status much higher and nobler than a laborer, an industrialist, or even a soldier. A pioneer may work in many jobs, changing roles and status, but he must never be wholeheartedly committed to the "class interest" of the group to which he technically belongs. As far as he is concerned, he should see himself as an actor, executing the role assigned by the director. The name of the play is "We Are Building a Jewish State," and the director is "The Idea of the State." One day he plays his role with spade in hand, tomorrow he may act as a teacher, and the day after tomorrow as a combatant. He is playing his roles with honesty and probity. But he himself is neither teacher nor soldier, neither bourgeois nor proletarian. He is all those things at the same time. For he is a pioneer.

NOTE

1. Brit Trumpeldor (the covenant of Trumpeldor) better known by its acronym Betar, was the Zionist Revisionist youth movement founded in Riga, Latvia, in 1923. The movement was named after Joseph Trumpeldor (see document 38), a Jewish officer in the Russian army, who lost his left arm in the Russo-Japanese War. Trumpeldor became an ardent Zionist and was instrumental, with Jabotinsky, in the creation of the Zion Mule Corps in 1915, which as part of the British army saw battle in Gallipoli, and in 1917 in the formation of the Jewish Legion, which took part in some of the final battles against the Turks in Palestine. Jabotinsky embraced the legacy of his former collaborator Trumpeldor and named the Revisionist youth movement after him. (Jabotinsky also used to sign his letters with "Tel Hai"). While Betar was an acronym of Brit Trumpeldor, Betar was also the name of the last Jewish fortress to fall during the Bar-Kochba rebellion against the Romans in 135 CE.

24

Betar and the Zionist Revolution (1932)

YEHOSHUA HESCHEL YEVIN

Yehoshua Heschel Yevin (1891–1970) was one of the leaders of the maximalist, or radical, wing of the Zionist Revisionist movement and one of the founders, along with Abba Achimeir and the poet Uri Zvi Greenberg, of Brit ha-Biryonim (the league of thugs). Born in Russia, Yevin was trained as a physician and served as a surgeon in the Red Army. Yevin was initially active in socialist Zionist circles, but in 1928, captivated by Jabotinsky's militaristic and revolutionary zeal, he joined the Revisionist movement. The maximalists (in the years 1932–33 as part of Brit ha-Biryonim and later as a faction within the Revisionist movement) were provocative in their rhetoric and action. While Jabotinsky was engaged in broad Zionist politics and represented his movement internationally, Yevin and his colleagues, unencumbered by the rules of diplomatic decorum, were able to articulate more purely the Revisionist message of blood and glory in the name of the national cause. In this article, Yevin addresses the members of Betar (see document 23n1). The young members of Betar were expected to lead the heroic fight for national liberation; Yevin here calls on them to ignore the universal promises of socialist and liberal Zionists, and instead to cultivate and uphold the ethos of strife and sacrifice.

Source: *Homesh Beitar*, January 3, 1932. Translated by Marganit Weinberger-Rotman.

The bankruptcy of Old Zionism is more than just a bankruptcy of a failed system. Failed systems can be fixed by repairs, by restorations, or by some basic improvements, which make them as good as new. But Old Zionism cannot be fixed by simple "renovations," because the bankruptcy of Old Zionism goes much deeper: it is a bankruptcy of Weltanschauung.

Old Zionism, from its very inception, was inspired by liberalism, which at the time was prevalent all over Europe—including socialist circles. Liberals believed in universal progress; the world is, slowly but surely, advancing towards a reign of justice. Thus, it was possible for Zionism to base its tenets on a simple, childish syllogism: the world is progressing towards justice and the realization of just ideas.

Zionism is a just idea.

Ergo, the world will inevitably progress toward the realization of Zionism.

Thus, the question of realizing the Zionist idea was basically a matter of explaining to the world how just and worthwhile the movement is in order to ensure its success.

The First World War has mercilessly wiped out these liberal assumptions. In the trenches, in the communal graves, where ten millions were buried, this cozy, optimistic belief in "the reign of justice" was also laid to rest. It is clear that the world does not progress toward universal justice, and that justice without accompanying armed legions belongs in the garbage heap of history.

This was well understood by world leaders. Pilsudski,[1] Masaryk,[2] and other national liberation leaders were quick to amass legions as they espoused the idea of universal justice. The Zionist leaders did not see this; they allowed themselves the luxury of remaining loyal to their liberal beliefs twenty years after the words "liberalism" and "progress" became a laughingstock around the world. This is why the "spies," Aharonson and his friends,[3] were outsiders in the movement, which had become anachronistic and, similarly, the idea of the Jewish Legion was rejected by those who "championed justice."[4] This is also why they saw the Balfour Declaration not as a call for forging a national Jewish army, but as corroboration of their effete belief that "the just Zionist cause is bound to triumph."

If the rivers of blood caused by the war and the revolution did not open our eyes to the truth, it is time that the events in Hebron and Safed[5] and the Passfield White Paper[6] opened our eyes. The cheery old Zionist syllogism is as false as its opening phrase; the world is not progressing toward universal justice! To them the bayonets of Hebron murderers are more "just" than mounds of murdered children and old people. Here's our dilemma; either give up Zionism altogether, or seek a Zionism of Power—justice, yes, but justice accompanied by battalions: A Betar kind of Zionism.

This is the revolution that Betar[7] represents, which is not the same as the ideas of the ZHR.[8]

The ZHR talks about revision, about repairing and mending; whoever is not pleased with Weizmann for one reason or another calls himself a "revisionist." But Betar has an altogether different significance. Our movement is not based on the thinking of Martin Buber,[9] Macaulay,[10] or John Stuart Mill; it is inspired by Gush-Halav, Massada,[11] and, mostly, Betar, the bastion of the last king of Judea. Betar means a new kind of Zionism that harks back to Bar-Kochba. We must never cease from fighting for our ideal, even in a world that is bloody and wicked. We will forge the power of the Jewish people, knowing that one day the strength of a small people will prove mightier than the strength of bigger nations, as can be witnessed by the rise of nations like the Czechs, Latvians, and Serbs.

But the idea of Betar is not just preparation for "Doomsday," the great day of Zionism. Betar means day-to-day battles for the honor of our people. It means building a wall with our bodies to shield the House of Israel from marauders and destroyers. This is why Betar pioneering is such a broad concept; it includes not only agriculture and construction but also a willingness to lay down one's life.

There is still much to change and improve in the Betar movement and in the Betar education—mostly in the spiritual sphere. The new Zionism, Zionism of heroism and rebellion, is also entrusted with fostering the renewal of the Hebrew spirit. The cohorts of Ahad ha-Am were wrong when they spoke of a contradiction between "state" and "spirit." Those who are politically bankrupt are even more bankrupt spiritually. They are destitute, both in action and in spirit. Betar must become a refuge for the Hebrew vision, a celebration of national revival and Israeli fury, because there is no other alternative to the devastation of the ruling Zionism.

There is much to be done and to improve, we know. The pioneering way of Betar is replete with obstacles, which are not acknowledged by the old fashioned, liberal, effete, overly optimistic Zionist movement. But the foundation has been laid for the revolutionary liberation movement of the Jewish people.

NOTES

1. Jozef Klemes Pilsudski (1867–1935) led the fight for Polish independence. He served as Poland's chief of state (1918–22). He returned to power in 1926 in a coup d'état and ruled the country as a de facto dictator until his death in 1935.

2. Tomás Garrigue Masaryk (1850–1937) was a leader of the Czechoslovak national liberation movement during the First World War and then served as the country's president between 1918 and 1935.

3. Yevin alludes here to Nili (acronym of the biblical phrase *Netzakh Yisrael Lo Yishaker* "The glory of Israel will not lie" [1 Sam. 15:29]), a Jewish espionage group that assisted the British against the Ottomans in Palestine. The leaders of Nili were Aharon and his sister Sara Aharonson and their friend Avshalom Feinberg.

4. Yevin alludes here to the Jewish units that were created as part of the British army to fight against the Ottomans. (Jabotinsky and Trumpeldor were the driving force behind the creation of these units.) In 1915 the Zion Mule Corps was formed in Egypt, composed primarily of volunteers who were deported from Palestine by the Ottomans; for political considerations, the unit did not participate in battles in Palestine and instead saw action in Gallipoli. In 1917 and 1918, battalions that included primarily Jewish volunteers—known as the Jewish Legion—participated in battles in the Jordan Valley in Palestine.

5. In August 1929, Arabs in Palestine attacked Jews in different communities throughout the country. On August 23–24, sixty-seven Jews were massacred in Hebron; on August 29, eighteen Jews were massacred in Safed.

6. Issued in October 1930 by the colonial secretary Lord Passfield, the Passfield White Paper set new guidelines for British policies in Palestine following the events of August 1929. The White Paper had a distinctly anti-Zionist tone and set new restrictions on Jewish immigration to Palestine.

7. The Revisionist youth movement (see document 23n1).

8. ZHR or Ha-Tzohar, an acronym for ha-Tzionim ha-Revisionistim, the Union of Revisionist Zionists.

9. Martin Buber (1878–1965), a philosopher and Hebrew University professor, was one of the founders of Brit Shalom that called for the creation of a binational state in Palestine.

10. Yevin is likely alluding here to the English historian Catharine Macaulay (1731–91) who was a supporter of the French Revolution and a champion of republicanism.

11. Gush-Halav and Massada were two of the most important Jewish fortresses during the major Jewish revolt against the Romans (66–73 CE).

25

The Strike at the Froumine Biscuit Factory (1932)

In October 1932, the Froumine food factory in Petakh-Tikvah hired a worker who was not a member of the Histadrut (see document 18n2). The Histadrut responded by declaring a strike at the factory. In return, the Revisionists, who had long objected to the monopoly of the Histadrut over the labor market, reached an agreement with Froumine's ownership that Revisionist workers would replace the striking Histadrut members, and that some of these non-Histadrut workers would be guaranteed employment after the strike's end. The struggle between the strikers and Revisionists turned violent on several occasions, revealing the deep antagonism between the Laborites and the Revisionists. At the height of the battle some Laborite circles published a special pamphlet titled "The Biscuit Front," in which they provided quotes by several Revisionist leaders that expressed fascist sentiments.

To the Working Public

The strike at the Froumine biscuit factory is already in its second week. Mr. Froumine undertook a holy mission: to fight his workers and the Histadrut. He is probably envious of his predecessors in this "holy" war that the public here remembers well from other acts of "bravery" in previous labor disputes . . . and he wants to secure for himself a place of honor in this history.

Source: Poster issued by the General Federation of Workers in the Land of Israel, October 18, 1932," Lavon Institute Archive, 4/36/6. Translated by Eran Kaplan.

And Mr. Froumine, who for years was as sweet as honey in his negotiations with the Histadrut, yet he routinely failed to accept a single demand to improve the status of his workers—this Mr. Froumine decided, apparently, to show his strength and many talents and suppress his workers' struggle.

And scabs are not to be found. They could not find hungry, poor people whose consciousness would not prevent them from agreeing to sabotage their comrades' struggle and break the strike. The war of the workers in the Land of Israel, which has been going on for years, has enlightened the minds of many workers and taught even the most reactionary among them the meaning of solidarity—and scabs are hard to find. In Jerusalem there are no more scabs!

But there are those who are willing to fill in the gaps. There are those who fear that the "holy" mission of strikebreaking won't be fulfilled, and it might disappear from our world. Therefore they took it upon themselves the task of finding public institutions that would do what private sources could not do this time. The organizers of the prospective scabs—the Revisionists and Betar,[1] which were created for this very role, have taken it upon themselves to carry out this task! They recruited and sent twenty-five of their members—most of them not even laborers—who are brainwashed and delusional, and sent them to fight the workers, whose struggles and hardships they have never experienced. The dangerous game into which they are driven by callous people—a holy war against the treacherous Histadrut—culminated with a lot of blood being spilt.

This is the first instance in the history of labor disputes in the country that an organization supplants striking workers. Froumine has nearly thirty workers and the twenty-five members of Betar came to take their place during the strike and ended up taking over their jobs permanently! And now they speak of their "right" to work in a place that allows its veteran workers only a limited number of work days a week!

Can the workers, who see themselves attacked both by the employer and by groups of scoundrels, not react to the vicious attack on their meager source of livelihood? Many workers went out to defend their jobs, and it should surprise no one that they clashed with these scabs. The bloody events should open everybody's eyes to see clearly what is going on here, and what the actions of this reckless gang can lead to. The responsibility for everything that happened here falls squarely on the shoulders of Froumine and his Revisionist underlings!

A strictly economic battle was turned by them into a bloody war. Out of pure malice this war was given a political character, a war between two labor organizations allegedly. But this deception will not succeed. The working public knows how to cut the hand that is raised against it; it will not be intimidated by a gang of hoodlums that tries to destroy it and will repel with all its might the attack against it.

The entire public will unite with the Histadrut and join its battle. This is a war over our most cherished possessions, and by the measure of the things that are going to go against it—so the strength and effort of the working public and its allies will avail itself and lead to victory.

NOTE

1. On Betar, the Revisionist youth movement, see document 23n1.

26

Labor Disputes and Acts of Violence (1934)

DAVID REMEZ

David Remez (1886–1951), né David Drabkin, was born in Belarus and immigrated to Palestine in 1913. He served as director of the Public Works Office of the Histadrut (see document 18n2) from 1921 to 1929, and from 1930 to 1946 he was the Histadrut's secretary-general. In this document, which is a summary of an address Remez gave before a meeting of the Yishuv's National Committee, Remez discusses the ongoing labor disputes between Labor Zionists (and their supporters in the Histadrut—the General Zionists [see document 22]) and the Revisionists when it seemed as if these tensions might tear the young Jewish community in Palestine apart. In 1934 the leader of the Labor movement, Ben-Gurion, and Jabotinsky, the Revisionist leader, negotiated an agreement in London to ease tensions between their respective movements—but their pact was not ratified by the Laborites. At the time of Remez's address in 1934, the Revisionists were still members of the Zionist Organization, but they would leave that body a year later to form an alternative body—the New Zionist Organization—thus making any potential agreement with them to calm tensions in the labor market all the more difficult. In 1936, however, the Arabs in Palestine began what would be called the Great Arab Revolt and the focus of the Yishuv shifted from internal conflicts to the struggle with the Arabs.

Source: "Statement by Mr. David Remez, representative of the Histadrut at the meeting of the Va'ad Le'umi," on March 14, 1934, Lavon Institute Archive, 4/104/49/2/109. Translated by Marganit Weinberger-Rotman.

As the representative of the Labor faction in the National Committee, Mr. Remez has agreed to place this issue at the head of the agenda; when it was approved, he said the following:

"We need to conduct a serious discussion of this painful question, but in muted tones and with no acrimonious accusations that are repeated in one meeting after another to no conclusion. It seems to me that the dispute in Petakh-Tikvah is a typical one, and it can be instructive. When the conflict in Petakh-Tikvah reached its climax and things got out of hand, not only did the National Committee step in, but also the leadership of the Jewish Agency. They handed down a decision, but noted contractors and the ZHR [Revisionists] disregarded that decision. It turned out that the other side does not recognize the national authority when it does not suit it, but not so when the shoe is on the other foot. . . .

The Histadrut Executive has previously announced that, regardless of the political differences and the political public debate between the Histadrut and the Revisionists, the Executive is always willing to open negotiations with Betar[1] regarding work, division of labor, and the elimination of competition among workers. The same agreement existing between the Histadrut and Ha-Po'el Ha-Mizrahi[2] can be applied to the Revisionists. How did Betar and ZHR (Revisionists) react? They declined the offer."

Here the speaker raises his voice, "I demand a clear statement from Betar and ZHR regarding their position on organized labor and organized labor relations. We are for organized labor relations, first of all, among workers. Just as small businessmen declare boycotts against intruders, we demand the same right for workers who object to unrestricted markets and unorganized labor. We will not allow lawlessness and anarchy in the work place. If Betar and ZHR think they can force the Histadrut to relinquish its fight for organized labor, I am here to tell them that this will never happen. We will never surrender on this fundamental issue.

"In view of our declaration that we are willing to negotiate about cooperation and division of labor, I declare, judging by their positions on the market, that we regard Betar and ZHR as deliberately refusing to enter negotiations with the Histadrut to resolve this issue. Their motive is clearly to blame the Histadrut in Palestine for barring other organizations from access to work." Here Remez states again, "The offer is on the table, why don't you sign it?" A subcommittee (comprised of Zuchovitzky,[3] Sofersky, and Remez) prepared a joint proposal for healthy work relations, but now Mr. Weinstein informs us, speaking for the ZHR and Betar, that their organization refuses to accept the proposal, demanding that the arrangements be made by the administration, not by the workers; in other words, every municipality and local council should appoint an official to settle work issues. Mr. Remez opposes this for several reasons. First, these councils deprive organized laborers of their right. Settling work issues by appointed officials purporting to be a neutral employment office is nothing but fraud. These issues can be resolved only between worker and worker.

What are the revisionists' demands as preconditions for negotiation?

Pressure from the National Committee and public opinion must have prevailed on the other side to open negotiation with the Histadrut. I was summoned to negotiations with a representative of the ZHR–Betar organization to try to resolve the issue of work relations. Instead of trying to be rational and accommodating, this representative was even more extreme in his demands than was Mr. Weinstein. He said that the World Revisionist Executive decreed that no negotiation with the Histadrut should take place until three preconditions had been met: (1) the Arlosoroff murder trial,[4] (2) the issue of immigration certificates; (3) a declaration by the Jewish National Committee condemning the Histadrut and blaming it for acts of violence. I asked the representative to explain his demand concerning the Arlosoroff murder, and he replied that the Revisionists will not trust the Histadrut until they resolve the matter of the trial.

"Why the Histadrut? Because, to the Revisionists, the Histadrut is everything: police, justice system, etc." These demands, Mr. Remez stressed, were presented to a neutral personality in the Yishuv. One wonders, are the Revisionists really interested in resolving matters, or do they merely want to annoy and harass the Histadrut so that they can accuse it of violence. We must not allow them to do this.

For the record: the Workers' Histadrut is willing to come to an accommodation with the Revisionists, as with all other organizations, ignoring all other political problems. The other parties should lend a helping hand in bringing this matter to a just and proper resolution. ZHR–Betar organization must accept the dictate of the national authorities. It may choose not to comply but, at the moment, we see no other way. If we do not resolve this matter, you will be held responsible.

The integrity and authority of the Zionist Organization requires the administration to insist on the following rules:

1. All members of the Zionist Organization are equal in rights and duties. There is no half or conditional membership.
2. A member of the Zionist Organization who is a member of another organization owes his first allegiance to the Zionist Organization and must submit to its rulings regarding Zionist

principles, policies, and funds. The governing bodies of the Zionist Congress—the Congress and the Zionist Executive—will determine the parameters of these policies and how to enforce compliance.

3. The Jewish Agency is the sole representative of the Jewish people vis-à-vis the British government, the League of Nations, and other world governments regarding the issue of a national home. The Executive cannot consider any proposal that is at variance with these resolutions.

If ZHR refuses to accept these conditions and decides to leave the Zionist Organization, thus invoking the organizational sanctions mandated by its governing board—even then, for the sake of peacekeeping and cooperation—the administration is willing (a) to maintain contact, and (b) to return to the *status quo ante* with ZHR provided that the latter (1) does not challenge the authority of the Agency and refrains from appealing to the government in an attempt to undermine the Agency; (2) will endorse the two agreements concerning the use of underhanded means in the political war and the settlement of labor issues; (3) will not interfere in the activities of the Zionist Funds.

NOTES

1. On the Revisionist youth movement see document 23n1.

2. Founded in 1922, Ha-Po'el Ha-Mizrahi was a national religious movement that operated under the slogan *Torah ve-Avodah* (Torah and labor). The movement participated in the Zionist settlement effort by founding religious kibbutzim and moshavim, and it represented the interests of religious workers.

3. Shmuel Zuchovitzky (1884–1968) was a member of the General Zionist Party, one of the founders of Magdiel in the Sharon Valley, and a member of the national command of the Haganah. Yehoshua Sofersky (1879–1948) was also a member of the General Zionists and a member of Tel Aviv's city council.

4. On the Arlosoroff murder trial, in which Revisionist activists were accused of murdering the labor leader in April 1933, see document 41.

27

Rabbi Herzog
on the Chief Rabbinate
(ca. 1948)

Isaac Herzog (1888–1959) was born in Poland and moved as a child to England where his father was a rabbi. Herzog served as a rabbi in Belfast and Dublin and became the Chief Rabbi of the Irish Free State in 1921. In 1937 he assumed the position of Ashkenazi Chief Rabbi of Palestine, succeeding Abraham Isaac Kook.

Religious Zionists like Herzog, who were dedicated to both the existence of a Jewish state and the Jewish religious tradition, hoped that the constitution of the state would be based on Jewish law. Because Jewish law discriminated between Jews and Gentiles, and men and women, Herzog attempted to introduce changes to certain areas of Jewish law to make it more likely that it would be accepted by the international community and the secular Jewish majority in Palestine. He wrote a book about the constitution of the new state, which remained unfinished. In this extract from that book, almost certainly written in 1948 before Israel declared its independence, Herzog attempts to navigate between his commitment to Jewish law and the practical considerations of creating a modern liberal constitution. This text illustrates ongoing tensions within Religious Zionism of the pre-state period as it sought to navigate a path fundamentally different from those of any of the streams of secular Zionism as well as the anti-Zionist Orthodoxy of the Agudat Yisra'el.

Source: Isaac Herzog, *Constitution and Law in a Jewish State According to the Halacha*, comp. and ed. Itamar Warhaftig, 3 vols. (Jerusalem: Mosad Ha-Rav Kook, 1989), 1:2–4. Translated and annotated by Alexander Kaye.

(1) The Zionist administration, or more precisely the [Jewish] Agency,[1] has declared again and again that the Jewish state, which is going to be founded by the authority of the approval of the United Nations, will be absolutely democratic, which is to say that its constitution and laws will guarantee complete equality for all its citizens.

Against this, not the slightest hint of reservation, organized or not, is heard from religious Jews within the Zionist Organization who are not associated with Agudat Yisra'el. This does not mean that we are not afraid, but that we are also optimistic and have risen up to a level of faith in the Redeemer of Israel and in the People of the Lord that everything will turn out well, with the help of God. As for Agudat Yisra'el, no specific reservations have been heard regarding the democratic nature of the future Jewish state. But it is known that most of them too, like us, are both afraid and optimistic, only their fear is greater than their optimism. Firstly, most of them are apparently deterred from the idea of a Jewish state altogether. In my opinion the main reason is because of the difficulty of establishing a Jewish state according to the Torah, which is also democratic in the real meaning of that term. And who can dismiss this concern with a wave of the hand? Although its leaders have spoken of a government of Torah, they have not needed to solve the problem of the harmonizing a government of Torah with democracy.

(2) Ostensibly, if a large and decisive majority of the Jewish population of Palestine was faithful to the Written Torah and Oral Torah[2] and believed in it with a full faith like all our ancestors until about fifty years ago, there would not be any problem here. In such circumstances we would have said to the Nations: Return to us our land and we will establish on it a state according to the Written Torah and Oral Torah beginning from the Torah of Moses, the Mishnah,[3] etc.,[4] the Talmuds,[5] the early jurists with our teacher Moses Maimonides at their head, the later jurists with our teachers Rabbi Joseph Caro[6] and Rabbi Moses Issereles[7] may their memories be for a blessing at their head. Say what you will! Say that this will be a theocracy! Look at Saudi Arabia! You all recognize it and you all chase after it because of its oil, and it maintains a government, and a penal and legal system that is absolutely theocratic. So it seems to be.

(3) But in truth it is not so. The great majority of the people of Israel is dispersed among the nations and wherever they are their situation is more or less precarious. So it is clear that if we would found the Hebrew state with all its executive, judicial, and legislative functions run according to how the simple meaning of the *halachah*[8] appears at first glance, in such a way that non-Jewish residents would be discriminated against to a large degree, we would endanger the situation of our brothers in exile,[9] and expose them to retaliation. You

might say that it would not be so terrible to suffer the denial of known civil and political rights in the exile. This is not so, for in this era known as modernity, dishonor will eventually result in total contempt and total contempt will bring the contemptuous to thoughts, which will result in actions, that the members of this people are denied human rights and that their blood and possessions are free for the taking.

(4) So however it *could* have been, we have to make allowances for current reality, and it has two aspects. Unfortunately, today is different from half a jubilee ago.[10] Those Jews who are one hundred per cent faithful and believing— whether we like it or not—do not constitute the majority. And it is our duty to draw this majority towards Torah and faith, to observance of the *mitzvoth* between man and God with ties of brotherly love (and, on rare occasion with rebuke, like that of a father to his son), and it is impossible for us to ignore this actual reality. On the other hand, "the rights of the religious and national minorities will be the responsibility of the UN." (Dr. Z. Warhaftig,[11] Memorandum no. 1.) "In general the wording of the rights is taken from the minority and national rights that the Versailles Treaty guaranteed to many of the states that were established after World War One." (Ibid.) So the establishment of the Jewish state is largely dependent on the guarantee of those rights in the spirit of that treaty. If so, then let us clarify the legal and political status of the non-Jewish resident, that is to say a member of another people who is also a member of a non-Jewish faith or in any case not a member of the Jewish faith, in a state that is under a Torah government.[12] (This discussion leaves aside the convert, who is a non-Jew who has accepted upon himself the Jewish faith in its entirety, who is a righteous convert, and about which more will be said later.)

(5) Before we can get to this question we have to answer the question: What is the character of a Jewish state according to the Torah; is it a theocracy or a democracy? First of all, what does "theocracy" mean? This is a word made up of two Greek words: *theos*, God, and *kratia*, government. That is to say a state whose constitution and laws, at least in the main, declare themselves to be from a supernatural, supra-human source. This does not mean that the term is only fitting for a state where there is no place for the human factor to be expressed and revealed. Already the term " in the main," which we used here, hints that this is not in itself the meaning of the term "theocracy." What is clear is that this term is only fitting for a state in which the human factor, in the context of the constitution and laws, can only be expressed and revealed within the limits of a supra-human command and according to the authority that is given to it by that command.

From this point of view, is it necessary for the Jewish state, which recognizes the decisive rule of the Torah, to be a theocracy? The answer is clear and simple: Absolutely yes! Surely it is a foundation of the faith of Israel that the written Torah is given by God through the hand of Moses. And that is true also of the transmitted Torah, the Oral Law, albeit not to the same degree as the Mosaic law. And this double Torah includes within it the foundation of foundations. That is to say the general principles of legislation, and the law in its general principles and, to a known degree, in details.

(6) The Form of the State. I will not deal here with history. My aim is not to give any sort of picture of the Jewish state as it really was in antiquity, in all the periods that it existed, or even in one of those periods. I am dealing here not with the practicalities of the past but with theory, that is to say with the question of how the state should come into being and continue to exist according to our authoritative sources of *halacha*.

From this perspective the form of the state is a theocratic monarchy. At the head of the state stands a king. He himself is placed under the authority of the Torah, just like the king of a democratic state is placed under the authority of the constitution and the law. He has, it is true, broader authorities than such a king, but they themselves are derived from the divine constitution, the Torah. We will speak about the details later, with the help of God. At the side of the king, who is the head and the first person of the state, there is the rule of the Torah—the Great Rabbinical Court, the Great Sanhedrin.[13] Although they must also have a perfect knowledge of [foreign] languages and other branches of knowledge, the principal qualification of the members of the Great Rabbinical Court is their expertise in the Torah in theory and in practice. We will talk of the details later, with the help of God.

There is no mention in our sources, the [M]ishnas, *beraitas*, *toseftas*, [T]almuds or Maimonides, to a parliament. Rather, everything is presided over by the king (who, it is understood, has advisors) and the Great Rabbinical Court. It is notable that the Great Rabbinical Court is the parliament and the senate together.

(7) With regard to the future,[14] the king will again appear at the head. But he has to be from the house of David.[15] According to the essence of the constitution, the coronation of a Jew from another tribe, other than the household of Aaron,[16] is not totally forbidden, although there is fundamental resistance by the prophets to the perpetual inheritance of the monarchy by his descendants. However, the future king at the time of the rebirth of Israel, which is foreseen by the faith of Israel, will be a descendant of David.

NOTES

1. The body that represented Jews and their interests in Mandate Palestine. After the Declaration of Independence it ceded most of its duties to the state of Israel but retained its responsibilities over immigration, land settlement, and other functions.

2. The Jewish legal corpus is divided into the Written Law, which is the Five Books of Moses, and the Oral Law, which comprises the traditions contained in the rabbinic literature. In this context for Herzog, faith in the Written and Oral Law signifies adherence to traditional Jewish faith and practice.

3. A body of rabbinic laws and sayings edited ca. 200 CE.

4. Herzog is referring here to collections of rabbinic legal literature contemporary with the Mishnah known as *beraita* and *tosefta*.

5. Collections of rabbinic literature (edited ca. eighth century CE) from Palestine and Babylonia.

6. Joseph Caro (1488–1575) compiled the *Shulhan Arukh*, a code of Jewish Law.

7. Moses Isserles (1525 or 1530–72) was a Polish rabbi whose gloss on Caro's *Shulhan Arukh* is authoritative for Ashkenazi Jews.

8. Jewish law.

9. The word *galut*, exile, can refer to the world in its pre-messianic state or, as here, to places outside of the Land of Israel.

10. I.e., twenty-five years ago.

11. Zerah Warhaftig (1906–2002) was a lawyer and member of the Mizrahi, one of the framers of the constitution of the Provisional State Council, and a signatory of Israel's Declaration of Independence. Herzog here is quoting from Warhaftig's memorandum, which dealt with the demands of the UN on the state-to-be.

12. Herzog does not discuss this issue in the extract presented here. A significant portion of the rest of the book outlines Herzog's system for providing equality for all citizens in the state in a way consistent with Jewish law.

13. The supreme religious and judicial body in Israel according to Talmudic tradition.

14. In the messianic era.

15. A descendant of the biblical King David.

16. That is, a priest.

28

Public Announcement (1938)

THE NETUREI KARTA COMMUNITY OF HAREDI JEWRY

Until the large-scale immigration waves after World War I, the majority of the Yishuv was Orthodox and a substantial minority were *haredim*—adherents of a fervently anti-modern and anti-Zionist Orthodoxy. Even those haredim who immigrated to Palestine after 1881 considered themselves to be the continuation of the pre-Zionist Yishuv. The haredim were aligned with the international Agudat Yisra'el (founded in Kattowitz in 1912)—an umbrella political party that represented ultra-Orthodox Jewry—and in 1919, Jerusalem's ultra-Orthodox Jews formed a separate communal organization called the *edah haredit*. Agudat Yisra'el did not take part in elections (largely due to women's suffrage) or the Yishuv's governing structure, and it did not recognize the authority of the Chief Rabbinate, a position created by the British and associated with the Zionist institutions.

Agudat Yisra'el began to soften its rigid anti-Zionist stand after the riots of 1929, in which their members lost life and property, and even more so after 1933, when it needed to cooperate with the Zionists to get immigration certificates for its members who were suffering persecution at the hands of the Nazis. Tensions rose between moderates and extremists within Agudat Yisra'el, and around 1935 an irreconcilably anti-Zionist faction in Jerusalem broke away from the party and called itself Ha-hayim (Life). In 1938, tensions grew worse as the Yishuv leadership imposed a new public excise tax, called *Kofer ha-Yishuv*, to pay for enhanced security services in the face of the Arab Revolt. The Haganah, the Zionist militia under the authority of the Jewish Agency, held military exercises on

Source: Placard in private collection of Menachem Friedman. Used with permission. Translated by Eran Kaplan.

the Sabbath and Jewish holidays, thus exacerbating long-standing haredi anger about Zionist institutions practicing violations of the Sabbath (e.g., cargo transportation). While Agudat Yisra'el was reluctant to publicly condemn the new tax, the extremist faction that adopted the name "Neturei Karta" had no qualms about doing so, as shown in this document, which, in the traditional fashion of communication in the haredi community, took the form of a street poster. In the years leading up to creation of the State, Agudat Yisra'el, while politically and theologically opposed to the Zionist idea, cooperated with the Zionist establishment, whereas the more radical Neturei Karta maintained their vehement anti-Zionism. After the creation of the state, Agudat Yisra'el participated in the Israeli political system (though between 1952 and 1977 it did not sit in the cabinet) while Neturei Karta refused to recognize Israeli sovereignty or cooperate in any way with the Israeli establishment.

A new ominous monster has arisen of late over our Holy Land.

In light of the terrible situation and great calamity that the Jewish community in our Holy Land and in the Diaspora has been battling for several years, the only option before us is to unify our nation's reserves and return to our original faith, seek ways to come back to our Father in heaven, destroy the pagan altars, which are the libertine schools that are based on heresy and apostasy (heaven forefend), to mend all the Jewish communities throughout the land according to Jewish family law, to abstain from forbidden foods and violating the Sabbath and holidays; for this is our true protection from all of our enemies and shall be our only salvation in this dire hour.

And what do we see today? Instead of the only refuge by means of repentance and good deeds, the reliable remedy of many generations since we became a nation until this very day, we see that the libertines who go against the Torah, the leaders of the Va'ad Le'umi,[1] who in their fear lest the people shall turn away from them because of all the failings that they have brought on the Yishuv since they disseminated their venomous ways, have raised a monster and a new pagan altar to poison the Jewish community, promoting a system of their own (heretical) hubris, that is, under the guise of Kofer ha-Yishuv, which undermines the very nature and spirit of our holy Torah for the following reasons:

(a) The very thought of defending the Yishuv by force of hand is heretical (heaven forefend), all the more so since this would bring destruction as we have already seen in the time of Bar-Kochba[2] who had tens of thousands of soldiers mighty and strong and brave, yet from the moment he mistook to rely on his own force without the help of God (Blessed Be He), his downfall began, as did the destruction of our saved remnant; [this certainly holds true for] the initiators of Kofer ha-Yishuv who are well-known heretics (heaven forefend), profligates, who in all of their written and oral pronouncements never mention God's name and only speak of relying on the force of their own hand, filling their mouths with heresy (heaven forefend).

(b) The very way they think of defending the Yishuv is false as it has already been proven by the misfortune and harm that we have experienced everywhere, especially the incidents in Tiberias, Ramat ha-Kovesh, and Ramat Rachel.[3]

(c) The defiling of the Sabbath and holidays and the consumption of forbidden foods that are carried out directly and indirectly in the name of Kofer ha-Yishuv by the conduct of public ceremonies and by smoking cigarettes on the Sabbath and holidays and everything else that they do and that we have witnessed.

(d) The Va'ad Le'umi's libertine coercion of the Haredi community under the guise of Kofer ha-Yishuv is forbidden to us *a priori*.

(e) The very handing over of funds to people who forfeited their right to manage public funds since the beginning of their influence in our Holy Land, as we have seen in respect to: *Keren ha-Geula, Keren ha-Ezra, Ezra u-Vitzaron*[4] and now Kofer ha-Yishuv, in the name of which they collected staggering sums of several hundreds of thousands of Palestine pounds without providing the public with a report approved by His Majesty's Government's certified accountant, including the Kofer Yishuv initiative, which during the last few months enabled them to collect fifty thousand Palestine pounds without proper public reporting about expenses. Moreover people who by their leadership and methods of governance brought a calamity on the Jewish community by straying and leading others astray from the only truth that our leaders already proclaimed: "Except the Lord keep the city, the watchman waketh but in vain; except the Lord keep the city, the watchman waketh but in vain. [Psalm 127:1]" Such men do not aid the Yishuv in any way since what motivates them is hunger for power and influence that poisons their work. We therefore appeal to the greater haredi public and ask:

How long shall we be under the foot of the power hungry libertines?
How long shall we bow our heads before all that the Va'ad Le'umi, forbidden to us according to our ancient sages, foists upon us?

And to the leadership of Agudat Yisra'el we pose this open question: How long will it hesitate and vacillate, and we remind it and demand of it that it fulfill its duty as a haredi organization and raise high the flag of our holy Torah and come out against the merchants of blood who always know how to exploit every disaster (heaven forefend), which befalls the Jewish community for their own advantage, who always prosper from the destruction of the Yishuv by increasing their powers and further poison the young generation, diverting it from the ways of the Lord. And to the haredi public we say the following: All who hold their family dear and wish to preserve the purity of their spirit and soul are bound by holy duty to exert their utmost influence over all their neighbors and friends and warn them of the danger (heaven forefend) in the Kofer Yishuv propaganda. And all those who fear the Lord must act to publicly ban any and all effort whose initiators and promoters are known as enemies of religion and the Yishuv!

We must remind the public over and over again that each and every penny given to Kofer ha-Yishuv adds to the pagan altar and to heresy (heaven forefend).

Say ye not: A conspiracy[5] concerning all whereof this Va'ad Le'umi do say: A conspiracy. "Some trust in chariots, and some in horses; but we will make mention of the name of the Lord our God. [Psalm 20:7]" And by virtue of our faith and our trust in God (may His Name be blessed) we shall live to see the redemption of Israel and His land and the coming of the righteous redeemer in our times.

The Neturei Karta[6] Committee of Haredi Jewry

NOTES

1. The Jewish National Council, the chief governing body of the Yishuv.

2. Leader of a failed revolt against Rome from 132 to 135 CE, and a venerated figure in Zionism as a fighter for national liberation.

3. Jewish communities and settlements attacked by Palestinians during the 1929 disturbances and the Arab Revolt that had begun in 1936.

4. Public fundraising campaigns in the Yishuv during the 1920s and 1930s.

5. Isa. 8:12

6. For the first time this extremist faction calls itself Neturei Karta, a name it has retained to this day. The name is derived from an ancient rabbinic story reproduced at the top of the poster. The story tells of two rabbis who arrive at a Jewish community in the Land of Israel and ask to meet the town guards (*neturei karta*, literally meaning "guardians of the city"). When presented with armed men, the rabbis reply that such men are not the guardians of the city but rather its destroyers. The true guardians, they say, are those who study Torah (and, by implication, keep its commandments). The connection with the Kofer Yishuv tax, and the armed guards whose training the tax is to support, is clear.

SECTION III

Tel Aviv City Hall, 1930s (Stanford University Libraries)

FORGING A MODERN
HEBREW CULTURE
IN THE LAND OF ISRAEL

When the first Zionist pioneers arrived in Palestine in the early 1880s, they were motivated by two similar and largely overlapping visions: a social ideal that sought to create a new Jewish society, which unlike the Jewish communities in the Diaspora would be based on a new division of labor in which Jews would engage in manual work; as well as a spiritual or cultural desire to rejuvenate Jewish life, to escape the perceived decadent life in the dark alleys of the Jewish ghetto and to rediscover the Jews' physical (masculine) qualities through a return to the land and to nature. The early Zionist pioneers sought to create a new social order that would redirect the course of Jewish history and make Jewish society self-sufficient and self-reliant, and they also wanted Jews to reengage in physical activities as a way to invigorate the Jewish psyche. These similar, yet at times competing, tendencies continued to inform Zionist ideology for the next several decades and led to some of the more charged early debates among different Zionist camps.

For Theodor Herzl, Zionism was a solution to the Jewish problem in Europe, which was a socio-economic and political problem. To Herzl, anti-Semitism could be explained according to recent developments in European society—the rise of modern capitalism, the dismantling of older social orders and protections—and the only viable remedy to European anti-Semitism, Herzl argued, was a political one: the creation of an independent Jewish state, in which Jews would be able to control their historical destiny and become like any other normal nation. Herzl's brand of Zionism came to be known as "political Zionism"; to him culture or spiritual quests had little to do with social remedies. In his utopian novel *Altneuland* (Old New Land), in which he described the future Jewish society

167

in Palestine, the country exhibited all the characteristics of high European culture, but there was nothing uniquely Jewish (or national) about it. What made the society described in *Altneuland* unique were its social and political institutions; culturally it was just an outpost of European civilization in the Levant.

One of Herzl's fiercest critics was Ahad ha-Am, who was the leader of what was called "cultural" or "spiritual" Zionism. Ahad ha-Am did not believe that a political solution could address the needs of the entire Jewish people. Instead, he believed that Palestine should be developed into a spiritual center that would revitalize all of Judaism. Ahad ha-Am wrote a scathing review of *Altneuland*, in which among other things he blamed Herzl for creating a cold mechanistic image that would not inspire people. He accused Herzl of not providing the society described in the novel with a uniquely Jewish character, or for that matter with a Jewish national language.

Indeed, the question of language was one of the most critical cultural issues that the early Zionists faced. For many of the early Zionist pioneers, Yiddish was the Jewish vernacular, while others spoke various European languages. A small number of intellectuals and activists, led by Eliezer Ben Yehuda, who settled in Palestine in 1881, believed that a revolutionary movement that aims to upend the course of Jewish history should not rely on the languages of the Diaspora but rather resurrect the ancient Jewish national tongue, Hebrew. Zionists were not the first to call for the resurrection of ancient Hebrew. *Maskilim*, members of the Jewish Enlightenment or *Haskalah*, a century earlier began this process in earnest. Much like the humanists of the Renaissance era, who wanted to rescue Latin from the clutches of the Roman church and reclaim its original literary and scientific qualities, maskilim wanted to return to the beauty and grace of ancient Hebrew and rediscover its more secular (literary, intellectual) qualities. But while the project of the maskilim was limited by and large to the realm of books and journals, Zionists were faced with more practical considerations—to turn Hebrew into a living, everyday language. And here intellectuals and writers, who created dictionaries, grammar books, and institutions aimed at the propagation of Hebrew as well as new literary creations in Hebrew (chief among these intellectuals alongside Ben Yehuda was Chaim Nahman Bialik, the great Hebrew poet), were joined by the broader Jewish population in Palestine that by the second decade of the twentieth century in their schools, public institutions, and their homes embraced Hebrew as their national language. Despite the fairly decisive victory of Hebrew over other languages at a time of massive Jewish immigration to Palestine, some of the Yishuv's political and cultural leaders feared the language's dominance; several organizations—among them the Hebrew Language Brigade as well as writers' associations—tried to make sure that foreign languages did not dominate the Yishuv's public sphere.

The early divisions between political Zionists and cultural Zionists were fierce and emotionally charged, but they were mainly theoretical in nature; on the ground in

Palestine, however, the reality was more nuanced—the development of social and political institutions went alongside the cultivation of cultural institutions. Yet the question of culture continued to inform ideological divisions in the Zionist camp. The Revisionists, under Jabotinsky's leadership, preached the urgency of achieving political independence (with military force) over developing social institutions—and they claimed to be Herzl's true ideological heirs; yet for them (unlike their proclaimed ideological forefather) culture played a crucial ideological role. To Jabotinsky and his followers, culture was a way to instill in the Hebrew youth such virtues as discipline, resolve, and self-confidence, all of which, they believed, would be useful in the national struggle for independence. Jabotinsky and other Revisionists leaders such as the poet Uri Zvi Greenberg were writers and intellectuals, and to them the written as well as the spoken word had a critical role in shaping the contours of the national body; they translated great works into Hebrew and contributed original works that aimed to enhance the sense of national grandeur and pride. Laborites had a more spartan cultural outlook than their Revisionist counterparts. Their cultural imagination was informed by the values of labor and agriculture. To many of them high culture was associated with Jewish life in the Diaspora—a return to the land meant a return to a more basic culture that derives its inspiration from the material conditions of the new land. The austere farmer, rather than the hunched yeshiva student, was their ideal type. Yet under the hegemony of Labor Zionism, culture flourished in Jewish Palestine. Publishing houses, newspapers, theaters, orchestras, cinemas, and even a fledgling film industry, which produced mainly documentaries that celebrated the accomplishments of the Yishuv, helped create a vibrant cultural scene that turned modern Hebrew culture into a viable national culture.

One of the most intricate questions that the new Hebrew culture in Palestine had to contend with was its relationship with traditional Jewish culture. This was the case with the Hebrew language, which in traditional Judaism was limited to the liturgical realm and in the new Zionist community became the vernacular. And it was also true of Jewish holidays. The traditional Jewish holidays, including the Sabbath, continued to provide the backbone of the new Zionist, and later Israeli, calendar (in addition to a few new civic holidays and days of commemoration, such as the day commemorating the fall of Tel Hai)—but the celebration of some of the traditional holidays was altered to reflect the values of the new society. For such holidays as Sukkoth, Passover, and Shavuot, in kibbutzim, moshavim, and schools all over Jewish Palestine emphasis was placed on the agricultural aspects of these holidays, marking the achievements in this area of the new Yishuv. In this respect, some of the celebrations of the Jewish festivals in Palestine underscored their pre-monotheistic origins. If traditional Judaism developed in the Diaspora, the new Hebrew culture, which sought to negate the legacy of the Jewish Diaspora, returned to some of Judaism's pre-exilic traditions, which, like Zionism, were tied to the land itself as a source of inspiration.

In this section, documents 29 and 30 explore the revival of modern Hebrew and the struggle to establish Hebrew as the new national language. Document 31 looks at the public Purim celebrations in Tel Aviv and the way a traditional Jewish festival was molded to reflect the new values of the Yishuv. Documents 32 through 35 examine the emergence of new cultural institutions in Palestine and the debates over the kinds of themes and values that the new Hebrew culture should aspire to. Document 36 looks at the Hebrew University, arguably the Yishuv's cultural crown jewel—an institution whose cultural impact was felt in the Jewish world well beyond the boundaries of Palestine.

29

Plain Language Association (1889)

ELIEZER BEN YEHUDA

Eliezer Ben Yehuda (1858–1922) was born in Lithuania to a traditional Jewish family and was one of the major contributors to the revival of modern Hebrew—in fact, in the Yishuv and later in Israel he was known as *mehayeh ha-safa ha-Ivrit* (the "reviver" of the Hebrew language). After completing a traditional course of Jewish education, which included the study of classical Hebrew, he attended the Sorbonne in Paris. Ben Yehuda became a supporter of Zionism and a champion of the use of the Hebrew language, and when he settled in Jerusalem in 1881, Hebrew was the only language that was used in his house. In 1884 Ben Yehuda established *Ha-Zvi*, a Hebrew newspaper, and in 1890 he founded the Hebrew Language Council, which later became the Hebrew Academy. Arguably, Ben Yehuda's most important contribution to the revival of the Hebrew language was the seventeen-volume *A Complete Dictionary of Ancient and Modern Hebrew*, on which he worked relentlessly and which was only completed by his wife, Hemda, after his death.

The Plain Language Association (Hevrat Safa Berura in Hebrew) was founded in 1889 by Ben Yehuda and several other community activists, including Ya'acov Meir, Haim Hirschensohn, and Haim Kalmi. This document contains the guidelines and goals for this association, namely the dissemination of a clear and grammatically sound Hebrew language throughout the Jewish community in Palestine.

Source: *Yisra'el le-Artzo u-le-Leshono: Kol Kitvei Eliezer Ben-Yehuda, Kerech Rishon*, ed. Itamar Ben Avi (Jerusalem, 1929), 201–3. Translated by Marganit Weinberger-Rotman.

> They say that when a child begins to talk, his father speaks to him in
> Hebrew; if he does not speak Hebrew to him, it is as if he has buried him.
>
> Rashi

> Whoever lives in the Land of Israel and speaks Hebrew is guaranteed
> a place in the world to come.
>
> Yerushalmi, Shabbat 78:3[1]

A. We are setting up an association in Jerusalem named "Plain Language." An association made up not of intellectuals or zealots, not engaged in controversy and schisms, but merely a Hebrew association with no other affiliation, dedicated to one purpose only.

B. The purpose of this association is to eradicate from the Jewish population in the Land of Israel the use of inferior vernacular dialects, such as the jargons spoken by Ashkenazi and Sephardic communities,[2] which separate the speakers and sow division in their hearts, causing such distinct manners, customs, and beliefs, that a Sephardi considers only other Sephardis Jewish but not Ashkenazis, and vice versa. This division is detrimental to the healthy physical and spiritual existence of our community. These inferior dialects have made us a laughing-stock and an object of scorn and derision in the eyes of our neighbors and other nations, and they have fostered animosity and acrimony among the various ethnic groups, thereby rendering us incapable of fulfilling our duty to our mother-land and to our esteemed and august government.

C. The association will have two kinds of members:

1. Supporting members whose monetary donations will help maintain the association.
2. Active members who will assist the association in carrying out its vision.

Note: A one-time donation of five napoleons[3] will confer on the donor the title of "esteemed founder," a one-time donation of three napoleons will confer the title of "esteemed member," and a donor of a lesser amount will become a member in good standing. A person donating much time and effort to the association will be awarded the title of "esteemed member" or "esteemed founder" by the committee, according to his or her work.

D. The central committee of the association will be in Jerusalem, with local branches in all other Jewish towns and settlements. The central committee will maintain contact with affiliated associations abroad that support our vision.

E. The central committee will elect an executive board to carry out the resolutions of the committee.

Here are the means the association will use to achieve its objectives:

1. The Association will hire Hebrew-speaking women (several who already live in Jerusalem can start working right away). These women will teach spoken Hebrew, as well as reading and writing, to women and girls in all the households that are interested in this project. Hebrew will also be taught at the Girls Schools of the *"Maestra."*[4] The Committee will see to it that no extra burden is imposed on the girls and that their work is not disturbed as a result. The association will look for women in other towns as well, and it will make special effort to extend the study of Hebrew to *Talmud Torah* [religious schools] and co-ed educational facilities.

2. Depending on resources, the association will publish a dictionary of limited scope that will include practical vocabulary for household and commercial usage. For this purpose a special literary committee will be established whose mandate is to examine literary and other books submitted to the association to determine their conformity to the association's mission; if books are found suitable, the association will finance their publication and pay the authors.

3. The literary committee will scour all the Hebrew sources and archives to compile a list of Hebrew words and words close to Hebrew and publish them so that people can get to know them. The committee will also coin new words after consulting with the best grammarians and authors in the language.

4. The association will encourage and assist anyone who wishes to introduce Hebrew into his household, and it will do its utmost to find ways to facilitate the process.

These are the principal measures we mean to use to achieve our goal, but we will also look for other devices and means; experience will teach us what to do and what roads to take.

We do not delude ourselves that our goal can be achieved in a short time; we know full well that the task is hard and demanding, and it will not be accomplished in five, nay even ten, years. We are aware of all the obstacles, stumbling blocks, and obstructions that await us along the way, and we know that many years will elapse until we begin to see the fruit of our efforts. But we are confident that, eventually, we will reach our goal, and that our endeavor will bring unity and brotherhood to our nation. We must launch this great project—a holy task that will confer honor and glory on all who engage in it; their names will be inscribed in our national chronicles for eternity.

May the God of Israel lend us succor, and may we live to see the fruit of our efforts, be it soon or in years to come.

NOTES

1. Ben Yehuda is paraphrasing, not quoting directly, from his rabbinic sources. In the original sources, speaking Hebrew and dwelling in the Land of Israel is inseparably linked with complete observance of the religious commandments. The secularist Ben Yehuda altered theses canonical texts in order to fit his cultural-Zionist agenda.

2. Yiddish and Ladino, respectively.

3. Presumably the text alludes to the colloquial name of a gold coin of twenty francs, which was first introduced in 1801.

4. This term refers to an old Sephardic custom of entrusting young girls to old women—known as *maestras*—to teach them language and reading.

30

How to Spread the Use of Hebrew (1927)

MENACHEM USSISHKIN

Since the inception of the Jewish national movement, the role of Hebrew as the national language was frequently debated. In fact, for Herzl, the question of which language would become the national language was of secondary, if any, importance; in his 1902 utopian novel *Altneuland*, in which he described the future Jewish society in Palestine in the year 1923, the different inhabitants of the New Society seemed to be speaking the various languages of their native, European countries. With the onset of Zionist settlement in Palestine, Hebrew began to emerge as the preferred language among the new settlers. New educational institutions started to adopt a Hebrew curriculum, and a growing number of Jews in Palestine, following the example of Eliezer Ben Yehuda, began to use Hebrew as their everyday language. Yet a substantial number of Jews continued to speak Yiddish or other European tongues, and some of them also made an ideological plea that Yiddish or in other cases German or Russian should be the vernacular used in the future Jewish state, while Hebrew should remain a religious language. In 1913, the Jewish community in Palestine witnessed what would become known as the "War of Languages." In that year, the Hilfsverein der deutschen Juden (German-Jewish Aid Association) sought to establish an engineering school with German instruction—generating an angry reaction

Source: Menachem Ussishkin, "Ha-Derech le-Hashlatat ha-Safa," in *Gedud Meginei ha-Safa be-Eretz Israel 1923–36*, ed. Shimon A. Shor (Haifa, 2000), 63–64. Translated by Marganit Weinberger-Rotman.

from many sections of the Jewish community; instead of a German-speaking school, the Technion, a Hebrew technical institute, was founded in Haifa. This was seen as a symbolic victory for Hebrew and a validation of its emergence as the undisputed national language of Jewish Palestine. After the First World War, however, with the growing influx of Jewish immigrants, some leaders in the Yishuv feared that Hebrew might again lose its dominance. For that purpose, they created in 1923 Gedud Meginei ha-Safa (the Brigade of the Defenders of Hebrew) to promote the use of Hebrew, but this organization was disbanded in 1936. The brigade's slogan was *Ivri daber Ivrit!* (Hebrew person, speak Hebrew!); its members organized Hebrew classes for new immigrants, they launched propaganda campaigns against institutions that used foreign languages, and they attended public events guaranteeing that only Hebrew would be spoken there. At times their tactics included intimidation, even assaults.

Avraham Menachem Mendel Ussishkin (1863–1941) was a member of Hovevei Tsion and an early champion of the revival of Hebrew as the national Jewish language. Ussishkin, an engineer by training, served as Hebrew secretary at the first Zionist Congress. Ussishkin moved to Palestine in 1919, and in 1923 he was elected the head of the Jewish National Fund. Ussishkin was also instrumental in the establishment of the Hebrew University in Jerusalem.

After all the greetings delivered here, I would like to discuss some practical matters. The fact that a Brigade of the Defenders of Hebrew exists, and that it operates not in Soviet Russia—where The Great "Ham"[1] rules—but here, in our own country, where the best and the brightest of the nation have gathered— this very fact is significant and instructive. A brigade of the defenders of Hebrew, indeed!

The name is very apt. Not a brigade of distributors, but a brigade of defenders. What does this tell us? When you have an association of Sabbath observers, the implication is that there are also those who desecrate the Sabbath. If you have a Zionist organization, it follows that there are also non-Zionists. And if you have a brigade of defenders of the language, it means that there are people who need to be reminded of their obligation to speak Hebrew. We must be vigilant and defend our language.

If we examine the history of the *Hibbath Tsion* [love of Zion] movement, we'll see that just as there was a dispute about the territory, there was also disagreement about the use of the Hebrew language. There were times when the Jewish land was in Uganda, in Argentina, and now in the Crimea.[2] These are weighty questions for our movement, but the question of the language is crucial to the entire movement. How did the Zionist leader regard this question? I mean the late lamented Herzl. Twenty-three years after his death, we may raise this painful question again. If you read his diaries, you'll find the passage where he asks: What language should be spoken in the Land of Israel? His answer: German. And he adds that if the zealots who champion the use of Hebrew succeed in their campaign, then the nation will be relegated to a remote corner of human culture. Throughout the history of the Zionist movement and in the Congresses, we tended to regard the Hebraists as a bunch of idlers, slackers, and daydreamers detached from the real world. Years have passed, Hebrew has won the battle, and opinions have changed. Hebrew is the spoken language, and it is used in ceremonies, lectures, etc., but the victory is not complete; when it comes to assigning positions in the Zionist movement, the requirements are always professional proficiency, education, general information, articulateness, etc., but not knowledge of Hebrew as a pre-condition for a job in the Zionist administration. Hebrew is necessary, perhaps, in some remote village, but not inside the organization. This attitude has permeated throughout the entire Zionist world in eastern and western Europe. Have you forgotten how they treated Hebrew speakers in Israel not long ago? I think they referred to them as "*schmendricks*" (good-for-nothings in Yiddish), and Ben Yehuda's household, the only one in Jerusalem where Hebrew was spoken, was despised and denigrated. Some vestiges of this attitude can be found to this day. We are regarded as "natives," even though the Congress has adopted a resolution that every Zionist officer must demonstrate proficiency in Hebrew no later than one year after assuming a position in the Zionist administration. This condition has been fulfilled only in the institute where I am the head. There was also a call for the Congress to be conducted in Hebrew. And what do we see? Even those who know Hebrew are speaking in foreign languages. Why? Because if you start speaking Hebrew, people start leaving the hall, led by the "high priests." A question arose where the executive committee should be located. Some demanded that it be moved to Jerusalem. I was the only one who objected. It is bad enough that our meetings abroad are marred by a hodgepodge of tongues; let us not import this mess to the Land of Israel. Spare us this indignity. We must put an end to this unfortunate state of affairs once and for all.

Building the Land of Israel requires people, capital, and a change of attitude toward Hebrew language and culture. The first two conditions are not hard to come by; Jews volunteer to build the country, and they come here in person, invest capital, energy, etc. But when it comes to the language, it is too big a sacrifice to undertake because habits acquired in exile are not easy to shake.

Many languages prevail in the country these days. Let us see which ones we should beware of most. We should watch for two languages in particular: English

and Yiddish. The first is attractive because many depend on it for their livelihood, and the second because it has a well-known ideology attached to it. It is
Yiddish that caused Hebrew to decline in Poland and in other places. English
has become the language of the upper class and the privileged. It is also the
language of culture and employment. I am sure it won't be long before every
man and woman in the country speaks English. What measures can we take to
countervail these trends? We should not boycott the foreign languages themselves; there is no point in that. We must declare a public boycott against those
who refuse to acquire our language. The requirement to speak Hebrew should
become a sine qua non for all participation in the building of the land, in any
capacity. If we strive hard enough, we will eventually see the day when delegates
to the Congress are not just Zionists but speakers and devotees of Hebrew. You
cannot be a delegate in the Parliament without speaking Hebrew. What we
accomplished at the Elected Assembly[3] can and should be accomplished at the
Zionist Congresses. We no longer have living among us such geniuses as Herzl
and [Max] Nordau, whom we allowed to speak foreign languages in the
Congresses. If someone does not know Hebrew, let him sit at home for a year
and learn it. It will not be a great loss to the Jewish people.

I have presented the question of the battle for the language in a political context. You are the decision makers. You will attain your goal, not by distributing
flyers saying, "Hebrew person, speak Hebrew!" but by exerting influence on
those who turn their backs on Hebrew, making sure they cannot obtain the
position they desire.

There was much applause here tonight in celebration of Hebrew letters.
But you must also defend and prize Hebrew culture. We can also create general
culture in Hebrew. We do not value only the mechanical language and the
letters. We must pay attention to Hebrew culture as a whole. There are people
overseas who regard the language as an outward shell emptying it of its
content. This is unthinkable. The Jewish nation that supports the revival of the
land must not renounce the content of Hebrew culture. This is particularly
relevant in our country. We now have 160,000 Jewish workers. Thousands of
them speak Hebrew. But we do not see the complete Hebrew person. To create
such wholeness is much harder than to grow bread out of the soil of Kibbutz
Ein Harod.[4]

I extend my best wishes to you. Keep your spirits fresh and they will
accomplish more than the "big shots" can. When our language becomes the
common heritage of the nation, like all our other national properties, only then
can you rest on your laurels and disband the brigade. But that day is still distant,
and you have your work cut out for you. Continue with resolve and determination
as befits young people. Work hard and prosper!

NOTES

1.   Ussishkin is referring here to Stalin. Ham was the youngest of Noah's three sons, who was cursed by his father (Gen. 9:25). In the Jewish tradition, Ham has been a symbol of evil.

2.   In 1924, the American Jewish Joint Distribution Committee (JDC) set up the American Jewish Joint Agricultural Corporation (Agro-Joint), which was an initiative carried out in cooperation with the Soviet government to settle "non-productive" Jews as farmers on agricultural settlements in Ukraine and the Crimea in order to ameliorate the social and economic condition of the Jewish population. About 70,000 Jews had been resettled through this program by 1936.

3.   Asefat ha-Nivharim (the Elected Assembly) was created in Palestine in April 1920 as the prominent elected political body, or National Assembly of the Yishuv in pre-state Palestine. Representatives were elected based on party affiliation.

4.   Founded in 1921, Ein Harod is a kibbutz located near Mount Gilboa in northern Israel.

31

Purim Celebrations in Tel Aviv (1931)

The first Purim Carnival in Tel Aviv was organized in 1912 by the Herzlia Gymnasium art teacher Avraham Aldemah; several students and adults in costumes marched from the school building to the train tracks on Herzl Street. Meir Dizengoff, Tel Aviv's first mayor, understood the civic significance of such an event, and on the following year he turned the march into a Hebrew festival. Since then annual Purim festivals were held in Tel Aviv, as long as the political situation allowed it to go on (in 1920 the carnival was canceled following the events in Tel Hai and the death of Joseph Trumpeldor; see document 38). In the late 1920s, the city decided to turn the carnival into a more organized institution that would last three days and include a variety of events. In 1931 the city sought suggestions from the public for themes for the celebration, and in 1932 the name *adloyada* (in Hebrew "until they will not know"; the name was taken from a passage in the Talmud that instructs people to celebrate the Purim holiday to the point when they will not know the difference between the evil Haman and the righteous Moredcai), which was proposed by the writer S. Y. Agnon, was adopted as the celebration's official name. The four adloyada celebrations that took place between 1932 and 1935 were grand public celebrations that included street festivals, activities for children, and special theatrical productions. The celebrations also included satirical themes aimed at British policies. In 1936, because of the Great Arab Revolt, the adloyada was canceled. Only in 1955 did the annual Purim celebration return to Tel Aviv on a regular basis until the late 1960s. In this document, the city of Tel Aviv provided an outline of what the official celebration would include with an emphasis on celebrating the spirit and achievements

Source: Tel Aviv-Yaffo Municipal Archive, C-4-3219. Translated by Marganit Weinberger-Rotman.

of the Jewish community in Palestine. While this was an urban carnival, great emphasis was placed on celebrating the achievements of the Yishuv's agricultural sector.

Objectives

1. Dispel the gloom enveloping the public and lift its spirits.
2. Attract out-of-town visitors to alleviate the economic slump and encourage commerce, transport, etc.
3. Demonstrate progress in industry, agriculture, and crafts.

Background

1. The carnival and the other Purim celebrations must be the creation and expression of the general public, unlike the rest of the year when the public is a passive observer. The committee must encourage and urge the public to participate.
2. The holiday of Purim should be an occasion of mirth and optimism for the Yishuv. This spirit should characterize all the preparations: we will assist not only those groups that put on satirical skits and critical sketches, but also groups that will spread good cheer, joy, and merriment.
3. Masquerades and other forms of entertainment should be humorous, witty, and done in artistic and tasteful manner.

Schedule

The holiday opens with the reading of the Megillah [Book of Esther], on the eve of the fourteenth of Adar and ends the next day, *Shushan Purim*,[1] the fifteenth of Adar, in the evening. Thus, there are three parts to the festival: (a) opening night; (b) the fourteenth of Adar—Children, Youth and Sports Day; (c) the fifteenth of Adar—Carnival Day.

A. Opening Night

1. Ushering in the holiday—At nightfall, a long siren will be sounded from the silicate factory, fire station, and the ships docked in the harbor that day. We

must, however, secure the captains' permission beforehand and make sure they point the projectors toward the city. The siren will last three minutes and will be immediately followed by a trumpet salute. For this purpose we need to recruit the best trumpeters from schools, youth organizations, and orchestras, about twenty-five in all, who will be placed on rooftops along Allenby and Nahlat-Binyamin streets. A special ten-minute-long tune should be composed for the occasion. When the music starts, torches will be lit on all the balconies and roofs of Herzl, Allenby, and Nahlat-Binyamin streets, which will add to the festive atmosphere, but are also emblems of ancient holidays. The committee will have to come to an agreement with landlords regarding this arrangement. When the trumpet blowing is over, two groups of torch bearing "satraps"[2] on horses, camels, and motorcycles, will ride from both ends of the city toward the main square in front of the opera house. They should be accompanied by an orchestra of wind instruments and carry banners with quotes from the book of Esther, such as, "It came to pass in the days of Ahasuerus," " The Jews had light, gladness and joy," etc. These riders will call on the inhabitants to join the festivities, and they will also display a sign with a humorous invitation. They will wear the costumes of ancient Persian officials.

They will reach the square, followed by a throng of thousands. From the balcony of the opera house, members of Ha-Ohel [the tent] and other theatrical troupes will recite verses from the book of Esther explaining the meaning of the holiday, written by one of our authors. Next, the opera chorus will sing *Shoshanat Ya'akov*.[3] If this cannot be arranged, we'll have to make do with the band playing familiar tunes and having the audience participate in the singing. Next will come a collective reading of humorous Purim texts by members of the *Matateh* (broom) satirical troupe, who will also invite the spectators to an open contest of comic presentations. After that, people can dance to the music of the band or do as they please. In order to disperse the revelers around town, one group of "satraps" will return to the center of town where a record player and a megaphone will invite the public to dance.

B. Sports and Youth Day

The race that ushers in the adult festivities will begin at three o'clock. One party will take place in the yard of the high school and the other on the hill near Ha-Carmel Street. Participation is open to all, but (free) tickets need to be obtained beforehand.

The program includes: band playing, high jumps, sack race, mock sports contests, comedians, and recitation by youth drama clubs. Since we cannot provide a stage, they will perform on the platform of a truck. Dances and gymnastic performances will take place simultaneously in different parts of town to prevent crowding and to offer people a variety of events.

At night the festivities will move to the streets. The town should be divided among the various youth associations, each entertaining the public in a different section. If possible, magic lanterns should be stationed on a couple of roofs, showing scenes of life in Palestine, or just funny pictures. Perhaps we could lease space on these shows to advertisers for a fee.

We should take advantage of the proximity of the city to the sea to organize cruises. The boats will be lit up with colorful lanterns and feature choirs singing popular songs and bands. Other activities could include: boat races, hitting targets on shore, and throwing toys for the spectators to catch.

C. Carnival Day

From early morning the public's attention will be drawn to surprises and attractions, such as decorated cars with information about upcoming events scouring the city, leaflets with comical messages, riders tooting various instruments, and other devices that will draw the public's attention.

Those who wish to participate in the carnival should register at least three days before the event. A day before the carnival, they will receive a number indicating when they should enter. Shows presenting foreign material will not be admitted.

In order to activate and involve the public, the musicians will be dispersed along the parade, and the public should be encouraged to join in, even though this may be a little risky. At any rate, bikers and motorcycles riding on both sides of the parade must wear special Purim helmets.

The themes of the shows will be: *Purim*, local agricultural and industrial production, *Keren Kayemet* cattle growing, the dairy industry, settlement and renewal in the Land of Israel, Diaspora and Israel, and entertainment. We need to negotiate with various agencies to undertake these performances and encourage the general public to contribute their own initiative to the parade.

Prizes should be awarded in each of the three events of the festival.

These are general outlines; each part of the festivities and the carnival requires further development and enhancement, which will be done by the special committees.

In order to promote a spirit of hilarity and merriment, we recommend changing the street names to names of characters in the Megillah to be used in all publications (of course, with the mention of the real names in parentheses).

Similarly, mock municipality with mock officials, banks, post (with humorous stamps) could also be suggested to various agencies.

NOTES

1. *Shushan Purim* is the day after Purim. It commemorates the day when the Jews of *Shushan*, the Persian capital, rested after defeating their enemies.

2. Satraps were provincial governors in the ancient Persian Empire.

3. *Shoshanat Ya'akov* is a traditional hymn recited in synagogue after reading the Scroll of Esther on Purim.

32

The National and Cultural Importance of Bezalel (1930)

JOSEPH KLAUSNER

In this article, Hebrew University professor Joseph Klausner (1874–1958)—a historian, one of the chief editors of the Hebrew Encyclopedia, and a literary scholar whose work covered such wide-ranging topics as Second-Temple Jewry, early Christianity, and modern Hebrew literature—celebrated the achievements of Boris Shatz (1866–1932) and Bezalel, the art academy that Shatz founded in Jerusalem in 1906. Shatz was born in Lithuania, and in 1889 he moved to Paris to study art. In 1895 he was invited by the Bulgarian Court to establish an art academy in that country, which he headed until 1906. In 1903 Shatz met Herzl and became an ardent Zionist. He immigrated to Palestine in 1906, where he founded what would later be named Bezalel (named after the architect of the Hebrews' desert Tabernacle in the book of Exodus)—the first modern Hebrew art academy. Shatz sought to develop in Bezalel a national Jewish artistic style that would combine modern European techniques with traditional Jewish and Middle Eastern themes and forms. The younger generation of teachers and students, though, resisted Shatz's vision in favor of a more modernist approach, and eventually their ideals prevailed. Until this very day, Bezalel is Israel's premier art and design academy and

Source: Joseph Klausner, "The National and Cultural Importance of Bezalel: On the 25th Anniversary of the Bezalel Academy of Art," *Ha-ʿolam*, May 27, 1930, vol. 22, 428–29.

plays a critical role in the country's artistic life. In this article, Klausner, who in addition to his academic work was also active in Zionist affairs and was associated with the right-wing Revisionist movement, discusses the importance of art and culture in the Jewish national movement, a common theme in the Zionist Revisionist discourse of that period.

We came here to build a national home, not with a sword and not with blood. We have no army and no government, and our physical force is smaller than that of the other inhabitants of the land. It will take decades for us to achieve economic independence and to become a majority.

What, then, is our hope, our aspiration for full national renewal? What will enable us to turn "Palestine" into the Land of Israel?

I think there is one strong foundation for such a hope.

A land does not belong to those who conquer it with fire and blood, nor to those who happen to settle it. The land belongs to those who leave their imprint on it. And that imprint can only be our national culture. We do not have—nor can we possibly entertain—any evil intent of dispossessing the Arabs of any of their rights. What is left, then, is free competition. This competition is bound to be difficult in the political and national arena, and even more so in the economic arena, but it may be easier and more feasible in the sphere of national culture.

We are a nation of culture. Our prophets and sages in Asia and our fore-fathers and brothers in Europe have bequeathed to us a vast cultural heritage that is both old and new, Eastern and Western. The Arabs used to have a culture—but it is gone. It will take them many decades to revive the culture they fostered in medieval Spain and blend it with modern European culture. Until then, it is merely Levantine, not national-humanistic, culture.

We are the only ones in this country who possess such a culture.

This is not arrogance—it is a fact. If there is theater in Palestine, it is Jewish.

If there is an academy of arts—it is Jewish. If there is a university, it is the Hebrew University. If there are lectures, courses, concerts, music, painting, sculpture, etching, pure and practical sciences, poetry, and worthwhile literature—it is all produced or imported by Jews. In short, the Jews are already leaving their mark on the cultural scene of this country—in science, literature and art. If this trend continues, the country is bound to acquire a Jewish-Hebrew identity, without, however, impinging on Arab culture. Rather, with help and encouragement from us, the Arabs will either develop their own culture or participate freely in our endeavors and achievements, without restriction and quotas.

One of the chief institutes contributing to the flourishing of Jewish culture in Palestine is Bezalel Academy of Art.

In the last hundred years, until the establishment of Bezalel, there was no modern art in this country, neither Jewish nor Arabic, Eastern or Western. Bezalel was a "temple in the desert." Professor Schatz was a pioneer, a trailblazer who tried to create Jewish art, and more generally, Palestinian art.

Professor Schatz understood this great secret: for a nation to be redeemed, its soul has to be redeemed first. And a national soul is made up of aesthetics as well as intellect. And he recognized another principle: the union of nation and country can come about only with a magical wedding ring of national art, which is the essence and embodiment of national culture.

But such national art—where can it be obtained?

Professor Schatz had the right answer, which is the only answer: the national art is scattered everywhere, but nobody collects or assembles it. The remnants of ancient art, recognized by archeologists, together with old artifacts produced over thousands of years of migration and diaspora—decorations, religious ornaments, sumptuous arks, ornate curtains—the spiritual beauty created by a nation of victims and martyrs, together with the extraordinary nature of the Land of Israel and the sublime aesthetics we brought with us from Europe, learned from the classical masters of Italy, Holland, and France—all these disparate elements must come together and blend to become something new, a supreme synthesis which is Hebrew and humanistic, Eastern and Western. This will be the new art of the Land of Israel.

This kind of synthesis is not easy to achieve and it cannot be done in a hurry. New ways must be sought and the seekers must be impelled by artistic, creative instincts. But Bezalel has already taken the first step. All over the Jewish world, the works of Bezalel are accepted as Jewish art, and there is a consensus that they embody our soul.

But Professor Schatz conceived another great idea.

Some art is individualistic art. The nation may be proud of it, but it does not belong to the people and the people do not enjoy it. It does not leave its mark on public life because it is outside the masses' ken, removed from national interests and popular acceptance. Such art remains in the private domain, cherished and appreciated perhaps, but essentially a buried treasure.

The other kind is popular art—art that has uses for the home and for the synagogue, for a mansion and for a humble shack. This art must have roots in scripture, in custom, in history, in momentous events in the past, in the nation's leaders and heroes and, in religious practice. This kind of art has relevancy and leaves its mark on the entire community and on the entire country. Bezalel has given our nation such an art, by fostering and developing twenty different kinds of arts and crafts culled from various ethnic communities. Whenever you find an objet d'art in a Jewish home, it is bound to be a product of Bezalel or one of its imitators. A synagogue or an exhibition in need of an especially elegant artifact turns to Bezalel. Bezalel products can be found all over the country. Even Franciscan monks and the Young Christians Association use Bezalel when they are looking for art in Palestine.

But this institute is now closed because it cannot garner 2,000 pounds a year! This is incredible![1]

Have we become so obtuse and hard-hearted that we cannot grasp the cultural and national importance of the Bezalel Academy? The thousands of pounds spent on Zionist propaganda cannot generate the love, appreciation, and interest that the works of Bezalel bring when they are sent around the world, to Jews and Gentiles alike.

Nothing can turn Palestine into the Land of Israel as the popular, national-humanistic art of Bezalel [can]!

On this 25th anniversary—half a jubilee celebrated by the entire people—how can we allow Bezalel to mark the occasion with its gates closed?

NOTE

1. In 1929 Bezalel was closed because of a budgetary crisis. The academy was reopened in 1935 by a group of teachers and students who came from Germany; many of them were Bauhaus graduates.

33

The Hebrew Stage:
Moriah, not Acropolis (1926)

AVIGDOR HAMEIRI

Avigdor Hameiri (1890–1970) was born in the Transcarpathia region of Hungary (today in Ukraine). He began writing Hebrew poetry in his late teens and published his first book of Hebrew poems in 1912. He immigrated to Palestine in 1921, where he worked for the daily newspaper *Haaretz* and several other literary and cultural journals. In 1927 he founded the short-lived satirical theater *Ha-Kumkum* (The Kettle) and wrote most of its skits and songs. In 1928, *Ha-Kumkum* was closed and Hameiri founded *Ha-Matateh* (The Broom), a satirical troupe that became a staple of Yishuv culture. Early in his public career in Palestine, Hameiri was closely allied with the Revisionists and their brand of heroic, militaristic Zionism. His poetry at the time conveyed a sense of prophetic anger and a call for a life based on the virtues of beauty and sacrifice. His 1930 novel *Ha-Shiga'on ha-Gadol* (The Great Madness) was based on his military experience during the First World War. From the late 1930s, though, Hameiri's political views began to shift to the Left. In 1968 he was awarded the Israel Prize for his literary achievements. In this article, published a year before he founded his own theater group, Hameiri criticized what he saw as attempts by modern Hebrew dramatists to adopt foreign forms and themes, and instead called for an authentic Jewish theater that would celebrate the uniqueness and vitality of the Jewish spirit.

Source: Avigdor Hameiri, "Ha-bimah ha-Ivrit: Moriah ve-lo Akropolis," *Teatron ve-Omanut*, vol. 4–5 (Jerusalem, 1926). Translated by Marganit Weinberger-Rotman.

Our era, marked by a national renaissance, is also the age of imitation, or to use A. Druyanov's[1] definition, the age of translation. Instead of creating art out of an impulse to express ourselves, we try to "become a nation," to enter the great family of nations, and to adapt our intellectual heritage to theirs. This is attested to not only by the literary genres we employ, but also by the ideas that are represented by our various literary forms.

If the mighty have succumbed, how will the weak emerge unscathed? What should those among us who care about the theater do? Can we possibly hope for anything but imitation of European theater—that "non plus ultra of all sublime ideals"—when we come to establish a Hebrew stage in the Land of Israel?

And yet, surprisingly enough, all those who worry about the Hebrew theater maintain that the Palestinian theater must first and foremost take into account the nature of the Land of Israel, i.e., accommodate itself to the climate and to the soil, and to build an amphitheater suitable for these conditions even better than that of Greece, the home of classical amphitheater. And yet, these people ignore another nature, no less important, which demands our attention and consideration, i.e., the nature of the Hebrew people itself, which rejects Hellenistic rituals and is vehemently antagonistic to all their manifestations.

It is the historical Jewish position, which calls for "redemption of the world in God's Kingdom" rather than in the wretched kingdom of beauty, a kingdom that has brought us to moral bankruptcy. We are worshipping these aesthetic idols, adoring Raphael's angels and babies and bowing reverentially to marble "*mater dolorosas*" [sorrowful mother—the Virgin Mary], ignoring the fact that at the same time those high priests of beauty set up new Inquisitions and poison Jewish babies, watching their slow death and intoxicating their rarefied blood. Had our "Hellas worshippers" looked more closely, they would have found that drunken Hellas itself, despite its moral turpitude and degeneration, gave rise to high-minded thinkers who were able to expose their country's failings and preach morality, godliness and salubrious art; catharsis instead of narcosis. Hedonistic, intoxicated Greece turned a deaf ear to its prophets' preaching, and it paid for it dearly.

And now, 3,000 years after the fierce battle with foreign gods and beauty-worshipping Hellenism, we are suddenly confronted with the great favor the Gentiles wish to confer on us: acceptance into their noble family. Instantly, we are willing to empty our coffers, disarm ourselves, and jettison our Hebrew heritage and the teachings of our much-touted prophets. But I doubt this will be easily accomplished. Our stubborn *Shechina* [divine spirit] will not put up with such charlatanism. Our Shechina champions ethics and humanism, not aestheticism and artistic inebriation. Judaism fosters social conscience, commitment, and humanitarianism.

The mission of the Hebrew theater is a Jewish one: to improve and exalt the humanity in us, without concessions and without aberrations. Since prophecy is no longer practiced in our midst, the theater is our only recourse to influence the masses and win their hearts. We must seize the moment and start defending our Hebrew heritage in the land of the prophets. We must cultivate conscientious and ethical authors and, through them, a healthy, moral, Hebrew society.

Theater is not an exclusively Hellenistic creation. To claim this is a ridiculous mistake. While the Greeks took a long and circuitous way to develop their dramatic arts—and were never able to rid themselves of the vulgar hexameter with its unnatural rhythms—Hebrew culture, from its very inception, used public means and devices, appealing directly to the people and using natural speech.

As for the concept of the stage and its development, anyone who has studied recent constructivist-expressionist[2] trends in contemporary Europe will surely recognize the tendency in the best theaters to return to the Bible in one way or another. The great socialist thinkers preach ethics in art, instead of the bourgeois "art for art's sake," which aims only at titillating the well-heeled and well-fed. The great dramatists and directors of the day are still fumbling in the dark, looking for the secrets of constructive creativity, of monumental theater in which nature itself is a backdrop: the spectacles of Mount Sinai, Mount Ebal, and Mount Gerizim,[3] or the scene where the doyen of prophets stood on Mount Tabor preaching to the whole nation and to the entire world[4]—a spectacle no Hellenistic master could ever conjure up.

It is time we, too, learned something from our own culture and heritage. No need to stagger and sweat trying to climb the lowly Acropolis when we can just as well ascend the heights of Mount Moriah.[5]

As for learning from others, it is basically a question of how far we have come from the time of the Exodus to the era of Reinhardt, Mayerhold, and Tairov.[6] How should we use European techniques and dramatic devices for our own purposes, for the creation of a Hebrew theater inspired by the Prophets?

[...]

As for content, the Israeli theater should deal with ethics and morality, in the spirit of the Prophets. As for form, it should use pathos, fury, screaming, and clamor; expressionism rather than realism. Not imitation or replication of life but a re-creation of life. Constructiveness. A representation of a better, more worthwhile life than the one we are mired in. Prosaic, realistic life is what we encounter in the marketplace, at home, in society. We do not want to see them duplicated on the stage; we want to see an improvement of them, in form as well as in content.

[...]

From its early stages, Palestinian theater demonstrated its potential to teach and educate; it is a first-rate tool for instilling moral, social, and artistic principles. What are these principles?

First and foremost is the issue of content, which, in this era of national revival, romanticism, and pioneering, should focus on national heroism, ideals of universal redemption, and historical Jewish salvation. This principle implies we rid ourselves of exilic attributes or, at least, ignore them. We must reconnect with our ancient Hebrew roots, the bedrock of our nation, the period of the Bible. The purpose of theater in the Land of Israel is to eradicate the small-mindedness of the Jewish shopkeeper and to foster a new generation imbued with heroism, religious faith, and supreme morality, a generation possessing a healthy, collective bond, a sense of mission in life, and loyalty to nation and to humanity. This generation of individual talent and superior intellect must have a collective goal and a readiness to sacrifice itself for the general good. Such a theater cannot be realistic and cannot employ naturalistic devices. Heroism demands a broad vision, not fussy attention to picayune details. It must follow the example of the Prophets.

The second principle has to do with stagecraft; there must be complete co-ordination between an actor's speech and his movements, between the soul and the body. In this respect, we have a great advantage (which anti-Semitism, however, has presented—even in our own eyes—as—a disadvantage): our body language. A Jew who lives and speaks truthfully does not prevaricate, quibble, or use diplomatic lies. He speaks not just with his mouth, but also with his body. His bones express his emotions. A Jew is not a diplomat, just as our forefathers the Prophets were not diplomats. The Israeli theater must enhance and amplify this aspect of our nature.

[...]

And finally, the principle of language. We must restore our downtrodden language to its pristine splendor, and raise it from the status of argot to being the music of the Jewish soul.

The clear and elegant language used by the theaters has already made a difference; it has had a beneficial effect on the spoken language, spurring people to improve and enrich their speech. But no less important is the effect of theater on our creative intelligentsia who tend to disdain our beautiful language in prose and poetry. Lately, their literary output has been marked by lack of style and polish. Not everything printed in short lines is poetry. Having rejected rhyme as redundant, some poets are showing contempt for the artistic soul of poetry, the inner music of the words. If the Palestinian theater continues to uphold the principle of style and elegance, it may force our wordsmiths to use a more graceful style and to polish their verse in a fittingly artistic manner.

NOTES

1. Alter Druyanov (1870–1938) was born in Lithuania and settled in Palestine in 1921. Together with Chaim Nahman Bialik and Yehoshua Hone Ravnitzky, he edited the first four volumes of *Reshumot* (1919–26), a Hebrew journal devoted to Jewish folklore. Druyanov's most celebrated achievement was his three-volume anthology of Jewish humor, *Sefer ha-Bedicha ve-ha-Chidud* (Book of Jokes and Humor).

2. The term "expressionism" describes a style of painting that reacted against late nineteenth-century naturalism and impressionism. Applied to the theater, it represented a protest against the existing social order. The language of expressionist drama was stark and exclamatory, preferring short scenes to longer acts. Constructivism was a modern-art movement that started in Russia in the 1920s and featured the use of industrial materials to form nonrepresentational, geometric objects.

3. Mount Ebal and Mount Gerizim are two mountains overlooking the city of Shechem (Nablus). Mount Ebal is the site where Joshua built an altar after the battle of Ai (Josh. 8). Mount Gerizim is sacred to the Samaritans who regard it, rather than Jerusalem's Temple Mount, as the site chosen by God for his holy temple.

4. Hameiri alludes here to the biblical story of the prophetess Deborah (Judg. 4 and 5) who called upon Barak to summon 10,000 soldiers to defeat the army of the Canaanite General Sisera.

5. Located between Mount Zion and the Mount of Olives, Mount Moriah is where, according to the Jewish tradition, the Temple's Holy of Holies was located. It was also the site of Isaac's binding (Gen. 22).

6. Max Reinhardt (1873–1943), born Maximilian Goldmann, was a Jewish-Austrian theater and film director. Until the rise of Nazism he worked as a director for various German and Austrian theaters. He migrated to the United States in the late 1930s where he had a brief but productive artistic career. Vsevolod (Emil'yevich) Meyerhold (1874–1940) was a Russian theorist, stage director, and actor. An innovative and experimental director, he served as the director of the imperial opera and drama theaters in St. Petersburg. His work foreshadowed many themes that would become staples of Russian Futurism. Alexander Tairov (1885–1950) was a prominent Jewish-Russian theater director. His chamber theater was widely popular in Russia and throughout Europe in the 1920s. In the 1930s, under constant pressure from the Stalinist government, his group was sent to work in Siberia. In 1941, Tairov joined the Jewish Anti-Fascist Committee (JAC) in Moscow.

34

Mordechai Golinkin and the Palestine Opera (1927)

This article is a tribute to Mordechai Golinkin (1875–1963), founder, director, and conductor of the Tel Aviv Opera House. Golinkin, born in the Ukraine, studied composition and conducting in Warsaw and became a conductor at the Marinskaya Opera in Petrograd. In 1917 he wrote the essay "Citadel of Art in Palestine," and in May 1923 he came to Palestine to realize his dream of creating a Jewish opera company in the country. On July 28, 1923, in Tel Aviv, the Palestinian Opera was launched with a production of Verdi's *La Traviata.* There was no opera house in Palestine at the time, and the company performed in movie theaters. Golinkin directed the Palestine opera for four years. In 1927 the opera company faced budgetary problems, and Golinkin left for the United States to raise money for it. In the 1930s there were very few operatic productions in Palestine, but things changed after the Second World War with the arrival in Palestine of the American soprano Edis de Philippe, who created the Israel National Opera. Golinkin joined the board of the Israel National Opera and conducted several productions. The article celebrates Golinkin's achievements, but it also reveals the vitality of the cultural and artistic life in Tel Aviv, the first Hebrew city. The article also shows how cultural activities were regarded as an integral part of the Yishuv's political efforts.

It is commonly accepted that the Palestine Opera is the most accomplished of all the performing-arts institutes in the country. It was four years ago that Golinkin came here and, in one fell swoop, took us out of the dilettantism that

Source: *Haaretz*, August 23, 1927. Translated by Marganit Weinberger-Rotman.

had pervaded the profession. How miraculous it seemed that only four to five months later, the opera *Faust* was performed in its entirety. And then *Samson and Delilah, Aida, Judas Maccabaeus, The Huguenots,* etc. — seventeen of the best operas in the world. Only now that the opera has been silent for some time do we begin to fully appreciate its existence. How could such a miracle happen? And four years ago!

All this happened because Golinkin brought three things with him: skill and experience that he had honed for thirty years; talent and inexhaustible energy; a capacity to work tirelessly and relentlessly. The population appreciated all this, and Golinkin garnered much recognition, affection, and admiration from all sectors of the Yishuv, with no exception.

The Opera House was appreciated also as a political agent. "We have an opera house," you'd hear the inhabitants, mayors, and administrators brag at political receptions and celebrations. The opera was considered one of our "conquests" in the country. Even the High Commissioner could not ignore it and he mentioned it in his report to the League of Nations.

But the real value of his efforts was internal. Instantly, the level of musical performances in the country rose immeasurably. Golinkin pushed us forward relentlessly to greater triumphs and musical conquests. The need to forge ahead and progress is one of the reasons that impelled Golinkin to travel far and wide, in order to help expand, develop, and improve this project.

We know that a whole range of operas could not be staged here because we lack performers. We also know how much time and energy the conductor had to invest attending to small matters — creating the basic conditions without which no stage performance, especially not a gigantic production like an opera, could exist. It so happened that during the time of crisis, Golinkin undertook the difficult task of expanding and improving the Opera House. But we hope that the troubles are over and that we will soon rejoice in the renewed work and construction, and that Golinkin himself will go from strength to strength, because he is one of our most diligent and dedicated builders; no burden is too heavy for him.

Tel Aviv, where the opera and its creator are located, the city that benefited most from his work and that watched the project from its inception — Tel Aviv today thanks Golinkin for four years of dedicated work. Tel Aviv cheers him on and sends him off on his way with blessings and good wishes. We are saying to this excellent man, "Good luck on your mission. We hope to see you back soon on the stage that you graced with your talent, energy, dedication, and true love of our homeland."

35

The Cinema Controversy in Tel Aviv (1932)

The first movie house in Tel Aviv, Eden Cinema, was opened in 1914. Initially, the city's governing body opposed the idea of opening a cinema in the city—they regarded movies as decadent and vulgar. The entrepreneurs behind Eden Cinema, using their influence among the city's leaders, were able to finally get approval for their project, and they also secured exclusive rights that prevented other venues from showing films until 1925. In the late 1920s and early 1930s several other movie houses began to operate in Tel Aviv. This document shows the suspicion with which this development was greeted by the city's cultural establishment, but it also reveals the dynamic changes that the city was undergoing in the 1930s.

A public trial of the cinema (talking films) took place on November 16, 1932, at Beit Ha'am Hall[1] in Tel Aviv. It was sponsored by the Writers' Association[2] and was attended by thousands who listened to the indictment, the prosecution, the defense, and the witnesses. The verdict (published in the weekly *Moznayim*)[3] included this excerpt:

1. We recommend the establishment of a control board with a mandate to inspect all films to decide which should be shown and which should be banned. The municipality, together with

Source: "Tel-Aviv Municipality and the Cinema," *Yediot Iryat Tel Aviv* 1, October 1932. Translated by Marganit Weinberger-Rotman.

the educational institutions, should find the best ways to prevent children under sixteen from going to the movies, except to see films approved by the board. The municipality and the schools should take steps to bring in science films, suitable for youth, to prevent exposing children to harmful performances.

2. Cinema can be beneficial when it is goes together with literature, theater, and artistic magazines, but not when it aims to supplant them. Therefore, the municipality and the cultural institutes must create the necessary conditions for the development of high quality music, theater, literature, and newspapers, to offset the pernicious influence of nefarious and harmful films. The municipality should not shy away from imposing taxes on light entertainment for the benefit of important and high-minded forms of art and culture.

NOTES

1. Beit Ha'am Hall in Tel Aviv, which was opened on Ben Yehuda Street in 1925 and hosted a variety of cultural events, also served as a cinema.

2. The Hebrew Writers' Association (Agudat ha-Sofrim ha-Ivri'im), the professional association of Hebrew writers and poets in Israel, was founded in 1921 by Chaim Nahman Bialik.

3. *Moznayim* is the journal of the Hebrew Writers' Association. The first volume appeared in March 1929. Bialik was the journal's founding editor.

36

The Hebrew University (1925)

CHAIM WEIZMANN

The idea of creating a Jewish, or Hebrew, university was an integral part of the Zionist program from the movement's very beginning. Chaim Weizmann (1874–1952) served as president of the Zionist Organization from 1921 to 1931 and again from 1935 to 1946, and after the creation of the state of Israel he served as the country's first president. In addition to his political activities, Weizmann was a renowned chemist. He taught at the University of Manchester, where he discovered a process to develop acetone, which was used to manufacture cordite explosive propellants that were crucial for the British military cause. Already in 1903 Weizmann championed the idea of a Hebrew university in Palestine. Weizmann was joined in this cause by other leading Zionist activists and ideologues, and the 11th Zionist Congress in 1913 adopted a proposal to establish a university in Palestine. The laying of the cornerstone for the university took place in 1918 at the top of Mount Scopus, and on April 1, 1925, the Hebrew University was opened in a grand ceremony attended by Zionist leaders and British officials. Weizmann chaired the university's first Board of Governors, which included also Albert Einstein, Sigmund Freud, Martin Buber, Chaim Nahman Bialik, and Ahad Ha-am. By 1947 the university had over 1,000 students and more than 200 faculty members. After the 1948 War, Mount Scopus was cut off from Israel and the campus was relocated to the Givat Ram neighborhood in Western Jerusalem. Some departments of the Hebrew University recommenced operations at the Mount Scopus site in 1968, and the Faculty of the Humanities returned to a renovated campus there in 1981.

Source: *The New Palestine*, Hebrew University Issue, March 27, 1925, 1.

As the first Jewish university on the hill overlooking the City of Jerusalem is being dedicated, many of us will have our thoughts cast back to the great historic scenes associated with Jerusalem; scenes that have become part of the heritage of mankind. It is not too fanciful to picture the souls of those who have made our history participating in this dedication, inspiring us, urging us onward, to greater and ever greater tasks.

The university begins to emerge after many years of dreaming and scheming. It seems at first sight paradoxical that in a land with so sparse a population, in a land whose reconstruction has only really begun, in a land still crying out for such simple things as plows, roads, and harbors, we should begin by creating a center of spiritual and intellectual development. But it is no paradox for those who know the soul of the Jew. It is true that great social and political problems still face us and will demand their solution from us. We Jews know that when the mind is given fullest play, when we have a center for the development of Jewish consciousness, then coincidentally we shall attain the fulfillment of our material needs. In the darkest ages of our existence we found protection and shelter within the walls of our schools and colleges, and in devoted study of Jewish science the tormented Jew found relief and consolation. Amid all the sordid squalor of the ghetto there stood schools of learning where numbers of young Jews sat at the feet of our rabbis and teachers. Those schools and colleges served as large reservoirs where there was stored up during the long ages of persecution an intellectual and spiritual energy which, on the one hand, helped to maintain our national existence, and, on the other hand, blossomed forth for the benefit of mankind when once the walls of the ghetto fell. The sages of Babylon and Jerusalem, Maimonides,[1] and the Gaon of Vilna,[2] the lens polisher of Amsterdam[3] and Karl Marx,[4] Heinrich Heine,[5] Paul Ehrlich,[6] and Albert Einstein are some of the links in the long, unbroken chain of intellectual development.

I do not wish to enter here into the history of the university idea—the less so as Reuben Brainin[7] rehearses this elsewhere in this publication. I would say, however, that the university was made possible only when the Zionist movement entered upon its new phase of intensive reconstruction in Palestine. But in spite of the fact that immigration is going on on a much larger scale than was believed possible in 1918, we are still justified in limiting ourselves to the original projects for the university; that is, to begin with a research institute.

No teaching can be fruitful nowadays unless it is strengthened by a spirit of inquiry and research; and a modern university must not only produce highly trained professional men, but give ample opportunity to those capable and ready to devote themselves to scientific research, to do so unhindered and undisturbed. Our university will thus become the home of those hundreds of talented young Jews in whom the thirst for learning and critical inquiry has been ingrained by heredity throughout the ages, and who in the great multitude of cases are at present compelled to satisfy this their burning need amid un-Jewish, very often unfriendly, surroundings.

There are people who would like to see a complete university instituted at once.

No complete university has ever been built up all at once. It is not only extremely costly, but even if the funds were forthcoming, Jewish Palestine is much too small to carry an organism of this kind.

It is essential that the university should fit into Palestine, become part of it, and grow together with it. In order to ensure the latter, the institutes must not only play an important part in developing and fostering science and art in their abstract forms but, as a living organism, must take part in the actual development of the country. The university must lead the way in solving the important problems that present themselves in connection with the reconstruction of the country. Thus, for instance, the Institute of Hebrew and Oriental Studies may play the same role for Hebrew in Palestine as the Académie française[8] plays for the French, purifying the language, molding its terminology and, in conjunction with the Publication Society that will grow up around it, creating the Jewish book.

The medical school, apart from doing original research, will set the standard in the work of hygiene and public health, and in the investigation of diseases prevailing in Palestine and neighboring countries as well as in subtropical regions generally. It will further unite all the sporadic attempts in this line of work, done by separate bodies — sometimes in ways that do not commend themselves to the scientific mind.

The outstanding danger from which we must steer clear, the particular danger threatening Palestine, is the danger of Levantinism. Levantinism in this case would be the facade, which would have all the appearance of European science, without the honesty, depth, many-sidedness, and meticulous exactitude that scientific study requires. At all costs this scourge must be avoided. Scientific modesty and self-abnegation must prevail, even at the cost of not producing "results" quickly.

It is true that there is no Jewish physics, or Jewish chemistry, but it is only true to a certain degree. The method of approach toward the solution of scientific problems may be different in England and in France, and in an atmosphere in which a normal Jewish life is developing, a scientific institute taking root side by side with this normal life may also approach the great problems of science in its own way. The Jewish scientist, in contradistinction to others, has been divorced from the stream of Jewish life and its realities. Who knows whether the great vitality permeating the unprecedented effort in Palestine may not inspire the scientific workers toward new and original tracks?

Thus, at a time to come that will be determined entirely by the growth of the Jewish national home, the Alma Mater will arise on the Scopus, and shelter within its walls teacher and discipline animated by the spirit that they are all building a home for Jewish science, for Jewish values that will not only be the soul and the guide of our effort in Palestine, but will radiate out its influence into the world, and make its contribution to humanity.

NOTES

1. Moses ben Maimon (1135–1204), perhaps the most influential Jewish jurist and philosopher of the Middle Ages.

2. Rabbi Elijah ben Shlomo Zalman (1720–97) was a prominent halachic scholar and kabbalist and was known for his fierce opposition of Hasidism.

3. Weizmann is referring here to Baruch Spinoza (1632–77) the prominent early-modern Jewish philosopher. Spinoza earned a living in Amsterdam as a lens polisher.

4. In this list of prominent Jewish thinkers, it is worthwhile to point out that Karl Marx's (1818–83) parents were Jewish, but they converted to Christianity before Marx was born.

5. Heinrich Heine (1797–1856) was one of the greatest German romantic poets. Born and raised as a Jew, he converted to Christianity in 1825.

6. Paul Ehrlich (1854–1915) was a leading German-Jewish scientist, known for his research on autoimmunity. He was awarded the Nobel Prize in Physiology in 1908.

7. Reuben Brainin (1862–1939) was a writer and publisher. He wrote for several leading Hebrew periodicals, including *He-Tsefirah* and *Ha-Shiloah* and published the periodical *Mi-Mizrah u-mi-Ma'arav* (From East and West).

8. The Académie française was founded in 1635 by Cardinal Richelieu. It consists of forty members and is the authoritative body on all matters related to the French language. In Palestine, a similar institute, Va'ad ha-Lashon ha-Ivrit (the Hebrew Language Committee) was established by Eliezer Ben Yehuda in 1890. In 1953, the state of Israel founded the Hebrew Language Academy.

SECTION IV

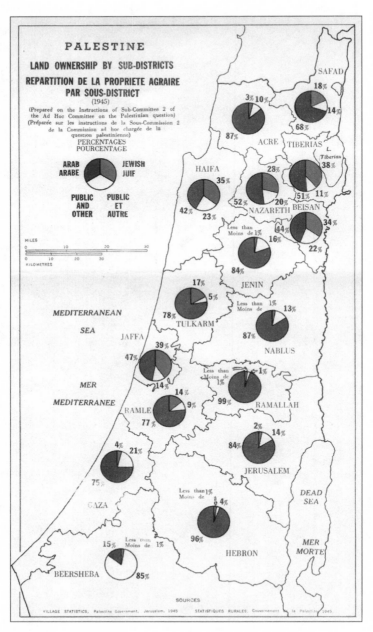

Landholding in Palestine, 1945 (United Nations Map no. 94b [1950])

JEWISH–ARAB CONFLICT
AND ZIONIST RESPONSES

Palestinian nationalism defined itself largely in terms of opposition to Zionism. To be sure, even without Zionism, a Palestinian nationalism would still have developed, just as Arab nationalism took on specifically Egyptian, Syrian, and Iraqi forms. Throughout the Middle East, Arab nationalism was shaped by a paradoxical combination of resistance to European rule and the use of the colonial political divisions as a sort of container into which nationalist ideology flowed like water. Arab nationalisms varied widely in form and content, but they shared a perception of Zionism as an aggressive form of European imperialism that sought not merely subordination of Arabs but also their expropriation from a land holy to Christian and Muslim Arabs alike. In Palestine, Zionism had a particularly galvanizing effect, creating a sense of shame over Arab weakness, on the one hand, and of mortal danger, on the other.

In 1918 there were about 600,000 Arabs in Palestine; thirty years later they numbered well over one million. Some of the increase was due to immigration from neighboring lands, as Arab laborers were attracted by jobs in construction and agriculture in the Yishuv. Most of the increase, however, was due to a sharp drop in infant mortality, caused by improvements in health care and a rising standard of living. Most inhabitants were peasants, but by the 1940s about 100,000 were urban wage laborers. There was a traditional elite of landowners, urban merchants, and Ottoman-era officials. During the Mandate period, the urban middle class grew considerably. Political power was largely concentrated in the hands of the old elites, particularly a handful of families in Jerusalem. As a predominantly Muslim and traditional society, the Palestinian community was responsive to religious authority, and for this reason in the early 1920s the British created a Supreme Muslim Council to regulate Palestinian affairs. They appointed as its president Amin al-Husayni, a Muslim cleric from one of Palestine's most distinguished families and a man known for strong nationalist sentiments.

Expressions of Palestinian nationalism first appeared a few years before World War I. Palestinian delegates to the Ottoman parliament made clear their opposition to Zionism and their fears of being displaced by Jewish immigrants from Europe. Palestinians were bitterly disappointed by the Balfour Declaration, which supported a Jewish national home in what Palestinians considered their own country. The Balfour Declaration also promised to protect only the civil and religious, not the national, rights of the land's non-Jewish inhabitants. Other Arab lands were under League of Nations mandates, but only in Palestine was the Mandate protective of the national rights of non-Arabs.

Even before the war, Zionist land acquisition became a flashpoint for conflict between Jews and Arabs, and it intensified during the Mandate period. Arable land in Palestine was scarce and fetched high prices. During the 1920s, the Arab sellers of land were mostly wealthy absentee owners who had been hurt financially by the war and needed capital to maintain their lifestyles. During the 1930s, economic difficulties in Palestine caused an increasing number of estate owners and some small holding peasants to trade in their land for cash. As a result of these transactions many thousands of Palestinian sharecroppers and tenant farmers were forced to leave their holdings, usually with minimal compensation. There were, however, other causes of Palestinian Arab landlessness. In Palestine, as throughout the Middle East, capitalist forms of agriculture gradually replaced peasants with hired labor, thus creating a landless proletariat. (Palestine's thriving citrus industry, which was well developed before the first Zionists arrived, was based on hired labor.) Zionist land purchases, however, unlike universal economic processes, were attributable to a single, highly visible source.

Palestinians viewed Zionists through a religious as well as political lens. The former made Arabs susceptible to propaganda that Jews wished to take over Jerusalem's Temple Mount and destroy the Al-Aqsa mosque. These suspicions were nourished by Zionist efforts throughout the 1920s to buy up the property surrounding the Western Wall of the Temple Mount. Also, Zionist postcards of Jerusalem depicted the Temple Mount crowned by a Star of David flag. In 1928 and 1929 tensions rose between Zionists and Palestinians over Jewish access to, and prayer practices at, the Western Wall. The establishment of the enlarged Jewish Agency for Palestine exacerbated Arab anxieties. In August 1929, a demonstration by right-wing Zionist youth at the wall touched off mass panic among the Arabs, who rioted throughout Palestine, killing 133 Jews, including 67 in the ancient community of Hebron. One hundred sixteen Arabs were killed, mostly by British forces.

Shortly after the riots, two British governmental commissions toured Palestine, and their recommendations were incorporated into a White Paper that recommended sharp restrictions on Jewish land purchases and immigration. The White Paper was harshly criticized by Zionist and key British officials, and the British prime minister, Ramsay Macdonald, wrote a letter to ZO president Chaim Weizmann that effectively undermined the paper's content. But the British and Zionists were now well aware that it would be impossible to implement the Balfour Declaration without arousing massive Arab opposition.

During the 1930s, Palestinian militancy grew, as the Fifth Aliyah more than doubled the size of the Yishuv. Palestinian leaders complained that they were being forced to pay for European anti-Semitism and the rest of the world's refusal to take in Jewish refugees. As neighboring Egypt and Syria moved steadily toward independence, and the progress of Palestinian nationalism was blocked by the Balfour Declaration and the Zionist Yishuv, Palestinian leaders decided to take radical action. In 1936 all five of Palestine's Arab parties formed an Arab Higher Committee, led by Amin al-Husayni. The AHC proclaimed a general strike, a tax revolt against the British authorities, and a boycott of British goods. Armed assaults against Jewish settlements soon followed. The Palestinian Arab Revolt had begun.

The revolt entered a lull in November but started up again in the fall of 1937. Between then and January 1939, Palestine fell into near anarchy, as Arab guerilla bands killed British officials, Jews, and rival Arabs, especially those who favored a more moderate, pro-British stance. The British responded with massive force against the Palestinians. All told, about 10 percent of both the Palestinians and Jews were killed or wounded. The Arab Revolt led the British to realize that they could not possibly hand Palestine over to the Zionists and maintain Arab goodwill, which they sorely needed with the approach of a second world war.

The first solution, proposed in 1937 by a commission headed up by Lord Robert Peel, was the partition of Palestine into Jewish and Arab states, with Jaffa, Jerusalem, and a corridor between them to remain in British hands. The Arab Higher Committee rejected partition in principle, and it refused to accept the transfer of hundreds of thousands of Arabs from the proposed Jewish state into its Arab counterpart. The next solution involved abandoning the Balfour Declaration altogether. In May 1939, the colonial secretary Malcolm MacDonald issued a White Paper declaring that in ten years' time Palestine would become an independent state. Political power would be shared between the two peoples, but since Jewish immigration would be sharply curtailed during this transition period, Palestine's Arabs would be a solid majority of at least two to one.

Arab leaders dismissed the White Paper for allowing any further Jewish immigration and land purchase, the ten-year delay in the attainment of statehood, and the stipulations that Jews and Arabs would share power.

Zionist reactions to the White Paper were even more bitter. Instead of a state in all of Palestine, they were being offered, or so it seemed to them, a ghetto surrounded by hostile Arabs. Ben-Gurion threatened to unleash a Jewish revolt against British rule, while he and other leaders of the Yishuv believed a war with the Arabs over Palestine was inevitable. These dark views were a far cry from earlier, more hopeful approaches to the Palestinians.

In the Zionist labor movement of the teens and twenties, armed force was conceived of as purely defensive, an extension of pioneering values of settlement and farming. After the war, the Zionist paramilitary body Ha-Shomer was disbanded, replaced with a national militia, the Haganah. The Haganah's activities and scope remained quite modest until the 1929 riots and the 1936–39 Arab revolt. Until the revolt, Arab violence was regarded by many Labor Zionists as the work of powerful Arab landowners who set impoverished Palestinian peasants against the Jews in order to distract attention from their own oppressive practices. In time, Labor Zionists hoped, Arabs would come to see Zionism as a force for economic liberation and a source of modern technological know-how. At the same time, most Zionists favored steady immigration, settlement, and land purchase that would some day produce either a Jewish majority or at least a substantial Jewish minority (reckoned as at least a half-million), large enough to constitute a fait accompli with which the Arabs would have no choice but to live in peace.

During the 1930s, the Haganah grew in size, procured weapons from abroad, and began to manufacture them at home. Its activities were clandestine but occasionally quite open, for during the Arab revolt the British trained and collaborated with Haganah field squads in raids against Arab villages. In 1937, the possibility of a partition of Palestine into Jewish and Arab states led to a flurry of new settlements in the Negev desert and Galilee, far from the coastal population centers of Tel Aviv and its environs. Even though the 1937 Zionist Congress rejected the Peel proposal, it did accept the principle of partition, and so the makers of Zionist settlement policy worked with the Haganah to create kibbutzim that could stake out and defend the borders of the future state.

Not all Zionists accepted the idea of partition. Some on the Far Left demanded nothing less than a purely socialist state in all of Palestine, for the benefit of Jews and Arabs alike. Others, associated with the small organization Brit Shalom (f. 1925) and its successors, explored various forms of binationalism. On the Right, the Revisionists never veered from their demand for a Jewish state in all of Palestine.

In general, there was a correlation between maximalist territorial demands and an embrace of militarism as a positive value. Within the Labor movement, moderates who were willing to compromise on the demand for a Jewish majority in Palestine and favored maintaining good relations with Britain were also reluctant to authorize the use of force against Arabs. Those who insisted on a Jewish state in all of Palestine were likely to be involved in Haganah military operations during the Arab revolt and to favor military over diplomatic solutions to the Zionist–Palestinian conflict. Among the Zionist Right, the situation was more complicated in that Jabotinsky, who idealized military service as a source of national cohesion (and who liked to be photographed in his World War I uniform), called upon Jews to learn how to shoot. He also remained attached to Britain until his death in 1940. But Jabotinsky was largely disconnected from the Palestinian Revisionists, as the British banned him from entering the country for leading Jewish military actions against Arabs during the 1929 riots. The Palestinian Revisionists tended to be more extreme, in part because of their political weakness, which encouraged the growth of an underground mentality, a self-image as a group that had to employ violence to make itself heard.

The difference between Labor and Revisionism was not that the former shunned the use of force and the latter glorified it. Rather, Labor did a better job controlling its members and regulating the use of force. The Haganah, for example, was at first under the supervision of the Histadrut and then, after 1929, the Jewish Agency. By the late 1930s, the Haganah numbered some 20,000 members and had a well-organized national command. The Revisionists, however, never possessed such authority over a military group. In 1937, about 1,000 Haganah members dissatisfied with Labor control founded a new militia known by its acronym, Etzel (also known as the Irgun). The Irgun was not under Jabotinsky's authority but rather that of local commanders. During the Arab revolt, Irgun members killed Arab civilians in revenge for attacks upon Jews, while the Haganah focused on attacks against guerillas and their bases. Nor did Labor feature the extremism to be found in the Zionist radical right, which flirted with fascism, as shown by a group founded in 1932 and known as Brith ha-Biryonim (the League of Thugs). This small group disrupted lectures on Arab–Jewish reconciliation at the Hebrew University, attacked the German consulate in Jerusalem, and was implicated in the assassination in 1933 of the head of the Jewish Agency's Political Department, Chaim Arlosoroff. The group's leader, Abba Ahimeir, was a visceral anti-communist and romantic nationalist who openly admired Fascist regimes.

To be sure, Labor had its share of factionalism. Socialist purists and opponents of Ben-Gurionist machine politics were a constant source of friction, and there formed within Mapai a Faction B, which in 1944 seceded to form its own party. All the Yishuv's political factions, however, agreed that the 1939 White Paper dealt a dreadful blow to the Zionist enterprise, and they were confronted with a painful dilemma: whether to undermine Britain for having forsaken the Jewish national home or to join forces with her against the greatest enemy the Jews had ever known.

This section's documents focus on the Yishuv's response to Arab violence against Jews, which Yishuv leaders were slow to recognize as manifestations of a coherent nationalist sensibility. Document 37 depicts the origins of the Haganah in the uncertain environment of immediate post–World War I Palestine. Documents 38 and 39 deal with the tragic events of March 1920 at the settlement of Tel Hai, which became a legend and symbol of Zionist defense against Arab violence. Document 40 provides a Labor Zionist assessment of the 1929 riots, while document 41 reveals the increasing desperation of the Yishuv's political fortunes in their wake. Document 42 offers a good example of the terms of debate about partition of Palestine in the mid-1930s. Documents 43 and 44 explore alternatives to partition from the Zionist Left, while documents 45 and 46 offer a variety of Revisionist views on Arab nationalism and the role of force in the achievement of Zionist aims.

37

The Need for Defense (1919)

YITZHAK TABENKIN

Yitzhak Tabenkin (1888–1971) was a leader of Ha-Kibbutz ha-Me'uhad (United Kibbutz movement). Although primarily associated with his kibbutz, Ein Harod, and the kibbutz movement, Tabenkin was a member of the first Zionist militia, Ha-Shomer (see document 9 for more information), and served as a Palmach commander during the 1948 War. Tabenkin believed that a Jewish state with expansive borders was necessary for the establishment of a viable, secure, socialist polity that would benefit Jews and Arabs alike. Tabenkin's thought thus represented an eccentric combination of what we would consider "dovish" and "hawkish" views.

This essay was written in the summer of 1919, before the attack on Tel Hai in March 1920 (see document 38) and, two months later, Arab riots in Jerusalem that claimed eight Jewish lives. After the attack, Jewish attention focused on the safety of the Yishuv, as evidenced by the founding in June 1920 of a Zionist militia, the Haganah, under the purview of the labor movement's chief economic and political arms (the Histadrut and Ahdut Ha-Avodah party). But Tabenkin's remarks focus on the fluidity of, and threat posed by, Palestine's as yet undetermined borders in the wake of the British conquest. The British military occupation government was either unwilling or unable to secure order in northeastern Palestine. Arab clashes with Jews were in part acts of brigandage, but they also expressed nationalist yearnings for a Pan-Arab state under Feisal, the son of Sharif Hussein, who had allied with the British against the Ottomans during the war.

Source: "Me-ha-galil," *Kuntress*, 26 Tammuz 5679 (1919). Reprinted in Israel Halpern, *Sefer ha-Gevurah: Antologiyah Historit-Sifrutit* (Tel Aviv, 1977), 4:283–85. Translated by Marganit Weinberger-Rotman.

In our land, even at a time of national revival, we find more and more signs of Diaspora mentality. With the conquest of the Galilee, after the liberation (from the Turks) we disarmed ourselves, giving up the few weapons we had. When we were under mortal threat, in a state of war, persecuted and distrusted, and under oppressive military Turkish rule, we guarded our weapons and increased them, because we saw arms as a guarantee to our security. But now that liberation has come, we have entrusted our security to the conqueror. It is no secret that our neighbors did not do likewise. Fleeing Turks and Germans left behind a trove of weapons, which has greatly increased our neighbors' arsenals. In addition, the victory of Sharif Hussein has given them British arms. We, the Jews, were the only ones to obey the order to surrender our arms. Half an hour walk from our settlements, we suddenly discovered a new border: near Milhamia and Degania.[1] Before the country was even partitioned, new administrative changes were introduced; ignoring the inhabitants and their needs, part of the Tiberias region was handed over to the Sharif's territory. On that border, hordes of rowdy people come and go, trafficking in weapons. This arms trading is extensive and open for all to see. The villages surrounding us are stockpiled with firearms, some the spoils of war, others obtained from the occupier. And we had put our trust in the new regime to protect us from outside. Inside, instead of setting up popular self-defense, we trusted in lobbyists, politicians, officials, and boards of representatives.

Every day we detect new suspicious signs, signs of Diaspora mentality, both outwardly and inwardly. Our actions are evaluated by the authorities not for themselves but for their effect on the neighbors, the "natives." For example, consider an ancient popular religious ceremony, which we had celebrated uninterrupted for decades under oppressive Turkish rule—Rabbi Meir the Miracle-maker's Festival of Lights[2]—it is now summarily canceled by edict of the local authorities. The reason given: this custom of lighting fires in public may cause annoyance to the neighbors. Those neighbors, you may note, are fully armed, and are liable to express their anger both by popular action and by pronouncement of their local leaders. The local government understands that public expressions of Jewish life may irk the neighbors, and it acts accordingly. Jewish defense, with weapons that for years protected our property and honor, is suddenly called off and declared outlawed. And again, for the same reason: openly defending ourselves against theft and robbery may infuriate our neighbors. You can no longer see a Jewish policeman in the villages and on the roads, because augmentation of the Jewish police can be "irksome." A Jewish battalion of the British Army briefly stationed on the border detected a convoy of arms smugglers walking hither and thither. Even that raised an objection, and the neighbors petitioned to get rid of this battalion and its mission. The neighbors have no fear and no restrictions. They even interfered in the deployment of the British army: they objected to the Royal Fusiliers[3] being given a certain mission, and a few days later that unit was redeployed to the desert, and other units replaced them in guarding the border of the Galilee.

The result of this state of affairs is that armed Arab marauders cross the "border" near Yavniel[4] unimpeded, in broad daylight; all they have to do is ask an Arab worker in the moshava if there are any military or police in the area, or if there are armed guards in the fields, and when they are satisfied that they will encounter none, they attack Jewish workers, rob them, and murder them, as they did to Ephraim Kamil.

Less than two weeks after that incident, another attack occurred, near Merhavia and Tel Adash.[5] About fifty armed robbers were involved. Two of them assaulted the teacher S. who was on his way from Merhavia to Tel Adash, took his mare, and stripped him of his clothes. Then they committed acts of robbery and plunder in the neighborhood before disappearing behind the "border" where they found safe haven. It is a disgrace; our security is at stake. We, the Jewish inhabitants, need to take action, to defend our lives and our honor. Where is the battalion of volunteers who will defend our land?

NOTES

1. Degania is at the southern tip of the Sea of Galilee: see document 7; Milhamia (in 1921 renamed Menachemia) lies eight kilometers (five miles) to the southwest.

2. An ancient tomb on the Sea of Galilee near Tiberias is traditionally associated with Rabbi Meir Ba'al Nes, a second-century sage. The reference is probably to pilgrimages to the tomb on Rabbi Meir's *hillula* (celebration), 14 Iyyar (mid-spring), which coincides with the minor Jewish festival of Pesach Sheni.

3. Jewish battalions of the British armed forces. See document 38n4.

4. Six miles (10 km) southwest of Tiberias.

5. Merhavia and Tel Adash (renamed Tel Adashim in 1923) are in the Jezreel Valley, about ten kilometers (6.2 mi) apart.

38

Tel Hai (1920)

Y. H. BRENNER

After World War I, the northeastern corner of the Galilee, home to the Jewish settlements of Tel Hai, Metulla, and Hamra, temporarily lay beyond the boundaries of either British or French colonial control. Despite this power vacuum, and the killing of two settlers in December 1919 and February 1920, the communities were determined to hold on to their lands. They were commanded by Joseph Trumpeldor, a charismatic former Russian army officer who, during World War I, had organized Jewish fighting units for the British army. On March 1, 1920, Arabs requested and were granted entrance into the Tel Hai stockade under the pretense of inspecting it for French soldiers. In fact, they planned to seize the settlement's weapons. The settlers fired the first shots; Arabs both within and outside of the stockade fired back, and in the battle Trumpeldor and five other settlers were killed. The surviving settlers abandoned Tel Hai and Kfar Gila'di, but in December 1920, the upper Galilee was placed within the borders of the British Mandate for Palestine.

Yosef Chaim Brenner (1881–1921) was one of the greatest Hebrew writers of his generation. He moved from his native Russia first to London and then in 1909 to Palestine. An anxious and troubled man, Brenner saw in the Tel Hai battle an ominous sign of pervasive and murderous Arab hostility, one of many forces that, he feared, would doom the Zionist enterprise to failure. A year after the fall of Tel Hai, Brenner was killed by Arabs during riots in Jaffa.

Source: *Yalkut Ahdut ha-Avodah* (Tel Aviv, 1920), 2:212–13; repr. in Yisrael Halpern, *Sefer ha-Ggevurah: Antologiyah Historit-Sifrutit* (Tel Aviv, 1977), 4:249–50. Translated by Marganit Weinberger-Rotman.

The arithmetic was clear: a few dozen workers could not hold out against thousands of Arabs equipped with mountains of European weapons,[1] even hundreds of fighters on our side could not have prevailed. It was equally clear that promises of Arab "rebel" leaders that they would not lift their swords against *Yahud* settlements had no merit, because an Arab's word cannot be trusted. The arithmetic was clear, but the heart, the faithful heart believed in miracles; believed that the love of the land could move mountains. And the will to believe created its own arithmetic of wishful thinking; we are not facing a regular army . . . we are merely defending ourselves against marauders, and if we have enough men, we can protect ourselves. . . . Had we been more numerous, a great commander would not have fallen.

Yes, a commander, and this has consequences. . . .

And besides, if we hasten to flee any place where danger lurks, then we might as well abandon all the settlements, and then where would we go?

We were told that help might be sent from the south to the north, so the combatants should stand guard until the last moment. There should be no talk of abandoning the post.

And they stood firm. They confronted an enemy ten, twenty times stronger than they. On that fateful day, about thirty Jewish workers defended their post against hundreds of attackers led by "officers" who invaded the post with weapons and bombs. By ruse and deception they penetrated the site, pretending to be the authorities, speaking words of peace, but spreading fear and menace—

But this realization, that the nation possesses desperate courage, and the significance of Tel Hai itself, have cost us dearly, incurring losses that we cannot afford within the borders of "Dan and Beer-Sheba."[2]

Joseph Trumpeldor, beloved and pleasant, this excellent, heroic man, symbol of selfless courage, was slain, his blood spilled by villains, and with him five more souls: Binyamin Munter, Sarah Chizik, Devora Drechler, [Ya'akov] Tocker, [Wolf] Scharff,[3] inseparable in death as in life.

The best among us; their blood spilled by marauding villains.

What we feared is upon us. We have been dealt a crushing blow.

The question I am asking now is this. Do we, the survivors, deserve such sacrifice? We, who are mired in corruption and meaninglessness, do we dare lift our eyes to look at these pure-hearted and brave warriors, who laid down their lives and willingly confronted their attackers? We watch from afar, from newspaper reports, how hundreds of young pioneers are eager to immigrate from east and west, but are repelled, prevented by lack of funds and entry permits, while we here sit idly not lifting a finger to facilitate their coming here. We, who watched Regiments 38 and 39 being turned away,[4] kept quiet as if it had nothing to do with us; do we have the right even to utter the name of Tel Hai on our lips?

What's next? Front-line fighters without a home front, avant-garde without a rear guard? Such an arrangement cannot hold for long. If there was a miracle there, it was the fact that they were not all killed, that a few survived. And what happens now? Danger lurks from all directions, and when tomorrow, or after tomorrow, we are attacked, will we know that there is no other way? Will we be able to rise to the challenge? When the moment of truth arrives, an ordeal perhaps harsher than the one we had five years ago—since then we faced an enemy government[5] and now we are facing hostile neighbors—will each one of us then, with Trumpeldor's name on our lips, be able to face his destiny?

Tel Hai was burned down, but the heart of Israel lives. Our brothers and sisters there, those who were killed and those who survived and reached us, showed us that that heart still lives, purified by fire, and they showed us where that heart is located. Scattered and weak as we are—will each one of us be able to say, I am a hero, and will we be heroes?

Tel Hai. The heart of Israel lives. But what about the rest of its parts? Will they live, too? Are we all prepared to live with this pulsating heart until we breathe our last? Are our motives clear in these perilous days, which are not likely to end soon? Have we all heard the echoes of the one-armed hero's exalted cry? "It is good to die for one's country"?[6]

Good! Blessed is he who dies with such a conviction—with Tel Hai at his feet.

NOTES

1. The number of attackers was in the hundreds, and they had one machine gun as well as small arms and hand grenades. There were at most sixty Jewish defenders, armed with rifles.

2. A phrase employed frequently in the Hebrew Bible to connote the boundaries of ancient Israel in terms of its northernmost and southernmost settlements.

3. The first names of these two victims were not immediately known.

4. A reference to the First World War and the Briitsh Army's Thirty-eighth and Thirty-ninth Battalions of Royal Fusiliers, which were drawn primarily from Jews from the United Kingdom and North America, respectively. Together with the Palestinian Jewish Fortieth Battalion, they took part in the British conquest of Ottoman Palestine. After the war, they were discharged and dispatched from Palestine. It is not clear how many wished to remain, but Zionist activists considered the British actions to be a sign of hostility to the Zionist project despite the promises made in the Balfour Declaration.

5. A reference to the Ottoman Empire's hostile and at times harsh treatment of Palestinian Jews during the First World War.

6. Alleged to be Trumpeldor's last words, this phrase closely resembles the famous Latin dictum, "dulce et decorum est pro patria mori"—it is sweet and fitting to die for one's country.

39

Yizkor (1920)

BERL KATZNELSON

Berl Katznelson (1887–1944) was one of the founders of the Labor Zionist movement in Palestine. A prolific writer and editor, after World War I Katznelson served as the chief ideologue of Ahdut Ha-Avodah and then of that party's successor, Mapai, founded in 1930.

In this short text about Jewish settlers killed at Tel Hai, Katznelson evokes but transforms the traditional Jewish memorial prayer for the dead, the Yizkor, into a secular commemoration of heroes of the nation. (On the battle of Tel Hai, see document 38.) God does not appear in the prayer, and Israel, the Jewish people, will be the agent of the land's future redemption. The eight fallen men and women are presented as tillers of the soil, determined to acquire the Land of Israel for the Jewish people through gradual settlement, not violent conquest. (As one of the fallen, Aharon Sher, put it, "A place once settled is not to be abandoned."[1])

Let the people of Israel remember the pure souls of its sons and daughters:

Shneur Saposnik,[2]
Aharon Sher[3]
Devora Drechler

Source: *Kuntress*, vol. 29 (Adar 1920), repr. in *Yalkut Ahdut Ha-Avodah* (Tel Aviv, 1920), 1:211. Translated by Marganit Weinberger-Rotman.

Binyamin Munter
[Wolff] Scharff[4]
Sarah Chizik
[Ya'akov] Tocker[5]
Joseph Trumpeldor

Loyal and brave, men and women of peace and labor, who tilled the land and sacrificed their lives for the honor and glory of the people of Israel and for the Land of Israel.

Let the nation remember them and be blessed with such progeny. Let us bemoan the flowering youth, the glorious valor, willing sacrifice, and total dedication that were lost in the heavy battle.

Our mourning shall not cease or abate until the day that Israel redeems its despoiled land.

NOTES

1. Anita Shapira, *Land and Power: The Zionist Resort to Force, 1881–1948* (New York, 1992), 102.

2. Saposnik had been killed earlier, on December 12, 1919.

3. Three weeks before the battle, Sher was killed in a confrontation with Arab marauders in Tel Hai's fields.

4. First name missing in original.

5. First name missing in original.

40

Response to the Arab Riots (1930)

THE GENERAL FEDERATION OF LABORERS
IN THE LAND OF ISRAEL

This document applies the most cherished principles of Labor Zionism to the understanding of Jewish–Arab relations in the Yishuv and the origins of Palestinian–Arab
violence against Jews. The doctrine of class conflict and belief in the trickle-down benefit
of technological progress underlie this representation of Arab resistance to Zionism as
the product of ignorance and manipulation rather than national consciousness or fears
of displacement. This analysis is very different from the one the Revisionists applied to
the Arab–Jewish conflict in Palestine at the time, which they viewed through a nationalist
and political prism: as the struggle of two competing national movements for control
over the land (see document 45).

I.

About two months ago, our country was the scene of murder, bloodshed, looting,
and severe attacks upon towns and villages. Ghastly murders were committed,
for the most part at Safed and Hebron, two old Jewish Communities, the residents

Source: Executive Committee of the General Federation of Labor in Palestine, "Memorandum
on the August Disturbances, Submitted to the British Labour Party and the Socialist International,"
in *Documents and Essays on Jewish Labour Policy in Palestine* (Tel Aviv, 1930), 69–87.

of which are either tradesmen or divinity students who have lived in peace with the Arabs for many generations. Recent immigrants, and especially workers, not yet having settled in these two places, there was a total absence of any element capable of self-defense or able to prevent bloodshed. Over eighty persons were murdered here, without offering any resistance, both men and women, aged and children. Hundreds were wounded. Houses were burned. Stores and warehouses were ransacked. The Jewish inhabitants were removed from their homes to government buildings. Their property left unprotected was destroyed. Gruesome murders were perpetrated in one of the Jerusalem quarters, and in the agricultural settlement of Motza, near Jerusalem, where there was no self-defense. Other small settlements, which had been evacuated, were looted, burned, and completely destroyed. On the other hand, at many places the assailants were met by the Jewish self-defense, which succeeded in throwing back mob attacks and preventing a repetition of the Hebron and Safed horrors in other parts of the country. In twenty-seven points attacked in Jerusalem, in all Jewish quarters in Haifa, in the Jewish city of Tel Aviv, in the Jewish agricultural settlements, even in the most distant, isolated, and sparsely populated spots, the settlers resisted either the fierce attacks of hordes, kindled with the fire of religious fanaticism, or of bands especially summoned to rob and loot, which had been assured by their instigators that Jewish blood might be shed and Jewish property looted without fear of government interference.

The work of the Jewish defense saved not only those positions where it was directly active, but prevented attacks on other points, so that the majority of the strong, centralized Jewish settlements were not exposed to mob attacks. However, those nine days of rioting in the country cost hundreds of lives, over 130 Jews and the same number of Arabs having been killed, and hundreds of Arabs and Jews wounded. Besides these human sacrifices, the nine days of rioting caused heavy loss of property: hundreds of houses were burned, whole quarters and settlements were looted and destroyed, shops and warehouses that had afforded a livelihood to scores of families, were burned and demolished; settlements built by pioneers at a tremendous effort went up in flames.

2.

This bloodshed and destruction is not an outgrowth of strained relations and quarrels of long standing between Jews and Arabs. The last years have seen quiet and steady development whereby the economic ties between all sections of the population have been strengthened. Jewish immigration brought labor and capital into the country, and, in their wake, progress in all branches of life. During the last ten years, about 90,000 Jews have come to Eretz Israel from various countries, bringing in capital amounting to at least £15,000,000. Sandy wastes have been transformed into orange groves. Swamps, formerly hotbeds of disease and pestilence, have been drained and made habitable. During this period, the plantation area increased fourfold, land already cultivated was improved, and agricultural methods modified and perfected. This progress was not confined to sections of land under Jewish control. Old Arab villages, influenced by the new colonies in their vicinity, introduced modern methods of cultivation. Likewise, Arabs living on land bought by Jews from the owners— the *effendis*—were enabled to improve their position and adopt better working methods thanks to the money they received. It must be remembered that Jewish land purchasing agencies not only pay the effendi from whom they buy, but also reimburse the Arab tenants who were eking out an existence on the land.[1] Hand in hand with this agricultural progress went the expansion of business and industry; exports and imports increased, modern factories were built, and a more extensive exploitation of water and natural resources initiated. The national income rose with this economic development. In 1921, the government revenue was £1,878,000; in 1927 it was £2,495,000. In Transjordan, which was separated from Palestine, the revenue for this same period remained stationary at about £300,000. Palestine is the only country formerly under Turkish rule that has paid off its share of the Ottoman debt and has met all expenses incurred, and investments made, during the British Military Occupation. Now it not only covers its own expenditure, but in addition meets part of that of Transjordan. With this increase in revenue, public works and utilities have gone forward, means of transportation have been improved, more and more Arab schools (mainly supported by government funds) have been opened, and sanitary and medical institutions enlarged. The cultural level of the entire population has been raised. During this period, the feeling of security was greatly strengthened. Robberies that had previously been a normal occurrence in Palestine practically disappeared. On the whole, workers' wages increased. The Jewish workers established a strong organization with a membership of 25,000, embracing over one-fourth of the entire adult Jewish population. The Histadrut succeeded in introducing European conditions of work and organization into the trade and industry of a country, where cheap labor is employed. The standard of living for the agricultural workers was raised 100 percent. Urged by organized labor, the government introduced elementary laws for the protection of workers. A chain of social and financial institutions for mutual aid was established by the Labor Organization, and producers' cooperatives consisting of hundreds of members were organized in the cities. The agricultural colonization of workers on National Fund land made much headway. Collective farms were founded, on the basis of a community of life and work, as well as individual farms on the principles of mutual aid and cooperative endeavor, to the exclusion of hired labor.

The organization of Jewish workers resulted in improved living conditions for Arab workers in towns and villages. In this respect, the Histadrut has been of help both in its regular activities and by special action whenever the occasion demanded. Assistance was given to Arabs in some of their strikes and everything possible done to organize Arab workers.[2] Arab Clubs were tendered help. A newspaper was published in Arabic. A definite plan was developed of establishing a federation of Jewish and Arab workers, organized in national sections. A number of Arab railway, post and telegraph workers . . . join[ed] the national union of workers in these services, which is affiliated with the General Federation of Jewish Labor. The improvement in the general standard of civilization and economic conditions has tended to reduce emigration to America, so extensive in prewar days. From 1921 to 1926, 7,400 Arabs (i.e., 1 percent of the population) left the country. During the same period 57,000 Arabs (i.e., 2 percent of the total population) left Syria and Lebanon.

The whole trend of economic and social life has resulted in improved conditions for all the inhabitants. It strengthened the desire for peace and encouraged common endeavor. Every resident was forced to recognize that the Jewish population had brought in wealth and progress. Yet certain elements were disturbed by this tendency to peace and by the development of common ties among all sections of the population. They left no stone unturned to destroy these conditions.

3.

Though the Arab effendis, owners of large estates, and rich merchants have also profited by the increased wealth, and particularly by the sale of their surplus land, nevertheless they are hostile to Jewish colonization. They fear that the introduction of another civilization will set up new standards for the masses and stimulate them to free themselves from the authority and influence of their exploiters. This class fear has been one of the main factors in arousing enmity against the Jewish population. The effendis have been joined by Arab officialdom in their anti-Zionist agitation among the Arab masses. This agitation has fallen on fertile soil because there are no clear-cut class divisions within the Arab population. Among Bedouins, all the members of a tribe accept the leadership of the Sheikh. The same conditions prevail among the *fellaheen* in the villages. Similarly, in the towns, the leading families dominate the poor folk, both spiritually and materially. While a social structure of this kind unites all the different classes for the protection of the rulers' interests, it also leads to internal dissension. The passion for power in every Bedouin Sheikh or village chieftain, the rivalry among the "notable" families in the towns, the lack of culture, and of a deep-rooted national consciousness—all these have undermined all attempts to present a united Arab national front. Most assemblies of notables, grandiloquently called Congresses, ended with internal conflicts. The mobilization of the masses for anti-Zionist demonstrations or attacks, as in the troubles of 1920 in Jerusalem and of 1921 at Jaffa, was only a temporary success that dribbled away entirely with the growth of economic relations and the strengthening of mutual understanding between the Arab and Jewish masses.

The most reactionary and influential group of effendis saw only one way of creating a united front and of strengthening their hold on the people, namely, by arousing religious animosity, a stimulus to which Oriental masses invariably respond. During the past year, they concentrated all their effort upon this device, being on the lookout for incidents likely to awaken a religious conflict between Arabs and Jews.

The natural allies of the effendis in this work were the Muslim religious leaders. United with the effendis by family ties and a common dread of seeing the country raised to a higher cultural level, the clericals were interested on their own account in arousing religious hatred, whereby it might be possible to organize Muslim masses in Palestine and elsewhere. The Muslim leaders in Palestine had reason to believe that under certain favorable circumstances Jerusalem might become the religious center for the whole of Islam. The fall of the Turkish Caliphate[3] and the setting up in Hejaz of the Wahabis[4] who, on account of religious differences, do not enjoy the unalloyed confidence of other parts of the Muslim world—left Islam without a religious center. The Grand *Mufti*[5] sought to utilize this situation, to focus the attention of the Muslim world upon Jerusalem, and only a religious conflict, wherein the Mosque of Jerusalem would figure as being in danger, could achieve his ends.

Moreover, the Mufti and the Muslim Supreme Council, of which he is the head, had material reasons for arousing hatred and linking up these fanatical sentiments with the institutions under their control. The Muslim Supreme Council was created ten years ago by the High Commissioner for Palestine, to administer the land and property left without a trustee with the fall of the Turkish regime in Palestine. This institution has grown; its field of activity and influence have expanded. It employs many officials who act as its political tools. The Muslim Supreme Council has succeeded in organizing collections for the support of the Holy Places of Jerusalem in many Muslim countries. A religious conflict in Palestine would, of course, be most valuable propaganda for a successful money-raising campaign. Furthermore, the Grand Mufti and his family, Husseinis, were personally interested in bringing about a religious war. The great power that the government concentrated in their hands had awakened considerable jealousy and called forth strong opposition. The most suitable way of crushing this opposition or, at least, of bringing it into abeyance for a time, and of mobilizing the masses about the present regime was again to awaken religious fanaticism. In this the effendis and the clericals saw eye to eye, and the Palestine government gave them a suitable pretext for the realization of their designs.

The conflict of the past year originated at the Western Wall. The Western Wall (called the Wailing Wall) is a remnant of the Jewish Temple, which was destroyed by the Romans. It is a Holy Place for Jews who come there from the whole world. It is located within the limits of the property supervised by the Muslim Supreme Council. The place of worship at the Wall is a narrow alley that serves as a passageway for the Moroccan Arabs living in the neighborhood. The exposed position of this place, holy to Jews the world over, leaves it open to constant incidents, and Arab neighbors, as well as the Muslim Supreme Council, have done their utmost to disturb the worshippers and to provoke the Jews to a remonstrance that might lead to religious conflict.[6] These designs not meeting with success, the Muslim Supreme Council demanded that the government tamper with the religious affairs of the Jews. In this respect they were successful.

Last year, on the Day of Atonement, the holiest day in the Jewish calendar, the police, by order of the Governor, forced their way to the Wailing Wall and removed the screen, which, according to Jewish custom, separated men and women at prayer. They took possession of the screen by force, insulting and beating the worshippers. This was done under the pretext that the presence of the screen constituted an infringement of the status quo at the Wall. The Governor of Jerusalem had not thought fit to wait until the prayers were ended and the holiday over, before settling the matter. This deed, and above all, the roughness of these police, awakened the indignation of all Jews. The storm of resentment against the government was intensified when the very status quo, in whose name the police had dared to maltreat Jewish worshippers on their holiest day at their holiest place, was violated on the part of the Muslim authorities by building additional layers on the Wall and by opening a door that made the sanctuary an open thoroughfare.

The whole Jewish population, irrespective of their religious convictions or class distinctions, was deeply wounded by the attitude of the government, disregarding their feelings and ignoring their rights. The government was warned that, in a country where it takes so little to arouse religious and racial conflicts, such offences might render the Muslim religious fanatics even more bellicose and lead to a serious outbreak. The warning not to do anything that might lead to a "holy" war was not only given to others, but acted upon by the Jews themselves. The workers' representatives in all national institutions made an effort to prevent demonstrations and acts that might lead to friction between Jews and Arabs in connection with the Wailing Wall. All the Jewish protests concerning the Wailing Wall were thus addressed to the government alone, being limited to negotiations with the government and press comments. However, those who wanted it found a pretext for exciting religious animosity. On Tisha B'Av (the Fast of the Destruction of the Temple) of this year, a demonstration was organized by several hundred Jewish youths, with the permission of the government, but against the advice of all Jewish institutions in the country. The procession was insignificant. It proceeded quietly through the streets of Jerusalem, without disturbing anyone, to the Wailing Wall. Arab instigators, however, found a suitable pretext in this procession, and on the next day they organized, again with the government's permission, an Arab demonstration at the Wailing Wall. The participants forced the Jews who were praying there to disperse, injuring a few and destroying prayer books. From that day on, provocations increased, false accusations multiplied, and unfounded rumors spread over the whole country that the Jews had attacked the Mosque of Omar and killed hundreds of Muslims.

[…]

9.

The British officials who came here after the occupation had served for the most part in Egypt, the Sudan, or other colonies. They were accustomed to dealing with natives. A European-Jewish community in the Orient was a strange and disconcerting novelty. The effendis, to whose society British officials in the east are accustomed, and the official personnel, consisting largely of the sons of Arab effendis, helped to inculcate an unfriendly attitude toward the

Zionists. With a large majority of the British officials the feeling is increasing that Jewish colonization interferes with the peaceful administration of the country and is responsible for the strained relations between the authorities and the Muslim population. This attitude has resulted in constant vacillation and a failure to carry out recent promises as well as previous obligations. . . .

During the First World War, the British military forces in Palestine included three Jewish battalions. After demobilization a special gendarmerie was formed, composed of Jews, Arabs, and Circassians in approximately equal numbers. But in the course of years, the Jews have gradually been dropped from all the forces responsible for the protection and security of the country. This special gendarmerie has been replaced by a frontier force in which there are only a few Jews among hundreds of Arabs. In the general police force the percentage of Jews has always been small. The conditions of work, the rate of pay, the relations between officers and subordinates, and particularly the attitude toward the Jewish minority and the disregard of Hebrew, have resulted in frequent resignations on the part of Jewish policemen. . . .

10.

The British Government undertook to assist Jewish colonization while guaranteeing the interests of all the inhabitants of the country. A policy destined to fulfill this twofold obligation would necessarily have reconciled these aims, for all work that helps Jewish colonization improves economic conditions and raises the cultural level of all the inhabitants. Moreover, every act furthering the economic interests of the whole population, ipso facto diminishes the obstacles interfering with the colonization of Jewish workers on a large scale. The rise in the economic and cultural level of the Arab workers, the increase in wages, the campaign against the exploitation of women and juvenile workers, the war against usury (which has impoverished the agricultural workers), the introduction of agrarian reforms to help place the small farmer on a firm footing, the establishment of credit institutions and mutual societies, and all work to reduce the frightful poverty and destitution prevailing among the Arab masses, both in the villages and towns—all this is of vital importance for the exploited Arab masses, as well as for the Jewish workers who must compete with cheap labor. Even the industries employing Jewish workers and accustomed to European standards and wages are interested in raising the economic level of the Arab workers, because their products must compete in the open market with the output of industries employing cheap labor. Every endeavor in this direction on the part of the government would receive the assistance of the Jewish and Arab masses, and would lead to a common effort and peaceful relations between the two groups. It would emancipate the Arab masses from their exploiters, whose helpless victims they are today, the same men who direct them to loot and murder after deliberately arousing their religious and racial hatred.

Once the cultural level of the Arab working masses is higher and they are capable of directing their own affairs, a solution for the political problems of the two nations can be found by peaceful means. The workers of both nations have no interest in either nation ruling over the other or dominating sections of the country not inhabited by their people. The national aspirations of the proletariat cannot be other than full autonomy for each group. The Jewish workers do not wish either to control the affairs of other inhabitants in the country or to ignore their rights. Their aim is solely to establish a Jewish working population, which will create its own economic and cultural life, help the Jewish masses to return to agriculture and other productive work, and seek to obtain self-government in all matters pertaining exclusively to the Jewish settlements and to the internal questions of all the Jewish inhabitants of the country.

Self-government is not in contradiction to the interests of any other sections of the population and can be given to both nations who live and will live in the country. In a large measure, self-government for the two nations in Palestine can be advanced by developing and strengthening local autonomy, for the trend of colonization is toward concentrated settlements of each nation. To carry this principle of self-government further, it will be necessary to develop a system of national autonomy, both for the solution of internal questions and for the management of those affairs that have a national significance. If these local and national self-governing bodies are set up on democratic principles, there is no doubt that the Arab workers will develop to the point where they will be able to insist that the true interests of the majority be respected. They will no longer serve as tools in the hands of their exploiters. It will then be possible to find a common language for the two nations. Each will become accustomed to recognize the rights of the other in the country. Each will make an effort to secure freedom and live a full national life without infringing upon the rights of others. Then only will it be possible to create a federation of the two nations, not on the premise that one dominate the other, but with the understanding that each of the two nations carry on its own affairs, and that together they manage those affairs of the country which concern both.

An important condition for unhampered development and the achievement of mutual understanding between the Arabs and the Jews is that the Mandatory Power, which is responsible to the League of Nations, fulfills the obligations imposed by the Mandate, to establish a Jewish national home, to protect the interests of the Arab inhabitants, and to guarantee the free development of the country as a whole.

For hundreds of years, Palestine has been forsaken and desolate. It is to the advantage of the effendis, the sheikhs, and the religious leaders who dominate the masses, that the land remain poor and that the doors be closed to those who wish to develop its resources. In general, the aspirations of the effendis are in opposition to the needs of a civilized people and cannot be sanctioned in any case, especially not in a country with which the lot of another people is bound up.

The Jewish people have not broken their bond with Palestine for thousands of years. Jewish settlements have been destroyed and rebuilt in all periods of history from the time of the Roman occupation until the present. However, in the last fifty years, Palestine Jewish colonization has received a new impetus and assumed a new character. Palestine has become one of the main countries of immigration for Jews, who are forced to leave the country of their residence. Other countries are gradually closing their doors, and even when partially open, they lack those conditions that make for a concentrated Jewish settlement and an economic, cultural, and political renaissance. When Jewish colonization in Palestine was begun, parallel attempts were made in Russia, as well as in North and South America, to render the masses productive and to establish concentrated Jewish settlements. However, the mighty pioneer forces required for changing the way of life and occupation have found expression only in the colonization of Palestine, that country of tradition, of hope, and of faith in the past and future of the Jewish nation. Only here settlements were established, which are developing and creating new forms of work and living and attracting the attention, the hope, and help of the Jewish masses the world over. Even the Jewish settlements in South America and the large labor unions in North America, who have attempted in their own way to change the mode of living of the Jewish masses and to direct them to productive work, have rendered great assistance to Palestine colonization in recent years. The return of the Jewish masses to their country with the help of the whole Jewish nation has become a vital factor and an active force in all countries in which Jews reside. For the Jewish nation Palestine is no longer the land of the past; it has become a country in which the nation is once more creative, and a place for the concentration of Jewish masses.

The International World [*sic*] must guarantee the development of Palestine by means of Jewish immigration and colonization; it must fulfill the hopes of the Jewish nation and raise the standard of the other inhabitants or the country. This duty the British government has taken upon itself. If it is carried out in the proper spirit, the British government can, in the course of years, help the Jewish people and the other inhabitants of the country to work for common ends growing out of the common interests of all workers, while preserving the right and freedom of every section of the population.

NOTES

1. A cautious and indirect reference to the removal of Arab sharecroppers from their lands after they had been purchased by Jews.

2. The Histadrut established an Arab union, the Palestine Labor League, in the belief that organized Arab labor would increase its wages and thus reduce the cost differential between Arab and Jewish labor.

3. In 1924, the recently established Turkish republic, led by Mustafa Kemal Attatürk, formally abolished the position of caliph, or supreme religious leader, that had been held by Ottoman sultans for over four hundred years.

4. Between 1902 and 1926, Abdul Aziz ibn Saud conquered much of Arabia, including the Hejaz, home to the holy cities of Mecca and Medina. The Saudi dynasty adhered to the fundamentalist Wahabi strain of Sunni Islam.

5. Mohammad Amin al-Husseini (1897-1974), was the political leader of the Palestinian Arabs during the Mandate period. The title "grand mufti" was invented by the British and bestowed upon him in 1921.

6. This treatment of the 1929 riots does not note the sanctity of the Western Wall to Islam (according to which Muhammad tethered his horse al-Buruq to the wall when he undertook a heavenly night journey between Mecca and the Temple Mount). Nor does it note that Zionists had indeed attempted to purchase the area around the wall.

41

The Future of Zionist Policy (1932)

CHAIM ARLOSOROFF

Chaim Arlosoroff (1899–1933) was one of the founders of Mapai and the head of the political department of the Jewish Agency. Arlosoroff was born in the Ukraine; his family relocated to Germany in 1905, and he received his doctorate in economics from the University of Berlin. His dissertation focused on Marx's theory of class struggles. Arlosoroff criticized the materialist, reductionist tendencies that influenced more dogmatic readings of Marx at the time, and instead emphasized the role of national–cultural consciousness among the working class. This relationship between the analysis of material forces and national consciousness would inform Arlosoroff's brand of socialist Zionism or "people's socialism": the realization of socialism, according to Arlosoroff, is tied to specific historical developments of a particular ethno-cultural group.

After moving to Palestine in 1924 and joining the leadership of Labor Zionism there, Arlosoroff adapted his general socialist formulations to conditions on the ground and became a chief advocate of constructivist socialism. Arlosoroff believed that analyzing the situation of the Yishuv from a strictly class perspective was meaningless; the national battle was the critical struggle, he maintained, and only after "normal" national conditions have materialized should the emphasis shift to more traditional socialist concerns. Moreover, from Arlosoroff's perspective, the national cultural struggle would elevate the condition of the Jewish workers and enhance their institutions.

Source: Chaim Arlosoroff to Chaim Weizmann, June 30, 1932. Central Zionist Archive, Jerusalem, Microfilm AM 1012/795.

While still in Germany, Arlosoroff joined Ha-Po'el Ha-Tsa'ir. However, unlike that party's spiritual father, A. D. Gordon, Arlosoroff continued to describe himself as a socialist. In 1930, Arlosoroff played an important role in the merger of Ha-Po'el Ha-Tsa'ir and Ahdut Ha-Avodah to form Mapai, which became the dominant party in the Yishuv.

In the spring of 1933, Arlosoroff who since 1931 had been head of the political department of the Jewish Agency, traveled to Germany to negotiate an agreement with the Nazi government to allow Jews to leave for Palestine with their property. The Revisionists in Palestine launched a campaign against the proposed agreement and against Arlosoroff. On June 16, 1933, two days after his return from Germany, Arlosoroff was murdered on the beach in Tel Aviv. Three members of a radical Revisionist group were charged with assassinating Arlosoroff. Two were acquitted by the district court; one was convicted by the lower court but later was acquitted by the Supreme Court for lack of corroborating evidence. The case has never been resolved and has continued, for years, to fuel the animosity between Laborites and Revisionists.

One of the chief ideological differences between Laborite and Revisionist Zionists had to do with the question of when the Zionist movement should move ahead and create the Jewish State. Laborites believed in a gradual approach: first the proper social and political conditions on the ground should materialize (a Jewish majority in Palestine and a strong social and economic infrastructure), whereas the Revisionists believed in immediate independence that would be achieved by developing Jewish military power. In this letter to Weizmann, Arlosoroff, in considering the rising tensions between Jews and Arabs in Palestine and the growing dangers for Jews in Europe, develops the idea of a revolutionary phase, by which the Jewish minority in Palestine would no longer pursue a gradual move from one stage of development to another but rather declare independence and allow Jews from Europe to come to Palestine. This formulation that, as Arlosoroff acknowledges in this letter, comes close to the Revisionist position, would become the mainstream Zionist position as articulated in the Biltmore Program of 1942 that called for the establishment of a Jewish Commonwealth in all of Palestine.

Arlosoroff was on close terms with Weizmann and sent this letter to him in confidence, without the knowledge of Ben-Gurion or other Zionist leaders. So far as we know he did not receive a written reply. Weizmann was concerned with maintaining close relations with Britain and presumably did not find the proposals in the letter to be helpful or feasible.

❖

Dear Dr. Weizmann,

Without waiting for a reply to my long letter of a few days ago I sit down today to write again. I am afraid it is going to be a rather curious piece of literature, and I hope you will not mind if I take up your time with something which may contemptuously be dismissed as an abstract dissertation on Zionist policy. However, the matter does not give me rest and the conclusions to which I am forced are such as to make it desirable to pave the way for an oral discussion which I hope may take place when I am in London.

In my last letter, in speaking of the political method which we are following at present I said that, in the last analysis and although we have, for the time being, no alternative method at our disposal, it cannot be regarded as more than a palliative, and that to achieve by this method the political aims of Zionism would seem to be difficult, if not impossible. I may describe this method as evolutionary and synthetic Zionist policy, and I do not think any other comments are necessary to make my meaning clear to you.

Nor do I propose to enter upon a discussion of what the aims of Zionism may be taken to mean. I still maintain that there is on this point no real difference of opinion between Zionists of different sections. I for one would be prepared at any moment to accept for my personal use the formula printed by the Revisionists on the back of their dinar receipts, just as I should be prepared twenty more times to vote against such a formula in Congress, even if it be in a *namentliche Abstimmung* [roll-call vote]. Yet, even if there was a Zionist who would in his heart of hearts dispute this definition and substitute another, less pretentious one, it is clear that, if we do not want just to reproduce Diaspora conditions in Palestine, we must aim at a settlement of hundreds of thousands of Jews to be achieved within a relatively brief period of time, so that at least a real equilibrium between the two races in Palestine might be established. A settlement on such a scale would require an effort differing in no essential from that needed in order to establish a "Jewish State on both sides of the Jordan." So to all practical interests and purposes the discussion of aims and objects does not matter at all.

I am forced to the conclusion that with the present methods and under the present regime there is hardly a possibility of working out a solution for this problem of large-scale immigration and settlement. Why not? The assumption upon which our policy is built is that it would be necessary and feasible to achieve our aim step-by-step and stage-by-stage. That this method was the only correct one in the past becomes clear if we realize that any other method which may suggest itself at present is based upon the actual strength of the Jewish Yishuv in Palestine, and that this strength itself has been achieved by the policy of gradualism which we have been following. The thing which I here call "stages" is not any concrete point to be defined either by logic or statistics or else by a diplomatic or legal formula, but a certain degree of development in the balance of real power between the two contending races in Palestine. This power may be based upon social weight, economic positions, technical or financial equipment, military organization or the fighting qualities of the grown-up male population of each community. The present "stage" which we have reached, by slow evolution and without any explicit definition, is one at which the Arabs are no longer sufficiently strong to destroy our position, yet at which they believe to be still powerful enough to enforce the establishment of an Arab State in Palestine without having regard to our political claims, while the Jews are sufficiently strong to hold their ground, but not powerful enough to enforce the continuous growth of the Yishuv by immigration and settlement and to safeguard peace and order in the country during the process.

The next "stage" will have been reached when the balance of actual power will exclude any possibility of the establishment of an Arab State in Palestine, that means when the Jews will have won that additional plus of real power which would automatically block the road to an Arab coup d'état. The "stage" following that would be the one at which the continuous growth of the Yishuv by immigration and constructive economic activities could no longer be checked and at which the Arabs, by this unceasing increase in Jewish strength, would be driven into a negotiated settlement. The "stage" following that would be a real equilibrium between the two races based upon actual power and a settled agreement. Now, the test for the evolutionary method of Zionist policy within the framework of the British Mandatory Regime would be whether the nearest "stage" could still be reached by it. If it could, it would be statesmanship and common sense to disregard all difficulties and troubles, to blind oneself to one's own bitter feeling and disappointment, and to carry on persistently and unwaveringly in adding strength to strength so that the nearest *étape* [stage] may gradually be attained. If it cannot—all this effort is in vain, the evolutionary method of Zionist policy becomes untenable and the faith and morale of the Zionist movement cannot be maintained on its basis. I tend to believe that it cannot.[. . .]

Nevertheless and in spite of everything it might be argued that for lack of anything better there is nothing for us but to continue to proceed step by step, adding what little strength we would be able to add to our present strength, entrenching ourselves more and more safely in the few important positions which we hold and waiting for "something to turn up"—for a new juncture to come from unknown quarters. I should have been prepared to follow that road without grumbling had I seen the prospect of a few decades of peace and more or less stable conditions in Palestine during which we might gradually continue to grow. Unfortunately, the political situation in the world remains so unsettled and the fermentation in the Middle East is growing at such a pace that there is little hope for any such optimistic assumption.

The first fact which we shall have to face will be the crumbling away of the "A" mandates,[1] with all its implications. As far as the Palestine situation is concerned, you can give the process three or five or seven years, that does not alter the fact. Then we have the process of revising the political boundaries in the Middle East which also has not come to an end yet. A Syria and Iraq united under one ruler may exercise quite a different pressure upon us than would the separate states to our north. Whether the Emir of Transjordan may not after all succeed, by taking advantage of occidental developments, to expand toward the south and incorporate in his domain parts of the Arab Peninsula is today a more serious question that it was even half a year ago. Add to that the repercussions which all those events are bound to have on the strength of the Istiklal [independence] movement, particularly among the youth. We should not forget that in the meantime the Palestine Arab movement has learnt all the tricks of Zionist politics from Congresses, presidents and *Geschäftsordnung* [bylaws] down to banks and fund collection. It has succeeded in focusing to a certain extent the attention of the Mohammedan and Arab world upon Jerusalem and Palestine. A policy designed to isolate the Palestinian Arabs today has to overcome a stronger resistance than it might have had ten or even five years ago. Moreover, I need not remind you that the non-Jewish population of Palestine grows rapidly. The problem of our majority or of an equilibrium was a problem of 500,000 ten years ago, is a problem of 600,000 today, and will be a problem of a million and a quarter fifteen years hence. The area of Palestine being after all (even within wide limits) of fixed magnitude, the pressure upon the basis of subsistence must in consequence also grow apace. I do not say it cannot be overcome: it can be overcome, but it will need larger means and an even more single-minded Government in order to overcome it.

These developments would come to a sudden climax if, on top of all that, a new international armed conflict would break out in which the British Empire would be involved. Can there be a doubt in anybody's mind that we are heading for a new great war? You may give it five years or ten. We may not know in what definite setting it will break out, whether it come as a concentration against Soviet Russia (partly to prevent Bolshevism from spreading) or in another constellation. "History," to use Bismarck's phrase, "does not allow me to look into her cards." But whither we are going can no longer be doubted. Take the British Labour Government's international policy which was as pacifist as any. Henderson[2] may preside at as many Disarmament Conferences as he likes. Either the British Labour Government spent a hundred and fifteen million pounds a year on armaments just for nothing, then they were madmen; or they were not madmen, and we shall have war as certainly as winter follows autumn.

On the day of the declaration of war the Mandates system will collapse and the League of Nations adjourn for a summer vacation. As far as Palestine is concerned it may (on the precedent of Cyprus and Egypt in 1914) be formally annexed to the British Empire. At any rate, if we allow matters to drift in the direction they are drifting now, at that stage we shall have either a clear-cut Arab–British alliance, or an Arab rising. Moreover, if we postpone decisive action to that date we shall have to take into account the fact that our communications with world Jewry, our hinterland for the supply of men, money and material, will be cut off.

Apart from all that, it becomes more and more manifest that with our present methods of policy we shall not be able to raise money on any scale that would enable us to carry through a systematic immigration and colonization program worth its name (even if political conditions would allow us to do so). Our budget, based on voluntary contributions to national funds, is crumbling away and for years to come (those precious years which once they pass will be irrecoverably lost) we shall be tied up with the tedious task of clearing away the debts of the past. As to the big financial corporations and the wholesale private investment—I do not see them yet, and if I see them I do not know in what direction they would finally work out in the conditions of Palestine. All big loan schemes under the Jewish Agency have, in the present circumstances and with the violent fluctuations in the income of our funds, passed out of our reach, unless we should be in a position to speak on behalf of a political entity recognized by international law.

And one word more: with all the strong Palestine sentiment which has manifested itself and continues to manifest itself in world Jewry there is no doubt in my mind that with the methods of evolutionary Zionist policy we shall not be able to maintain our strength in the face of the cruel facts. The facts are that the economic conditions of the Jewish people are so rapidly deteriorating that the interest in a Palestinian venture which does not offer any material solution for the needs of the Diaspora must dwindle—unless, of course, the lack of a substantial material relief is counterbalanced by an outstanding political and national value. Despite the enthusiasm which the Yishuv evokes in the heart of every Jewish tourist, I am afraid that the gradualist system offers neither. On the other hand there is the alluring call of Soviet Russia with her gigantic constructive program and her strong appeal to our youth. How long can we expect to keep them hoping against hope and snatching up hungrily the crumbs of certificates which once in every six months fall from the table of the Palestine Government? Why should Palestine, in the face of these facts of disintegration, repulsion, and attraction focus for another twenty or thirty years the thought of the Jewish people all over the world? We are compelled to throw overboard all makeshift replies and face the real issue.

I know you will have grown very impatient by now (if you have at all managed to read the foregoing pages) and be asking yourself nervously: what is the upshot? What are the conclusions to be drawn from all that?

There seem to me to be four possible sets of conclusions that offer themselves: The one is to say that it is no more than a popular prejudice to assume that there must be a solution to every problem, and that all accounts must square. In fact they don't. We have just to carry on, drifting on an uncharted sea and not knowing exactly which way the land lies. We have to carry on even if we had to stand with our face to a wall which appears insurmountable. We have to gather as much strength as we are able to. We do not know what may happen and what new chances the future may bring after all. The "Poritz [a Polish landowner] may die," as the famous Jewish story has it, "the dog may die," and there are other possibilities. In the meantime hold on. It is an extremely Jewish attitude; I should say, the specifically Jewish form of heroism, but I do not think it is a Zionist attitude. It is the drift of the Zionist movement from the plane of political action (which calls for a thought-out policy and a constructive program) to the plane of Jewish fatalism (which is a heritage of age-long passivity). In this sense Zionism was always to me a rebellion against Jewish tradition. For lack of anything better we may have to go back to it. But that, I am sure, would apply only to the band of militant Zionists who have fought all the battles of the movement and for whom there is no life without it. It would not, I feel certain, apply to the Jewish people at large, particularly not to the young generation yet to be won for Zionism, the generation which looks into the world of the mid-twentieth century with the clear and disillusioned eyes of postwar youth, and asks for a clear lead.

The second possible conclusion would be to say that in the circumstances of this world, the Zionist ideal cannot be turned into a reality, and that the Zionist program is bound to go through a continuous process of liquidation—flourishing, inspiring, and singularly fascinating as the life of the young Jewish Yishuv of 180,000 Jews in Palestine may be. The truth of the Zionist diagnosis has been proved the world over, from Soviet Russia to the United States of America. The truth of the Zionist cure has been proved in the few drops of national life—labor, soil, and speech—which the Yishuv has produced, but objective conditions of the world, of the Jewish people and the present population of Palestine obstruct Zionism in its progress toward its goal. I include in this category all recent experiments in the re-interpretation of Zionism, all pseudo-Zionist platforms and compromise proposals, whether they be termed "cultural

Zionism," or Brit Shalom.[3] I am not surprised at all to find that a group like Brit Shalom, or—*lehavdil* [to differentiate]—like *Ha-Or*,[4] are rapidly disintegrating and getting assimilated into either a communist faction with an outspokenly anti-Zionist attitude or else a group of religious romanticism. It is one of either: either these people take their own Zionist formula seriously, then they must cope with the same difficulties which our Zionism has to face. Or else they do not, then they drift off to new shores which have for them a stronger lure. Unless, however, one is prepared to face any of the other possible policies there is something to be said in favor of this conception because it might save thousands of lives which through a policy of drift may be endangered.

The third theoretical possibility would be to maintain the fundamental principles of Zionism but restrict their application to certain districts or areas of Palestine. This is the line along which run all the canton schemes or Dr. Jacobson's program of a Jewish State in Palestine (instead of Palestine as a Jewish State). The idea is to create, within the limits of a definite zone, by the establishment of a national sovereignty over that part of the Palestinian territory, all those possibilities of unhampered development which are dependent upon the application of state methods in administration, colonization and finance, and to use this as a strategic basis for a possible advance in the future. In spite of all the noise of our press there is no doubt in my mind that there is a sound core to all these schemes. They contain the elements of territorialism and political self-determination which are the fundamental truths of Zionism. All these schemes however are in my opinion foundering on the rocks of four difficulties:

(a) The limited size of Palestine
(b) The problem of Jerusalem
(c) The unfortunate geographical configuration of the areas of Jewish Settlement (Coastal Belt, *Emek*, [Jezreel Valley], Jordan Valley, Upper Galilee)
(d) The fact that even in the above-defined districts the Jews form no more than a minority so that the problem is altered only quantitatively and not qualitatively.

The fourth possible conclusion would be that Zionism cannot, in the given circumstances, be turned into a reality without a transition period of the organized revolutionary rule of the Jewish minority; that there is no way to a Jewish majority, or even to an equilibrium between the two races (or else a settlement sufficient to provide a basis for a cultural center to be established by systematic immigration and colonization, without a period of a nationalist minority government which would usurp the state machinery, the administration and the military power in order to forestall the danger of our being swamped by numbers and endangered by a rising (which we could not face without having the state machinery and military power at our disposal). During this period of transition a systematic policy of development, immigration, and settlement would be carried out. This conception may run counter to many beliefs we have been holding for many years. It may come dangerously near certain popular political creeds with which we never had much sympathy. It may at first sight appear impracticable, even more, fantastic. It may seem to contradict the conditions in which the British Mandate places us. All this needs a discussion which I do not care to put into writing. All I feel, and with overwhelming force, is that I should never accept the defeat of Zionism before an attempt was made which would be equal to the grim seriousness of our struggle for national life and to the sacredness of the trust which the Jewish people has laid in our hands. And don't forget that any turn of events in the world or in the Middle East, any cruel contingency may force upon us a course which we would be loath to choose of our own free will. Our preparatory measures must take that into account irrespective of what we may or may not like to decide with regard to our policy.

I hope I need not emphasize that my trend of thought is today just as remote from what is called Revisionism as it ever was. I continue to regard its tactics, politics, and educational tenets as downright folly. If I had to devise in my fancy a movement for the purpose of preventing "the Jewish State on both sides of the Jordan" from coming into being I should invest it with the specific characteristics, language, and actions of the Revisionists. I have said before that the so-called *Kolonisationsregime* of the Revisionists under which the English would snatch the chestnuts out of the fire for us in keeping the Arabs down by their bayonets is an utterly unreal slogan. The Revisionist press, with their wholesale provocation which is not backed by any real power, produces militant reactions on the Arab side, stirring up and (indirectly) organizing forces which on the day of crisis will confront us. The mind of our youth, which through the toll of a few decades had been slowly turning toward the grim realities of our situation, is by Revisionist propaganda stuffed again with illusions and their mouths are filled with empty talk. Moreover, all I stand for is based upon the actual strength of the Yishuv while the Revisionists are at present engaged in vague searchings for a strategic basis between Paris, Warsaw, and Rome. Of course, they too might have chosen the Yishuv as their base if they ever would have had a chance of relying upon organized labor in Palestine which, whatever may happen, remains the "iron brigade" of Zionism for any policy.

I hope you will not be angry with me for writing letters of such abominable length and will not think that I am getting out of my senses either. It is now months and months that my mind is constantly tracing and re-tracing the name road, and there is no one to whom I would consider myself to be under greater obligation of reporting than to you.

Yours ever,
(Signature)

NOTES

1. Class A League of Nations Mandates were areas in the Middle East that were formerly part of the Ottoman Empire and were deemed to be close to achieving national independence and would be administered by Mandatory Power until such time that they were able to stand alone. The Class A Mandates included territories under British control: Mesopotamia, which would become Iraq, and Palestine, whose eastern portion became Transjordan and whose western part was designated as the future Jewish national home. In the north, Syria (including Lebanon) was under French control.

2. On Arthur Henderson, see document 17.

3. Brit Shalom (Covenant of Peace) was a small movement of Jewish intellectuals, many of them affiliated with the Hebrew University in Jerusalem, which was founded in 1925 and called for the creation of a binational Arab–Jewish state in Palestine. Among the group's members were Martin Buber (1878–1965), Gershom Scholem (1897–1982), and Hugo Bergmann (1883–1975).

4. *Ha-Or* was a small Trotskyite journal that was published in Palestine in the 1930s. The journal's motto was: "A political, economic, and literary bi-weekly dedicated to issues of the workers without distinction by nation, people, religion, or race."

42

On the Partition of Palestine (1937)

DAVID BEN-GURION

This letter, written by Ben-Gurion from London to his adolescent son, Amos, has acquired a good deal of notoriety in Middle Eastern historiography. It has been cited as evidence that Ben-Gurion consciously planned the expulsion of the Palestinians a decade before Israel's War of Independence. The letter is published in full here for the first time.

The factual background to this letter was the Peel Commission's recommendation in July 1937 that Palestine be partitioned into Jewish and Arab states. The Peel Commission also recommended that where possible Arabs were to be moved from the Jewish to the Arab state and vice versa. In fact, the population transfer would be almost entirely unilateral, with more than 200,000 Arabs being moved versus just over 1,000 Jews.

The proposal divided the Zionist leadership. Some accepted it; others rejected partition in any form; and still others were willing to accept partition in principle but were discontent with the amount of territory allotted to the Jewish state. Ben-Gurion cautiously adopted the first position, arguing to his party's executive committee that a Jewish state within the biblical Land of Israel was not a final goal and that some day the state would include Transjordan and southern Lebanon.[1] The third position prevailed at the World Zionist Congress that met in Geneva in August. Amos took the second, fully oppositional position. At the time, Amos belonged to a Zionist youth movement, Ha-Mahanot Ha-Olim (the Ascending Camps), which was affiliated with Ha-Kibbutz ha-Me'uhad (United Kibbutz movement), whose leader, Yizhak Tabenkin, believed that

Source: Ben-Gurion Archive (correspondence), Sede Boker, October 5, 1937. (Many thanks to Motti Golani for this document.) Translated by Marganit Weinberger-Rotman.

socialist values and territorial maximalism were mutually reinforcing (see document 37). A minuscule Jewish state, it was feared, would lack the resources and the security to develop a stable socialist economy and society. Moreover, unlike Ben-Gurion, many Zionists on the left as well as right of the social spectrum were unwilling to make even a pragmatic concession to the Jews' historic claim to the entire Land of Israel.

Ben-Gurion wrote a prodigious number of letters and diary entries, which he usually viewed as a form of self-documentation for dissemination and eventual publication (as was, in fact, often the case). Thus this letter could be seen not as a private exchange of ideas between father and son so much as a political statement, or an attempt to convince not only Amos, but many others, of the viability of partition, particularly in terms of the quantity of land that would be available for Zionist settlement. According to this interpretation, Ben-Gurion's territorial maximalism would have been purely rhetorical. Whether or not this is true, in years to come Ben-Gurion tried to conceal his earlier support for taking territory east of the Jordan River, and this letter was deleted from the 1968 Hebrew edition of Ben-Gurion's correspondence.[2] Similarly ambiguous was the intent of—and intended audience for—Ben-Gurion's musings in this letter on the possibility of forcibly transferring Arabs from Palestine in the case of partition.

Dear Amos,

I was not mad at you; I was only very sad not to have received an answer from you. I cannot accept your excuse that you had no time. I know you are busy at school, in the field and at home, and I am pleased that you are studying, but one can always find a free hour when there's need. Not only on Saturdays, but during the week, too.

Similarly, your excuse that I wander from country to country is not convincing. You can write to me in London. Here, they always know where I am, and they forward my mail regularly.

As for the question of my membership in the Executive Committee,[3] I will explain it to you when we meet in person, if I find you still in Tel Aviv on my return. I will only comment briefly on the split between logic and feeling when it comes to matters of state. Politics is not a matter of sentiment. The only consideration is what's good and beneficial for us. Which road will lead us to our goal. Which policy will strengthen us, and which will be a detriment.

I have feelings too, or I would not have been able to endure this difficult work for dozens of years. And my feelings are not hurt by the idea of establishing a Jewish state, however small. It goes without saying that I do not favor the partition of the land, but the land to be divided is not in our hands; it is in the hands of the British and the Arabs. We hold only a small fraction of it, less than what is offered for the Jewish state. If I were an Arab, my feelings would be seriously hurt. But the fact is, in the partition plan, we receive more than what we own, though less, much less, than what we deserve and want. But the question is whether we would get more without partition? If the status quo remains, will our "feelings" be satisfied? What we want is not to keep the country one and whole, but that the one and whole country will be Jewish. I have no use for a Greater Palestine that is Arab.

For us, the status quo is poison; we need a change in the situation. How will this change come about? How can we establish our own state?

The crucial question is whether the establishment of a Jewish state would help or prevent turning this country into a Jewish country?

My assumption is—and this is why I am an ardent supporter of establishing a state even if it involves a partition now—that a Jewish state on part of the land is not a final status; it is just the beginning. When we purchase a thousand or ten thousand dunams, we rejoice and our feelings are not hurt because we did not purchase the entire land. The purchase is important not only in itself; it also helps us go from strength to strength and this empowerment helps lead us to purchasing the entire country. Establishing a state, even a partial one, maximizes our forces, and it will contribute to our historical effort to redeem the entire country.

We will admit as many Jewish immigrants as we can. We firmly believe that we can bring more than two million here. We'll establish a multifaceted economy: agricultural, industrial, commercial, naval, etc. We'll build sophisticated armed forces, an excellent military—I am sure our army will be among the best in the world—and then we'll be able to settle in the other parts of the country, either through mutual agreement with our Arab neighbors or through other means.

We mustn't lose sight of some basic facts that enable us to settle in Palestine; it is not the British Mandate, nor the Balfour Declaration—these are corollaries, not causes, temporary, ephemeral events. They could just as well not happen. Were it not for the First World War or the way it ended, the mandate and the declaration would not have occurred. But there are fundamental historical facts that are immutable as long as Zionism is not fully realized. These are:

1. The afflictions in the Diaspora, which impel Jews to immigrate to Palestine.
2. The fact that the land is largely uninhabited. There is great potential for settlement in areas that the Arabs don't need and are not capable of settling (because they do not need them). There is no problem of Arab immigration, there is no Arab

Diaspora and the Arabs are not persecuted. They have a country, a vast country of their own.[4]

3. Jewish talent and inventiveness (a result of reason No. 1), the Jews' ability to make the desert bloom, create industry, build an economy, develop culture, conquer the air and the sea using science and pioneering efforts.

These basic facts will be greatly helped by the existence of a Jewish state in part of Palestine, just as the Zionist movement is helped by every conquest, small and large, every new school, factory, boat, etc.

If we have a state, we'll be able to populate the land, outnumber the Arabs, and accelerate building and expansion. The more our forces grow, the sooner the Arabs will realize that they cannot and should not oppose us. They will rather take advantage, both politically and materially, of the Jewish presence.

I am not a dreamer and I do not like wars. I have always believed—even before the option of a state materialized—that when we are strong and numerous in the country, the Arabs will realize how beneficial an alliance with us can be; if they let us settle in all parts of Palestine, they can benefit from our help. The Arabs have many countries, sparsely populated, undeveloped and unprotected. Without France, Syria could not withstand Turkey for one day. The same applies to Iraq and the new state. They all need the protection of France and Britain. But such protection implies subjugation and dependence. The Jews could be equal allies, true friends, not conquerors and tyrants.

Let's assume that the Negev is not included in the Jewish state. It will remain a barren desert because the Arabs do not need it and are incapable of developing it. They have plenty of other deserts, and they lack the manpower, the money and the initiative. It is quite possible that in exchange for financial, military, organizational, and scientific aid they will allow us to develop and build the Negev. But then again, maybe not. Nations don't always act according to reason and in their best interest. Just as you maintain that there is a dichotomy between reason and feelings, perhaps the Arabs will be motivated by counter-productive nationalistic sentiments and will tell us: "None of your honey, none of your sting, we'd rather the Negev stayed barren and desolate than have Jews settle in it." Then we'll have to speak to them in another language. And we will have that "language" which without a state could not exist. We should not accept that large uninhabited areas, which can accommodate thousands of Jews, would remain empty; we should not accept that Jews wouldn't be able to return to their homeland because Arabs choose not to allow either nation to settle there. We will have to expel the Arabs and take their place. Our national aspirations are based on the assumption—proven right since the start of our settlement here—that there is enough room for both the Arabs and ourselves in Palestine, and if we need to resort to force—not in order to dispossess the Arabs of the Negev and Transjordan, but in order to guarantee our right to settle there—then we will have the power to do so.

It is quite possible in that case that we'll have to deal not only with the Palestinian Arabs but with the neighboring countries which will rush to help them against us, but we will be more powerful, not only because we are better organized and better equipped, but because our forces will be greater in both quantity and quality. We have a reservoir of troops in the Diaspora. Our younger generation now living in Poland, Romania, America and elsewhere will rush to join us if and when this conflict flares up—and I hope it never does. The Jewish state will not depend only on the Jews living within its borders, but on the entire Jewish people all over the world, on the millions who want and must live in Palestine. There are no millions of Arabs who want or must settle in Palestine. Of course, adventurers and Arab gangs from Syria and Iraq may come in, but they are no match for the hundreds of thousands of Jewish youths for whom the Land of Israel is not just a matter of "feelings" but also a question of personal and national life.

This is why I attach so much importance to reclaiming land from the sea, to building a Jewish port and a Jewish navy. The sea is the bridge between the Jews in Palestine and the millions in the Diaspora. We must prepare conditions that will allow our ships and our sailors to bring in thousands of youths, so we can train them—even while they are still living abroad—for any possible task in Palestine.

I am confident that establishing a Jewish state, even in part of the country, will allow us to accomplish that. If we build our own state, we will rule the sea, and much will be achieved.

This is why there is no split in my heart between reason and feeling. Both tell me: build a Jewish state now, even if it is not in the entire territory; the rest will come later—it must come!

When are you going back to Kedouri?[5]

Write to me.

Show this letter to your mother and to your sisters.

Best,
Dad

NOTES

1. Nadav G. Shelef, *Evolving Nationalism: Homeland, Identity, and Religion in Israel, 1925–2005* (Ithaca, N.Y.: Cornell University Press, 2010), 30.

2. Ibid., 38.

3. Of the Jewish Agency.

4. Ben-Gurion's acceptance of Pan-Arab doctrine of a single, united, Arab nation well served Zionist purposes as it denied Palestinian Arabs a national identity and national rights.

5. An agricultural school in the Lower Galilee.

43

Platform for Judeo-Arab Accord (1930)

CHAIM MARGALIT-KALVARISKY

Chaim Margalit-Kalvarisky (1867–1947) was a veteran of the First Aliyah and devoted his life to the seemingly contradictory causes of Zionist land purchase and Jewish–Arab coexistence in Palestine. Before World War I, while working as an administrator and land-purchase agent for the Jewish Colonization Association, Kalvarisky developed close ties with many rural Arab notables, and during the 1920s, he was the Zionist Executive's chief Arabist. Kalvarisky simultaneously bought land from Arabs (including lands whose tenants were forced to leave) and strove to purchase Arab goodwill through bribery. Yet he shunned any alliance between Zionism and Western imperialism and sought to maximize Jewish and Arab integration in what he thought would be a common Semitic homeland. In 1925, Kalvarisky was a founder of Brit Shalom, a group of a few score Jews, most of them Central European, who were willing to renounce the claim to an autonomous Jewish national home in favor of a binational polity.

This document, written in the shadow of the 1929 riots, is typical of many manifestos penned by Kalvarisky in its energy, optimism, and curious blend of far-sightedness and wishful thinking.

Source: Central Zionist Archive, Jerusalem, A113/13. August 4, 1930. Translated by Marganit Weinberger-Rotman.

Of all the ancient Semitic tribes and races who had reached the apex of development in antiquity and had founded powerful kingdoms—Babylonians, Assyrians, Aramaeans and Canaanites, Jews and Arabs, only the two last mentioned have survived. Aram and Canaan have long disappeared, while Assyrians and Babylonians are mere names in the archaeological records. The Arabs have conquered a large continent extending from the Taurus Mountains to the Persian Gulf as far past as the Indian Ocean, and westward as far as the Straits of Gibraltar, including the whole continent of North Africa. They have evolved a high civilization wherever they went, and when Europe went through its darkest period of history, the Arabs and the Jews who lived in their midst were practically the sole carriers of the torch of enlightenment in the world. Those were the heydays of Arab civilization. Since then a gradual decadence set in. More powerful and virile forces have since overpowered them. Many of them came under foreign tutelage, but to this day the Arab race remains strong. It numbers several millions and occupies expanses of land in several continents that are comparable in magnitude to those of the greatest Empire in recorded history. Their rich language, which is a kindred language to Hebrew, but which is distinguished for a variety of dialects, is the link that unites the Arabs and renders them into one compact bloc.

The fate of the other Semitic tribe that has survived and that in one time played a prominent role in the history of the world was very different. The Jews have not only lost their political liberty but were expelled from their land by Romans, Babylonians, and Byzantine conquerors who treated them cruelly and scattered them to all the four corners of the world. This long Diaspora has had a double effect upon them; a good effect and a bad effect. Under the influence of European nations who have attained a high pitch of economic and cultural development, the Jews too have attained considerable height in wealth and in culture. In Europe, the Jews are distinguished in all spheres of human endeavors. Economically, too, they play a leading and prominent role. While the anti-Semites' allegation that the Jews monopolize the key position in the economic life of their respective countries is certainly exaggerated, there is no denying their considerable influence upon the economy of the world.

Nor do they take a back seat in scientific and intellectual endeavors, and their influence on the press and literature is particularly marked, while their influence on political life, though smaller, is not at all negligible. All these are favorable factors from which individual Jews have benefited from the ability and industry of the Jews [sic].

But the Jewish Diaspora was not without its negative aspects. It has adversely affected the development of the Jewish people as a nation. In order to exist within the nations whose hospitality they enjoyed, the Jew had to adapt himself to the mentality and habits of his environment, to speak the language of his neighbor and, what is worse, he very often had to abandon his Jewish and Semitic mentality and adopt that of his Aryan neighbor, and not infrequently to think like his anti-Semitic neighbor. He gradually came to abandon his national faculties, to forget his language and national traits, and to assimilate those of his neighbors. The link between one Jewish Territorial Concentration and another has gradually weakened, and there is a danger of this Semitic race completely disappearing from the world. The best minds in the Jewish people have viewed the future of this people with grave anxiety but it was beyond their power to check the disintegrating process. Most European and American states granted their Jewish citizens civic emancipation and the process of assimilation wrought havoc in Jewish quarters; many were the Jews who sought salvation in apostasy and many more, who formally remained faithful to their religion, endeavored to look like the non-Jews in whose midst they lived.

In these dire days of stress, some of the Jewish intellectuals raised the banner of Zion. They pleaded that as long as Jews remained in countries alien to them, among alien cultures of non-Semitic people, so long will they assimilate the national characteristics of those people until they will ultimately reach a stage of complete self-effacement. They pleaded that there was no other way open to them save that of return to their original land, to the Orient, to their ancient homeland that was in part inhabited by their brothers in race, the Arabs, with a view to the resettlement, cultivation, and the restoration of their own culture in an unadulterated national atmosphere. This was the only course open to the Jews if they were to save the Jewish Semitic race from complete national extermination.

The early pioneers of fifty years ago were confident that their Arab brethren would welcome this, and they were not be disappointed. Did not the Russian slave [sic] aid their Bulgarian brethren in their fight against their Turkish overlords?[1] Did not nations aid nations? I have had occasion to state elsewhere that but the help given us by Arab officials before the war in the consummation of our colonization endeavors, we would not have managed to survive the numerous administrative restrictive measures devised by the Turkish Authorities against Jewish colonization.

The Arabs had instinctively felt that Jewish immigration to this land, so far from resulting in any injury to them, was indeed highly beneficial. During the war [World War I], when all mankind underwent untold misery, when both Jews and Arabs were literally straying in the streets of Palestinian towns, they extended to one another a helping hand. In several places Jews opened soup kitchens that catered to the poor and the needy irrespective of race and creed, and in other places they opened schools for Arab children only. There was a true and sincere rapprochement and educated people on both sides took to planning a system of mutual cooperation and even a political concordat between the two people. Some of the leaders of both parties have even discussed the possibility of an autonomous Palestine within the Arab Confederation, something along the lines of Croatia, within Hungary, or Galicia in the defunct pre-war Austrian Monarchy. Had these discussions been allowed to continue normally and unhampered, it may be assumed that the two races would have reached a true rapprochement and would have helped one another in the attainment of their goals. I am confident that had the Arabs been a truly independent nation, then they would have been moved by their national instincts and by considerations of national interests to secure a rapprochement with the Jews and aid in their effort to achieve national restoration on the land of their common ancestors. But to our regret the Arabs are not independent and have grown extremely suspicious since the war. (In his aspirations to full political liberty he fails to see or refuses to see that the Jews do not come to Palestine as conquerors seeking predominance over anybody, but as true sons of their country returning to their homeland in order to restore it to its erstwhile glory by sheer hard labor in conjunction with the people settled in it.) The Arab is well aware that Jewish immigration to Arab territories in general and to Palestine in particular is unlikely to endanger his position; yet he continues to fear that the Jew in Palestine is a tool in the hands of European imperialists who seek to dominate them, through the Jew. This is indeed at the root of Arab opposition to Jews.

As a matter of fact, the Arabs are not afraid of the Jews, and in their heart of hearts are indeed sympathetic to them because of a racial and religious affinity with them and because of a common mentality, but they are chary of Europe and the Europeans. To remove this misunderstanding it is our duty first to declare that Zionism is not a tool for imperialistic ends. Zionism is an end in itself; a straight and honest objective in the realization of which all Semites are interested. This object is to enable a Semitic race, or rather to such section of the race as has remained loyal to the Semitic tradition and as has been unwilling or unable to assimilate with the peoples within whom it has lived; a safe refuge where it would work and develop its cultural life unhampered. We further have to declare that the ideal of the Arab nationalists to establish an Arab Confederation is not at all in conflict with our own ideal to establish in Palestine a national home for the Jewish people. Jews and Arabs are brothers and should be able to live together within the confines of one state and one federation. As in Russia and Germany, where there are Russians and Ukrainians, Prussians and

Bavarians, but are all of the same race, so here too the main factor should be that we are all of the same race. I believe that the Jews will have no objection to joining a federation of Arab states, provided the Arabs will not restrict their work in Palestine. They seek no special privileges in Palestine, but a strict equality of status. There should be one law and one authority for both of them. Palestine was once theirs, and in the millennia of dispersion they have never given up the hope to return to it. Thirteen centuries ago, you the Arabs have conquered this land from those who have conquered it from us. We are fortunate in that the legacy of our ancestors has not gone into altogether strange hands. The last decade or so has brought new reforms in its wake, but the road is open to us and we can both of us, worthy of both of us. Let us proceed and do it. You should know that we want to dispossess or oust no one, neither the *fellah*, nor the *effendi*, nor the Arab workman; we only want to occupy and develop that which is unoccupied and undeveloped.

I therefore propose a general Judeo-Arab Covenant on the following foundations:

(1) The two Semitic races, Jews and Arabs, undertake to help one another in all spheres of human endeavor, economic, social, and cultural.

(2) The Arabs welcome their Jewish brethren returning to the east, the ancient homeland, and throw open the gates of their extensive territories to Jewish immigration.

(3) In consideration of this, Jews will do their utmost in giving their resources, energy, and experience toward the development of the Semitic East and toward its progress to a great future.

(4) In all the Oriental lands where Jews will reside, they will have the same rights accorded to national minorities in the more advanced Europeans [*sic*], e.g., Czechoslovakia, etc.

(5) In view of its past and its association to the two Semitic peoples and to the three faiths, Palestine will form an autonomous unit with a special constitution. That constitution will postulate the formation of Palestine into a uni-racial but not a uni-national territory, which will belong not to one or another of the Semitic races, but to both of them jointly and equally irrespective of which of them forms the majority and which forms the minority at any given time.

(6) Within the boundaries of this territory, the Hebrew language shall have equal rights with the Arab language. Jewish culture

and Arab culture shall develop side by side in perfect and undisturbed harmony.

(7) The Jews shall declare that they have no intention of dominating anyone in Palestine nor of hampering the development of Palestinians other than Jews, but they will desire that no one shall dominate them or hamper their own development.

(8) The Jews shall undertake not to dispossess their Arab fellah nor prejudice the rights of the Arab workman. So far from their entertaining any such intentions, they will be a great cultural effort, endeavor to improve the deplorable condition of the fellah, and will offer the Arab workman employment where he has had none before. So far, the country at large and the Arabs in particular have benefited directly and indirectly from Jewish immigration. In future, Jewish organizations will have to be established with a view to enhancing the indirect interests of the Arabs in Jewish activity.

(9) The Jews undertake not to oppose national aspirations of the Arabs. Should a federation of Arab states be formed in the Near East, Palestine could form part of this federation because nothing will add more happiness to the Jew than the glory and regeneration of the Semitic race.

The above are the main clauses of an accord upon which the Judeo-Arab Covenant must be based. They form only a nucleus covenant to which other clauses may be added but from which nothing may be deducted.

The dangers to which the Arabs are allegedly exposed as a result of Jewish work are imaginary, not real. The penetration into Semitic countries in general and into Palestine in particular of a Semitic race will result in no danger to the Arabs. On the contrary, it will contribute to its vigor and to its inherent strength. We Jews shall not thrust ourselves an [sic] alien growth upon the body politic of the Arabs, as many extreme nationalists believe, but we shall form a beautiful ring in the chain of the United Arab Confederation. The Arab Confederation does not alarm us. Therefore the sooner the Covenant is signed between us, the better for all of us, for us Jews as well as for you Arabs.

The present fraternal strife now waging between us is ruinous to us as well as to you. Our heart goes out to the many innocent victims that fell last year on both sides. Will there be an abatement of this bloody strife? In my view the time is ripe for a truce to be declared, for a hand of peace to be extended by one side to the other. Some of the friends of the Arabs protest that the Jews stand in the way of Arab constitutional development and prevent them from a securing a legislative assembly; a handicap that is prejudicial to the interests of the people. To these protestations I shall counter by saying that time was when we Jews were anxious to have a legislative assembly[2] and you the Arabs refused to have it for various reasons. Now the tables have been turned. Is it any wonder? I think that in the present circumstances it is little wonder that Jews have grown apprehensive. But I believe that even on this issue an agreement may be reached provided there is mutual understanding. I admit that a legislative council may prove of considerable benefit to the country—if it conducts its work in a manner beneficial to all the people of the country, to its present as well as to its future population, but it can be a dangerous instrument if it conducts its work in a manner beneficial to one section only of the population. It can prove of invaluable benefit if it limits a full equality in the rights of the two races, but it will result in considerable injury if its promoters live up to the statement of one of their leaders before the Shaw Commission,[3] "We have not protested at the Seventh Congress at the Balfour Declaration, neither have we asked for its cancellation, because we have insisted on the establishment of a parliament, which amounts to the same thing." The Arabs had better know that no Jew could concur in a parliament that would invalidate the Balfour Declaration. But the truth is that those who have recommended at the Seventh Congress[4] that the Arabs should neither protest against the Balfour Declaration nor ask for its cancellation have not sought to deceive anyone. I know them well as of honesty and integrity. They have deplored and bemoaned the internecine strife that has been going on between the two parties and are anxious to form a bridge between the two Semitic races. It is with regret that I have to state that neither party was quick to seize the extended hand of peace, and meanwhile we have had the Wailing Wall issue that has resulted in many innocent casualties on both sides. The time has come for a proper appreciation for the situation and for each party to declare openly that which it believes. I say: Jews are not opposed to a legislative council. In our present situation as a minority in the country, we are not unmindful of the many handicaps of such an institution to the Jews. Nevertheless, we should not oppose it if we are given adequate guarantee that it will not be abused with a view to hampering the development of the national home in Palestine. That is, for the time being. And if after these lapse of a certain period of cooperation in the legislative forum and in the political life of the country we are satisfied that you have no intention of restricting our development, and we are convinced that the legislative assembly will prove of benefit to the two races alike, I am confident that we shall aim at an even greater measure of political cooperation with a view to widening the platform of joint political endeavor in the country.

NOTES

1. The Russo-Turkish war of 1877–78 resulted in, among other things, the emergence of an autonomous Bulgarian principality within the Ottoman Empire.

2. In the early 1920s, the British Mandatory government attempted to create a legislative body that would represent both Jews and Arabs, but it foundered over the issues of how delegates would be chosen (via governmental appointment or direct election), the ratio of Jews to Christian and Muslim Arabs, and, most important for the Arabs, whether participation in the council presupposed acceptance of the terms of the British Mandate, which promised to foster the growth of a Jewish national home. In 1928, leaders of the two main Palestinian political factions agreed to pursue the idea of a legislative council, and Arab support for such a body increased in the early 1930s, mainly as a means of putting a lid on Jewish immigration. It was precisely for this reason that most Zionists opposed the idea of a joint legislative council.

3. The British commission of inquiry that investigated the causes and events of the 1929 disturbances.

4. The Seventh Palestine-Arab Congress was convened in Jerusalem in June 1928.

44

Platform (1942)

IHUD

In 1942, as news of the genocide of European Jewry penetrated the consciousness of the Yishuv and American Jewry, most Zionists reacted by demanding full-blown Jewish statehood in Palestine. Their reasoning, reflected in the Biltmore Program, was that nothing short would provide a guaranteed refuge for the survivors. A small group of prominent Zionists, however, responded differently, by stressing the need for a binational, Jewish–Arab state in Palestine as part of an Arab federation. Nothing short, they argued, would guarantee a bloody and endless war with the Arabs.

This latter approach was that of Ihud. Ideologically, Ihud was a successor to Brit Shalom, but it was more politically active, both within Palestine and in the international arena. Counting at most two hundred members, Ihud gained attention through the prominence of its members (e.g., philosophers Martin Buber and Ernst Simon, Rabbi Judah Magnes, Hadassah president Henrietta Szold, Yishuv leader and writer Moshe Smilansky). Ihud members were condemned by both mainstream Zionists and Palestinian nationalists: the former for being willing to cede the principles of a Jewish majority and Jewish statehood in Palestine; the latter for insisting on ongoing Jewish rights and needs in the wake of the Holocaust for immigration to the future binational state.

As this document demonstrates, Ihud was influenced by not only Jewish–Arab strife in Palestine but also the cataclysmic events of World War II and striving to create a strong, viable international body to prevent future war.

Source: Yosef Gorny, *Mediniyut ve-Dimyon: Tokhniyot Federaliyot ba-Mahashavah ha-Medinit ha-Tsiyonit 1917–1948* (Jerusalem: Yad Ben-Zvi and ha-Sifriyah Ha-Tsiyonit, 1993), 188–90. Used with permission. Translated by Marganit Weinberger-Rotman.

The purpose of this brochure is to present to the Jewish public the facts about Ihud, its inception, and its objectives. We do not wish to engage in a meaningless debate with that part of the Palestinian press that incites against us and tries to silence our voice. Our purpose is to tell the truth to those in the Yishuv and in Jewry who, like us, agonize over what happens in this country, and to humanity in general, and those, like us, who are trying to forge a new pathway to a new world. Readers of *Problems of the Day* [1] are familiar with the tenets of the Ihud Association. Dr. Y. L. Magnes [2] has published four articles there describing the situation in Palestine viewed against the background of world events. In his last article, he raised the banner of "union," [ihud], first used by Abraham Lincoln. In order to promulgate this idea, a group of people has now convened, and this brochure presents their platform.

Our basic tenet is that we cannot triumph over the catastrophe now engulfing the world, unless we reject the unbridled nationalistic idea for a vision of cooperation and unity between nations, as expressed by President Roosevelt's "Four Freedoms." [3] The unchecked egotism of a single nation is bound to lead to wars and further devastation, if not to total annihilation.

In the world at large, we are now witnessing the awakening of a strong movement seeking a real new order—not Hitler's sham "new order," which was only slavery. Nations are admitting their mistakes and repent their past sins. This movement is particularly prominent in the United States of America. Its spokesmen, Roosevelt, Hull, [4] Wallace, [5] all speak in this vein. They emphasize that the US has made a grievous mistake in thinking only of its own interests and not about its obligation to the rest of humanity. The world must be rid of the tyranny of isolationism and narrow nationalism and replace it with cooperation between nations. In this issue we bring you testimonies to these ideas expressed by the leaders of the Allies. We see in these concepts a ray of sunshine in these dark days of human history. This movement, seeking true liberty, is also the only hope for freedom and happiness for small nations, Israel among them.

As a small group of Jews in a country remote from the centers of the world, we do not presume to make declarations for the whole world. We cannot be leaders and guides to all mankind, but we believe that it behooves all nations of the world to participate in this political and spiritual revolution, not to wait for others to bail them out. We call upon the Jewish Yishuv and the Zionist movement to wake up and, as free agents, to join the united universal movement. The pioneers of the new world are sailing toward new horizons; we, the Israeli pioneers in the Land of Israel, should not allow ourselves to be mired in provincial, narrow-minded policies, which may jeopardize our future and progress and isolate us from the vital forces of the Diaspora and from the best and brightest of the free world who are our only allies today.

We do not subscribe to the notion that only our nationality is sacred and worth preserving while battling against everyone else, including our friends. We see in the idea of unity—in Israel, in the Semitic world, in the entire free world—a means of salvation. Only unity and cooperation will bring long-lasting peace and happiness; only unity and cooperation will safeguard the essential national interests of the Jewish people.

At present, our main task is to take part in the war against the Nazis and their allies. Perhaps at the moment, no significant change is expected in the political arena, but we must prepare for the future, and it is quite possible that this future is closer than we think. Some in the British Parliament are saying that certain organizations are advocating a civil war in this country intending to conquer it by force in order to give it to the Jews; we deem this utter nonsense. No responsible nationalistic Jew would come up with such an idea, which is bound to bring disaster on the country and on the entire Zionist enterprise. The only way to ensure the future of the Land of Israel is by unity; we must redouble our efforts to enlist the help of those united nations that, after victory, will decide the shape of the world. We must prepare hearts and minds for that day; to lay the foundation for a radical change in international relations—these are the articles of faith of Ihud.

Ihud's Platform

The Ihud Association maintains connection to

a. The Zionist movement sharing its desire to establish a Jewish homeland in the Land of Israel.
b. The international movement that aspires to establish a new world order based on unity of nations, large and small, which will guarantee liberty, justice, and freedom from fear, oppression, and poverty.

In this spirit, the association approaches the fundamental questions of our country with hope for a unity between the Jewish and the Arab nations. We will seek ways for the Jewish world and the Arab world to cooperate in all aspects of life, social, economic, cultural, and political—for a renaissance of the Semitic world.

The major political aspirations of the "union" association are

a. Creating a political system based upon equal rights for both peoples.
b. Securing the support of the expanding Yishuv and the entire Jewish people for a federative union of the Middle East that includes the Land of Israel, which will guarantee the rights of all its member nations.
c. Creating an alliance between this federative union and the Anglo-American union as part of an alliance of all free nations, when it comes into being.

This alliance of free nations, acting as the highest authority, will be responsible for establishing and maintaining proper international relations in the new postwar world.

The association will work together with various groups represented in the Jewish–Arab League for Rapprochement and Cooperation;[6] it is also willing to work with other institutions and organizations in other areas.

NOTES

1. Between 1940 and 1942, this was the organ of the New Aliyah Party, which drew on recent Central European immigrants. In 1944 it became formally associated with the Ihud.

2. Judah Leon Magnes (1877–1948) was a prominent American Reform rabbi, the first rector of the Hebrew University, and a binational activist.

3. As laid out in President Franklin D. Roosevelt's speech of January 6, 1941, all humans have inalienable freedoms of speech and religion, as well as freedom from want and fear.

4. Cordell Hull (1871–1955) was a long-serving secretary of state under Roosevelt and a central figure behind the founding of the United Nations.

5. Henry Wallace (1888–1965), a prominent progressive politician, was vice president in Roosevelt's third term and held cabinet positions both before and after.

6. Brit Shalom dissolved in 1921, but much of its ideological legacy survived in the Jewish–Arab League for Rapprochement and Cooperation, which was founded in 1939. Like Ihud, the league's supporters came from not only Brit Shalom but also radical Zionist parties such as Ha-Shomer Ha-Tsa'ir.

45

On the Iron Wall (1923)

VLADIMIR JABOTINSKY

"On the Iron Wall" became one of the cornerstones of Zionist Revisionist thought. It was one of the first instances in which a Zionist leader addressed the Arab question in Palestine from a political and national perspective. The article underscored Jabotinsky's belief that force and military power should be at the core of the Zionist movement's policies, and it revealed his aversion to any sort of political or ideological compromise. (On Jabotinsky see document 23.) The article first appeared in *Rassvet* (Dawn), an émigré Jewish-Russian periodical, which was published in Berlin and later in Paris, and which Jabotinsky headed between 1922 and 1934.

Contrary to the good rule of beginning an article with the crux of the matter, I have to begin this one with an introduction, and a personal one too. The author of these lines is considered an enemy of the Arabs, a proponent of driving them out, etc. This is not true. My emotional attitude toward the Arabs is the same as to any other peoples—respectful indifference. My political attitude is dictated by two principles. First, I consider driving the Arabs out of Palestine, in whatever form, absolutely impossible; there will always be two peoples in Palestine. Second, I am proud of belonging to the group that formulated the Helsingfors Program.[1] We formulated it not for the Jews alone but for all peoples, and its basis is the equal rights of nations. Like everyone else, I am ready to swear, on

Source: *Rassvet* 42–43 (November 4, 1923). Translated by Denis Kozlov.

behalf of ourselves and our descendants, that we will never violate these equal rights and will never attempt driving out or oppressing [the Arabs]. As the reader can see, this credo is quite peaceful. However, the question of whether it is possible to achieve peaceful aims by peaceful means lies in a totally different dimension. Because this depends not on our attitude to the Arabs but instead exclusively on the attitude of the Arabs to Zionism.

Following this introduction, let us move to the crux of the matter.

I.

Voluntary reconciliation between the Palestinian Arabs and us is absolutely out of the question, whether now or in a foreseeable future. I state this conviction so harshly not because I like frustrating good people, but rather simply because they will not be frustrated: all those good people, except for those blind from birth, have long since realized themselves the complete impossibility of getting voluntary consent from the Arabs of Palestine to the transformation of that Palestine from an Arabic country into a country with a Jewish majority.

Every reader has a certain general idea of the history of colonization in other countries. I propose that he recall all the cases he knows; and let him, having gone through the entire list, find a single case when colonization proceeded upon the consent of the natives. There has never been such a case. Natives, be they cultured or uncultured, have always stubbornly fought against colonizers, be those cultured or uncultured. And the way the colonizer acted had no impact whatsoever on how the natives viewed him. The companions of Cortes or Pizarro or, for example, our forefathers in the days of Joshua ben Nun, behaved like robbers; however, the English and Scottish "father pilgrims," the first true pioneers of North America, were invariably people of highest moral pathos who would not want to hurt a fly, let alone a redskin, and who earnestly believed that the prairie had enough room for the whites and for the reds. Yet the natives fought equally furiously against good and bad colonizers. The question of whether the country had a lot of free land was of no significance either. In 1921, there were estimated 340,000 redskins in the United States; but even in better times, not more than three-quarters of a million of them lived in the entire colossal territory from Labrador to the Rio Grande. There was no one in the world then with an imagination strong enough to foresee, in earnest, the danger of newcomers "driving out" the natives. The natives fought not because they were consciously and definitely afraid of being driven out, but rather because no colonization, nowhere, never, and for no native, is ever acceptable.

Every native people, be it civilized or savage, regards its country as its national home, where it wants to be and ever to stay complete master; and it will not let in voluntarily not only new masters but even new companions or economic partners.

This refers to the Arabs as well. Conciliators among us try to convince us that the Arabs are either fools who could be duped by a milder formulation of our true goals, or a venal tribe that will yield its primacy in Palestine to us for some cultural or economic benefits. I categorically refuse to share this view of the Palestinian Arabs. Culturally they lag 500 years behind us; spiritually they have neither our endurance nor our willpower; but this is where our internal differences end. They are just as good psychologists as we are; and just as us, they have been raised by centuries of intricate disputation [*pilpul*]: whatever we tell them, they understand the depths of our souls just as well as we understand theirs. And they treat Palestine at least with the same instinctive love and organic jealousy as the Aztecs treated their Mexico or the Sioux treated their prairie. The fantasy that they will voluntary agree to the realization of Zionism in exchange for cultural or material conveniences, which the Jewish colonizer will bring them—this childish fantasy comes, with our "Arabo-philes," from a certain preconceived contempt of the Arabic people, from a certain sweeping image of this race as venal rabble ready to give away their motherland for a good network of railroads. This image is completely unfounded. They say that individual Arabs are frequently venal, but that does not mean that the Palestinian Arabs as a whole are capable of selling their zealous patriotism, which even the Papuans did not sell. Every people struggles against colonizers, as long as there is at least a spark of hope for getting rid of the threat of colonization. Palestinian Arabs act and will act that way as well, as long as they retain at least a spark of hope.

II.

Many among us keep thinking naively that a certain misunderstanding has happened; that the Arabs have not understood us, and that is the only reason why they are against us; but if one could explain them what modest intentions we have, then they would stretch out their hand to us. That is a mistake, which has already been proven many times. Let me remind you of one case among many. Some three years ago Mr. Sokolow,[2] while he was in Palestine, delivered a long speech there about this very misunderstanding. He proved it clearly how badly mistaken the Arabs were if they thought that we were going to take their property away, to expel them, or to oppress them; we do not even want a Jewish government, we only want a government representing the League of Nations. To this speech, the Arab newspaper *Al-Carmel*[3] responded with an editorial, the idea of which I cite from memory but accurately enough. The Zionists need not to worry: there is no misunderstanding. Mr. Sokolow is telling the truth, but the Arabs understand it perfectly without his assistance. Of course, the Zionists do not currently dream either of driving the Arabs out, or of oppressing the Arabs, or of a Jewish government; of course they presently want only one thing: that the Arabs not impede their immigration. The Zionists promise that they will immigrate only in numbers that the economic capacity of Palestine allows. But the Arabs have never doubted that: look, this is a truism; otherwise immigration does not make sense. The Arab editor is even ready to admit that the economic capacity of Palestine is very large, i.e., that the country can accommodate any number of Jews without driving a single Arab out. The Zionists want "only that"—and this is precisely what the Arabs do not want. Because then the Jews will become a majority; and then a Jewish government will naturally emerge; and then the fate of the Arabic minority will depend on the good will of the Jews; and Jews themselves tell very eloquently how uncomfortable it is to be a minority. Therefore, there is no misunderstanding. The Jews want only one thing—freedom of immigration; and that Jewish immigration is precisely what the Arabs do not want.

This reasoning by the Arab editor is so simple and clear that it would be worth learning it by heart and making it a basis, from now on, for all our deliberations on the Arab question. The problem is by far not in whose words—those of Herzl or those of Samuel[4]—we will explain our efforts of colonization. Colonization itself carries its own explanation, the only one, inseparable and clear to each healthy Jew and each healthy Arab. Colonization can have only one goal; for the Palestinian Arabs this goal is unacceptable; all this is in the very nature of things, and to change this nature is impossible.

III.

Many consider the following plan very attractive: to have Zionism recognized not by the Palestinian Arabs, since that is impossible, but rather by the rest of the Arabic world, including Syria, Mesopotamia, and Hedjaz, if not Egypt itself. Even if this were conceivable, it still would not change the principal situation: in Palestine itself the Arabs would keep treating us the same way. The unification of Italy was once purchased at a price of, among other clauses, Trento and

Trieste staying under the Austrian power; yet not only did the Italian inhabitants of Trento and Trieste not reconcile themselves to this, but rather they redoubled their efforts in struggle against Austria. Even if it were possible (which I doubt) to persuade the Arabs of Baghdad and Mecca that Palestine is for them no more than a small insignificant hinterland; even then, for the Palestinian Arabs, Palestine would still be not a hinterland but rather their only mother-land, the center and bulwark of their own national existence. Therefore, in that case as well, colonization would have to be carried out against the will of the Palestinian Arabs; that is, in the same conditions as today.

But an agreement with the non-Palestinian Arabs is also an unrealistic dream. In order for the Arabic nationalists of Baghdad, Mecca, and Damascus to agree paying us such a serious price as would be, for them, abandoning the maintenance of the Arabic nature of Palestine — that is, the land that lies at the very center of the "federation" and cuts it in two — in order for that to happen, we must offer them an extraordinarily valuable equivalent. Clearly, there are only two forms of such an equivalent: either money or political help, or both together. But we cannot offer them either the one or the other. As for money, it is ridiculous to think that we will be able to finance Mesopotamia or Hedjaz when we do not even have enough for Palestine. It is clear for a child that these countries, with their cheap labor, will find capital simply on the market, and they will find it much more easily than we will for Palestine. All talks on this topic of material support are either childish self-delusion or negligent light-mindedness. And it would be completely negligent on our part to talk about political support for Arab nationalism. Arab nationalism aspires to the same goals as, for example, Italian nationalism did prior to 1870 — to unification and national independence. Translated into plain language, this means the ousting of England from Mesopotamia and Egypt, the ousting of France from Syria, and then perhaps also from Tunisia, Algeria, and Morocco. On our part, helping this at least remotely would be at the same time suicidal and treacherous. Our basis is the English Mandate; and France has signed the Balfour Declaration in San Remo.[5] We cannot participate in a political intrigue whose goal is to drive England away from the Suez Canal and to annihilate France completely as a colonial power. Not only is it impermissible to play such a double game, it is impermissible even to think about it. We will be crushed — with all due shame — before we can even move in this direction.

To conclude: we cannot offer any compensation for Palestine either to the Palestinian or to any other Arabs. Therefore, a voluntary agreement is impossible. Therefore, people who consider such an agreement a *conditio sine qua non* of Zionism, may already now say, *non*, and abandon Zionism. Our colonization should either stop or continue against the will of the native population. And this is why it may continue and develop only under the protection of a force independent of the local population—an iron wall, through which the local population cannot break.

This is the essence of our entire policy toward the Arabs: not only "should it be the essence," but also it is indeed the essence, no matter how hypocritical we may be about it. What for is the Balfour Declaration? What for is the Mandate? Their meaning for us is that a foreign power has taken an obligation to create in the country such conditions of governance and security, under which the local population, however much it desires that, would not be able to obstruct our colonization, administratively or physically. And we all, without exception, daily urge that power to fulfill those obligations firmly and relentlessly. In this respect, there is no substantial difference between our "militarists" and our "vegetarians." Some prefer an iron wall to be made of Jewish bayonets; others prefer it to be made of Irish bayonets; others still, the proponents of an agreement with Baghdad, are ready to be satisfied with Baghdad bayonets (a strange and risky taste); yet all of us solicit the iron wall day and night. However, at the same time we, for some reason, undermine our own cause by proclamations about an agreement, trying to persuade the mandatory that the problem is not in the iron wall but rather in yet more and more talks. These proclamations ruin our cause; and therefore discrediting them, showing their illusory nature and their insincerity, is not only a pleasure but a duty as well.

IV.

The question is not exhausted, and I will come back to some of its aspects in the next article. Yet here I deem it necessary to make two more comments.

First of all, to the run-down reproach that the above standpoint is unethical, I respond: this is not true. It is one or the other: either Zionism is moral or it is immoral. We were to resolve this issue for ourselves before we took the first shekel. And we resolved it positively. And if Zionism is moral, which means just, then justice has to be done, regardless of anyone's agreement or disagreement. And if A, B, or C want to obstruct by force the rendition of justice, because they find it unprofitable for themselves, then it is necessary stand in their way, also by force. This is the ethic, and no other ethic exists.

Secondly, all this does not mean that *no* agreement is possible with the Palestinian Arabs. It is only *voluntary* agreement that is impossible. As long as the Arabs have a spark of hope to get rid of us, they will not sell this hope for any sweet words or any nutritious sandwiches, precisely because they are not rabble but rather a people, very backward, yet living. A living people yields in such enormous, fatal issues only when no single loophole is visible in the iron wall. It is only then that the radical groups, whose slogan is "never ever," lose their charm and influence passes over to moderate groups. Only then will those moderates approach us offering concessions; only then will they honestly bargain with us about practical issues, such as a guarantee against expulsion, or equal rights, or national peculiarities; and I believe and hope that then we will be able to give them such guarantees, which will assuage them; and the two peoples will be able to live side by side peacefully and in an orderly fashion. Yet the only way to such an agreement is the iron wall, i.e., the strengthening, in Palestine, of an authority inaccessible to any Arab influences, i.e., exactly that against which the Arabs are fighting. In other words, the only way for us to an agreement in the future is absolute rejection of all attempts at an agreement in the present.

NOTES

1. The Helsingfors (Helsinki) Program, which Jabotinsky helped draft, addressed both general Russian political issues as well as Jewish political concerns. The program advocated liberalizing Russian politics by introducing universal, secret ballots in the election of government officials. The program asserted the principle of states as federations of autonomous national groups. On the Jewish front, the Helsingfors Program called on the Russian government to recognize the Jewish nation as well as the right of Jews to self-administer various aspects of Jewish life. The program called among other things for the creation of a Jewish national assembly; the right to use Hebrew and Yiddish in Jewish institutions; and for recognizing the Sabbath as the Jews' day of rest.

2. Nahum Sokolow (1859–1936) was a Zionist leader, author, and journalist. Born to a rabbinic family in Poland, he began writing for the Hebrew paper *Ha-Tsefirah* at the age of seventeen (he later became the paper's editor and co-owner). In 1906, Sokolow became the secretary general of the World Zionist Congress. In 1921, he was elected chairperson of the Zionist Executive, and from 1931 until 1935 he served as president of the Zionist Organization.

3. *Al-Carmel* was an Arabic weekly newspaper that was founded in 1908 by Najib Nassar, with the stated purpose of opposing Zionist colonization and alerting the Arab public inside and outside Palestine of the dangers posed by the Jewish national movement. In 1911, the paper published a sixteen-part series called "Zionism: Its History, Objective, and Importance."

4. Herbert Samuel (1870–1963), a British Jew and a supporter of the Zionist movement, was appointed High Commissioner of Palestine in 1920 and served in that post until 1925. While his appointment drew sharp criticism from the British military leaders in Palestine, Samuel's tenure was marked by his efforts at neutrality in dealing with the Arab and Jewish communities.

5. The San Remo Conference (April 19–26, 1920) was a meeting of the Allied Supreme Council and attended by the prime ministers of Britain, France, and the host country Italy. The conference approved the framework of a peace treaty with Turkey, and it determined the allocation of Class A League of Nations Mandates over previously Ottoman-ruled regions of the Middle East.

46

On Militarism (1929)

VLADIMIR JABOTINSKY

This article reveals the great importance that Jabotinsky attributed to the virtues of militarism in achieving the goals of Zionism. Unlike the political and historical consideration that informed his analysis in "On the Iron Wall," in this article Jabotinsky does not explore so much the practical benefits of militarism to the Jewish national movement, but rather the type of qualities—order, discipline, strength, decorum—that militarism cultivates among the youth. One of the key terms that Jabotinsky employed in his writings was *Hadar* (splendor or glory in Hebrew). Jabotinsky wanted the members of Betar to develop a sense of Hadar—or as he wrote in Betar's anthem: "Hadar, a Hebrew if noble, if poor, if slave, if a simple man, was created a king, crowned in David's glory." Militarism (and militaristic education), according to Jabotinsky, was one of the prime means to develop Hadar among the Zionist youth—to instill in them the type of confidence and resolve that would be essential in the struggle for national liberation.

Militarism is a despicable word. But grownup people must not recoil from the sound of a word and should be required to analyze every concept and distinguish between its good and bad attributes. War is bad; it is the killing of young innocent souls. On this we are all agreed, and we hope that one day war will be unacceptable, just as in every civilized country cannibalism is unacceptable today, as

Source: *Haynt*, January 25, 1929, from Ze'ev Jabotinsky, *Ketavim, ba-derech la-medinah* (Jerusalem, 1959), 39–46. Translated by Marganit Weinberger-Rotman.

well as physical torture, which used to be the norm before the French Revolution. But is this really the only meaning of military life?

If this were the case, then all of humanity, or at least liberal humanity, would detest anything that has to do with military life. But lo and behold: even the most conscientious pacifists, the most extreme left-wingers are wont to use typically militaristic images: the "Salvation Army," which helps many unfortunate men and women alienated by society, calls itself an "army," with lieutenants, majors, and troops of soldiers marching as to war. Every progressive movement uses concepts such as "front," "trenches," and "standing guard" although metaphorically, but it is still military terminology. This surely proves that not everything about military life is despicable and objectionable. In everyday life, we do not normally use words borrowed from the terminology of slaughter-houses or brothels, because those are truly ugly and reprehensible, even when used only rhetorically in a discussion of some idealistic aspiration. But all idealistic movements derive at least half of their technical vocabulary and three-quarters of their propaganda rhetoric from military life. Which proves that it is not all that bad.

The truth is that only war is ugly; military life per se has many beautiful aspects that unfortunately are lacking in civilian life. First and foremost is the uniformity of army life, its spartan simplicity, and the equality between rich and poor. Second, the hygiene, outdoor life, and physical training; and third, military discipline, which requires further elaboration.

Quite often we repeat opinions that we no longer really hold. For example, ask an average person how he/she feels about military discipline, and you're likely to hear: "Fooey! They turn human beings into machines!" But in fact that same person will evince great enthusiasm when watching a troop marching in unison, like a well-oiled machine.

I have often quoted, both orally and in writing, a chapter from Masaryk's[1] memoirs (I no longer remember when or where I read it), but it is worth repeating again. It has to do with the first demonstration of the Czech youth movement Sokol,[2] which Masaryk, as a young man, saw in Prague. Several thousand youths stood in formation on the town square, keeping equal distance, like chess pieces on a board, all wearing uniforms and keeping completely still. Then their leader blew a whistle and they all stretched their left arms and right legs. Nothing more. They executed it in unison, like a perfect machine. Masaryk comments that he had never in his life been so impressed by national unity and the power of spiritual unity, when he witnessed his people capable of such performance.

It is a well-known fact that you can infect (at least for a moment) even the worst assimilationist with national, Jewish enthusiasm by using a simple measure:

take a few hundred Jewish youths, dress them in uniform and march them in perfect formation, all locked in one step, "like a machine." Nothing impresses us like the ability of a crowd of people to feel and act in unison, with one will and one tempo. This is the essential difference between a "crowd," a "mob," and a nation.

I do not claim that Tsar Nicholas I, in whose army's parades the soldiers could hardly breathe, transformed his troops into superior beings. In general, my comments refer only to organizations that are voluntary and not coercive (like real military regiments), organizations like the aforementioned Czech Sokol, or any sports association where a member may leave the group at any time. This is very different from a coercive organization, where a person is forced to become a part of the machine, by means of intimidation, torture, or imprisonment. In a voluntary organization, a person is motivated to join by a certain mood or desire, and forces himself to learn new techniques of standing, marching, etc., as part of a general structure. This is the basic difference between coercion and self-discipline: the former can be applied even to wild beasts, while the latter can be achieved only in an atmosphere of perfect civility.

There is another attribute of military discipline that typically merits negative reaction, even though we all know how much we, Jews, lack this quality in all aspects of life. I am talking about decorum and ceremony, the proper way to stand, greet, talk to friends and superiors. We, Jews, are deficient in form and proper etiquette. In the old ghetto, there were typical, though idiosyncratic, social customs, but lately, we have lost those customs, yet have not replaced them with new ones. The average Jew does not have any particular manners of walking, dressing, eating, and relating to others. This is especially lacking when it comes to respecting hierarchy, dealing with "foreign dignitary," or even a fellow Jewish "hero." Even when he wishes to show deference, he does not know how to do so without loss of self-respect, and the result often comes across as either impudence or excessive obsequiousness. But our lack of manners and ceremony is manifested in other areas as well, even in purely spiritual matters. Listen to a sermon by an old preacher in a synagogue. In wisdom he may be superior to gentile philosophers, but he is incapable of pursing a topic from start to finish: he jumps from subject to theme to theme, and what's worse is that this style actually finds favor in his listeners' eyes. They no longer have a need for orderliness, consistency, and they have lost the ability to discriminate between first and last in importance. [. . .]

Obviously, this cannot be achieved by taking shortcuts. At first, there may be some overreaching. The cult of physical fitness can sometimes, especially at first, lead to irresponsible and unnecessary use of force. It may encourage at first an excessive tendency to tasteless, gaudy uniforms. This is unwelcome but understandable as a phenomenon of young movements. The Enlightenment, too, at first had some unpleasant manifestations. Our fathers told us how they would hold literary parties on Yom Kippur merely to annoy their own grand-parents. And yet the Enlightenment movement made of us what we are today — modern, educated people, capable of creating a nation.

We must be patient, especially where youth is concerned; we should not be deterred by Latin words, even when the word is militarism. Hatred of wars is the spiritual legacy of our people: our Prophets were the first to denounce mass killing, and we all adhere to their teaching. Nobody wants to foster a generation that thirsts for war. But in an education that some critics can dub "militaristic," there is yet some aspects that can help us raise a better and healthier generation.

And this is the main point.

NOTES

1. Tomás Garrigue Masaryk was Czechoslovakia's first president after that country achieved independence in the aftermath of the First World War. Masaryk was well-disposed toward Jews, and he visited Palestine in 1927. The kibbutz Kafr Masaryk, which was founded in 1940, was named after him, as well as several streets and squares throughout Israel.

2. The Sokol was a Czech youth movement and gymnastics organization that was established in Prague in 1862.

SECTION V

Arthur Szyk, "Jewish Soldiers," 1942 (reproduced with the cooperation of The Arthur Szyk Society, Burlingame, CA, www.szyk.org)

WORLD WAR II,
THE HOLOCAUST, AND
THE YISHUV

s in 1914, so in 1939 Palestine became part of a Middle Eastern theater of war. The German-Italian Axis vied with an alliance of Britain, France, and, after June 1941, Russia for control over a vast territory from North Africa into Central Asia. Unlike the previous conflict, where the Allies gained Arab support by encouraging rebellion against their Ottoman rulers, this time around the Allies themselves were the rulers and thus liable to be perceived as the enemy. In order to assuage Arab anger over ongoing British control over Palestine, the British further tightened immigration restrictions by the 75,000 per year figure set forth in the 1939 White Paper. During the war, only about 50,000 Jews immigrated to Palestine, and at least 16,000 of them were smuggled in by sea by the Haganah, the Revisionists, and other groups. The British authorities were zealous in their attempts to prevent ships laden with Jewish refugees from entering Palestine. These efforts led to great tragedies, such as that of the *Struma*, which in February 1942 foundered at sea, killing all but one of the 768 on board.

Despite their coldness to the suffering of European Jewry, the British did much during the war to develop the economic and military infrastructure of the Yishuv. This occurred in response to British self-interest, not a change of heart toward Zionism. Palestine's central location in the Middle Eastern theater made it an industrial and commercial hub, and many Yishuv industries were placed on a war footing. Moreover, the Yishuv, with its educated and skilled population, much of which had military training, was a valuable manpower reserve for the British army.

After initial attempts to suppress the Haganah and imprison its commanders, the British military realized that the militia was needed in the increasingly desperate battle against Axis forces in the Middle East. In the spring of 1941, there was a meeting of minds between the Haganah, which wanted to beef up its forces in preparation for an Axis invasion of Palestine, and the British, who needed reconnaissance specialists for the upcoming Allied invasion of Vichy-controlled Syria. The result was the formation of the Yishuv's first permanently mobilized military force, the Palmach. (The Palmach operated within the framework of the Haganah and was responsible to the Haganah national command.) Palmach members served with distinction in Syria and Libya. The British also made use of Irgun members. In May 1941, the Irgun commander David Raziel died while fighting against an anti-British revolt in Iraq.

When the war broke out, the Jewish Agency, Haganah, and Irgun proclaimed support for the British struggle against Nazism. They not only saw Hitler as a terrible and common enemy, but they also believed that assistance to the British would result, after the war, in the rescinding of the 1939 White Paper. To that end, Weizmann demanded the formation of a separate Jewish army within the British forces. The British had no qualms about integrating recruits from the Yishuv into the British army, and they created de facto British battalions in Palestine, but the formation of a Jewish Brigade was delayed until 1944. More frustrating, the British attempted to disband the Palmach and suppress the Haganah after the Axis threat in Egypt and Palestine passed with the defeat of Nazi commander Erwin Rommel's North African forces at El-Alamein in late 1942.

During the first three years of the war, the residents of the Yishuv feared for their very existence. They anxiously followed the Axis' eastward advance across North Africa. Italian bombers attacked Tel Aviv and Haifa, killing more than one hundred Jews and Arabs. Jewish volunteerism for the British forces, however, was low, as many Jews wanted to defend Palestine rather than be sent abroad. As the threat to the Yishuv passed, there was even less of a motive to volunteer, but in June 1942 the British imposed a general conscription order, which the Jewish Agency was obliged to supervise. Some zealous Zionist activists beat up draft dodgers or doused them with castor oil, a punishment previously devised by the Italian fascists against their opponents. While approximately 20,000 Jews went off to war, the rest of the Yishuv lived more quietly than in many years. There were few clashes with Arabs, as the Palestinian leadership had been left in disarray after the Arab revolt. (Amin al-Husayni had been sent into exile, and from 1942 on he lived in Berlin, broadcasting anti-British propaganda to the Arab world and mobilizing Arab and Balkan Muslims into the Axis armies.) In the resulting power vacuum, a relatively modern and moderate political party, Istiqlal (Independence), gained influence. The Palestinian economy benefited from the war as a source of raw materials for British forces. And there was a general feeling that whatever the outcome, the post-war environment would favor the Arabs.

This respite in Jewish–Arab tensions did little to calm the Yishuv, however, as news of Nazi massacres against Jews filtered into Palestine. On November 27, 1942, the

Yishuv's National Council declared three days of public mourning for the Jewish dead in Europe. Grim reports of mass murder darkened the public mood during the remainder of the war. Some young kibbutzniks advocated the formation of "ghetto-busting squads" that would send the Yishuv's finest young men to Europe to engage in heroic rescue operations. Similar demands came from members of the Revisionist youth organization Betar. Ben-Gurion believed, however, that the Jewish Agency's limited funds should be allocated for the strengthening of the Yishuv and preparation for statehood, not engaging in rescue missions of dubious value. When, in 1944, he authorized the dropping of Haganah paratroopers in Eastern Europe, he had in mind not rescue but rather public relations. He hoped this dangerous mission's volunteers, the most famous of whom was the young Hungarian Zionist Hanna Szenes, would convince Holocaust survivors of the Zionist movement's concern for them and win their allegiance in the postwar struggle for statehood.

The Yishuv leadership has been criticized for not giving its all to thwart or mitigate the Nazi genocide. They should have done more, it is argued, to publicize the Holocaust in the international arena, promote immigration, and engage in rescue operations. We should keep in mind that until late 1942 the Yishuv's main concern was its own survival, and by then, the Nazi killing machine had been operating for more than a year and as many of two-thirds of the Holocaust's victims were already dead. Moreover, there is little that a half-million Jews in Palestine could have done to rescue substantial numbers of Jews trapped in distant, Nazi-occupied Europe.

Thus the main Zionist response to the unfolding disaster in Europe was to prepare for Jewish statehood. In May 1942, an emergency Zionist conference convened at New York's Biltmore Hotel and demanded immediate Jewish sovereignty for Jews in all of Palestine. This rejection of partition represented a triumph for Ben-Gurion and the American Zionist leader Abba Hillel Silver against the aging Chaim Weizmann. Weizmann continued to negotiate with the British for a favorable partition agreement, but in 1944 the Jewish Agency and the Yishuv's Representative Assembly firmly declared their rejection of anything less than statehood in the entirety of Palestine.

In that same year the Irgun called for a revolt against the British presence in Palestine. The Irgun had grown during the war owing to an influx of Jewish soldiers who had fled Nazi-occupied Poland, enlisted in the Allied armed forces, and been shipped to Palestine. With some 2,000 members, the Irgun launched a number of attacks, some lethal, against British installations in Palestine. Its new commander was Menachem Begin, former leader of Betar in Poland and a longtime opponent of Jabotinsky's emphasis on diplomacy and condemnation of terrorism. Under Begin's command, the Irgun broke ties with the Revisionist New Zionist Organization. Even further removed from Jabotinsky's worldview and the Revisionist movement was a splinter group led by Avraham Stern, which as early as 1940 had declared itself unwilling to declare a truce with the British because of the war against Germany. For eighteen months, the "Stern Gang" attacked British officials and supported itself through crime, including robbing the Histadrut's Workers' Bank. Stern was killed by the British in 1942, but in the following year some of his followers created a new underground movement known as Lehi. Its leaders were Yitzhak Jezrnitsky (Shamir), Nathan Friedman (Yellin-Mor), and Israel Scheib (Eldad). Lehi believed that all means, including assassination, had to be employed to expel the British. Such thinking led in November 1944 to the assassination of Lord Moyne, the British minister-resident in Cairo, by two members of a local Lehi cell.

Lehi's ideology was a strange brew of fascism and communism, racism and universalism. Its ideology was eccentric and its acts of violence spectacular. Ben-Gurion saw the Irgun as the far greater threat, however, because it was much larger and because he mistakenly believed it was the military arm of his political rivals, the Revisionists. Thus the Haganah focused on the Irgun when, in the wake of the Moyne assassination, it collaborated with the British in their crackdown against Jewish underground organizations.

Not only the underground militias but the Yishuv as a whole was radicalized by the war. Unlike World War I, which left the Yishuv depleted, this war had invigorated the Yishuv both economically and militarily. The Holocaust inspired the international Zionist movement and Yishuv leadership in the subsequent battle for a Jewish state.

In this section, documents 47 through 49 depict the anxiety and sense of impending destruction that faced the Yishuv during the first three years of the war. Documents 50 through 52 present the founding, operations, and ethos of the Palmach. Document 53 offers insight into the Zionist leadership's thinking about the relationship between the war and long-term Zionist goals. Documents 54 and 55 contrast the views of the Irgun and the left-wing party Ha-Shomer Ha-Tsa'ir on the war and the unfolding tragedy of European Jewry. And document 56 throws light on Lehi's outlook, which was more messianic than pragmatic, and arguably as different from that of the mainstream Zionist Right as from the Zionist labor movement.

47

Diary (1940–41)

ARTHUR RUPPIN

World War II affected the Yishuv in many ways. As discussed in the introduction to this section, until late 1942 it was under threat of invasion from German forces advancing from North Africa, and it also suffered bombing by Italian aircraft. Most of the Yishuv had close family and friends in Europe and anxiously followed news of Nazi atrocities against Jews. For the most part, however, Palestine was spared the ravages of war. Its economy flourished, and Zionist leaders devoted most of their efforts to immigration, land purchase, and settlement, to the extent that British regulations introduced in the wake of the 1939 White Paper made any of these possible. The Yishuv and the Jewish world as a whole were galvanized by British refusal to allow ships crammed with Jewish refugees into Palestine.

We already encountered Arthur Ruppin, the author of this document, in document 13. During World War II, Ruppin lived in Jerusalem, where he taught sociology at the Hebrew University, and in the town of Binyamina, near Haifa. Ruppin kept a diary throughout his life, and he dutifully recorded the events of World War II and his reactions to them almost until the day of his death in 1943. Ruppin's phlegmatic, understated tone conceals neither his anxiety about the fate of European Jewry and the Yishuv nor his dogged determination to advance the Zionist settlement projects that were his life's work.

Source: Arthur Ruppin, *Briefe, Tagebücher, Erinnerungen*, ed. Schlomo Krolik (Königstein/Ts.: JüdischerVerlag, 1985), 520–29, 533–34, 537–38, 541–42. Used with permission. Translated by Erin Hochman.

Jerusalem, 25 February 1940. In the evenings over the radio in the hotel we listened to Hitler speaking, screaming, barking from Berlin, but always only repeating the old phrases about Germany's right and the devilry of its enemies. How long will this man still rule the world?

Jerusalem, 1 March 1940. The day before yesterday the government publicized the restriction of land purchases by Jews (in the Land Transfer Regulations),[1] which was already announced in the White Paper. Only in the coastal areas may Jews buy unrestrictedly. In two other zones the purchase is limited or completely forbidden. In the Executive[2] there was naturally great commotion. One had hoped until the end that Churchill's[3] influence would succeed in preventing the law. Ben-Gurion wants to resign as the chairman of the Executive.

Jerusalem, 4 March 1940. In the last days many agitated sessions regarding the new land law. The day after tomorrow it should come up in the House of Commons.

   Jewish demonstrations in the streets of Jerusalem, Tel Aviv, and Haifa. The police used their truncheons. A young man has died as a result of a blow. A curfew in Tel Aviv.

Jerusalem, 18 May 1940. The events of the war come thick and fast now—after eight months of quiet. The Germans have invaded Belgium and Holland, have breached the Maginot Line,[4] and are said to have taken Brussels and Antwerp today. Thereby, with one blow, the position of the Allies has become very grave.

   The Germans are said to have superior numbers of airplanes and tanks and attack the Allies from behind with guns that are mounted on the planes. It is said a million soldiers have been killed in action—300,000 among the Allies, 700,000 among the Germans. The cruelty of this war eclipses everything that came before. One thinks that the end of the world is near. That I nevertheless do all my usual work is the result of my fatalism, which lets me regard the political events, against which I am powerless, just like I would an earthquake.

   For the time being, we still live in Palestine as in a paradise: no rationing of food, no conscription for military service, no acts of war. But who knows how fast it can change! In Haifa, sandbags for protection against air raids already lay in front of the big buildings; also blackouts are already being tried. Jerusalem is kept comparatively safe from air raids.

Jerusalem, 30 May 1940. The last two weeks have brought new surprising events in the theater of war. The Germans have succeeded in marching through

Belgium, breaking through the French-English front, and arriving at the English Channel. Dunkirk is in their hands. The day before yesterday, King Leopold III of Belgium capitulated and the Belgian army retreated from the battlefields. The situation of the French–British troops has thus become very critical. The governments of France and England openly admit this. . . .

In Palestine, the events of the war have caused quite a panic among the Jews. One believes in Italy's early entry into the war and fears a bombardment of Haifa and Tel Aviv. Shelters are hastily prepared against aerial attacks. The exchange rates on the Tel Aviv Stock Exchange have dropped a lot; the English pound is listed in New York at $3.13 (instead of the parity of $4.86). A strong depreciation of the pound seems unavoidable because the enormous war expenditures are even too great for England. . . . . .

I fight a hard battle in the Executive in order to devote the little money that we have not for political adventures,[5] such as a new resettlement of far-out estates of the JNF [Jewish National Fund] in Beersheba, but for the strengthening (irrigation equipment) of our already established settlements.

Jerusalem, 12 June 1940. The day before yesterday, Italy declared war on the Western Powers; it was expected daily for a long time. For the time being, they still have not attacked France; in contrast, the English have closed many Italian harbors by laying mines.

The blackout in the country (also in Jerusalem) now begins already at 7:45 p.m. We have made all windows pitch-dark with shutters or curtains and can have the lights on inside and work. Only on the streets is it pitch-dark.

I do not know whether I should praise or reproach myself that I do the usual work as always in this time of catastrophe. I work every morning in the garden (where I incidentally gathered wonderful peaches not long ago and will soon have plums and pears) and manage to record the memories of my youth.

Jerusalem, 17 June 1940. When I returned this afternoon from my university lecture, Dr. Frieda Wolf told me she had heard on the English radio station at 3 p.m. that the French cabinet of Reynaud resigned and Marshall Pétain[6] has asked the Germans for peace. I threw up my hands in despair; the events followed one another with such force and rapidity that the mind cannot follow. The consequences of France's collapse are enormous. What will happen now in Syria? Can England carry on the fight alone? Will the Arabs in Palestine try to revolt? Unanswerable questions and they proliferate endlessly. What seems to stand most solidly in the world is beginning to totter; we have nothing more that we can hold on to.

Jerusalem, 20 July 1940. Land warfare in Europe has stopped. All of central and western Europe is under German control. Only by sea and in the air is the battle continued. Italian planes have also dropped bombs on the oil refineries in Haifa a few days ago and thereby have destroyed a few tanks and killed a few people. In England, admiration for Churchill and the steadfast will to carry on the war prevails.

[. . .]

Jerusalem, 10 September 1940. The air raids on London last Saturday and Sunday were much more extensive than before and have caused hundreds of deaths and more than 1,000 injured. Yesterday afternoon, Italian planes dropped bombs on Tel Aviv. Until now, it was believed here that the Italians would have only zeroed in on the oil refineries in Haifa, which they have recently bombed three times. I drove early today to Tel Aviv. It has emerged that 107 Jews have been killed and that about just as many were seriously injured. I inspected the damage for myself with a member of the Home Guard as a guide. Only rubble has remained of many small houses; the roof or the balconies of others have fallen down. Window panes were shattered within a large radius; shutters on the doors and windows hang loosely on hinges or are torn off. I attended the burial of the victims at the new cemetery by Tel Rambam. The corpses were buried in four rows side by side. A few oriental [of Middle Eastern Jewish origin] women burst into convulsive crying and bawling. The corpses of the small children were particularly horrible. Almost all the palls were bloodstained.

Three houses away from Ruth's[7] apartment, a bomb has struck the third floor and has killed three people. Ruth and Bello have luckily gotten away with no more than a fright.

One thing is clear: the war approaches our doors. According to the official news, one can hardly doubt that the Italians are preparing an attack on Palestine either from Libya or Syria.

Jerusalem, 16 September 1940. Yesterday Italian troops pushed forward from Sollum [near the Egyptian-Libyan border] over the Egyptian border and they apparently have the intention to advance toward Cairo, which is 400 km [249 mi] away. The English, for the time being, do not offer resistance, but believe that the crossing of this stretch of desert will cost the Italians many victims and that it is better to make a stand against them near Cairo. In any case, we are already in a (Middle) Eastern war.

After long negotiations with the Jewish Agency, the Palestinian government has finally agreed to assemble special Jewish (and Arab) fighting units of Palestinian volunteers; for the time being only one battalion of 400 men.[8]

The only work, which still attracts me at sixty-five, would be the activities dealing with agriculture, the growing of subtropical trees, for which I tried shoots of mangoes, avocadoes, etc. in my garden, and experiments in genetics. But will I get around to doing it? Will this war still even allow regular work?

22 September 1940. The day before yesterday the Italians bombed Haifa again. The result: around thirty Arabs killed (incidentally not a single Jew).

Rafi[9] has enlisted as a volunteer for the 400-men-strong troop, which is now employed as a Jewish fighting unit in the British Army and will depart in the next few days for the training camp in Sarafand.[10] I am sorry that he must give up the work that has become dear to him in the Institute for Economic Research,[11] but it seems to me and to him an absolute duty to make himself available for the defense of Palestine. Hanna[12] also raises no objections.

Jerusalem, 30 November 1940. For the last three weeks, the Executive was primarily busy with the fate of some 1,800 illegal refugees from Germany, Austria, and Czechoslovakia (among them is my former legal colleague Michael Mayer with his wife). After a terribly exhausting and long journey over the Danube, they had departed on two small steamboats from Sulina, were picked up by the British en route, and were escorted to Haifa. They sat for three weeks in the harbor. The government did not want to let them land, but wanted to send them to Mauritius and had to this end already transferred them to another steamship, the *Patria*. All efforts by the government here and in London to prevent this did not help. There occurred on Tuesday an explosion in a hitherto inexplicable way, and it sunk the ship in fifteen minutes. The passengers jumped into the water (the ship was in the harbor); thirty to forty died, eighty were missing, the remaining 1,500–1,600 were saved and brought to the [British internment] camp in Atlith. The local government wanted to send the people to Mauritius despite this tragedy (an incomprehensible action against all the laws of humanity!), but yesterday they agreed, apparently due to [Chaim] Weizmann's intervention with Churchill, to leave the people here. This triggered a feeling of relief by the Yishuv because many have close relatives on the ship. Thereby, one does not think of the thirty or forty victims any more.

Jerusalem, 13 December 1940. In Tel Aviv there was a strike as a protest because the government indeed allowed the surviving refugees from the Patria into Palestine (so far already more than fifty dead have been discovered), but sent another ship arriving with 1,800 refugees to Mauritius. It is really a horrible measure for those who have their relatives in Palestine. The only consolation is that it will always still be better for them in Mauritius than in Germany, Poland, or Romania.

Binyamina, 23 May 1941. In an unexpected and unprecedented way, the Germans have brought more than 1,000 soldiers to Crete with airplanes and the help of parachutes and battle British troops. The outcome of the battle is still unclear. In Syria, German planes have landed with agreement from the French (Pétain) government. They have flown further to Iraq in order to help the Iraqi rebels in the fight against England.[13] More and more, the war approaches the borders of Palestine.
　[. . .]

Jerusalem, 9 June 1941. In the last two weeks, the Germans have kept quite still and have made no new advances. On the other hand, the Free Frenchmen[14] and the English marched into Syria early yesterday because allegedly many Germans have arrived in Aleppo as tourists and have occupied the local airport/airfield. The Free Frenchmen and the English have announced to the Syrians that the French mandate is repealed and Syria is an independent state. For the time being, they seem to have found little resistance in Syria.

　On the occasion of the ceasefire with the rebels in Iraq, the English Foreign Minister Eden has delivered a declaration to the Arabs that the English government is well disposed towards the endeavors toward the creation of a greater Arab federation. Nice, but where do we Jews and the Jewish national home stand?

Jerusalem, 12 June 1941. The son of settler Shmuel Dayan from Nahalal,[15] Moshe Dayan,[16] who was recently released after a one-year imprisonment, has had an eye shot out in Syria.

　The air raid warning sounded for the first time in Jerusalem the day before yesterday, and we all went next door to the shelter at Professor Roth's house. There was again an alarm tonight, but we stayed in our beds. Nothing happened in Jerusalem, but bombs were dropped on Tel Aviv and Haifa during the night. In Tel Aviv, many Jews were killed and injured (the occupants of a home for the disabled of all people). On the other hand, no one in Haifa is said to have died or been injured.

Jerusalem, 22 June 1941. As I arrived this morning from Binyamina in Jerusalem around 11 a.m., I met Sioma Ginsberg and heard from him that (a) Germany has declared war on Russia and the German army has already invaded Russia; (b) the English have occupied Damascus. Compared with the first piece of news, the second piece seems irrelevant. The war between Germany and Russia, however, can have enormous consequences for the world.

Jerusalem, 8 December 1941. . . . The news from early this morning that Japan has declared war on America landed like a bomb. There is a rumor that already many American and Japanese warships have been sunk and that places in Hawaii were bombed. Aside from Japan's entry into the war lengthening the war's duration, the provisioning of Palestine with food and other essential items will become much more difficult. So far, we lack nothing; however, the index for goods has increased on average fifty per cent.

Just now (8:30 p.m.), I heard (very clearly) on the radio Roosevelt's speech before the Congress in Washington, in which he announced the United States to be at a state of war with Japan and requested congressional confirmation of it.

Jerusalem, 31 December 1941. The year brought no deciding turn in the war, but there is no doubt that the situation of the Allies (and a year ago that meant almost solely England) was much worse a year ago than it is today. The entry of Russia and the United States into the war has immensely strengthened the powers fighting against Germany. The danger of invasion from Syria or Libya, which still threatened Palestine during the spring of 1941, is—at least for the moment—fully averted.

Until now, Palestine has not suffered in the war. Rather, the requirements of war production, as well as the presence of a sizable English army, have given both agriculture and industry a boost, and they are in full swing. Unemployment among Jews, which a year ago amounted to 15,000, has fully disappeared. The provisioning of necessary foodstuffs was satisfactory; in fact, nothing was lacking. We live nearly as we did in peacetime. The sole exception is that butter has become rare and has been replaced with margarine, which I am already accustomed to. Prices have risen considerably; the price index is now approximately 160 against 100 in August 1939. However, the great portion of our supply comes from India, Australia, and New Zealand, and it is therefore possible that the war with Japan will hinder or reduce imports so that we will lose our privileged position in provisioning.

[. . .]

My six brothers and sisters are all in Palestine; they are spared the atrocities that Jews in countries controlled by the Nazis suffer.

[. . .]

Jerusalem, 8 November 1942. It seems that we have reached a turning point in the war. In the battle of El Alamein, the Allies have won a decisive victory in Libya. They have driven the Germans and Italians from Egypt and have taken Tobruk. Still more important is that the Americans have landed in Algiers and Morocco and have taken the city of Algiers and many other places. France has broken its diplomatic relations with the United States. My brother-in-law David Hacohen, who spent a week in Egypt and returned today, said that of Rommel's 100,000 soldiers and many hundreds of tanks, only 10,000 soldiers and twenty tanks had been saved. At any rate, there is no doubt that Palestine is currently safe from a German attack and that in general the prospects for a victorious end to the war have risen.

Jerusalem, 16 November 1942. In the morning, exams at the university. Yesterday, I had invited Ben-Gurion and Kaplan to a discussion/conversation about post-war problems and the economic capacity of Palestine. He is convinced that we will obtain very sizable sums for Palestine in the United States, provided that we can show major projects for the accommodation of millions of Jewish refugees into Palestine. Ben-Gurion has in mind an immigration of two million Jews within two years. I answered him that a final placement of two million in all sectors of the economy would take at least ten to fifteen years. A temporary placement in public works on a grand scale could reduce this period, but the costs hugely increase. I explained that we do not have enough land available to resettle a sizeable portion of the immigrants in the country. The only way out would lie in the irrigation and cultivation of the Negev. However, until now, we cannot definitely say whether and how the Negev can be irrigated. As a first step, it would be important to invite a first-class water engineer from the United States in order to get a reliable and authoritative appraisal. In this way, we could perhaps win American public opinion and President Roosevelt for the large operation, which could be carried out by the United States and other democratic powers for the benefit of the Jews. Ben-Gurion was very enthusiastic and plans to telegraph his friends in the United States. Kaplan was also in favor of inviting an American expert.

NOTES

1. The Land Transfer Regulations, published in February 1940, limited Jewish land purchase to approximately 5 percent of the territory of Mandatory Palestine. Although the permitted territories included some of Palestine's most fertile land, Zionists saw these regulations, like the 1939 White Paper as a whole, as a betrayal of the terms of the Balfour Declaration and League of Nations Mandate for Palestine.

2. The Jewish Agency for Palestine's executive committee.

3. Winston Churchill (1874–1965) was a long-time supporter of Zionism and voted against the White Paper although he was a government minister at the time. After Neville Chamberlain's resignation in May 1940, Churchill became prime minister of the United Kingdom and served in that capacity throughout the duration of the war.

4. France's defensive fortifications along the German border.

5. Political in the sense of extending the borders of future Jewish statehood by settling regions such as the northern Negev, which was distant from the Yishuv's population centers on the coast and in Jerusalem.

6. Philippe Pétain (1856–1951) was one of France's highest military commanders in World War I and was a leader of France's short-lived counterattack against the German invasion in 1940. As France fell into chaos, he became head of the French government and surrendered to Germany. He then served as head of state in a fascist regime in the unoccupied zone of southern France.

7. Ruppin's daughter.

8. The "Palestine Buffs," as this unit was called, was supposed to be an equally weighted force of Jews and Arabs. But few Arabs signed up, so in the summer of 1942 the British gave up on parity.

9. Ruppin's son.

10. A British military base in central Palestine, today an Israel Defense Force base.

11. Ruppin had founded this institute in 1932.

12. Ruppin's second wife.

13. The reference here is to the 1941 coup by the pro-Axis prime minister of Iraq, Rashid Ali al-Gaylani. The coup led to a brief Anglo-Iraqi war, which restored the Hashemite monarchy and British control.

14. The French military forces in exile, organized out of London by Charles de Gaulle.

15. The first moshav in the Jezreel Valley (1921).

16. Moshe Dayan (1915–81) was to be the future chief of staff of the Israeli Defense Force and minister of defense. He served during World War II in the Palmach (see document 50). Ruppin is referring here to the actions of a reconnaissance force of Palmach members, Arabs and Australians that on several occasions carried out missions in Lebanon, and Syria. Dayan's injury forced him to wear a black eye patch, which became his trademark.

48

Introduction to *The Book of Valor* (1941)

BERL KATZNELSON

In 1941, as the Yishuv faced an imminent threat of Nazi invasion from North Africa, Labor Zionist leader Berl Katznelson (see document 39) decided that the Histadrut's new publishing house, Am Oved, should present as its debut book an anthology of texts documenting Jewish heroism over the millennia. The goal was to inspire the members of the Yishuv to sacrifice, partly in keeping with the traditions of their ancestors, but also as a new breed of Hebrew fighter, struggling for national freedom. In the introduction to the anthology, called *The Book of Valor*, Katznelson walked a delicate line between presenting the Yishuv's situation as identical to the desperate state that characterized much of Diaspora Jewish life and as something categorically superior. He identifies certain universal features of Jewish heroism but distinguishes between desperate and constructive heroism, the latter associated with the warriors of the Hebrew Bible, the time of the Maccabees, and the Zionist Yishuv. This short piece also testifies to Katznelson's deep Judaic literacy and his fear that the Zionist project was not sufficiently cognizant of the rich textual canon of Jewish civilization.

Source: *Sefer ha-Gevurah: Antologiyah historit-sifrutit*, ed. Israel Halpern (Tel Aviv: Am Oved, 1949), 1:9–12. Translated by Marganit Weinberger-Rotman. Thanks to Yitzhak Lewis for help locating the references for note 9, 15, and 16.

Our sages maintained that knowledge that has no foundation and knows not its provenance is worthless. In modern terms we could say that a culture that has no foundation is worthless. A popular movement, if it is not ephemeral, should not be an orphan but know its father's house. "Know where you come from and where you are going"[1] is not just a moral precept but a basic need; we need to seek the roots of our being, explore our sources; even when there are no answers, we must not cease asking.

How little do we know about our past. When we lost political freedom, we also lost the freedom to write Jewish historiography.

No regime fostered our historical memory. On the contrary, almost all those who ruled over us erased, burned, destroyed, and annihilated our records. We see now what wars, expulsions, and persecutions can do to national treasures. This has always been our lot, while years of peace and tranquility were but a short respite. Every transition from one exile to another destroyed the substance of the national memory, uprooted historical traditions, broke up families, severed ties, and demolished physical and spiritual assets. What do pogrom orphans know about their history? What do refugee children remember of their family traditions? How many national treasures have sunk into oblivion together with the severed limbs that carried them? One can only marvel at the amount that survived the devastations and still exists.

There is much forgetfulness and obliteration in Jewish history. Some is caused by devastation and martyrdom, some by tyrants' decrees and the fate of the defeated. What the long arm of external censorship has not wrought, inner censorship has brought about. Do we possess one line of the literature of the Zealots?[2] Feats of bravery that were not crowned with victory were obliterated. The fate of the defeated! We have records of Samson, Gideon, David and his warriors as well as the heroic exploits of the Book of Jashar,[3] but even the heroism of the freedom-fighting Hasmoneans was not captured and preserved in an original Hebrew book, and their memory is reduced to sporadic rumors and epitomized in the story of the miraculous cruse of oil.[4] Similarly, all the heroic deeds that took place after the destruction of the Temple, the attempts to fight oppression, to end the exile, to put an end to evil regimes, were all erased from memory or reduced to vague folktales and obscure idioms. They all became like faded flowers kept in the pages of a legend.

Only with the advent of Zionism has new light been shed on the defeated and forgotten Jewish heroism. The fighters at Masada were rescued from foreign texts, Rabbi Akiva, known to us only as an old sage and scholar, was revealed as the prophet of rebellion, and Bar-Koziba was restored to national consciousness as Bar-Kochba.[5]

The gigantic figures of Rabbi Akiva and Bar-Kochba (unburdened by the conflicts that surround Rabbi Yohanan Ben-Zakai and the Zealots),[6] represent the two aspects of Jewish heroism after the destruction of the Temple—exalted spiritual heroism and rejected physical heroism, sometimes united, often separated. Though they were regarded as being different, they were intrinsically the same. The miracle of Hanania, Mishael, and Azaria[7] did not happen to their martyred descendants who sanctified the name of God with their last breath . . . and the victories of the Hasmoneans were not granted to the fighters at Masada, or to Shemaiah,[8] Ahija,[9] Bar-Kochba, and the other freedom fighters in Israel and the surrounding countries centuries after the destruction. The glory of victory surrounds the Hasmoneans: "the weak triumphed over the mighty, few over many, pure over unclean, righteous over wicked."[10] Is there a greater paean that this? The fighters of Masada are enveloped in the tragic heroism of defeat: "We were the first to strike against them [the Romans] and we were the last to fight them—we know full well that our end will come tomorrow, but we can still choose to die like heroes—let our women die before they are defiled, let our children die before they become slaves."[11]

This has been the fate of Jewish heroism since the destruction. In essence, there is no difference between the fate of the rebels of the Galilee and that of the defenders of Tultchin,[12] between those who resisted Mohamed[13] and those who barricaded themselves against the Crusaders or the martyrs who died for their belief. They were all doomed from the start and their heroism was tragic. But not tragic like Saul or Samson who, when they died, knew that victory was not far off. Jewish heroism since the destruction is devoid of the chance of victory. They are heroes who persist in their struggle for their faith even though God does not countenance them; tortured heroes who know what awaits them in the battle against evil and iniquity, yet do not shy away. Job-like, even when they quarrel with God, they look inwardly, their conscience clear. The special prayer for martyrdom (there is such a prayer!) does not ask for escape or salvation, not even for release from pain, only for holiness and sanctity and the strength to withstand the ordeal: "Thou knowest my heart of hearts."[14]

Jewish heroism after the destruction achieved only one goal: that of being true to itself. It did not seek reward in this world. It followed it own dictates. Because of its tragic nature, it gained no acceptance. Chronicles written by our enemies (for which we should be thankful: their hatred helped preserve some names that would otherwise be forgotten; they also reveal the extent of our people's rebellion) and the contempt of enlightened people (who saw their brothers trample and rape us and saw our brothers take their lives in their hands yet shrugged at the sight of Jewish "madness"). This was our lot among the Gentiles. There is no glory or dignity in the heroism of the downtrodden.

Not only do Gentiles not appreciate the heroism of defeated Jews, many among us, too, do not understand it. After all, what is the point of heroism which does not bring victory, which is only momentary and cannot prevent raging hatred? This question has been posed by sober Jews from the days of the Zealots to this day. There is no forgiveness for heroism that brings no victory. It is not considered worth recording.

But even when it is not memorialized in books, this heroism is etched in the soul of the nation. Acts of valor and courage are the essence of our existence. There can be no Jewish life among hostile religions, warring kingdoms, wrangling classes, revolutions, and constant dangers. Without such stubborn heroism, would we be able to endure and hope for victory some day? The young Zealots of Roman times "endured inhuman torture by their tormentors who tore their flesh to pieces in an attempt to extract an admission that they submit to the Emperor, but none of them yielded and said that Caesar was his master."[15] The young zealots of our own generation guard the flame of Jewish life in undergrounds and in prisons—it is a burning fire that is never consumed.

And one wonders what will be the fate of Jewish heroism when we rebuild our national life in our country? Will we be like the Hasmoneans whose heroism was not just one of conscience but of actual victory?

"Never was a purer blood spilled than that of the plowmen of Tel Hai."[16] But in this country the plowmen and the defenders do not die like the desperate rebels and the martyrs of the Inquisition. We mourn them as we mourned Saul and Jonathan, founders of Jewish freedom. Their lives and their deaths tell us: Be consoled, my people.[17]

NOTES

1. From the Mishnah, tractate Pirkei Avot 3:1.

2. *Kana'im* in Hebrew. The most extreme of the Jewish factions fighting against Rome during the rebellion of 66–73 CE.

3. Book of the Upright. A Hebrew work of biblical interpretation from the Middle Ages or early-modern period. The book takes its title from a *Sefer Hayashar* that is referred to in Josh. 10:13 and 2 Sam. 1:18 and appears to have been a collection of war poetry, but it has not survived.

4. Katznelson is referring here to the Hasmonean dynasty of Israelites in Palestine in the second and first centuries BCE. Also known as the Maccabees, the exploits of the Hasmoneans are chronicled in the 1 and 2 Maccabees, which were not included in the Hebrew Bible. It has long been believed that 1 Maccabees, which relates the story of the Jewish uprising against the Seleucid dynasty and the rededication of the Temple, was originally written in Hebrew by a Jewish author, although it survived only in Greek translation. The story of the cruse of oil that miraculously lasted for eight days is of Talmudic origin.

5. Zionist ideology celebrated Bar-Kochba's tragically unsuccessful revolt against Rome (132–135 CE) as a struggle for national liberation. Rabbi Akiva, known in rabbinic literature as a

great sage and martyr at the hand of the Romans, was presented in Zionist thought as a herald of national redemption for his belief that Shimon Bar-Koziba was the Jewish Messiah and for bestowing upon him the name Bar-Kochba, "son of the star." (On the negative view of the Bar-Kochba revolt in the rabbinic tradition see document 28).

6.   Katznelson is invoking two extremes of Jewish political behavior. During the first Jewish revolt against Rome, R. Yohanan Ben Zakkai escaped from a besieged Jerusalem and negotiated with the Romans to allow for the continuation of Jewish religious life and study under rabbinic authority in return for Jewish obedience to Rome. The Zealots, on the other hand, fought to the last man and even assassinated Jews who cooperated with the Romans.

7.   From the book of Daniel, which relates that these three Israelite youths, educated in the court of the Babylonian king Nebuchadnezzar, refused to worship the royal idol and were thrown into a fiery furnace, yet emerged unscathed.

8.   Shemaiah was the head (Nasi) of the Sanhedrin (approximately 60–30 BCE) and the teacher of rabbis Hillel and Shamai. According to Josephus' *Antiquities* (book 14, chap. 9, sec. 4), when King Herod was brought before the Sanhedrin under accusation of murder, Shemaiah alone dared confront him.

9.   Ahija the Shilonite was a biblical prophet in the time of Solomon and his successors. In rabbinic tradition, he died as a martyr at the hands of Solomon's grandson Abijah, king of Judah.

10.   From the paragraph added to the traditional daily prayers for Hanukkah and Purim.

11.   Josephus, *Wars of the Jews*, book VII, chapter 8, section 6.

12.   A town in Ukraine and a site of a massacre of Jews by Cossacks in 1648 during Bogdan Chmielnitski's rebellion against Polish rule in the region.

13.   According to Islamic tradition, when Mohamed fled from Mecca to Medina and attempted to establish authority there, he encountered resistance from Jewish tribes. For example, one Jewish tribe, the Banu Qurayza, allied with Meccan forces against Mohamed, and when they were defeated, all the men were killed aside from a few who converted.

14.   In Hebrew, *atah yodea' matzpun libi*. This quotation may be from R. Yeshiyahu Horowitz (1565–1630), a central European Talmudist and mystic who used this phrase in prayers he composed.

15.   From Josephus, *The Jewish Wars*, book 7, chap. 10, sec. 1.

16.   See documents 38 and 39.

17.   Isa. 40:1.

49

On the Defense of Palestine and the Jews (1942)

DAVID BEN-GURION

During World War II, the Zionist movement attributed supreme importance to the formation of a Jewish army within the Allied forces. The Labor Zionist leaders of the Yishuv proposed it even before the war, and the Zionist Organization's president, Chaim Weizmann, did the same in a letter to the British government two days after the Nazi invasion of Poland on September 1, 1939. David Ben-Gurion continued to expound upon it from 1940 to 1942, thinking in terms of the fate of European Jewry, the defense of Palestine, and the postwar emergence of new states out of the British Empire. In the United States, Revisionist Zionists agitated for a Jewish army via mass rallies, newspaper advertisements, and theatrical pageants.

The British were pleased to take Palestinian Jews into their forces and spread them throughout Europe. By 1943 some 20,000 Jews served in a dozen units in Britain and North Africa. The British were reluctant, however, to create a distinct Jewish army. One concern was that such a force could turn against its masters and fight for the Zionist cause. (This did, in fact, happen, as in 1941 the Palmach was used by the British for operations in Syria—see document 51. After the Axis was defeated in the Middle East, the British tried unsuccessfully to disband the Palmach, which went underground and went on to spearhead the Zionist military forces in 1948.) A second concern was that a separate Jewish army would support Zionist claims to a distinct national status and to national rights over Palestine in a postwar settlement. Some 10,000 Palestinian Jews did

Source: David Ben-Gurion to Moshe Shertok (Sharett), July 8, 1942, CZA 74/14632.

serve as supernumeraries, largely in the police. But a Palestinian Jewish brigade was created only in the fall of 1944, and then not out of support for Zionism so much as a desire to shore up Jewish support for the Allies in the wake of the destruction of Hungarian Jewry.

The Zionist case for a Jewish army is laid out eloquently and briefly in this letter, written while Ben-Gurion was visiting Washington, D.C., and it was passed on to President Roosevelt through an intermediary. By emphasizing the need to keep the Yishuv's Jewish fighters in Palestine, as opposed to their being sent into the European or Pacific theaters, Ben-Gurion was thinking not only about protecting the Yishuv from an Axis invasion but also playing to his home constituency, as many kibbutzniks and youth movement members were willing to defend their homeland but were less enthusiastic about being sent abroad.

The Nazis are nearing the gates of Palestine. The invasion of that country by Hitler, even temporarily, may result in the complete annihilation of the Jewish community there—men, women, and children—and the total destruction of their work by the Nazis with the help of the *Mufti*. To the Jewish people throughout the world, this will mean more than the massacre of some 600,000 Jews; it will be the ruin of their Third Temple; the destruction of their Holy of Holies.

Repeated efforts and offers made since the beginning of the war by Jews of Palestine to mobilize all their resources alongside Great Britain were, with few exceptions, frustrated. With the Italian attack on Egypt in the summer of 1940, the British army required as many men as it could get. The Arab allies of Great Britain in the Middle East, Egypt, and Iraq, chose to remain neutral. Only Jewish Palestine was eager to provide the necessary manpower. But the Palestine Administration, pursuing a policy of appeasement toward the *Mufti* and his friends, saw to it that the services of the Jews should be limited and confined to noncombatant units. When the threat of invasion to Palestine came nearer and the Jews there insisted on their right to defend their country, the government could hardly resist this claim, and it was decided to form Jewish fighting units. But the appeasers qualified this decision by introducing the principle of "parity," which meant that only as many Jewish fighting units could be formed, as there may be Arab units. As the Palestinian Arabs showed no greater eagerness to fight on the side of the United Nations[1] than the Egyptians and the Iraqians [*sic*], the decision to have Jewish figuring units conditioned by parity could not amount to very much.

Australian soldiers in Palestine wondered why they had to be shipped from the other side of the world, when, on the spot, there were young Jews ready to fight. The official reason for the refusal to mobilize the Jews of Palestine was lack of equipment. But the Jews never requested preferential treatment. All they asked was the same measure of equipment supplied to British troops throughout the world. Another reason sometimes given was that the mobilization of Jews might upset the Arabs. What Arabs? Pro-Nazi Arabs (either because they hate the British, or believe in Hitler's victory, or sympathize with fascist ideals) cannot be bought off by sacrificing the Jews. Those Arabs who want the democracies to win must welcome an additional force fighting with the United Nations. Jewish units, which fought in Egypt and Lybia [sic], and those stationed in Palestine, upset nobody.

Jews of Palestine claim the elementary right, denied to no people in the world, to defend themselves and their country and fight the mortal enemy of their people and of humanity.

The number of Jews (men) aged from twenty to thirty-five is about 80,000; there are another 45,000 in the age groups between eighteen and twenty and thirty-five to forty-five. About 13,000 are already enlisted in special Jewish units in various military services: infantry, artillery, air force, navy, technical. An additional 7,000 are serving in the police, which is now militarized. Some 30,000 are engaged in works essential for the war effort. Thus, after deducting the physically unfit, there are available for further enlistment in Palestine about 60,000 Jewish men, many of whom have seen military service in different lands and do not require long training. If properly organized, the present Jewish units will constitute a single division. In addition, at least three more Jewish divisions can immediately be raised.

The war potential of Jewish Palestine may seem very little in the scale of this global war. But on the Palestinian front it may play a not inconsiderable, and, under certain conditions perhaps, a decisive role. A division of two may tip the scales in a crucial battle. Even if it does not assure victory, it may affect delay. And a delay of the invasion of Palestine may mean the difference between survival and destruction.

It may be that with all the Jews of Palestine fighting to the last, invasion and destruction cannot be avoided. But even then it will be a matter of supreme importance whether Jews of Palestine perish as soldiers and men fighting their enemies or are slaughtered like defenseless sheep. Should our people in Palestine be massacred, having been denied the right of self-defense by the Mandatory Power, it will not only be a most tragic disaster for the Jews. It will deal a fatal blow to the prestige of the British government and bring grave moral damage to the cause of the United Nations. Public opinion throughout the civilized world will be aroused against this wanton sacrifice of a people needlessly deprived of the means of self-defense.

There is no time to be lost. Only the friendly intervention of the president of the United States with his British ally can avert the catastrophe threatening Palestine. A word from the president should make possible the immediate and full mobilization of all Jewish manpower in Palestine, without preference and without discrimination, on a basis of equality of all other people.

NOTE

1. Ben-Gurion is probably referring here to the Allied Nations.

50

Origins of the Palmach (1941–42)

During the first half of World War II, the Yishuv faced threats on several fronts. Nazi forces were galloping across North Africa, and Syria and Lebanon had fallen under the rule of the collaborationist Vichy regime. Within Palestine, tensions between Jews and Arabs abated in the wake of British suppression of the Arab revolt, but the Yishuv leadership expected renewed Arab violence. In May 1941, Yizhak Sadeh (see notes 7 and 8) began to organize Jewish fighters into what he hoped would be a small standing military force attached to the larger Zionist militia, the Haganah. This standing force was known as the Palmach, an acronym for the Hebrew words *Pelugot Mahats*, meaning "shock companies." Even Palmach fighters were not full-time soldiers; they divided their time between working on kibbutzim and military training and operations. The Palmach was allowed to develop by the British, who needed them in the fight against Nazi and Vichy forces in the Middle East and North Africa. In the 1948 War, Palmach fighters would become the backbone of the Haganah and later, after the creation of the state, the IDF (Israeli Defense Forces).

A. Order of the Day No. 8[1]

A period of relative quiet after years of troubles, the establishment of mutual relations with our neighbors, the stationing of a large army in the country, and

Source: Appendixes 7 and 9 in Yehuda Bauer, *From Diplomacy to Resistance: A History of Jewish Palestine* (New York: Atheneum, 1973), 379–81, 385–86. Used with permission of the Jewish Publication Society.

the development of the war in Europe and the Middle East have fostered delusions among shortsighted people in the Yishuv as to the value of the role assigned the Organization [The Haganah] as an independent Jewish defensive force.

Many imagine that the "spear is only for when it's needed," as if it will automatically be there when the time comes. Many are misled and slight the Organization, get caught up in quarrels, resignation, and opposition.

The *Kofer ha-Yishuv* [2] is weakened. The money shortage has caused skimping and cutting down on operations.

Even within the organization's membership, the tension of personal effort has slackened.

Thanks to efforts mapped out and directed by the High Command, the Organization has succeeded in reinforcing its main force, even while going through this period of debilitation.

The plan for dividing the organization into regional commands has been carried through, preserving and even increasing the effectiveness of the work.

Defense plans have been worked out in detail and brought up to a high standard.

The level of training has been elevated, progress has been accelerated along with the branching out into special skills. Resources and equipment have developed and grown on a large scale.

Enlistments have been carried out that have strengthened the position of the Jewish soldier in the British Army.[3]

Knowledge of conditions and events in the Arab community has been deepened, as has that on the neighboring states and everything pertaining to the Organization and its interests in general.

Systematic contact with members and officers of the Organization has been ramified and reinforced.

The approach of the front, the revolt in Iraq,[4] the increased activity toward the rebirth of the Arab gangs[5] in Palestine, the preparation for attack, the return of gang leaders and men specially trained in a military school in Iraq for the needs of the Palestine "revolt,"[6] the activity of a fifth column and of Nazi espionage, the increase of incidents where travelers are injured, shooting at guards and other objectives—all these factors obligate the Haganah to stand tensely prepared, to remain on guard, to be in a battle-ready state.

Additional means have now been placed at the call of the High Command, though late and on a still insufficient scale; but, considering our resources, large enough so as not to warrant any additional loss of time.

Increased mass training and the thorough acquisition of skills

Feverish labor to add to equipment and fortifications

Completion and execution of plans for local and national defense

Improvement of communications

Enlistment and training of units for special duties, which may be
needed

Redoubled activity to bring in the youth, intensify and prepare it

General enlargement of the Organization

Strengthening of the means of spreading information

—These are the urgent tasks laid out by the High Command as a plan of action for the coming months. Orders have been given to carry out this plan.

The High Command is depending on the members of the Organization, on the Jewish settlements, and on their official institutions to make a redoubled effort in the volunteering spirit and in sacrificial devotion to establish the Organization as a fortified wall for the Yishuv. Our strength depends upon it.

B. Yitzhak Sadeh at Kibbutz Mishmar Haemek (1942)[7]

No one sent me here. And no one invited me either. I am a soldier and, as such, I want to say a few words. I have been in service since 1936.[8] I was jealous of other members. The time has come when I am no longer jealous. You have probably been talking about important things. But how have you done that? Could people in Russia get together and discuss such things? There is no healthy anxiety here. Today, things do not have to be pondered over. Everything is needed for defense only. There is only one means, and that is arms with which to fight for the blue and white flag and the red flag. You ask whether we are going to be able to do anything. Yes, we will. The whole war is not mechanized. Men have value. Mikhailovitch[9] in Yugoslavia is not fighting with machines, but with men. There is a war of men. Men have value, and all our effort is going toward that. Have we prepared better than Chamberlain[10]—the one we criticized? There is almost nothing more for me to say. We can mobilize 100,000 in Palestine,[11] the arms are there, but where are the men? You don't get a feeling of awareness of what is coming. We are enthusiastic about Russia's courage, but here I have been busy with recruitment for the Palmach—and every place I go, they start bargaining; it's amazing. If this is what happens right now—all the words are worthless. We are not free in this war. We have a partner who has power, but he has no talent, that's why all the exertion is necessary. We have the ability to defend the country, and the English see that. The Yishuv must emerge in full force. Therefore, I want you to prod us so that we won't be the ones making demands—you make the demands. We, for our part, are ready with thought and plans to call on everybody for the defense of our land.

NOTES

1. From the Haganah's National Command, dated Lag Ba'omer 5701 (May 15,1941).

2. The fund for support of Haganah training, purchase, and operations. See document 28.

3. By 1943, some 20,000 Jews, mostly from Palestine, were serving in the British military and stationed in one of the war's theaters. Another 10,000 served in Palestine, mainly in the supernumerary police.

4. In Iraq in 1941, Nazi Germany provided air cover for Rashid Ali al Gailani's putsch against the pro-British government of Nuri al-Said. A British invasion overthrew Ali and restored the previous government.

5. A term frequently used by Zionist and Palestinian sources to refer to each other's guerilla organizations and militias.

6. A reference to the forces organized by Fawzi al-Qawuqji, a Syrian military officer who organized an Arab volunteer force out of Iraq that fought in Palestine during the Arab revolt. Qawuqji would return to Palestine in 1948 as commander of the multinational Arab Liberation Army.

7. April 16, 1942. Sadeh (1890–1952) was a veteran Haganah activist and the Palmach's founding commander.

8. Sadeh organized the first Haganah commando units during the Palestinian Arab revolt (1936–39).

9. Dragoljub (Draza) Mikhailovitch (1893–1946) was a Serbian military officer and commander during World War II of the Chetniks, a Serbian nationalist guerilla force. Although at first dedicated to driving the German and Italian occupiers out of Yugoslavia, as the war progressed the Chetniks began to collaborate with the Axis against their common enemy, the Yugoslav Communist Partisans. At the time Sadeh made his remarks, Mikhailovitch would have been known abroad primarily as a resistance fighter.

10. Neville Chamberlain (1869–1940) was the British prime minister, notorious for his allowing Adolf Hitler in 1938 to annex the ethnic German portions of Czechoslovakia, the Sudetenland.

11. Although the Yishuv numbered just over a half million, the Haganah could theoretically mobilize most of its able-bodied men and women. In fact, at the height of the 1948 War, Israeli forces surpassed the 100,000 mark, although these numbers included some 20,000 recent arrivals from Eastern Europe as well as 5,000 volunteers, mainly from North America and South Africa.

51

The Palmach's First Operations (1944)

YITZHAK SADEH

In this text, Yitzhak Sadeh provides a detailed account of the Palmach's first action, a sortie into Vichy Syria in June 1941, involving some thirty fighters and two Australian brigades—underscoring the cooperation between the Yishuv and the British in the struggle against the Nazis and their allies. (On the Palmach and Sadeh see document 50.) The document also reveals the fears in the Yishuv at the time (1941) of a potential German invasion of Palestine.

Based on our cumulative experience as well as on the trust we have in our own people, we ventured to offer the Allies some far-reaching suggestions.

The thought of cooperation with the Allied Armed Forces first arose when it was suggested that two of our units take over the Litani bridges[1] in a coordinated operation—one taking control of the crags on the left bank of the river (Kala't Ashkif), and the other taking the bridges. We were confident that we could carry out such an operation successfully. For reasons that we cannot go into here, the operation was eventually more limited in military terms, but covered more extensive territory. We were charged with the task of finding a possible

Source: Y. Noded (Yitzhak Sadeh), "The Establishment of Our Regiment," *Alon Ha-Palmach*, 1944. Translated by Marganit Weinberger-Rotman.

connection between the northern roads of Palestine and the southern roads of Syria. Simultaneously, we were to cut off telephone communication along the entire front (from the B'not Ya'akov Bridge[2] to the Mediterranean). On the shore, we were required to transport an Australian military unit to a certain location in order to foil the French plan of blowing up the main highway. We regretfully report that the Jewish settlers along the Palestinian–Syrian border did not know the terrain; we had to use Arab and Circassian guides.

Our men were deployed in small units of two and three. They exhibited excellent hiking skills, quick orientation, and courage from the moment they set out on preliminary patrols until the end of the operation. When the test came, we passed it with flying colors. Every unit fulfilled its mission. When a serious military confrontation occurred—when our men and a few Australians were facing grave danger—our extensive training stood us in good stead. Our men engaged in hand-to-hand combat (using grenades and cold steel), and the commanders needed only a few minutes to familiarize themselves with the various weapons of the French. They showed great courage and initiative in the battle and were immediately put in command positions over the entire unit, including the Australians. Thanks to our men, one platoon was able to take over a command post, take prisoners, and destroy four times as many enemy soldiers as themselves. An entire enemy squadron, bent on foiling the invasion was disabled by a single unit of ours!

Telephone communication along the front line was disconnected, as per the instructions we received (this was the only means of communication of the French army). This action had serious consequences; it took the French by surprise and it contributed to the success of the invasion in the first days.[. . .]

When there was a threat of a German invasion into the country and the Allies recognized the importance of the Jewish presence, our way of thinking triumphed. We came up with a plan of attack in case of invasion and our plan was modified to conform to the general military plans for the region. The training and the modus operandi were designed for partisan operations with demolition activity and defense using partisan weapons. We established special units that trained for operations against both the Germans and our neighbors. Our men prepared themselves for work as operatives and demolition experts in neighboring countries as well, in case of a Nazi invasion there.

We often underestimate our own operations. In the case of the "German Unit," we heard from both the commanders and the ranks that the training was inadequate. But when two of the men were actually sent to operate as Germans among Germans, their success was unqualified!

At that time we heard a heroic tale of two Jewish soldiers who died in action. Dressed as Germans and accompanied by a German lieutenant (who worked with us but later betrayed us) they were transporting a few French fighters in an armored car to a German command post in the desert for the purpose of sabotage. During the operation, when our men realized that the German "guide" had betrayed them and they were attacked by a German unit, one of our men drew his machine gun and opened fire, killing many of the enemy soldiers. The other man, like Samson, lobbed his grenade at the explosive charges stored in the truck and died with the Philistines that surrounded him.[3] . . .

Miraculously, a French officer who was in the car survived the incident, and he told us all the details. German prisoners from that camp, who were captured later, confirmed the story.

This operation became the model for our "German Unit." It showed what could be expected of our men when there's call for action.

However, we suffered some damage from this "cooperation." We got used to working more or less openly and with advanced technology. It is hard for us to return to our modest ways, but time and reality will cure us of these ills.

During the Days of El-Alamein[4]

In those difficult and fateful days our regiment, though not yet sufficiently trained and consolidated, was required to report for duty on the southern front—and report we did!

What tactics should we apply in case of invasion? How could we face the enemy? We were so few, even when joined by other Haganah regiments and volunteers from the settlements. We were confused. But one thing we knew for sure: we would never surrender; we'd fight to the bitter end. We'd cause as many casualties to the enemy as we possibly can. We'd conduct surprise attacks, we'd bomb, shoot, and ambush them—We won't give up!

The tactical thinking of the Haganah was the following: to devise defense plans against an enemy whose forces were infinitely greater than any army that had ever attacked us—the unstoppable German hordes who are well versed in wars of provocation. All this was before the great massacre in Europe, and some in the Yishuv entertained a misguided hope that the Germans might need us, our agriculture, our industry, and our medicine. But we knew better; we realized right away who this enemy is. We had no doubt that if they invade our land, we'd have to barricade ourselves in Masada[5] again. We'd have to defend every settlement with the utmost determination. We'd have to operate partisan units in the mountains and in the plantations (hidden from the bombers). How long could we fight like this while still surrounded by local enemies?

This tactical concept was far-reaching: it focused on Haifa as the last bastion. Every able-bodied Jew who can wield a weapon would be recruited. In this scenario we assumed that the Allies would be interested in supporting our operations and would supply us with artillery, airplanes, and gun ships.

All this was before Stalingrad [6]—but our plan was definitely Stalingrad-like. We would have our own Stalingrad. In this war we played for time, anticipating the change in the balance of power on the global frontlines.

Fortunately, the balance of power did shift in favor of the Allies, not around Haifa but near El-Alamein. Our plans were never carried out. We are not sorry that they remained unused but we are pleased that we had them. Such plans are not merely theoretical, tactical exercises—they are formative, educational acts. In any future conflict that still awaits the Zionist movement, we will have recourse to these plans.

Our plans focused on Palestine, but from time to time we answered desperate calls from the Diaspora. We could not very well ignore them. We responded, not in accordance with our objective capabilities, but in compliance with what the other nations allowed us to contribute, by sending individual emissaries here and there.

We have often entertained the thought of establishing a Jewish partisan unit in the accursed Diaspora, a unit run by us, which would serve as a center of combat and resistance.

After the German occupation of Poland, we came up with the following idea, which at the time sounded crazy, but which today is obvious to one and all. Had Polish Jews fought from the start of the occupation in partisan units, this could have been their route to salvation, and for many an honorable death.

But we were prevented from carrying out this idea, and it was snuffed out. But every once in a while it flares up again. Our representatives offer our services, but until now the [British colonial] government's answer has always been NO.

But we have not given up. We hope to be able to translate our deep hatred of fascism into action, to avenge the murders of our brothers, and to prove our loyalty to our nation.

However, our basic tactical thinking should be geared toward possible battles that await us in Palestine. The difficulty of planning actions here—and consequently the difficulties of building units and training them—is the need to maintain maximum flexibility. We must be able to spread and diversify our forces to maximize attacks while maintaining a unified resistance front. We must be able to consolidate our efforts to build a serious striking force that will smite the enemy and destroy their supply lines.

Let us draw a lesson from our past experience: from the Arab–Jewish riots, from the successes—and failures—of our battle against the "White Paper,"[7] and from this war. Our members who are deployed on different fronts, in special operations in the Diaspora and in partisan activities—are all accumulating experience. The time of reckoning shall come. We must be flexible; we have weighty tasks in front of us. Our forces are limited, and thus our victory depends on the quality of our men and the merit of our actions.

NOTES

1. In Lebanon, some thirty kilometers (18.5 milies) north of the international border.

2. A bridge across the Jordan River, which divides the Galilee from the Golan.

3. An allusion to the biblical story of Samson, Judg. 13–16.

4. A reference to two major battles fought in northern Egypt, the first in July 1942, the second in late October and early November of that same year.

5. A Roman fortress in the Judean desert of Palestine. According to the Roman Jewish historian Flavius Josephus, during the first Jewish rebellion against Rome the fortress was captured by Jewish extremists. Besieged by the Romans, in 73 CE the fighters killed their family members and themselves rather than fall into captivity.

6. The Battle of Stalingrad, waged between July 1942 and January 1943, ended with a Nazi defeat and more than two million casualties.

7. The 1939 White Paper severely curtailed Jewish immigration to Palestine and proclaimed that in ten years' time a unitary, binational state would be created in Palestine.

52

The Palmach Anthem
(1941)

ZERUBAVEL GILAD

Zerubavel Gilad, a member of Kibbutz Ein Harod, was a poet, writer, and the Palmach's cultural officer. The anthem was written in the summer of 1941, and at first it was sung to the melody of a Red Army song, in keeping with the Palmach's self-image as a revolutionary vanguard closely tied to the Soviet project. In 1943, David Zahavi provided a less martial, more traditionally Judaic melody.

The storm rages around us
But our heads will not bow
Ever ready to obey all commands

We are the Palmach
From Metullah to the Negev
From the sea to the desert
Every able-bodied man is ready to take arms

Every man will stand guard!
The eagle has its path in the sky

Source: Zerubavel Gilad, "Shir Ha-Palmach," in *Gevurat Yisra'el be-Hazon ha-Dorot*, ed. Arieh Cohen (Tel Aviv: A. Zalkovitch, 1967), 257–58. Translated by Marganit Weinberger-Rotman.

The wild ass in the mountains
Our path leads us to the enemy

In crevices and cliffs
We are always the first
In daytime and in the dark
Always ready to heed the call to arms
We are, always, the Palmach.

53

Outlines of Zionist Policy (1941)

DAVID BEN-GURION

This document, written shortly before Ben-Gurion left the United Kingdom for the United States, consists of talking points for him to raise with American Zionist leaders. This and other documents were removed from Ben-Gurion's luggage and copied by British censorship officials, and it is possible that Ben-Gurion intentionally placed the documents in his luggage so that British authorities would know where Zionist policy was headed.[1] At the time Ben-Gurion wrote this document, official Zionist policy had not yet reached the point of clearly calling for full Jewish sovereignty—that is, an independent Jewish state—in Palestine. But as seen here, Ben-Gurion was definitely of this view, and in early 1941 Chaim Weizmann expressed it in print. This document thus provides background to the American Emergency Committee for Zionist Affair's Biltmore Program of May 1942, which called for the establishment of a Jewish commonwealth in Palestine at the war's end.

Moreover, the document throws light on the practical aspects of Zionist state-building: plans for immigration, speculation about the future state's borders, and the possible removal ("transfer") of the Palestinians into other Arab lands. Like Ben-Gurion's 1937 letter to his son (see document 42), scholars have quoted selectively from this document's discussion about the issue of transfer, but it has never been reproduced in its entirety, as is done here.

Source: Central Zionist Archive Z4/14632. Hand-dated October 15, 1941.

Private and Confidential
Chapter II: Jewish State

Our failure (so far) to achieve a Jewish Army should not, as Mr. Bevin[2] seems to think, move us to seek an immediate final settlement in Palestine. For friendly British Ministers like Mr. Bevin and Mr. Amery,[3] it is easier to talk—without of course committing the Government or themselves to any real degree—of the necessity of establishing a Jewish State in Palestine. For them it may serve as some sort of moral escape from the uncomfortable feeling lurking somewhere at the back of their minds that they have let down the Jews. But for us there is no point in looking for any such facile escape. So long as the war goes on—and perhaps only God knows how long it will go on—we must not give up our efforts to achieve a Jewish Army. The time has not yet come to open negotiations with the Government for a final settlement of the Palestine problem. While the British Empire is engaged in this life-and-death struggle, and especially while the tide still runs in favor of the Nazis, the British Government cannot be expected to effect or consider political changes in the Middle East—except to our disadvantage. No sane person can imagine that while Palestine and the Middle East are still not secure against Nazi invasion, a Jewish State will be established. Mr. Bevin's suggestion (to drop the idea of a Jewish Army and get instead some kind of Jewish State, or autonomy, in Palestine at once) indicates more lofty sentiment than sound judgment or sufficient knowledge. Our task for the present, so far as the future of Palestine is concerned, is rather the negative one of preventing, by all means in our power, the British Government from committing itself to the Arabs and from bringing Palestine within the orbit of the contemplated Arab Federation.

But while we have not yet reached the stage where any final settlement for Palestine can be practically discussed with H. M. Government, it is not too early to try and clarify the problem in our own minds, and to start educating public opinion, Jewish as well as British and American, in the direction of a Zionist settlement of both the Jewish and the Palestine problem immediately after the war.

1. Jewish State as a means,
not an end.

The first conclusion we must reach is that the establishment of a Jewish State has now become an indispensable means of achieving Zionism under the new postwar conditions. It is necessary to stress the word "means," since the object we ought to have now in mind is not the achievement of what is called in Zionist jargon the *Endziel* [final aim]. Apart from the serious doubt whether there is really, in history, such a thing as a final aim, I do not believe the time has yet come to achieve it—whatever it may mean. It must be clearly realized—and it is the task of Zionism to make the world realize (at least, the Anglo-Saxon world)—that immediately after the end of the war it will be faced with a mass exodus of Jews from Europe, and that these Jews, whatever the regime in Palestine, will surge irresistibly toward that country: Palestine will have to absorb the largest possible number of Jews in the shortest possible time.

A large-scale Jewish immigration and colonization in Palestine cannot be secured, otherwise than through a Jewish Administration, having power and responsibility for creating in Palestine such economic, administrative, and political conditions as may be necessary for the absorption and free development of a large new population.

Immigration into Palestine differs entirely from immigration into—e.g.,— the United States or any other rich and developed country. If the U.S.A. should after the war be prepared to open its doors freely to Jewish immigrants, no preliminary economic preparation would be required in order to enable large masses of Jews to establish themselves there. The existing economy would immediately be able to absorb a new mass immigration, just as it did in the past—before the last war. Palestine is not a country of immigration of the same type. The half million Jews who have come to Palestine were not absorbed by the existing economy, which they found on their arrival: Jews are not found in Palestine either in Arab villages or in Arab towns. They do not settle in these places for the simple reason that in Arab towns and villages there is no place for European immigrants, nor are they able to support additional population.

Immigration into Palestine presupposes new colonization work. In Palestine we have to build up a new industry, a new agriculture; establish new villages and new towns; in short, create economically, so to say, the country we are going to settle. Without new colonization there can be no immigration into Palestine. Large-scale immigration requires large-scale colonization. . . .

2. To what extent can a Jewish State in Palestine solve the Jewish Problem?

It is neither necessary nor possible that Palestine should take in after the war all the Jews in the world, and a Zionist solution to the Jewish problem has never meant, and does not now mean, the transfer of all Jews throughout the world to their Homeland. On the other hand, Zionism today can no longer mean what it has meant, to some Zionists, in the past forty years: the creation of a spiritual center in Palestine, effected through a moderate Jewish immigration. Zionism today no longer means even just a Jewish majority in Palestine, as the Revisionists maintained for some time—because the immediate need of the Jews for a country of their own is not to be measured by the number of Arabs who happen to be in Palestine, but by the number of Jews—many times greater—who have been completely and hopelessly uprooted from many countries of the Diaspora.

The practical problem which will face us after the war will concern between three and five million Jews. Given a Jewish State, I see no reason why such a number should not be absorbed there, not over a long period of years, but within a short time, that is within several years, as was done in Greece,[4] as an immediate, planned, State undertaking.

The prevailing poor notions, even in Zionist circles, about Palestine's absorptive capacity are largely the result of ignorance and mental inertia. Since Palestine has in sixty years of new Jewish settlement absorbed no more than 500,000 Jews, the deduction is made that the absorption of another 500,000 will require, if not sixty years, at least another ten or twenty. Those people forget that the growth of the Jewish community in Palestine has been taking place in geometrical progression: between 1882 and 1918 there were in Palestine only 60,000 Jews; in the first decade of the British Mandate, the Jewish population increased only to 175,000; and it was only in the second decade that another 300,000 came in.

There are three even more important points which are either ignored or overlooked:

(a) Before the period of the British Mandate, our work in Palestine was done under the worst possible conditions: Jewish immigration and acquisition of land were completely prohibited by Turkish law. Even under the British regime, with the Balfour Declaration and the Mandate, we received little assistance from the Government, which tended, even before the White Paper, to restraint rather than encouragement. Our settlement in Palestine was perhaps the first and only case of colonization undertaken by people who had neither governmental powers nor State means at their disposal. In this initial period we had also to overcome internal difficulties: our own complete ignorance and inexperience in matters of colonization; the almost insuperable handicap of having to settle on the land a people who for centuries had been town-dwellers. The historical significance of our achievement so far is thus to be measured, not so much by the number of people settled, but by the fact that successful settlement was achieved, and that we acquired experience and complete confidence in our own ability, and in Palestine's capacity, for large-scale settlement, in agriculture as well as in industry, and also— quite recently—in seafaring pursuits.

(b) In discussing Palestine, people—even Zionists—sometimes forget that so far we have settled 600,000 Jews not in the whole of Palestine, but in one-fifteenth part only of Western Palestine. So far we occupy only 1,400,000 dunams[5] of a total area of about 27,000,000 dunams. These figures would be meaningless were it not for the fact that Jews are settled in Palestine on the basis of an independent economy, founded on their own agriculture, industry, building, and trades, in their own, purely Jewish, areas, as if they were a normal people occupying a country of their own. While Jews in all other countries must settle among other peoples, and be entirely dependent for their whole livelihood on the economy of the peoples among whom they live, it is not so in Palestine. In the United States there is a Jewish community ten times as big as that in Palestine. But the daily existence of the American Jews is entirely dependent on the services they may render to, or obtain from, the 120 millions of non-Jewish Americans. Break off this daily intercourse, then America's five million Jews are doomed to immediate destruction. The situation of the half million Jews in Palestine is fundamentally different. Their economic existence in no way depends on the economic intercourse with the million Arabs in the country— neither on services rendered nor on services obtained. Economically, the Jews of Palestine are as independent of the Palestine Arabs as any other independent people in its own country is independent of the neighboring countries. Herein lies the great significance of the fact that so far we have built up an economy absorbing half a million Jews in a tiny part of the country— something like 7 percent of Western Palestine.

(c) The extent of available land: According to the official claim of the Arab Delegation at the London Conferences, Palestine (i.e., Western Palestine) has only 7,000,000 dunams of "cultivable" land, meaning that in the Arab view only 7,000,000 dunams of Western Palestine are or can be cultivated by the Arabs. The area of Western Palestine is 26,500,000 dunams. Consequently, according to the Arab admission, some 19,000,000 dunams of Western Palestine are uncultivable for Arabs. Some parts of this area are clearly uncultivable, even from the Jewish point of view, e.g., the stony desert near the Dead Sea, parts of the hill-country, and parts of the Negev. But all our colonization work so far goes to prove that tracts of land which had lain waste for centuries and had been considered uncultivable, can be cultivated and fertilized by us—for instance, the dunes of Ein Hahoresh, converted into the flourishing settlement of Rishon Le-Tsion,[6] the swamps of Shomron, now the prosperous settlement of Gederah,[7] the barren rocks near Jerusalem which have become Motza.[8] . . . Dozens of other instances could be cited. We have discovered water, and have irrigated lands which for centuries have been arid desert. Moreover, there is the whole of the southern part of Palestine—some fifteen million dunams, almost entirely unoccupied, and "uncultivable"—which awaits only the introduction of a water supply to make room for hundreds of thousands of new settlers, just as the intensification of cultivation and full irrigation in the plains will make room for more tens of thousands.

On the assumption that we can occupy only one-half of the soil of Western Palestine, there is no reason why the present agricultural population should not be increased sevenfold. This is a very conservative calculation, and admittedly, in the areas already in our possession, we could, by intensification, double and perhaps triple, the present agricultural population; we have been gradually increasing it during the past ten or twelve years.

While the area of available land is the objective limit to our agricultural expansion, the development of Jewish industry in Palestine is limited only by the available markets, and there is no reason why a Jewish Palestine should not become the industrial center of the whole Near and Middle East, and supply curtain products even so far afield as India (as it is, indeed, already beginning to do).

Jewish immigration and settlement in Palestine will always be limited by the economic absorptive capacity of the country. But this capacity is not static or fixed, and given modern technique and science, given creative initiative, large-scale planning, the urge and need of a desperate people, and whole-hearted support from the State, this capacity can be expanded beyond all present-day conceptions.

A large number of Jews—by which I mean some millions—can be settled in Palestine. There is no practical reason—given a Jewish State—why this number should not be settled in the shortest possible time, i.e., within a few years: What was done in Greece can certainly be done in a Jewish State.

3. Boundaries.

The distinction between the Jewish State as a means and the Jewish State as an ultimate aim is especially relevant to the question of boundaries. The formula "Palestine within its historical boundaries," attractive though it is sentimentally, cannot in my view be adopted by us as a political formula for present practical purposes. Apart from the fact that the expression "historical boundaries" is rather vague, and indeterminable, since the boundaries of Palestine, even more than those of other countries, have been subject to constant changes, if what it is taken to mean is Palestine including Transjordan, it is at present impracticable, and can therefore only do harm by antagonizing the Arabs still further, and by increasing our difficulties with England. So far there is no need to define the boundaries of the Jewish State which we claim must be established at the end of this war. We have not yet reached the stage of serious negotiations either with the Government or with the Arabs, and we are not yet called upon to define the area of the Jewish State. Therefore we should not use a formula which will either uselessly increase the number of our opponents outside, or unnecessarily raise discussions and difficulties within the movement. This means that on the one hand we should not make any explicit claim to Transjordan, while on the other hand we should in no way, either explicitly or implicitly, propose the partition of Palestine. As in 1938, I am still convinced that we were right in our attitude toward the Royal Commission's Report. But the position of the Jewish people, and perhaps also of the British in the Middle East, would now be quite different had a Jewish State been established in 1938, even in a partitioned Palestine. But while it was right to accept a Jewish State when a British Government offered partition, it would be an irreparable mistake to suggest partition as a way of establishing a Jewish State.

When we are asked what, in the way of territory, we mean by a Jewish State in Palestine, we should, in my view, make it definitely clear that what we have in mind is at least the whole of Western Palestine. The magnitude of the Jewish problem, the size of the imminent Jewish immigration, the sufferings and wrongs done to the Jewish people, the necessity for a "New Deal" after the war, the sweeping changes which will have to be made throughout the world, the vast and sparsely populated territories possessed by the Arabs, and in which they will become independent after the war, the smallness of Palestine, and the fact that this is the only corner of the world which the Jewish people has for ages regarded as its home—all these considerations make the establishment of a Jewish State in Palestine both necessary and feasible.

While we should not make extravagant and indefinite claims based on "historical boundaries," we should in no way claim less than the whole of Western Palestine.[9] We have to bear in mind that for the vitality of the Jewish State it is imperative that on the one hand we should be neighbors of Christian Lebanon, and on the other hand that our territory should include the vast unoccupied tract of the Negev and also the waters of the Jordan and the Litani.[10]

4. Status and External Relations.

In regard to status, even more than in regard to boundaries, we should for the present avoid any commitments, either as to an Arab Federation, or inclusion within the British Empire, or even as to complete sovereignty of the Jewish State. At the present juncture it is impossible to foresee the political circumstances which will prevail at the end of the war, or the main outlines—if any—of the new world order. While we should not be too much affected by the prevalent tendency to deprecate small States, we should also not lose sight of the real need and hope of the world for greater political unity and humanity, which implies the abolition of separate sovereignties. Our aim and our need is not to be separated politically from other people, but to be independent, i.e., to be the masters of our own fate and to work out our own salvation. What we need is a country—a homeland—affording us free and full expression of our national genius, our own economy, our own culture, civilization, society, ideals of life; all this is impossible so long as we are dependent on the mercy of others. But this does not imply a barrier between ourselves and other peoples, and the most far-reaching ideal of Zionism is entirely compatible with the abolition of States or the establishment of a single world-state, on condition that the Jews can settle millions of their people in Palestine and develop their own life there in peace and freedom.

The State we need, and which is in my view indispensable for achieving Zionism means merely the organized and recognized collective capacity of the people to order their life in Palestine in such a way that great masses of Jews may be able to settle there in safety and in accordance with their own wishes, needs, and ideals. But whether Palestine will be an independent sovereign State or merely an autonomous, equal member of a larger unit—Middle East Federation, British Empire, or World Federation—makes no essential difference for the main purpose of achieving Zionism.

But we ought not to commit ourselves to an Arab Federation, because

(i)   An Arab Federation is not our business and does not depend on us;

(ii) As long as the Arabs do not agree to a Jewish State, it can only weaken our position, without giving us any compensating advantage, if we agree beforehand to the inclusion of Palestine within an Arab Federation.

Almost the same reasons apply to the question of Palestine becoming a British Dominion.

It is rather questionable whether the British would agree to make Jewish Palestine a British Dominion, and our unilateral declaration to that effect can have no value; but by declaring beforehand that we want Palestine to become a part of the British Empire, we may unnecessarily antagonize the Arabs, and perhaps also other Powers, without thereby gaining any degree of sympathy or support from the British.

We should therefore leave entirely open the question of the external status of the Jewish State until we reach the stage of political negotiations with the interested parties.

Chapter III: "ARAB QUESTION"

With regard to the Arabs Zionist policy was based on the following four principles:

(i)   There is no Arab problem in the sense that there is a Jewish problem: i.e., there is no Arab homelessness; no need for Arabs to emigrate. More even than most other peoples, the Arabs are concentrated in their own territories, and if they have a problem it is that their vast territories are too sparsely populated, too underdeveloped—as for instance Syria and Iraq—and for their well-being and safety need a larger population, and would be rather helped than hindered if they were willing to absorb the whole or part of the Palestinian Arab population.

(ii) Palestine is only a tiny part of the huge territories settled by Arabs, and the Arabs of Palestine only an insignificant section of the Arabic-speaking peoples. But for the Jewish people through-out the world Palestine is the only homeland—both for reasons of past history, and for reasons of the present and the future.

(iii) Jewish immigration and colonization in Palestine on a large scale can be carried out without displacing Arabs; moreover, as has been proved and admitted, with actual benefit to the present Arab population of Palestine.

(iv) In a Jewish Palestine the position of the Arabs will not be worse than the position of the Jews themselves, and certainly not worse than the position of Arabs in other countries. They enjoy not merely equal rights, but will share in the general rise of economic and cultural standards in a Jewish Palestine.

In contemplating a Jewish State in the near future some further enquiry is necessary.

(a) Transfer: Some people, in England as well as in America, advocate the transfer of the Palestinian Arabs to Iraq and Syria as the best solution of the so-called "Arab Question." We must consider first whether such a transfer is practicable, and secondly whether it is indispensable.

Complete transfer without compulsion—and ruthless compulsion at that—is hardly imaginable. There are, of course, sections of the non-Jewish population of Palestine which would not mind being transferred, under favorable conditions, to some neighboring country—for instance, the Druses, several of the Bedouin tribes in the Jordan Valley and the south, the Circassians,[11] and perhaps also the Mutawalis[12] (a Shiite sect in the north of Palestine). It would, further be probably not too difficult to settle in neighboring Arab countries the section of the Arab population consisting of tenants and landless agricultural workers. But the bulk of the Arab population, the *fellaheen*, as well as the urban population (which is largely agricultural) could hardly be expected voluntarily to remove itself en masse, whatever the economic inducements offered.

That compulsory transfer of populations on a large scale is possible has been shown by the transfer of the Greek Turks after the last war, which involved millions of people deeply rooted in the soil. In the present war, the idea of transfer of population is steadily gaining in popularity as the surest and most practical means of solving the thorny and dangerous problem of national minorities. The war has already brought about the resettlement of large numbers of people in the east and south of Europe, and in the plans for a postwar settlement, large-scale transfer of populations in central, eastern, and southern Europe are taking an increasingly important place.

It would, however, be unsafe and unwise on our part to advocate, or even expect, a compulsory transfer of Arabs from Palestine. The Turkish–Greek exchange of populations was the result of a crushing victory by the Turks over the Greeks. The exodus of the Germans from the Baltic countries and from the Italian Tyrol at the beginning of this war was an item in a big political deal between Great Powers. Large numbers of the conquered peoples are at present being ruthlessly transferred by the Nazis, and it is probable that an Allied victory will enable the Poles, Czechs, Russians, and possibly some other victorious allies to remove large numbers of Germans from the liberated territories.[13] But the Arabs, while they have been rather unhelpful to the Allies, and more inclined to the Nazis, are practically not belligerents, and formally rather "friends" of the Allies, especially of Great Britain (at least so long as Hitler has not invaded the Near East). It can, therefore, hardly be expected that a victorious England will undertake the compulsory transfer of Arabs from Palestine merely for the benefit of the Jewish people. It would thus be a mistake, politically and even more morally, for us to advocate a compulsory transfer of the Arabs.

Can a voluntary transfer be contemplated? It would be rash to assert that in no circumstances and under no conditions can such a transfer take place. If the neighboring Arab States, especially Syria and Iraq, which have a vital interest in increasing their Arab populations and strengthening their economic and military position vis-à-vis Turkey and Persia, can be induced to cooperate in such a transfer, a certain number of Arabs from Palestine would perhaps be ready, in consideration of substantial economic advantages, to leave Palestine and settle in Syria or Iraq. Even then, transfer would be limited to a fraction of the Arab population. The majority of the Arabs can hardly be expected to leave voluntarily within the short period of time which can materially affect our problem.

It is my definite conviction that the presence of something like a million Arabs in Palestine, while it raises political difficulties and problems for the Jewish State, need not seriously hamper large-scale immigration and colonization (by which I mean the settlement of some millions of Jews in Western Palestine alone); the reasons for this view I have briefly set forth in Ch. II, section II above. We should not, therefore, burden our political action—already sufficiently complicated—with this more than doubtful point of Arab transfer. We must not, of course, discourage other people, British or American, who favor transfer from advocating this course, but we should in no way make it a part of our program. It can do nothing to facilitate our task, while it may easily undermine our moral position, and will, further, distort the real picture of the situation in Palestine and obscure the fundamental fact that Palestine, as it stands, can absorb, given a suitable political regime, many millions of Jews without removing or disturbing the Arabs. We are proud of the fact—admitted by all partial observers, as for instance the Royal Commission—that our colonization has not only not displaced Arabs, but had resulted in an increase of Arab population in the areas of Jewish settlement. It is also admitted by the Arabs themselves (as pointed out above) that more than two-thirds of Western Palestine are, from their point of view, uncultivable.

But while we must not in any way commit ourselves to compulsory transfer, we ought to work out plans for voluntary transfer—admittedly of limited numbers—with the assistance of the neighboring Arab States, and in our contacts with Arab leaders outside Palestine we should take soundings as to how far they would be prepared to cooperate in this.

(b) Arab consent: The establishment of the Jewish State cannot be made to depend on previous Arab consent, either from the Arabs of Palestine or of the neighboring countries. This does not mean to say that such consent cannot be obtained; on the contrary, I believe that when the Arab States are firmly told by Britain and America that the Jewish problem—one of the most disturbing problems of the world—must finally be solved, and that Palestine alone can provide a lasting solution, it may reasonably be expected that the Arabs will acquiesce without raising undue difficulties. But it would be illusory and dangerous to expect that if the establishment of a Jewish State is made dependent on the prior consent of the Arabs, such consent would be forthcoming. Even those of the Arab leaders who, for political or other reasons, might accept the necessity, or even desirability, of the return of the Jews to their ancient Homeland, would not dare to say so in public, as their rivals (and we should not forget the existence of numerous competing cliques, groups, and parties in all Middle Eastern countries) can too easily play up the religious and chauvinistic feelings of the populace against them.

In the present Arab world there is one leader who is more or less independent, and—in his own country at least—without overt opposition: Ibn Saud.[14] But apart from the fact that his influence in Syria, Iraq, and Palestine, as well as in Egypt, is not very great, for dynastic, religious, political, and economic reasons, he is the last man to consent voluntarily to the handing over of Palestine to the Jewish people. We should therefore beware of all friendly and unfriendly advice, whether from private or official sources, to obtain first the consent of the Arabs, and then ask the British Government for its blessing.

The Jewish problem, like the Palestine problem, is international in character, and not one between Jews and Arabs. It is rather between the Jews and the civilized world, or in the first instance with the Anglo-Saxon world, for the additional reason that England at present occupies Palestine, and that America has a large Jewish community whose fate and future are largely bound up with the lasting solution of the general Jewish problem. Our claim to Palestine is a matter of historic justice and international readjustment. The Iraqi, Syrian, or Egyptian peoples have no more historical, moral, or political rights in Palestine than any of the European, Asiatic, or American peoples. It will be the victorious Allies, with England and America at their head, who will be responsible for the new world order, and it is from them, and only from them, that we may rightly expect an understanding of our historic claim and right to return to our ancient Homeland. It is in their power, as they have the responsibility to achieve it. Our policy must therefore be not to arrive, through the consent of the Arabs, at a British decision, but the reverse; only a decision on the part of England and America can bring about the consent or acquiescence of the Arabs. This fundamental political principle must be clear, at least in our own minds.

But while adhering to this principle, we should not relax our efforts to maintain contact with the Arab leaders, to enlighten Arab public opinion—so far as such opinion exists—and to maintain and increase Jewish–Arab cooperation wherever possible, all the time making it clear to the Arab leaders what is our object in Palestine, and our determination to attain that object.

(c) Treatment of Arabs in a Jewish State: It follows from what is said above in paragraph (a) that in the established Jewish State we shall be confronted with the problem of a considerable Arab population. It goes without saying that a Jewish State can be based only on complete equality of all its inhabitants. But in my view mere civil and political equality is in this case not enough. Jews and Arabs in Palestine represent not merely two different nationalities, but rather two widely separated civilizations and standards of life: one perhaps the most modern and progressive in Europe or America, and the other still living in the Middle Ages. It will be a vital interest—moral, political, and economic—of the Jewish State gradually and consistently to raise the standard of life of the Arabs within it, and their social and cultural level, to that of the Jews. We can hardly expect to build up a healthy economy with a decent standard of living for our own people so long as we have in the country a backward population, easily exploited, illiterate, and socially unhealthy. The existence in the country of a primitive agriculture and industry, based on cheap labor, must hamper the normal development of Jewish industry and agriculture which is necessarily based on a much higher level.

The political life of our country may also suffer from the presence of a considerable illiterate and backward population, and so may our relations with the neighboring Arab countries, which may be affected by the situation of the Arabs within a Jewish State. Finally, as Jews we cannot ignore moral claims. Eretz Israel is after all the land of the prophets; for ages the Jewish people has suffered for refusing to renounce its faith and mission. It will be the duty of our restored people to live up to the moral implications of our history, alike in our internal life and in our relations with our neighbors—to achieve a society based on the fundamental teaching of Judaism: "Thou shalt love thy neighbor as thyself."[15] This must be the basis of the constitution of the Jewish State in Palestine, and our treatment of the Arab citizens of our State must be the same as our treatment of the Jews. That means not merely equality but equalization; helping them to raise themselves to the same level as our own, while preserving their national identity, language, and culture. It must be the mission of the Jewish State to see that the position of the Arabs in Palestine should be better than their position in the Arab States, so long as the Jewish State itself is on a higher level than its Arab neighbors. While the main purpose of the Jewish State must and will be to restore the Jewish people to their ancient homeland, and while until this object is achieved it must remain the mainspring and primary function of the Jewish State, we must treat the Arabs remaining within our borders exactly as if they were Jews.

NOTES

1. Ronald W. Zweig, *Britain and Palestine during the Second World War* (London: Royal Historical Society, 1986), 152.

2. Ernest Bevin (1881–1951) was a Labor politician, Secretary of Labor during the war, and became Foreign Secretary in 1945. Bevin supported Zionism during the war, but his views changed afterward, when he was saddled with the burden of solving the Zionist–Palestinian impasse.

3. Leo Amery (1873–1955) was a longtime Conservative MP and served during the war as Secretary of State for India. He was sympathetic to Zionism, perhaps in part due to his partial Jewish origin, which he concealed throughout his life.

4. Over the course of the Balkan Wars, World War I, and the Greco-Turkish War of 1919–22, some 1.5 million Orthodox Christians (Turkish as well as Greek-speaking) were driven from Turkish lands to Greece. Another half million were transferred by treaty in 1923. At the same time, some 500,000 Muslims, most of them Turks, were expelled from Greece to Turkey.

5. The dunam was an Ottoman unit of land measure, some 913 square meters, or about a quarter of an acre. Under British rule, the dunam was rounded up to 1,000 square meters and became known as a metric dunam.

6. See document 1.

7. A First Aliyah settlement about ten kilometers (6 mi) north today's city of Rehovot.

8. A village just west of Jerusalem, in the Judean hills.

9. West of the Jordan River.

10. The Litani flows entirely within Lebanon. At its southeasternmost point it comes to within four kilometers (ca. 2.5 mi) of the Israeli border.

11. Muslims originally from the Caucasus Mountain region who began to move to the Middle East in the mid-1800s.

12. The Alawites, concentrated mainly in Syria.

13. Ben-Gurion's statement was prescient; after the war some twelve million ethnic Germans were expelled from Soviet territories.

14. Abdul Aziz Al Saud (1876–1953) was the king of Saudi Arabia.

15. Stated twice in Lev. 19 and in many places in the New Testament.

54

Liberating Jerusalem (1942)

IRGUN TZVA'I LE'UMI

At the beginning of the Second World War, the Haganah halted all military operations in Palestine in support of the British fight against the Nazis. The Etzel—the paramilitary organization associated with the Revisionist movement—leadership decided to take part as well in the ceasefire but some Etzel members refused, withdrew from Etzel, and formed Lehi (see document 56). Other members of Etzel who remained with the organization claimed that British policies as well as activities of the Arab Palestinian leadership called for immediate action—but the mainstream leadership of the Etzel cooperated with the British and even participated in military operations with the British army against axis forces and allies in the Middle East. This document reflects the sentiments among Etzel members and their view of the changing political conditions in the region. The document also shows that while the Haganah and Etzel decided to pursue a common policy, tensions, suspicions, and mistrust between the two organizations continued. By the later stages of the war, Etzel activists clamored to resume their military activities in Palestine against the British to advance the creation of an independent Jewish state. In February 1944, under the command of Menachem Begin, Etzel declared a revolt against the British government in Palestine and resumed its military operations.

Source: *Bamah la-No'ar* (A Forum for Youth), vol. 4, May 10, 1942. Published in *Ha-Irgun ha-Tzva'i Le'umi be-Eretz Israel: Osef Mekorot u-Mismachim, Kerech 2* (Tel Aviv, 1992), 239–50. Translated by Marganit Weinberger-Rotman.

Jerusalem, David's capital, is waiting for its liberation.

Its sons, who day by day turn their faces toward her, are scattered across continents and seas.

Jerusalem, the regal city, is still widowed. . . .

A foreigner now occupies the seat of David. Jerusalem has no law or justice. The fleecing of Israel and looting of the poor are prevalent in it. It has become the source of spilled blood.

And for this it shall mourn.

Jerusalem, the capital of the King the Messiah, awaits its salvation. . . .

From the depths of despair and weakness springs the vision of the faith in a liberated Jerusalem.

Eternal is David's Jerusalem.

And in these days, days of blood for the freedom-seeking nations and a struggle for life and death, we are calling in these pages upon the Hebrew youth to join the underground of the regal Israeli army to prepare for the decisive battle for the liberation of Jerusalem.

This pamphlet appears on the anniversary of the death of the commander of the Hebrew underground—David Raziel.[1] He fell in battle. But his path was clearly laid out. For his soldiers, he will always remain a symbol of a great personality, a symbol of the willingness to sacrifice, a symbol of conviction and vision. . . . He was the first in command and the first in action. And he always set an example to the soldiers who followed him. We will honor his memory and continue in his path.

The Commander

He was the first real commander of the Hebrew youth. He was the first who rose from the national underground army. He emerged as a great military leader. Like the great generals who shaped their nations, like Garibaldi and Cromwell, Pilsudski, and Atatürk,[2] he too stood head and shoulders above his people. He did not need to employ any form of artificial or external discipline on his men; naturally they followed him, the way the heart and body, the will and the spirit operate, because his command was imbued with the spirit of the nation's leader, of God Almighty.

From his childhood he was a fighter. From his childhood he was a military person. But he was not content with the external manifestations of an officer. He studied the art of war in all its branches and all its languages. Just as he was a great scholar of Judaism, he spent days and nights mastering the sciences of defense and battle.

Such was the man who grew among us. And after we've become orphans with the passing away of our supreme commander Ze'ev Jabotinsky[3]—we pinned on him all of our hopes. In our minds we saw him standing and winning the decisive national battle, and we also saw him as the first politician and leader of our young kingdom when it is founded.

But God took him away from us. Providence does not wish upon us an easy path. Each one of us is called upon to acquire a sliver of the spirit of our late commander. Each one of us must become a fighting and brave Hebrew military person, "a genius and benevolent and cruel."

In place of the one thousands will come.

And the day of battle will surely arrive.

And the laurels of the victor we will place on the grave of David Raziel.

"To remember the shame"—this is the essence of the warlike consciousness of each and every one of us. Human beings are naturally disposed to remember primarily the good; the bad that one experiences gets washed out, blurred. It is more convenient to remember the good; if you remember the bad—you must determine the cause, to draw conclusions. Bad memories are tied to turbulence and the "man on the street" seeks quiet. There, in the subconscious he forgets the bad of yesterday and tomorrow he'll forget the bad of today.

But have mercy on the collective, the people, that forgets the bad that happens to it; pity the nation that does not remember its shame; it will never look for reasons, it won't draw conclusions and won't change the shape of things: forever it will be mired in its shame. . . .

The role of the rebels is primarily to remind us of the shame again and again; to inscribe it on the tablets of the hearts of the young generation, because only thusly a change is possible.

And to remind does not mean only words. That is not enough; only deeds tend to remind, to instill faith, to excite.

That is why the Italians appreciated Cavour[4] but believed in Garibaldi. That is why the Irish elected Cosgrave,[5] the diplomat and master of words, but they put their faith in the rebel and man of deeds de Valera.[6]

The late David Raziel remembered the shame. And because he remembered it he felt the shame and understood it. And because he understood its essence he rebelled against it in all of the coolness of his mind and the heat of his turbulent and free soul . . . Like Judah the Maccabi in his time, David Raziel knew that numbers do not carry an advantage, not even equipment. The one who carries the shame in his heart and is sick of it—will not be brought down by any kind of weapon. . . . He is gone. He will not return to us and teach us anymore. But the "theory of shame" that we acquired from him will be imprinted on our blood forever and ever. And the oath he made us take—to end the shame—still stands. And as we stand in attention in memory of our brave commander, quietly our lips will say: "we will remember the shame"!

When we heard that Ha-Ko'ach Vienna,[7] the football team, was about to come to the Land of Israel, he made the following speech in honor of the visitors: "Wonderful! Release the bones of this people that have been broken for 2,000 years since it was exiled from its land; straighten the hunched back, the legacy of the Diaspora. Show that the Jew can also be a man of matter, whose strength is in his waist and his vitality is in the muscles of his stomach. Until now they only knew the hunched and oppressed Jew, now show a second version of the Jew who takes his enemies by the back of their necks.

Don't be ashamed of your Jewishness, don't be athletes who are Jewish but Jewish athletes, accentuate your Jewishness, your nationality. . . . You must transform a people of shopkeepers, traders, and teachers to a people that can fight back—a people that will not be trampled by others."

Will there be an end to the recklessness of the police?

The [British] Palestinian police has raised its head. After the bloodbath that it perpetrated on a number of Hebrew youths in Tel Aviv, it now continues in this effort. Again we learned that it broke into a private residence in Jerusalem and a Hebrew youth was injured. The police feel it has a license to kill Hebrew youths without a trial and a verdict and without stirring up the Hebrew public. Have we really reached the point when there is no longer a judge and justice in Zion?

We mustn't accept these bloody deeds silently. Our silence will only vindicate the atrocities and prove that we surrendered to a verdict of annihilation that was imposed on us by the British administration. . . .

Jews Surrendering Their Brothers

In recent days we have witnessed an increase in the number of kidnappings. Every day we learn about Hebrew youths who are kidnapped from their homes at night, tortured in basements, and turned over to the British police. The number of occurrences and the nature of the activity show cooperation between "the force that knows how to defend" [the Haganah] and the British police. Jews are surrendering their brothers over to a foreign ruler. In addition to the meagerness and the moral servitude that surrendering Jews to the enemy entails, these Jews are helping to dismantle the strength of the Yishuv and are destroying with their own hands the hope for salvation of the suffering nation and are legitimizing the harmful acts of the government of Palestine.

Athens and Jerusalem

The visits of the Mufti in Berlin and Rome led to the creation of a national Arab government: Haj Amin al-Husseini,[8] the prime minister; Rashid Ali[9] (the instigator of the rebellion in Iraq) the foreign minister; and Fawzi al-Qawuqji,[10] the minister of war. These are going to be the activities of the "threesome" that is recognized by the Axis powers, and undoubtedly they will be very busy.[11] They will be situated probably in Athens, which will serve as the center for Arab propaganda. From there the venomous propaganda will spread to all the Arab countries in the Middle East. There they will train officers for their "liberation army," paratroopers, spy agents, propagandists, and so on. To aid the "threesome" and their plots, the Axis powers will send military trainers and veteran agents, planes and ships, and especially—money and arms.

The Land of Israel, Syria, Iraq, and even Egypt will serve as vast operational fields for these plots. To each member of this "threesome" are a great many supporters among the Arab population and they have great influence in a variety of arenas, including the political, economic, cultural, and religious, especially among the young. They will have everything at their disposal, and in due time also the weapons that have been collected in the battlefields of Syria or stolen from the British weapon depots in Israel.

The plan of this "government" was articulated in a proclamation to the Arab world promising that on the day of the victory of the Axis powers the eight million Arabs in the Middle East will get the chance to act out their revenge against the British and the Jews following the Hong Kong example (in Hong Kong the Japanese conquerors abused the British and their wives). . . .

In the mosques, the preachers are giving speeches and ignite the imagination of their followers; the teachers in the schools are fueling to Arab zealotry among the students; the scouts are preparing themselves for their national destiny; there is growing mobilization that is accompanied by desertion of Arab soldiers, with their weapons, from the British army; the British army depots are being cleaned out by "anonymous" Arabs; the Arab gangs are operating again though still on a small scale; the number of "Kafiah" wearers has grown; Arab officials in government offices are collecting important data. . . .

These things are taking place in plain view of the British authorities, and in some areas with their aid and support; because here also prevails the tendency [among the British] to turn the Arabs into a decisive factor, to create the illusion that the Arabs are opposing the "Axis" and support, allegedly, the British. And for this reason they are floating of the slogan of "Pan-Arabism" and appeasing the Arabs at the expense of the Jews. . . .

This [British] policy has resulted directly in the *Struma*[12] affair and all the venomous Arab propaganda against the Jews. . . .

To summarize, the mere attempt at appeasement increased the Arabs' appetite immensely, and it taught them to ask for more and more. And eventually the deciding force in the country will not be the British but the Mufti in Athens.

NOTES

1. In their attempts to quell an Iraqi rebellion in 1941, the British sent Jewish units, including an Etzel unit led by David Raziel, to Iraq. On May 20, 1941, Raziel was killed in that mission from a German aerial attack.

2. Giuseppe Garibaldi (1807–82) was one of the military heroes of the Italian battle for national liberation. Oliver Cromwell (1599–1658) was one of the leaders of the New Model Army that defeated the Royalists in the English Civil War (1641–51). After the execution of Charles I in 1649, Cromwell dominated the short-lived English commonwealth until his death. Josef Pilsudski (1867–1935) was a leader in the Polish struggle for independence after the First World War. From 1918 to 1922 he was Poland's chief of state. He returned to power after the May 1926 coup and ruled Poland as a dictator until his death. Mustafa Kemal Atatürk (1881–1935) led the Turkish national movement after the defeat of the Ottoman Empire in the First World War. He is the founder (Atatürk literally means the father of the Turks) of the Turkish Republic and served as its president from 1923 until his death.

3. Jabotinsky was Etzel's titular head but was not involved in its day-to-day operations

4. Camillo Paolo Filippo Giulio Benso Conte di Cavour (1810–61) was a leading figure of the Italian unification movement. He served as the prime minister of the kingdom of Piedmont, and for three months before his death he served as Italy's first prime minister.

5. William Thomas Cosgrave (1880–1965) served as the first president of the Executive Council of the Irish Free State from 1922 to 1932.

6. Éamon de Valera (1882–1975) was one of the more militant leaders of the Irish Republican Movement during the Irish Civil War. Later in his career he traded his early support for militarism with a cultural conservative agenda. He served as the president of Ireland from 1959 to 1973.

7. Ha-Ko'ach Vienna was a Jewish athletic association that was founded by Austrian Zionists in 1909. The association included swimming, wrestling, and track and field teams, but the most famous was the football team. Following the Nazi *Anschluss* in 1938, Ha-Ko'ach Vienna was shut down.

8. Haj Amin al-Husseini (1895/7–1974) was the Grand Mufti of Jerusalem from 1921 to 1948. Husseini emerged early on as one of the fiercest opponents of Zionism and Jewish settlement in Palestine, and he was the driving force behind the Arab Revolt (1936–39). In 1937 he fled Palestine

and found refuge in Lebanon, Iraq, Italy, and Nazi Germany. During the war he supported the Axis powers by broadcasting from Berlin, seeking to raise Arab support for the Nazi cause, and recruiting Muslim volunteers.

9.   Rashid Ali al-Gaylani (1892–1965) served briefly as Prime Minister of Iraq in 1933, 1940 and 1941. He led a short-lived coup in 1941 that was supported by the Axis powers and suppressed by British forces.

10.   Fawzi al-Qawuqji (1890–1977) served as an officer in the Ottoman army during the First World War. He later participated in a rebellion against the French in Syria (1925–27), and he led Arab volunteer forces in Palestine during the Great Arab Revolt. He supported Rashid Ali during his 1941 coup and spent the rest of the Second World War in Germany. He was the field commander of the Arab Liberation Army, an army of volunteers from different Arab countries, during the 1948 War.

11.   All three Arab nationalist leaders mentioned above: Amin al-Husseini, Rashid Ali, and Fawzi al-Qawuqji were in Iraq, leading anti-British activities, at the time that David Raziel was killed. All three Arab leaders were Nazi collaborators, and they spent the rest of the Second World War in Germany. They did not, however, create a "government." In fact, during the Arab Revolt in Palestine, Qawuqji and Husseini had several major disagreements over tactical as well as political matters.

12.   The *Struma* was a ship that was chartered by Betar to bring Jewish refugees from Romania to Palestine. The ship left for Palestine on December 12, 1941 — but because of faulty engines it was towed to Istanbul. While it was docked there, negotiations were carried with the British government in Palestine to issue entry visas to Palestine, but as the negotiations were being held, the Turks towed the ship out to sea where it was torpedoed by a Soviet submarine on February 24, 1942, killing all but one of the 769 passengers on board.

55

Four Years (1943)

HA-SHOMER HA-TSA'IR

Ha-Shomer Ha-Tsa'ir (the Young Guard) is a socialist Zionist movement founded in 1913 in Galicia, then part of the Austro-Hungarian Empire. The movement was heavily influenced by the writings of Ber Borochov, who combined Zionism with a Marxist historical approach. Members of the movement first settled in Palestine in 1919; in 1927 they founded Ha-Kibbutz Ha-Artzi (the National Kibbutz Federation). By the start of the Second World War, the movement had 70,000 members worldwide, mostly in eastern Europe. This article, written during the war, examines the devastating impact of the war on the movement as well as the heroic fight that many members of the movement led against the Nazis. Occupying the leftist flank of the Zionist movement (many members of Ha-Shomer Ha-Tsa'ir supported the creation of a binational—Arab and Jewish—state in Palestine), other Zionist factions frequently criticized the movement and questioned its Zionist credentials. This article addresses these criticisms, as it asserts the commitment of the movement to the fate of the Jewish people. The article also raises the question of rescue operations by the Yishuv and the commitment of the Zionist movements in Palestine for their brethren in the Diaspora, an issue that has become quite controversial in recent historical writings on the Yishuv's reaction to the Holocaust. After the creation of the state in 1948, Ha-Shomer Ha-Tsa'ir merged with Ahdut Ha-Avodah Po'alei Tsion to form Mapam (Mifleget Ha-Poalim Ha-Me'uhedet—The United Workers Party), a Marxist Zionist party with a pro-Soviet orientation, which won nineteen

Source: *Hedim: Le-She'elot ha-Hevrah ha-Kibbutzit*, vol. 8, 1943. Translated by Eran Kaplan.

seats in the first Israeli Knesset; it was the second largest party after the ruling Mapai party.

Four years have passed since that day, September 1, when the Second World War started. In the storm that ensued, the Nazi armies advanced from country to country, spreading death, destruction, poverty, and slavery. The entire European continent fell prey to the Nazi beast. And immediately the process of extermination began. They hoped to get rid of the Jews by diseases, plagues, starvation, by uprooting them. To that end they enslaved them, restricted their food rations, denied them medicines, crowded them in ghettoes, levied on them fines, and turned the local population against them. But all of these measures could not break the will and vitality of the Jewish masses.

With the outbreak of the German–USSR war, the methods of the destruction were changed. The Nazis realized that they could not defeat this stubborn people. And then began the systematic killing of Jews by gases, electricity, mass poisoning, and machine guns. One region after another was emptied of Jews. Jewry is being burnt on the stake. In the extermination camps in Treblinka, Mejduk [sic], in the forests and roads, in the ghetto streets and basements, inside the train cars slowly making their way to the extermination camps—thousands are killed every day. Nothing like that has ever happened in the history of human misery. Only the mind of a beast in the guise of a human being could invent such a satanic plan to destroy an entire people.

These four years were also the years of struggle for our right to save our brothers. Allies and foes alike erected a wall of alienation around us. We won't ever forget that the declaration of war against Germany was accompanied by British policemen shooting at the ships bringing immigrants. . . . At the price of 129 casualties, the refugees aboard the *Patria* won the right to land on the shores of the Land of Israel.[1] But the passengers of the *Atlantic*, which also docked at the port of Haifa, were turned back by the police and were shipped to the Island of Mauritius, a place where over 1,500 Jews are suffering under the harsh conditions of a concentration camp.[2] And there was also the *Struma*,[3] a ship of immigrants and pioneers from Bulgaria that docked in Istanbul, waiting for immigration permits from the British government in the Land of Israel. And when the government refused to issue the permits, it sailed away from shore, becoming easy prey for both the massive waves and submarines—all of the 300 people aboard were drowned. Even those who are trying to escape the Nazi horrors by small boats are turned away to Cyprus were they are detained in camps, held at the mercy of the authorities who might someday allow them to enter the land.

The Bermuda Conference[4] declared that for us, the Jews, they have no salvation. We have one option: the gallows. . . . A wall of malicious alienation shut off our scream from reaching the conscience of the world. Indeed, when it came to saving the Jews that conscience was silent.

Our Movement during the War

We were a movement of thousands, operating all over Europe. . . . In the major Jewish centers we became a major public force. . . .

The war did not undermine the pioneering spirit of commitment of our members. . . . Hundreds congregated in Vilnius to emigrate from there together. On the Romanian border we had emissaries, looking for cracks to blaze a path for immigrants. . . . In the Soviet Union members traveled to the Caucuses and the borders of Iran and Afghanistan to seek ways to reach the Land of Israel. . . . Only a few were successful and many failed and paid with their lives or in long prison terms for their bravery.

Our members did not succumb to destiny. . . . This is a time in which we are reconstituting the ruins of the Shomer farm in Chenstochov,[5] traveling from one place to another and organizing the different branches. Sisyphean labor was required to create something positive in the horrible reality of the Nazi regime, the underground, the hunger, the labor camps. . . . And not only in Poland and Galicia, these are the old and established centers, but everywhere in Europe there were instances of bravery and sacrifice. Our friends in Yugoslavia joined the ranks of the partisans, and they are distinguishing themselves in fighting the invading enemy. . . . Our friends in Antwerp are carrying out the rescue of tens of our members to neutral countries. And in Slovakia, where Jewish blood is spilled by the local population, small rescue operations are being arranged with our members playing a major role. This is the state of our movement until a change comes.

In the middle of 1942 the extermination commenced. For months we did not know. World leaders, for some reason, kept it a secret. They did not even give us this mercy of knowing the fate of our people. . . . All of our movement's leadership in Poland and most of our members have died in the defense effort. No one was spared. Some came back to Warsaw to take part in the fighting.[6] . . . We will also remember the leaders of our movement in Galicia who were put on trial for their Zionism in Lviv. Our members have defended valiantly and proudly their right to be Zionists in the Soviet Union. They turned the courthouse into a stage from which they described the virtues of socialist Zionism. They did not recant their past and declared publicly that they will continue to strengthen the Zionist-socialist creed among our members under the liberating regime of the Soviet Union. They are still imprisoned because the wall of alienation has yet to be breached, and there isn't yet a bridge of understanding between Zionism and the policies of the Soviet Union. They also have not given up. . . .

We never considered our pioneering education and our missions in the Diaspora to be contradictory. On the contrary, we always took upon ourselves the most pioneering of tasks. We demanded our members to be uprooted from their surroundings and make aliyah; because we consider aliyah the revolutionary act that will serve the interest of the Jewish masses. . . . Our ideological awareness commended us to pursue complete fulfillment of the pioneering mission for the benefit of the Jewish Diaspora. And it is this awareness that led our members, in the current historical period, to forsake the possibility of making aliyah and to return from Vilnius to the occupied Nazi areas and to die on the ghettos' walls. . . . We knew that all the empty talk by our adversaries about our lack of connection to our people is nothing more than folly. We know our movement and how it is tied, in an unbreakable bond, to the fate of the Jewish people, and that in trying times it will be one of the first to protect the Jewish people's honor.

Our Duty

We will participate in the aid and rescue effort. We will demand from the Yishuv and free Jewish communities to partake in aid and rescue operations that match the depths of the Jewish tragedy. It is still possible to save—this is the call that reaches us from our friends who are sitting at the gates of Europe. . . . In the first two years we did not do enough. The calls from the Diaspora fell on deaf ears. We did not adequately assess the danger. Also, at the time the Yishuv was under great pressure because the enemy directly threatened the country. However, the Land of Israel no longer faces direct danger, while the remains of European Jewry still does. . . . Our farms must be open and prepared to absorb children and youth, who might arrive soon or even immediately in the Land of Israel. We mustn't be too strict about the educational principles we employ when we will have to absorb the young, because they are our children. . . . We must struggle to ensure that the toll of this great effort is spread equally in the

Yishuv so we won't repeat the despicable spectacle, in which farms finance by themselves the absorption of the children, while in the cities landlords and speculators loot the refugees. . . . And lastly the Diaspora. When the day comes, we will send delegations from the Land of Israel to perform political tasks, and to provide medical and material assistance. . . .

After thirty years in existence, as we stand face to face with the destruction of Israel and the annihilation of our movement, we will have to start all over again. We will confront a new reality. We will have to collect the remains and infuse in them a new will to live. . . . Even on the eve of the war we were only thousands among millions. We mustn't be led astray by false optimism that the majority of Jews in the Diaspora who will survive would learn the right historical lesson from Hitlerism. We will not be alone in the Jewish street. We will have to fight over determining the intellectual character of this Jewry. . . . There will be the illusions of assimilation; there will be a renewed belief in the powers of democracy on the one hand, and on the other, a belief in the power of socialism to solve the Jewish problem abroad. The struggle would probably intensify, because we can assume that in the first years after the war Jews will be treated more liberally. With great force we shall have to go out to the Diaspora. Much effort will also be needed to blaze new ways to reach the shores of Israel. Our blood is cheap and no one but us will avenge it. Our revenge can be only one: to create in the land enough power that will assure that Jewish blood will never again be forsaken. We must invest all of our strength and stubbornness, and all of our capabilities in this revenge.

NOTES

1. The *Patria* was a French-built ship that carried 1,800 illegal Jewish immigrants who were deported from Palestine to Mauritius and Trinidad by the British mandatory authorities. In order to prevent the ship from leaving Palestine, on November 25, 1940, the Haganah planted a bomb on the ship. The bomb went off while the ship was in the Haifa Harbor causing hundreds of causalities (many more than this document indicates). Eventually, the more than 1,500 survivors were allowed to remain in Palestine.

2. The *Atlantic* carried 1,645 illegal Jewish immigrants to Palestine; it arrived on November 24, 1940. The British placed 134 of its passengers on the *Patria*; the remaining passengers were sent to the Atlit detention center just south of Haifa, and then on December 9, 1945, they were deported to Mauritius.

3. See document 54n12.

4. The Bermuda Conference was held on April 19, 1943. The United States and Britain convened the conference to address the plight of Jewish refugees in Europe. It failed to yield any concrete solutions.

5. In the summer of 1941, Ha-Shomer Ha-Tsa'ir members attempted to reconstitute the movement's training camp in Chenstochov, Poland. They were unsuccessful and instead they

established an agricultural farm on the nearby Zarki farm, which belonged to Jews. Several such farms operated in Poland; the Germans allowed them to operate as work camps, because they provided free agricultural labor in areas that were economically devastated by the war.

6.   Members of Ha-Shomer Ha-Tsa'ir played a critical role in the Warsaw ghetto revolt in the spring of 1943. One of the revolt's leaders, Mordechai Anielewicz, was a member of the movement.

56

Works of Avraham Stern and Lehi (1932–ca. 1943)

Avraham Stern (1907–42) was one of the leaders of the Etzel and later, from 1940 until his death, the commander of Lehi (Lohamei Herut Israel—Fighters for the Freedom of Israel). Stern was born in Suwalki, Poland, and came to Palestine at the age of eighteen. He enrolled at the Hebrew University in Jerusalem where he studied classical languages. As a student he joined the Hulda group—a student organization with strong nationalistic leanings. During the riots of 1929, Stern joined the Haganah. In 1931 Avraham Tehomi, Stern's commander, seceded and formed Haganah B, a Revisionist-leaning underground organization that adopted more proactive military tactics. In time this faction would call itself Etzel (Irgun Tsva'i Le'umi—the National Military Organization). Stern followed Tehomi to Etzel, and in 1932 he completed an officer-training course. It was as a member of Etzel that Stern adopted his *nom de guerre* Yair, after Elazar ben Yair, the leader of the Zealots in Masada during the Great Jewish Revolt against the Romans in the year 72 CE.

This collection of texts by Stern includes the poem "Unknown Soldiers" (*Hayalim Almonim*), which Stern wrote probably sometime between 1932 and 1934 and which served as an unofficial anthem of both Etzel and later Lehi. The poem serves as a clear indication of the type of nationalist pathos that one could also find in the poetry of Vladimir Jabotinsky and Uri Zvi Greenberg, the great Revisionist poet and ideologue, which celebrates the notions of sacrifice and blood on the battlefield in the name of national pride and freedom.

The second text in this collection, from April 23, 1937, was composed at the height of the Arab Revolt in Palestine, when the Peel Commission was exploring possible

Source: saveisrael.com. Used with permission.

solutions to quell the intensifying inter-religious violence in Palestine. Among the possible solutions, which later in the summer of 1937 became the committee's ultimate recommendation, was the idea of partitioning Palestine into two states: an Arab one and a Jewish one. In that same year, the Etzel commander Tehomi and the majority of his supporters returned to the Haganah, and Stern was appointed secretary of the rump Etzel command. Stern's short text reflects the drama that engulfed Etzel at the time of the split. A second split occurred in the summer of 1940. After the start of the Second World War, the Haganah and then Etzel decided to halt military operations in Palestine as long as the British were fighting the Nazis. A small group of radical Etzel members, headed by Stern, refused to stop the battle against the British and created Lehi. The final text in this collection outlines Lehi's basic ideological tenets. The text explores the type of commitment that the struggle for independence would require as well as some ideas as to what the future Jewish state might look like.

Stern was caught and shot by the British police in an apartment in Tel Aviv, which had served as one of his hideouts, on February 12, 1942. He was replaced by three men at the command of Lehi: Yitzhak Yezernitsky (Shamir), Nathan Friedman (Yellin-Mor), and Israel Scheib (Eldad).

Unknown Soldiers:
Anthem of the Fighters for the Freedom of Israel

We are unknown soldiers, uniforms we have none,
In death's shadow we march, in its terror,
Volunteering to sever to the end of our days,
Only death from our duty can us sever.
In days red with slaughter, destruction and blood,
Nights black with pain and despair,
Over village and town our flag we'll unfurl,
Love and freedom the message 'twill bear.
Not like slaves brought to heel were we dragged to the fight,
In strange lands our life's blood to squander,
And if we must die our people to free,
We are willing our lives to surrender.
In days red with slaughter . . .
With obstacles rising to block every move,
By fate cruelly sent to entrap us,
Neither enemy, prison or miserable spy

Will we ever permit to divert us.
In days red with slaughter . . .
Should we happen to fall in some building or street,
To be furtively buried by night,
Many thousands of others will rise in our stead
To defend and continue the fight.
In days red with slaughter . . .
With the tears of mothers bereaved of their young,
Sacred infant's blood want only spilt,
We'll cement the bricks of our bodies for walls
And our homeland will surely be built
In days red with slaughter, destruction and blood,
Nights black with pain and despair,
Over village and town our flag we'll unfurl
Love and freedom the message 'twill bear.

To Those Who Honor the Oath!

The Irgun Tsva'i Le'umi (IZL) in the Land of Israel was created because we believe the Hebrew state will not become a reality without relying on an independent military body.

The Jewish Agency now hopes to obtain approval for free action for those under its command in return for subjugation to the foreign rule and surrender to the cantonization plans for this land. The IZL in the Land of Israel is charged with the duty of acting as the only real force that will be called upon and will be able to fight for re-establishment of the Hebrew nation in the Land of Israel in the face of the plotting of the external enemy and the surrender to those who are willing to betray us from within.

The IZL in the Land of Israel has been forced by political reality to decide whether to surrender to the power of the government and the Jewish Agency, or to redouble its sacrifice and its risk-taking. Some of our friends were not up to this difficult task. They surrendered to the Agency and left the battlefield. The large loyal majority continues to uphold the original policy of the IZL. All the attempts by the former command of the Irgun to reach a merger with the Leftist organization have failed, since the Left has not negotiated on the basis of joining forces but of imposing one group's will on the other. Putting the IZL under the authority of the Agency, which is ruled by the Left, is the end of our organization.

There are two organizations today in this land: one is leftist, run by Left, and to our regret some of our men have joined it. The other is the IZL, which continues to fight for the dignity and the life of the nation being reborn. We believe in the mission of our movement and its power to reestablish the full independence within the historical borders of the Hebrew state. We believe in the youth of Israel's willingness to fight and to sacrifice, having set as its life's goal the might and the independence of the nucleus of Hebrew power.

Anonymous Soldiers!

The nucleus of Hebrew power is prepared for any order or sacrifice!

"Only death releases us from our duty!"

The Ideology of the Lehi
National Revival Principles (*Ha-Techiya*)
The Fighters for the Freedom of Israel (FFI)—The Lehi

1. The Nation

The Jewish people are a covenanted people, the originators of monotheism, formulators of the prophetic teachings, standard bearers of human culture, guardians of glorious patrimony. The Jewish people are schooled in self-sacrifice and suffering; their vision, survivability, and faith in redemption are indestructible.

2. The Homeland

The homeland is the Land of Israel within the borders delineated in the Bible ("To your descendants, I shall give this land, from the River of Egypt to the great Euphrates River." Gen. 15:18) This is the land of the living, where the entire nation shall live in safety.

3. The Nation and Its Land

Israel conquered the land with the sword. There it became a great nation and only there it will be reborn. Hence Israel alone has a right to that land. This is an absolute right. It has never expired and never will.

4. The Goals

1. Redemption of the land.
2. Establishment of sovereignty.
3. Revival of the nation.

There is no sovereignty without the redemption of the land, and there is no national revival without sovereignty.

These are the goals of the organization during the period of war and conquest:

5. Education

Educate the nation to love freedom and zealously guard Israel's eternal patrimony. Inculcate the idea that the nation is master to its own fate. Revive the doctrine that "The sword and the book came bound together from heaven." (*Midrash Vayikra Rabba* 35:8)

6. Unity

The unification of the entire nation around the banner of the Hebrew freedom movement. The use of the genius, status, and resources of individuals, and the channeling of the energy, devotion, and revolutionary fervor of the masses for the war of liberation.

7. Pacts

Make pacts with all those who are willing to help the struggle of the organization and provide direct support.

8. Force

Consolidate and increase the fighting force in the homeland and in the Diaspora, in the underground and in the barracks, to become the Hebrew army of liberation with its flag, arms, and commanders.

9. War

Constant war against those who stand in the way of fulfilling the goals.

10. Conquest

The conquest of the homeland from foreign rule and its eternal possession.

These are the tasks of the movement during the period of sovereignty and redemption:

11. Sovereignty

Renewal of Hebrew sovereignty over the redeemed land.

12. Rule of Justice

The establishment of a social order in the spirit of Jewish morality and prophetic justice. Under such an order no one will go hungry or unemployed. All will live in harmony, mutual respect, and friendship as an example to the world.

13. Reviving the Wilderness

Build the ruins and revive the wilderness for mass immigration and population increase.

14. Aliens

Solve the problem of alien population by exchange of population.

15. Ingathering of the Exiles

Total ingathering of the exiles to their sovereign state.

16. Power

The Hebrew nation shall become a first-rate military, political, cultural, and economical entity in the Middle East and around the Mediterranean Sea.

17. Revival

The revival of the Hebrew language as a spoken language by the entire nation, the renewal of the historical and spiritual might of Israel. The purification of the national character in the fire of revival.

18. The Temple

The building of the Third Temple as a symbol of the new era of total redemption.

SECTION VI

The United Nations' Partition Proposal, November 1947 (reprinted from Mark Tessler, *A History of the Israeli–Palestinian Conflict* [Bloomington: Indiana University Press, 1994])

THE STRUGGLE
FOR PALESTINE AND
THE ESTABLISHMENT
OF THE STATE

After the end of World War II the Zionists' attention moved to the one million Jews who had survived the war and remained within the borders of the former Nazi empire. They focused in particular upon 250,000 Jewish refugees in Displaced Persons camps that the Allies had set up in Germany and Austria. The Zionist leadership claimed that Palestine was the only logical destination for the refugees. The Zionists demanded the immediate admission of 100,000 DPs, and in August 1945 the American president Harry S Truman publicly endorsed this proposal.

Britain wished to maintain close relations with the Arab world, but, bled white by the war, it could no longer afford a massive Middle Eastern military presence. The British were determined to retain control over the Suez Canal, which they hoped to protect by maintaining a military force in Palestine's Negev desert. Thus Ernest Bevin, the British foreign minister, saw little benefit in a pro-Zionist position.

Britain's pursuits of its own best interests appeared to the Zionists as betrayal. Despairing of diplomatic solutions, the Haganah in October 1945 joined forces with the Irgun and Lehi in attacks against British targets in Palestine. Lehi focused on murdering British soldiers. The Irgun did this occasionally but it, like the Haganah, concentrated on destroying trains and military installations. The most audacious attack was the destruction in July 1946 of the British military headquarters at Jerusalem's King David Hotel. The operation was performed by the Irgun, but the Haganah played a role in planning the attack.

In addition to engaging in guerilla warfare at home, the Haganah and Irgun made heroic efforts to smuggle Jews from Europe to Palestine. Between 1945 and 1948 some

70,000 illegal immigrants attempted to reach Palestine. Almost all the ships were intercepted by the British and their passengers interned. About half of the refugees were allowed to enter Palestine under previously established immigration quotas. The illegal immigration movement was thus not a pragmatic initiative to get Jews into Palestine so much as a gesture of the Yishuv's determination to take matters into its own hands. It was also a public relations strategy to expose world opinion to the spectacle of British soldiers boarding ships filled with Holocaust survivors and interning them in Mauritius, Cyprus, or the open-air prison at Atlit in Palestine itself.

International pressure, the escalating toll from the Zionist guerilla war, and Palestinian demands for Arab independence pushed Bevin in February 1947 to turn the Palestine matter over to the United Nations. The UN's Special Committee on Palestine, like the Peel Commission a decade before, recommended partition. This time around, though, the Jewish state would gain the virtually empty Negev, and the Arab state would have much of the Galilee, which had a large Arab population. The Zionists accepted the proposal, although they were distressed by the loss of Galilee and of Jerusalem, which would be placed under international trusteeship. The Arab states led what appeared to be a sufficiently large opposition to defeat the proposal within the General Assembly. Yet when put to a vote on November 29, 1947, it received just over the required two-thirds majority (thirty-three for, thirteen against, and ten abstentions). American backing was crucial, not only for the one vote it cast for partition but also for the pressure that the United States placed on some of the other countries to follow suit. No less crucial was the support of the Soviet Union, which saw in the Labor-dominated Yishuv as a possible socialist ally in its search for a broad Middle Eastern sphere of influence. Finally, the Latin American countries, which voted solidly for partition, appear to have been motivated by a sense of solidarity with a small group of historically oppressed people.

A recommendation by an international body without coercive power could not automatically result in Jewish statehood. Palestinian Arab leaders and a core of Arab fighters were committed to fight against partition, and there was massive popular support throughout the Arab world for a war against the Zionists. The Zionists had long felt that independence could be won only via military confrontation. That conflict took place in two stages. First, there was a war between Jews and Arabs in Palestine between November 1947 and May 1948, when the British formally vacated Palestine and the state of Israel proclaimed its independence. Then, between May 1948 and January 1949, Israel fought a series of short wars, punctuated by truces, against the armies of five Arab nations, principally Egypt and Jordan.

In the autumn of 1947, the leaders of the Arab states bordering Palestine privately expressed inability to prevent the establishment of a Jewish state should the United Nations vote for partition. The Palestinian Arab Higher Committee, however, proclaimed confidence in the military option, and on the day after the UN vote, Arab attacks on

Jews flared up throughout Palestine. Although the Zionists had formally accepted the UN partition resolution, they felt that its borders were a strategic nightmare, and the Haganah quickly pushed beyond them to take land in the Galilee, coastal plain, and Judean hills.

By endorsing the Partition Resolution, the Zionists appeared to be implicitly supporting the creation of a Palestinian state. In fact, the Zionists, the British, and King Abdullah of Jordan did not welcome such a prospect. Abdullah wanted the land designated for Palestine for his own kingdom, and the British vastly preferred Abdullah, who had been their client for decades, over the anticolonial Palestinian leadership. The Zionists, too, saw in Abdullah a relatively trustworthy neighbor, and in negotiations carried out between 1945 and 1948 they suggested that he annex the central Palestinian hill country, the heavily populated heartland of the designated Arab state. Negotiations between Abdullah and the Zionists did not, however, lead to any formal understandings, and Abdullah did not offer to recognize a Jewish state in part of Palestine, nor could the Zionists and Abdullah agree on the fate of Jerusalem. Also, it is doubtful whether Abdullah would have opposed the Palestinian leadership had it accepted partition.

The Zionists were aware that the Arab armies were much larger on paper than the actual numbers of men they could put into the field. Still, they were concerned about the strength of the Jordanian and Egyptian forces, and even more so about their own military shortcomings. The Haganah (including its elite unit, the Palmach) could mobilize some 50,000 fighters, but they were for the most part poorly armed and equipped. The Haganah was a militia, not an army, and many of its civilian commanders belonged to Mapam, a party to the left of Mapai. Thus the command structure of the Haganah was not fully responsible to Ben-Gurion. In May, Ben-Gurion dismissed the Haganah national command and created a standing army, called the Israel Defense Force (IDF), led by a regular officer corps.

The Palestinians outnumbered the Jews by a two to one ratio, but the former did not have a credible army. Bitter rivalries divided forces loyal to Amin al-Husayni from a multi-national Arab Liberation Army under the veteran commander Fawzi al-Qawukji. The vast majority of Palestinians did not take up arms against the Jews, and many Arab villages signed nonaggression pacts with nearby Jewish settlements. Nonetheless, in the winter of 1948 Palestinian Arab guerillas killed hundreds of Jews by sniping, bombing, and commando raids. Arab control of the roads cut off rural settlements from one another and placed Jerusalem under siege. In response to this crisis, in March 1948 the Haganah formulated a plan to secure the borders of the future Jewish state before the British withdrawal in May. In this plan (known as Plan D), the securing of roads and Jewish settlements demanded the conquest of the Arab villages from which the guerillas were operating. Expulsion of the villagers was sanctioned if field commanders deemed it necessary.

The plan was quickly implemented in the Judean foothills in order to break the siege of Jerusalem. The most notable Palestinian military leader, Abd el-Qadir al-Husayni, was killed in the battle for the village of Qastel. Palestinian morale was weakened further by mass killing of the inhabitants of Deir Yasin, a village on the outskirts of Jerusalem. The Irgun and Lehi perpetrated the operation, but the Jerusalem Haganah command knew and approved of the planned conquest. At least 120 Arabs were killed, some of whom were unarmed civilians.

The massacre at Deir Yasin augmented an already sizable wave of Palestinian flight. During the spring of 1948, most of the Arabs of Haifa and Jaffa fled in the face of battle. In these cities the Arabs were not expelled by the Zionists, but expulsions occurred in cities later in the year and in rural areas that came under the purview of Plan D. The largest single expulsion, involving as many as 100,000 Arabs, took place with the Israeli conquest of Lydda and Ramle, along the Tel Aviv–Jerusalem road and adjacent to the Jordanian-held West Bank. (The expulsion was even reported in the American Jewish press, via the euphemistic term "evacuation.") In general, the Israeli army's emphasis was on conquest rather than depopulation. Christian and Druze villages in the Galilee, which put up less resistance than Muslim ones, were much less likely to be emptied through either flight or expulsion. An IDF senior officer ordered the expulsion of the Arabs of Nazareth, but the commander on the scene countermanded the order, and his decision was upheld by Ben-Gurion. On occasion, Palestinian leaders forced Arabs to clear away from villages facing attack, lest they attempt to surrender or otherwise impede the course of battle.

Zionist military successes in the spring led Ben-Gurion to believe that the Yishuv should declare independence, even if that meant facing a multinational Arab invasion. Several members of the government demurred, but the majority supported their chairman. On the afternoon of May 14, several hours after England's formal surrender of control over Palestine, Ben-Gurion read the Declaration of Independence from the Tel Aviv Museum. The message was broadcast on radio throughout the country, except in Jerusalem, where electricity had been disrupted because of the war. The following day, armed forces from the bordering Arab states entered Palestine. Arab leaders had mixed feelings about going to war, but Arab public opinion demanded that the Jewish state be crushed. The battle plans of the Arab states were poorly coordinated and they often fought at cross-purposes, but during the first month of fighting they inflicted heavy losses on Israel. The new Jewish state lost thousands of men and barely held its own. Thanks to massive infusions of money from Diaspora Jews, Israel was able to purchase weapons from France, Italy, and Czechoslovakia, and unlike the Arab states, Israel had its own home industries for the manufacture of munitions. In July, the Arabs unilaterally broke a UN-imposed truce, but Israel routed its opponents and took land in the western Galilee that had been designated for the Arab state. By the beginning of January 1949, Israel had secured the Negev.

Israel emerged from the war with about 20 percent more territory than the UN had allotted it. But 5 percent of its population had been killed or wounded, and there were some 60,000 internal refugees. Palestinian society, on the other hand, had been decimated— between 600,000 and 750,000 Palestinians had become refugees, mainly in the West Bank, Gaza Strip, Syria, and Lebanon. At a peace conference in Lausanne in 1949, Arab representatives belatedly accepted partition, but in return for peace they demanded that Israel retreat to the original UN partition boundaries and repatriate the Palestinian refugees. At this time, masses of Jews from Europe were streaming into Israel, in need of homes, workplaces, and farmland. In Israel there was little sympathy for the Palestinians, and a good deal of fear of them, and the new state commandeered their land for the new immigrants.

The documents in this section focus on how Jews in the Yishuv perceived the tumultuous events of the period. Documents 57 through 59 depict the public mood during the fighting, and documents 60 and 61 present the wartime views of the Irgun on the conquest of Deir Yasin and other controversial events. The final document, 62, deals with relations between secular and religious authority in the Yishuv—an issue that arose at the very beginning of the New Yishuv (document 2) and remains contentious to this day.

57

The Silver Platter
(1947)

NATHAN ALTERMAN

Poetry was a revered form of expression about many aspects of Yishuv life, particularly those associated with struggle, challenge, and loss. We saw one example of this in Nathan Alterman's "Song of the Valley" (document 15), a paean to the pioneers and fallen heroes of the Zionist labor movement. Similarly, Alterman's "The Silver Platter" quickly assumed an iconic status in Israel, symbolizing the courage and sacrifice of the Zionist forces in 1948, and it is probably Alterman's best-known poem outside of Israel.

In a number of sources the poem is dated to the spring of 1948, shortly after Israel's Declaration of Independence. The poem's pathos, power, and depiction of fateful battle appear to reflect the fledgling Israeli state's desperate fight against the multilateral Arab invasion in May and June 1948. Yet the poem was, in fact, written several months earlier and was published just three weeks after the United Nations' Partition Resolution of November 29, 1947. In December, the Yishuv was already engaged in numerous skirmishes with Palestinian forces, and although scholars disagree about which side was on the offensive in these battles, there was undoubtedly a great deal of anxiety within the Yishuv about its future as the British prepared to vacate the country. Moreover, Alterman's poem reflects an ethos of martial valor and sacrifice that had been forming among the

Source: First published in *Davar*, December 19, 1947. Translated by Derek J. Penslar. Thanks to Arieh Saposnik for translation suggestions.

Yishuv's youth for at least two decades, since the 1929 riots. Alterman's poetry had long expressed this ethos, as in his epic poem cycle *The Joy of the Poor* (1941):

> A night of straits, a night of trial.
> And you, ready and experienced.
> I saw you desperate, I saw you armed,
> My brazen remnant.
> I saw you and understood how thin is the line
> Between the verge of catastrophe and the eve of jubilation.[1]

Yet whereas *The Joy of the Poor* was a complex work with a limited audience, "The Silver Platter" was published in the Yishuv's most important newspaper and immediately taken to heart by the Zionist public.

> And the land grows silent.
> The heavens' red eye fades on borders of smoke.
> And a nation will stand—torn at heart but still breathing,
> Accepting the miracle—one, and no other . . .
>
> It prepares for the rite. It faces the moon
> And stands, ere daybreak, clad in feast-day and fear.
> —Then from across come a lass and a lad
> And slowly they step towards the throng.
>
> In battle gear, shoes heavy with grime,
> They ascend the path, wordless . . .
> They did not change clothes, they did not wash away
> The remains of the day's toil and the night of hot battle.
>
> Weary without end, deprived of repose,
> Dripping with dew drops of fresh Hebrew youth—
> Silently come forward
> And stand without moving.
> No sign if they're alive or shot through
> Then the nation, awash in enchantment and tears
> Shall ask "who are you?" And the two then in silence
> Shall answer, We are the silver platter
> Upon which you will have the State of the Jews.

Thus they speak and, wrapped in shadow, fall at its feet.
And the rest will be in Israel's annals retold . . .

NOTE

1. Taken from "Leyl Ha-matsor" (Night of Siege), in *Simhat Ha-'Aniyim* (The Joy of the Poor) (Tel Aviv, 1957), 87.

58

A Jewish Child's Letter
to an Israeli Soldier (1948)

The mobilized, militaristic ethos embodied in the previous document was not limited to a narrow elite of politicians and intellectuals, nor to the domains of the Labor movement or the Yishuv's militias. It percolated into middle-class and Orthodox–Zionist circles, and it was found among children as well as adolescents and adults. This letter was written by a ten-year-old boy, Eliezer Don-Yehiye, who lived on Kfar-Hasidim, a moshav near Haifa. (Don-Yehiye grew up to become a prominent professor of political science at Bar-Ilan University.) This letter was one of many that were composed by Jewish children during the 1948 War and published in the children's supplements to the daily newspapers. Such letters were not fabricated by adults or coerced; they reflected a collectivist and patriotic spirit that had been inculcated into Yishuv youth from their earliest years. Don-Yehiye was himself from an Orthodox farming community, and the newspaper in which this letter appeared was affiliated with the National-Religious Mizrahi Party.

Greetings to you, my brother, my Hebrew soldier, wherever you are, in the mountains or in the valley, in outposts or on the front. I greet you and your comrades in arms who are fighting the Arab enemy threatening to destroy our homeland. You who fight on the front, spilling your blood for our country, battling against savages from the desert, Bevin's[1] mercenaries, dodging the fatal

Source: "Letter to a Hebrew Soldier 'Somewhere,'" *Hatzofeh li-Yeladim*, July 8, 1948, reproduced in "Itonut Lohemet: Hishtakfut Milhemet ha-Atzma'ut be-Itonei ha-Yeladim," in *Am be-milhama: Kovetz Mehkarim al ha-Hevra ha-Ezrahit be-Milhemet ha-Atzma'ut*, ed. Mordechai Bar-On and Meir Chazan (Jerusalem: Yad Ben-Zvi, 2007), 441–65. Translated by Marganit Weinberger-Rotman.

bullets. I who live here in the village, peacefully and without fear, send you, the Hebrew freedom fighter, this letter. I am well; here in the village there is no danger of British soldiers and Arab marauders. But even though our life is peaceful and calm here, we do not forget you. We, the children, are collecting books to send to the Hebrew warriors, for your hours of rest and recreation. I hope that when the war is over, we'll have a chance to meet. If I were as old as you are, I would take a Sten[2] in my hand and smite the enemies of our people. I try to conjure up your image as you stand with a roaring weapon in your hands, striking the enemy. Hebrew warrior! Be strong and of good courage![3] Be not affrighted! Have the might and valor to destroy our enemies. I hope you return soon from the battlefield unscathed. From me, here on the homefront,

Eliezer Don-Yehiye

NOTES

1. Ernest Bevin (1881–1951) was the British foreign secretary at the time of the 1948 War and widely believed among the Yishuv population to be anti-Zionist and even anti-Semitic.

2. An inexpensive British submachine gun, widely used by Israeli forces during the 1948 War.

3. Joshua 1:9. This famous biblical phrase is a general exhortation to bravery but has a special meaning here, as it was uttered by God to Joshua, successor to Moses, as the Israelites prepared to conquer the Promised Land.

59

Public Opinion during the 1948 War

There are limits to the capacity of published sources to reflect authentic public opinion, in the Yishuv or anywhere else. Thus public opinion surveying, which dates back to the early twentieth century, can be extremely valuable, although one must carefully examine the survey's sampling techniques and possible biases of the observers. In the winter of 1948, crude but highly suggestive public opinion surveys were compiled in the Haifa area by the Haganah's Branch for the Study of Public Opinion. The samples were usually quite small, usually consisting of only a few dozen, and the evidence is more anecdotal than quantitative. But the opinions reported here have the value of reporting a wide range of views held by ordinary people in extraordinarily difficult times. We see that the Yishuv was bound by high levels of solidarity, but that noble heroism was perhaps less common than a sense of grim determination, even desperation. We also see how disputes between the various Yishuv militias affected the public mood.

In the passages below, some of the headers have been deleted or changed, and at times text has been moved in order to enhance its flow and accessibility

Source: Archive of the Haganah, Tel Aviv, file no. 80/54/2. Translated by Marganit Weinberger-Rotman. These surveys were carried out in the Haifa area by the Haganah's Branch for the Study of Public Opinion. Some of the headers have been deleted or changed, and text has been modified and moved in order to enhance its flow and accessibility.

Question: What is the mood in your neighborhood toward the second phase[1] of the war? (Second Report: February 24, 1948)

This survey includes forty-six [people] who represent many dozens of members of the community. Since the question was broadly formulated, the answers refer to almost all aspects of public life. Most noteworthy is the readiness to assume any role and to sacrifice one's life. There is also a demand for a fairer division of responsibility and for recruitment of additional segments of the public (who have not yet been called up, or who are slackers). There is great enthusiasm for every military initiative and for giving more benefits—economically and socially—to enlisted persons.

An engineer: The second phase of the war reveals a deterioration of the situation due to (1) large scale attacks by the Arabs, and (2) "preventive actions" by our forces. Add to these factors disturbances and troubles from "the third party."[2] The engineer reports total readiness and accurate assessment of the difficulties from his immediate surroundings. There is an unshaken belief that we will triumph in the end and achieve our goals.

As far as military matters are concerned, the conditions are satisfactory . . . but the situation on the home front receives severe criticism. Why is part of the Yishuv still living a life of comfort and luxury? Why don't our troops have welfare services like the British "Garrison Club"? Why are many capable and willing people not allowed to contribute to the war effort beyond night watch, vehicular services, and the Civil Guard? Where do you go to volunteer? Why is there no action against draft dodgers, however few they may be?

More cooperation and shared responsibility will assist the military machine, give satisfaction to those willing to work, and lift public morale.

A civil servant: His milieu: Government and municipal workers and professionals: There is willingness to carry the burden, to support the continuous war effort, and to take the initiative despite the sacrifices. There is a feeling that this is the most effective way to shorten the confrontation and to assure victory. Casualties breed anger when there is enemy action after a period of inaction on our part. There is dissatisfaction with disruption of public transportation to downtown and to Tel Aviv, even though it is known that the "third party" is the source of difficulty. Still, it is clear that despite the resentment, there is staunch readiness to continue fighting to the end. An action like the one taken on Friday, February 20,[3] greatly boosted morale.

A municipal official:

A. An extensive Arab attack is expected. The respondent and his
   neighbors have no illusions in this respect, and they are confident
   that this battle will determine whether we live freely or lose our
   liberty. Thus, all agree that sacrifices of both lives and property
   are expected, and they are willing to fight to the bitter end.

B. We need to initiate a military offensive. Our aim should be to
   strengthen the moderates among the Arabs and weaken the
   extremists. Thus, we need to retaliate for every action on their
   part. Only when they are made to pay several times for every
   attack, will we see the moderates take over. An example of such
   an effect is the action that took place on February 20. There
   were four casualties and fifty wounded and that strengthened
   the moderates and weakened the extremists. The flight of the
   Arabs on the following Saturday and Sunday overwhelmed the
   Arab population in Haifa. That attack is unanimously viewed as
   a preemptive measure that will prevent a future attack by the
   enemy.

A doctor in a state hospital: He thinks (and assumes that others around him
share his opinion) that a massive Arab attack is in the offing. He believes we can
withstand the attack, because no withdrawal is possible and negotiation is no
longer an option. He is not sure that we are fully prepared for the assault (for
instance, for hundreds of wounded). Yet he believes in "miracles" and trusts
that at the last moment, the right people will be at the right place because
our youth can do it, if only we train them properly and supply them with the
necessary equipment. He does not dare entertain another option. It is best to
take the initiative, but this requires organization and planning, not just for battles
like the ones we have experienced so far, but for total military warfare.

A construction worker (near the Electric Company and Tnuva dairy
cooperative): He meets about eighty people at work and talks to them during
work and after. His conclusion from these conversations: there is no fear! The
most popular topic among the workers is the operations of the Haganah, their
equipment, and modus operandi. Each new operation is received calmly and
without much excitement. One major topic of conversation these days is the
activity of the Dissidents (Revisionists). Some among the workers support the
Dissenters. As for raising money, it is easier to recruit fighters than donors. Every
drive gives rise to harsh discussions. Eventually, people give, but reluctantly,
because of the high cost of living.

Regarding transportation: At first, there were many complaints, but people now understand that these are the constraints of the situation, and they accept it. They even got used to being shot at on buses. After each incident they ask each other jokingly, "How was it?" then focus on the main issue: How many Arabs got killed? The number of casualties suffered by the enemy is of much interest to the public, even more than the destruction of their positions. The attacks on buses do not deter people from going to work, and most people report to their jobs regularly. One worker remarked that he is reluctant to go to a dangerous place; his boss and colleagues berated him, saying that everyone has to go wherever they are needed if there is an order, and even if there is no specific order, "you still don't abandon your position." Many of his friends work in mixed Arab–Jewish facilities, such as the slaughterhouse. There are places where three Jews work among fifteen Arabs, yet they still don't abandon their jobs. Two days ago, some workers were building a roof when shooting started with bullets flying all around. A cement mixer was blown up. The workers got off the roof and when the shooting stopped, they climbed back and continued working. They were afraid, but they kept working.

A mother of two enlisted sons: She is not afraid. She was not afraid when they fought in World War II, but she was constantly worried. She scans the papers every day fearing she might see her sons' names mentioned. She knows the war will produce casualties and she may be directly affected, but she also recognizes that there is no alternative. It is a struggle of life and death.

A mother, fifty, whose only daughter is a commander in the Galilee: She knows what awaits her. She is expecting news every day, but what can she do?

A mother, whose daughter is in Nir-Am, crying: Why are so few people serving in the Negev? Only 1,500. We don't need so many people here in the city. She, her husband, and her daughter are enlisted, but she knows many families who have not signed up.

A woman whose husband has many guard duties: Why is the burden of guard duty not evenly distributed? Some workers don't guard at all while others serve frequently. Her neighbor sleeps at home every night while her husband goes on guard duty four times a week.

Another woman whose husband is enlisted: There are many tenants in her house, but only a few men go on guard duty. This causes resentment and hurts feelings.

[Subject] No. 20 adds: . . . The population in the Lower Town and the Commercial Center should be better provided for. They are mostly people from Salonica and Sephardic communities that will not be easily relocated. But they complain bitterly of being abandoned by the authorities. Nobody comes to lift their morale; they have no public meetings or places of assembly. Except for soldiers in their outposts, they don't see any official representatives. Why don't they build a supermarket in the area? Or an assembly hall? The same complaint was voiced by Hadassah[4] nurses at the Well Baby Clinics who report to their duty regularly. They mention neglected children.

A wealthy Sephardic merchant: Admits that the London resolution regarding the Palestinian lira[5] is not altogether clear to him, but he trusts that commerce will continue without serious interruptions and that the market will not be shaken.

Two truck drivers: One of them says: We'll go on. I don't deal in high politics. What's my choice? Go back to Poland? I'll continue working wherever I can and make sure I get paid properly.

A taxi driver: Complains that his nerves are shot. The night rides, especially to the harbor area, scare him because they are extremely dangerous. Asked why he agrees to go there at all, he says, What should I do? I can't leave Jews in an Arab neighborhood over night. There's danger lurking. Asked if he charged extra for these rides, he answered that he is no war profiteer. This is a war zone!

Two property owners: They play cards a lot, complain about taxes, and say they would flee if they only knew where to. "It's either win or die, and we don't want to die, so it's better to donate money and win."

Two bank clerks: The public is unshaken. The reaction to the changes in the currency proves it. Anywhere else in the world such upheavals would have lead to panic and speculation, but here the "regular folks" behave decently.

A cleaning lady: What can I say? My son is a soldier, and I work. I wish they would call me up [for military service]. I would wash the feet of our brave boys. Never mind the present difficulties. In six, twelve, or eighteen months, we'll have our own state.

Supplement: The Mood among Immigrants from Central European Countries

Since [s]urveys . . . indicated that there are pessimistic outlooks among people who emigrated from Central Europe, [one of our agents] undertook a special investigation to determine this subject. Here is [the summary of] his report:

> Based on these interviews and my own experience with immigrants from Central Europe, my conclusion is that most of them react with their intellect rather than their feelings. They lack the inner conviction

that comes from a warm Jewish heart. The reason, as we know, is that these Jews were not brought up in close-knit Jewish congregations and did not receive the Zionist or traditional education common in East European Jewry. On the other hand, they are well disciplined, and they share the sense that this war is unavoidable. Moreover, these Jews are used to obeying authority. They believe that we already have a Jewish administration, and will, therefore, be loyal citizens to this regime, just as they were obedient citizens in other foreign regimes under which they lived. The first informant is correct in saying that being less emotional, they are also less given to bouts of depression.

What is the mood in your neighborhood at this stage of the war? (Third report, March 2, 1948)

In the two previous surveys we interviewed seventy subjects who represented scores of other members of the public. In this survey we interviewed thirty more people, including the interviewers themselves who summed up opinions in their immediate environment. Noteworthy themes in this survey are: The mood of the general public is bleak; the main reason is the lack of agreement with the Dissidents and the fear of internecine wars. On the bright side, the actions of the defense forces boost people's morale.

A journalist who interviewed six cab drivers, four small business owners, and three different clerks: The businessmen and the clerks were more disheartened than the laborers because the slump in business is affecting them. Recent attacks by the Haganah (both offensive and defensive strikes) were much appreciated and greatly lifted morale (especially successful was intercepting an explosive device in an Arab garage). These strikes somewhat offset the grim political news from America.[6] On the whole, there is a general sense that "we shall overcome"; except for few cases, the public is not depressed.

Secretary of the Commerce Department: Even though the economic situation is serious, there is no room for panic. His main worry is that we might lose Haifa.

A lawyer: This is a tough question to answer because the mood among our people is volatile — either excessive elation or depression. The news from Lake Success[7] confuses people, and the press with its wild speculations does not help stabilize people's mood. Strikes by our defense forces are the only news that lifts people's spirits. There is also concern about casualties and lack of agreement with the Dissenters. These are the topics that engage people these days.

A butcher's wife, about fifty years old: She has been working hard for many years. In her opinion, the war is just starting, and will doubtless be very hard. She already experiences a slump in business. Her seventeen-year-old son will soon leave the house, making it harder on the family. But she realizes that there are no easy wars. In the Diaspora, we lost our youths in vain; now, at least, we are fighting as a nation (not profiteering from war as Jews did in the past). Everyone must sacrifice both body and soul. She regrets not getting a red card like her son; she would gladly serve. In her estimation, there is some dejection in the public, and it is important to cheer up the simple folks.

A judge: The general opinion is that the Yishuv should depend only on itself. At present, there is a greater sense of security than before and the sense is that, given proper equipment, the Yishuv will be able to triumph without international military aid. Organization in the Yishuv is improving, though it has not yet reached the highest level of efficiency. There is more consolidation of manpower, but many potential forces have not yet found their use, and many good candidates are disqualified for worthless political reasons.

Two merchants (Sephardic) from the city: Morale is low because of inner conflicts and political rifts. This jeopardizes our political future. On the other hand, our economic future is promising and there are good chances that we will come through, provided the conflict does not last more than six to seven months.

Two merchants (Ashkenazi) from the city: Even though one is from Germany and the other from Poland, their views are similar. We have no choice but to fight the Arabs, and the British, if necessary. We have considerable strength in the knowledge that we have no alternative. But if our leaders do not put an end to the internecine fighting, we will soon perish.

A stevedore: The situation is grim, although the port relations with Arabs and Brits are not too bad, but this may last only as long as the fruit season is on; afterwards, matters may worsen considerably.

Postal clerk (war veteran): In his opinion we are quite strong. The Arabs fear us more than we fear them. Two bank managers, who took a leave of absence for more than six months, went overseas claiming that they prefer being jobless than in constant danger. At the post office, relations between Jews and Arabs are quite good. Asked if Jews are leaving their jobs at the post office, he said he does not think his workplace is more dangerous than any other in town. We must suffer until we have a state, and then everything will be fine.

General Impressions: The mood among the dozens of people he talked to is grim. The reason is common to all: most people are willing to withstand a long war with the Arabs, some are even ready to fight the British, if necessary. But the ever-deepening rift with the Dissenters and the fact that we are facing an out-and-out civil war is causing great consternation and despair. The reaction to the "Iron Fund"[8] drive was also interesting; people expected unruly behavior from the Lehi members, but then were pleasantly surprised by their politeness and, consequently, the attitude toward them changed somewhat. One Technical University professor said that he had been prepared to suffer blows and damage to body and property rather than give them a cent, but was then amazed to find that his refusal to donate was not met with rowdy behavior but with respect. It seems that Lehi members knew how to use this good impression for their benefit. If there were instances of improper behavior, they should be made public. Out of dozens asked if they had donated (one pound each), only three said they did. Perhaps there were others who gave, but were ashamed to admit it. A rather strange phenomenon is noted: even though the Dissenters are almost universally condemned, and their damage to national interests stressed, the members of the dissenting organization themselves elicit certain affection.

Interviews reveal that the number of those willing to flee the country for the duration is increasing. The interviewer witnessed a young man falsifying documents in Yiddish for a friend who sought permission from the authorities to leave the country in order to visit his supposedly gravely ill mother.

In this respect, more countermeasures are needed, such as publishing the names of young people trying to leave the country who were taken off the boat. This may deter future deserters. Many buy tickets from Arab or British travel bureaus.

Suggested ways to fight profiteering
[Separate survey of 250 respondents]:

1. Strict control (by supervisors and detectives), checking inventories, fines, imprisonment, publication of offenders' names: seventy-eight respondents.
2. Same as 1 except jail time only for the offenders (fines are paid by consumers . . .): thirty-nine respondents.
3. Same as above plus confiscation of goods and appropriation of business by the state (plus send offenders to the front): thirty-four respondents.
4. Same as above, except both black marketers and customers should pay fines: eleven respondents.
5. Impose rational order on the market, organize the consumers (issue cards, etc.): thirty respondents.
6. Open co-ops across the board: fourteen respondents.

7. Lectures and publicity campaign for Austerity (don't buy on the black market, consume less, etc.): eleven respondents.

8. Shoot black marketers (or, alternatively, hang them): nine respondents.

9. Only open markets and free competition will lower prices: four respondents.

10. There is no way of fighting profiteering (it only makes things worse): eight respondents.

11. No opinion: twelve respondents.

Total: 250
Notes:

1. There are many calls for replacing officials in charge who are riddled with corruption and cannot put an end to it.

2. Many want a specific address where complaints can be lodged, even by phone.

3. Some (especially small businessmen) see big businessmen as the main culprits.

4. Several stevedores see only one solution: beat the hell out of offenders. If only THEY were in charge, everything would be okay . . .

NOTES

1. The term "second phase" refers to the mobilization of soldiers. In December 1947, men between nineteen and twenty-three were ordered to register for service; in February 1948, they were called up to serve on a one-year term. It is likely that the public opinion surveys were done at this time in order to measure the public mood as the Yishuv moved closer to all-out war. Many thanks to Moshe Naor for this information.

2. A euphemism for the British.

3. A major Haganah attack against the offices of the Arab National Committee in Haifa; this is described later in the document.

4. The Women's Zionist Organization of America.

5. On February 20, the Palestinian currency was removed from the global sterling currency union. Palestinian bank holdings in UK banks were frozen.

6. In February the United States government appeared to be moving away from support for the partition of Palestine in favor of a United Nations trusteeship.

7. Seat of the United Nations.

8. A fundraising campaign by the Irgun underground militia.

60

Radio Broadcasts from The Voice of Fighting Zion (1947)

Relations between the Yishuv's Labor Zionist leadership and the Irgun reached a nadir in the winter of 1945. The Yishuv leadership and the militia under its jurisdiction, the Haganah, favored cooperation with the British in the war effort against Nazi Germany. The Irgun, however, had in 1944 declared a revolt against British rule in Palestine and was attacking British forces (see document 54). Over a period of about three months, the Haganah assisted the British in locating hundreds of Irgun members, who were then arrested and often jailed. This period became known as the *saison*, or hunting season, and incurred bitter rage on the part of the Irgun against the Haganah and Yishuv leadership. After a ten-month period of cooperation between the Irgun and the Haganah tensions between the organizations flared again after the Irgun bombed the King David Hotel in Jerusalem on July 22, 1946. This anger was further inflamed in 1947, when Haganah and Irgun forces competed in Europe for control of illegal immigration and for influence over the United Nations' Special Committee on Palestine, which was convened in May.

These radio broadcasts by the Irgun from late 1947 reflect the organization's fury at the military action taken against it and the real possibility of civil war within the Yishuv at this time. They also register the Irgun's fierce resistance to the partition of Palestine and the loss of what they believed to be inalienable Jewish territory to a Palestinian-Arab state.

Source: Transcripts of the Irgun Tsva'i Le'umi be-Eretz Yisra'el, Haganah Archive, Tel Aviv, 20/76. Translated by Marganit Weinberger-Rotman.

A. October 26

The incited rioters continue to run amok in the towns and villages of our country and feed the fires of fratricidal war.

    a. In Rishon Le-Tsion, as in Rehovot, the rioters employed arms against our men, engaged in putting up our notices. Twice our young soldiers withstood the fire without retaliating. But they warned the men of the "sacred arms"[1] that if they continue using them against Jews, disseminating their creed amongst the people, our comrades would be forced to return fire with fire. The rioters persisted in their wanton behavior in an attempt to frighten our men.

    b. Early Friday morning, October 24, our men were again fired on in the southern settlements. Two of our men in Rishon Le-Tsion were wounded; others returned the fire, in defense of their comrades and themselves, against the murderous fire of the attackers. The responsibility for the blood spilt in Rishon Le-Tsion falls on those inciters who *gave the orders* for our men to be shot at.

        During Friday night the incited rioters played havoc in the settlement, made an attempt at kidnapping, and fired into Hebrew homes indiscriminately.

    c. A unit of "shock troops"[2] was dispatched into Benyamina in order to attack the local youth. (The rioters have not enough numbers within the colony itself.) Five youths were attacked with iron rods, axes, and clubs by scores of rioters who were also armed with guns. All five were badly wounded.

    d. In Tel Aviv the rioters—with the help of the manager of the "Atara Café"[3]—set a trap for one of our men. The manager of the café had promised to give us a donation. But that was a wanton lie. When our man arrived at the office of the café he was set upon by five rioters who *tortured him for a whole hour.*

    e. At Bat-Yam one of our men was attacked by tens of rioters who did not desist until they had left him on the road, bleeding and unconscious.

The list of facts is not complete and we hereby announce that we shall not overlook even one of them.

We do not want to clash with the Haganah but in no circumstance will we permit them to interfere with our organization, to shut our mouth, or to attack our comrades. We shall retaliate for every attack and every act of torture. And we shall return fire with fire.

We announce and warn:

We do not want civil war. But it is becoming ever clearer that Ben-Gurion is driving to civil war, wants it, is longing for it.

If Ben-Gurion wants civil war—he shall have it.

We are not to be intimidated by threats. We are not to be overcome by fire or by death. The man does not exist who will succeed in subjugating the comrades of Dov Gruner.[4]

These are days of anxiety for the people. The enemy is weaving his plots. He does not even conceal them. His official representatives and his unofficial commentators say explicitly that we are doomed. They are preparing our destruction.

And in these days Ben-Gurion is preparing an internal bloodbath. He is doing his utmost to bring about armed clashes between groups of Hebrew youth. The arms in his possession were once proclaimed to be "sacred arms," to be used *only* for defense. But with these "defensive arms," bought by good Jews for defense against an enemy, it is permissible and necessary, according to Ben-Gurion, to attack . . . boys pasting up posters and to smash the heads of all those who refuse to submit to the dictatorship of retreat and hysteria.

"We shall speak to them in the only language they understand—the language of force," said Ben-Gurion in one of his oratorical outbursts. You hear these words and are astounded. True, we have always known that Ben-Gurion's mouth is larger than his brain—but that he should underestimate the spirit of his opponent—that we did not expect. Does Ben-Gurion expect to intimidate *us* by force? Has he not seen how others, greater and stronger than he, have not succeeded in overcoming us, neither with threats, nor with torture, nor with the gallows? Did he not himself write to Cunningham[5] that "it is clear that hangings do not frighten the terrorists"?

But Ben-Gurion forgot his "Biltmore"[6] speeches and has also managed to forget his utterances before the head of the oppressive regime. He announced a war of extermination against the "dissidents" because he yearns for a fratricidal war. He believes now is the time for such a war. He must show the world that *he* is the ruler in the Jewish ghetto. He presumes that the masses of the people will look on passively for fear that should he, Ben-Gurion, really become the ruler of the "sovereign" ghetto, he will take revenge on them . . .

But Ben-Gurion is mistaken. Among the many things he has forgotten he's also forgotten who it is that faces him. He's forgotten that the young men who went to Acre, that forced the "Schneller" fortress,[7] wrought havoc within the

British security zones—will not retreat before any force in the world, not even before the Tommy guns and Stens of the "men of defense." This youth does not want a fratricidal war. They were brought up to love their brothers and hate the enemy. But they were also taught *not to surrender under any circumstances.* And should a traitorous hand be raised against them, *they will but it off or die. But they will not surrender. They will never surrender.*

There is no doubt that should Ben-Gurion persist in his lunatic behavior, a fratricidal war—with all its horrors—will break out.

And we warn the masses of the people, at home and in the Diaspora, against this danger.

B. November 19

We have repeatedly warned that the knife that the Jewish Agency [8] put into the hands of foreign nations with which to dissect our homeland, would continue slicing away at it. The miserable partition plan recommended by the UNSCOP [9] became the *Jewish maximum* from which additional slices were to be taken in order to "do justice to the Arabs." And that is just what has happened. During the past weeks we have witnessed one of the most painful and most shameful procedures. Our homeland has become a piece of cloth in the hands of her indifferent traders. They cut here; they slice there. They measure. They compare sizes. Further cuts are made. Jaffa has gone. Beer-Sheba has gone. Part of the Negev has gone.[10] Jerusalem will remain "abroad." There is cut out and comes into shape a "Jewish State" minus 95 percent of all those historic places on which our unalterable claim to this country is based, which for 2,000 years molded its character and became an eternal part in our nation's history.

A caricature comes into being. And the men of the Jewish Agency, who have collaborated in its creation, pretend to be "heroes" fighting for every inch of our homeland and order the people to dance—dance on the *grave* of its independence, on the grave of the hope of once again being reunited in our homeland.

For it is nothing else than deception when the dissectors of our homeland talk of a million and a half new repatriates within a few years. There is not, and there will not be, place for them in a "state" composed of a crowded ghetto; a *tiny* area whose density of population is even now greater than that of the European industrial countries, together with a larger area that has always been waste desert. True, the Negev too is part of our homeland. The Negev too is dear and the peddling of its area, which is being so flippantly conducted by Mr. Shertok,[11] hurts us no less than the peddling of other parts of our country. But it is a fact that the "partitionists" asked for the inclusion of the Negev into the Partition State only for its psychological effect, only so that they might the more easily deceive the people and get them to accept partition, even joyfully. Thousands of square kilometers . . . Our State is not so small . . . We have room for expansion . . . There is room for new settlements . . .

But the truth is—and the partitionists *know it*—that tens of years will pass before it will be possible—if indeed it will ever be—to settle any substantial number of people in the Negev. And in the meantime the pressure of the Return to Zion will continue from the countries of the Diaspora. Hundreds of thousands, maybe even millions, will pound at the gates of the "Jewish State" and Ben-Gurion himself will be forced to lock it—just as the cunning Crossman suggested to Bevin.[12] And we may yet witness a fratricidal war on the shores of our homeland. . . .

But this is not yet the *whole* tragedy. For even for this caricature of a state we shall be forced to pay with *blood*, much blood, with the blood of the best of our sons. And there is no doubt that the blood tax, which will be collected from us in order to enforce *partition*, will be no less that [*sic*] what we would have had to pay for the *liberation of our entire homeland*. And the conclusions to be drawn from these facts are self-evident.

In our comment on the slaughter at Raanana,[13] written immediately after the event and published in yesterday's issue of *Herut*, it was assumed that the informer who brought the gang of Nazo-British murderers to the grove at Raanana was a Jew. Much to our joy it now appears that this assumption was not correct. The informers, who told the British enslaver that the youngsters were training there, were *not* Jews.

We repeat again—Milo Friedlich, a refugee from Rumania aged twenty-six, was one of the four refugees kidnapped by the agents of Ben-Gurion's Gestapo in Europe and was tortured by them for weeks, *until he died*. Milo Friedlich, whose photograph we shall shortly release, was murdered in Grunwald on the Austro-Italian border by sadists who claim that they "serve the nation."[14]

The sadists are—as usual—also despicable cowards. They "deny" the murder and think that their denial is payment enough for their torture and their murder by torture. But they are mistaken. Public opinion—Jewish and non-Jewish—knows what value to place on their announcements and denials. And public opinion will demand the immediate setting up of a public committee of inquiry to go to the DP Camp in Austria, there to uncover the facts and deal with those responsible for the triple crime committed by emissaries of the Haganah.

C. November 23, 1947

With the approaching end of the UNO discussions on Eretz Israel, the criminal lunacy of the acceptance by the Jewish Agency of the country's dissection of the national territory will remain an everlasting political and historic fact, remorselessly pursuing and avenging itself upon our people. Yet its direct, immediate effect will be neither increased repatriation nor real Hebrew rule, but—war, bloody war which will threaten our very existence.

Today, after Cadogan's announcement and Martin's explanations,[15] nobody can doubt any longer that the British are preparing for the *coming months*—and these will be decisive—a bloodbath in Eretz Israel. True, neither of them revealed anything new, but they confirmed finally the warning which we issued immediately after the British declared their intention of evacuating Eretz Israel. They have confirmed that:

a. The British pirates are to continue their blockade on the sea;
b. Neither increased repatriation nor the entry of war material will be permitted;
c. The land frontiers will stand wide open for unlimited penetration by their mercenary forces, whether uniformed or disguised as "partisans" of Qawuqji[16];
d. The Nazo-British forces, imposing their direct rule on all the strategic key positions, will restrict the freedom of movement of the Jewish forces and will even continue to send to concentration camps or to the gallows holders of "illegal" arms.

In these circumstances we shall have to face attacks both frontal and from the rear, and the military aid from UNO, which the partitionists hoped for, will—as we warned—prove to be a mirage, just as the "settlement of millions in the Negev"[17] is a mirage of the desert's sandy wastes.

The threat of war or the necessity to fight it does not, of course, invalidate any political programme for the redemption of our people, just as the prospect or the promise of peace do not make acceptable any plan that frustrates our national aspirations. But this war, which we shall enter, or—to be more precise—into which we are going to be dragged with the hump of partition on our backs—what is its significance and what is its purpose? For there will, after all, be only two possibilities: either a military victory over the Nazo-British enemy's mercenaries or the overwhelming and destruction of our forces. In the second case, even partition upon which UNO may decide will not come into being. In its place there will be *complete* surrender by the Jewish Agency. In its place there will be imposed in full the British plan of enslavement and destruction.

But in the case of victory, which, too, will demand a very heavy price in blood, we should—with the consent of the nations—be able to liberate the *whole* of the country, bringing redemption to our people and *lasting* peace to our homeland. We *should* be able to—but then Nemesis will appear and demand expiation of the crime of those blind "leaders" who undertook before the world to regard Jerusalem and Hebron, Jaffa and Beersheba, the hills of Judea and of Galilee as everlasting *foreign territory*.

Has a people ever faced so cruel an alternative? Has any people on earth ever been dragged into bloody war in which, while defeat means destruction, victory spells defeat?

How the "leaders" have sinned! And the price of their sins and their blindness will be paid by the people both in its blood and in its future. But however clear their guilt may be, it does not alter the fact that we shall, in the coming months, face a decisive British effort to crush us and turn us either into slaves or into lambs for the slaughter.

. . . It is a disgrace, a disgrace to a Hebrew society which prides itself on its progressiveness, a disgrace to the institutions, which have money for everything—especially for employing hundreds of parasites to shadow Hebrew fighters—but which cannot find the means to house completely destitute brothers.

A regime that tolerates such spectacles of poverty as we have seen these last days on the Tel Aviv beach[18] is rotten to its foundations, and no phrases about progress and socialism can cover its rottenness.

This disgrace must be ended. And without delay. If those who have been entrusted with the peace and living conditions of the people do not fulfill their responsibilities—we shall do so. And let them not tell us that the matter does not concern us. It concerns us very much. Those who lie in the cold of the night on the wet sands of the beach are our brothers, children of our people. And we have not shed our blood so that in the Jewish state our children shall go hungry, shivering with cold and boil-ridden. We are devoting our lives for a state in which justice shall be the supreme ruler, and we do not intend to tolerate such a disgrace as that of the Tel Aviv beach.

We say simply: if the city Fathers do not in the next few days find accommodation for the Jaffa refugees, we shall help them find homes. And we shall find them.

NOTES

1. A derisive reference to the Labor Zionist code of *tohar neshek*, or "purity of arms," an ostensible commitment to employ violence only when necessary and without hatred or bloodlust.

2. Palmach fighters. "Shock troops" is a literal translation of *plugot machatz*, from which the acronym "Palmach" is taken.

3. A famous establishment and gathering place for the Yishuv's literati.

4. Irgun fighter, executed with three others by British authorities at Acre prison in April 1947.

5. Sir Alan Cunningham, the last British High Commissioner in Palestine, 1945–48.

6. A conference of Zionist and other Jewish organizations was held at the Biltmore Hotel in New York in May 1942 to discuss the catastrophic situation facing European Jewry. Whereas previously the mainstream Zionist groups had been vague about the precise nature and borders of the desired Jewish national home, the conference clearly called upon the British to establish a Jewish commonwealth in the entirety of Palestine.

7. A British army compound in Jerusalem, taken by Jewish forces in 1948.

8. The Jewish Agency for Palestine was the governing body that linked the Zionist Organization, non-Zionist Jewish philanthropists, and the Yishuv. Its Palestine executive was effectively the government of the Jewish state in the making.

9. The United Nations Special Committee on Palestine convened in May 1947. In September, its majority recommended partitioning Palestine into Jewish and Arab states, with Jerusalem, Bethlehem, and their environs to be under international administration.

10. The partition proposal brought before the UN's General Assembly in November 1947 moved Beersheba and its environs from the Jewish to the Arab states, and made Jaffa into an Arab enclave within the Jewish state.

11. Moshe Sharrett (originally Shertok) (1894–1965) was at this time the head of the Jewish Agency's Political Department, akin to a state's foreign ministry.

12. Richard Crossman was a Labor MP, a Zionist sympathizer, and on the Anglo-American Committee of Inquiry, which recommended in 1946 that 100,000 Jewish refugees in Eruope be allowed to immigrate to Palestine. British foreign minister Ernest Bevin rejected these recommendations.

13. On November 11, British forces killed five Lehi fighters in Ra'anana, northeast of Tel Aviv. (On Lehi see document 56.)

14. Friedlich was working as an Irgun operative in the Austrian–Italian border region, engaged in illegal immigration activities. The Haganah was engaged in illegal immigration work of its own and did not welcome Irgun involvement. Haganah forces kidnapped Friedrich along with three others, but in fact, Friedrich was not killed, as he escaped his captors and eventually reached Palestine.

15. Sir Alexander Cadogan was Britain's representative to the United Nations; M. Martin was the assistant undersecretary of state for the British Colonial Office.

16. Fawzi al-Qawuqji (1890–1977) was a Syrian military commander who fought for a number of Arab nationalist causes. In 1936, while based in Iraq, he headed a band of some two hundred Arab guerillas who took part in the Palestinian Arab revolt but operated independently of the Palestinian guerilla forces. At the beginning of 1948, he returned to Palestine as commander of the multinational Arab Liberation Army.

17. A reference to Ben-Gurion's vision of transforming the Negev into habitable and arable land and settling millions of Jewish immigrants in it.

18. This is a reference to Jewish refugees who fled rioting in Jaffa and became homeless.

61

Deir Yassin (1948)

THE VOICE OF FIGHTING ZION

This document is a transcript of a radio broadcast by the Irgun's broadcasting service that reported on the battle of Deir Yassin, a village on the western outskirts of Jerusalem.

Before 1948 there existed good relations between Deir Yassin and Jewish Jerusalem. In the wake of the United Nation's resolution to partition Palestine into Jewish and Arab states, Palestinians and Jews began to fight, and local Arab forces were joined by units of volunteers from Arab lands. The alleged presence of Arab fighters in Deir Yassin led Etzel and Lehi units to attack the village. The leaders of the Haganah, as well as the leaders of the Jewish Agency, condemned the massacre and lay blame squarely on the rightist underground organizations. However, as this report indicates, units of the Palmach, the Haganah's elite force, joined the Lehi and Etzel fighters in the latter stages of the battle. More recent analysis of the historical records suggests that indeed Haganah fighters took part in the battle.

The massacre of Deir Yassin intensified the already existing sense of fear among the Arab population in Palestine, and historians such as Uri Milstein and Benny Morris have argued that it contributed to the growing numbers of Arabs who fled the country. As the report indicates, at the time, it was believed that during the battle over 240 local Arabs were killed by Jewish military forces. (On April 13, 1948, the *New York Times* reported 254 civilian fatalities). More recent historical accounts by both Arab and Jewish-Israeli scholars suggest that the number was closer to 100.

Source: The Broadcasting Service of Etzel—The National Military Organization in the Land of Israel, April 11, 1948. Haganah Archive, 20/76. Translated by Marganit Weinberger-Rotman.

Fighting units of Etzel and Lehi attacked and occupied the village of Deir Yassin, west of Jerusalem. Deir Yassin was base to a dangerous gang of marauders that harassed the western neighborhoods of Jerusalem with persistent sniping. Intelligence sources reported that reinforcement of Iraqi and Syrian combatants had arrived in the village preparing to attack the western neighborhoods. On Friday night, the 29th of Adar II, 1948, at 2 a.m., our forces, divided into four units, set out for Deir Yassin. When the units arrived at their appointed destinations, the command to attack was given at 4:30 a.m. Despite the heavy enemy fire launched at our forces from fortified positions, our units advanced in military order, stormed, and captured most of the enemy positions. After evacuating the women and children, the barricaded positions were blown up and dozens of enemy combatants were buried under the rubble. During the attack, a loudspeaker urged the women and children to leave the village and seek shelter on the slopes of the mountain. Consequently, many women and children were thus able to save their lives. The battle continued. Two of our armored vehicles advancing into the village were stopped by a ditch [a] meter and half deep. With great effort, under incessant enemy fire, a detail of sappers was finally able to fill the ditch. A house-to-house battle ensued inside the village, until our forces were able to take over the entire village. The surviving irregular combatants, who had fled in panic, barricaded themselves in a house outside the village, on the road to the Castel.[1] In the meantime, a large Arab reinforcement had made its way into the village. A group of irregular combatants came from Ein-Karem[2] and positioned itself on the ridge facing Yefe-Nof,[3] launching intense firepower from heavy machine guns. However, during the shelling, two fully equipped Palmach units joined our forces.

The village of Deir Yassin was captured and is in our hands. Our casualty count: four dead, three seriously injured, twenty-eight suffered light wounds. So far, 240 Arab casualties have been counted. The battle was for every single house in the village. Prisoners were taken.

NOTES

1. A peak in the Judean hills and an Arab village ten kilometers (6 miles) from Jerusalem.

2. An Arab village on the southwestern outskirts of Jerusalem. In 1948, it was captured by Israeli forces and incorporated into Jerusalem.

3. A Jewish neighborhood in western Jerusalem, close to Deir Yassin.

62

The Status Quo Agreements (1947)

Labor and Religious Zionists had a long history of political cooperation. At the 1935 Zionist Congress, Mapai drew the Religious Zionist party Mizrahi into a coalition government by offering support for Sabbath closings in the Yishuv. Relations were more tense, however, between Mapai and the ultra-Orthodox Agudat Yisra'el, which opposed Zionism in principle. During the 1930s and Second World War, many leaders of the Agudah endorsed pragmatic cooperation with the Zionist authorities. As these two documents show, the Holocaust and its aftermath at first weakened, and then strengthened, the Agudah's position vis-à-vis the fledgling Israeli government.

Toward the end of 1946, when a declaration of Jewish statehood was appearing increasingly likely, the Agudah demanded from David Ben-Gurion that the future state follow the dictates of Jewish law, but Ben-Gurion and his allies in the Jewish Agency Executive refused. The first document reproduced here, a letter of June 1947 from the Jewish Agency Executive to the Agudah, is couched in generalities and does not guarantee the maintenance of existing legislation within the Yishuv regarding the public observance of the Sabbath, holidays, and dietary laws, as well as rabbinic control over marriage, burial, and conversion.

The Agudah's position was strengthened in the wake of the 1948 War and Israel's declaration that West Jerusalem, which the United Nations intended to be part of an international trusteeship, would be Israel's capital. The Israeli leadership feared that

Source: Menachem Friedman, "The Structural Foundation for Religio-Political Accommodation in Israel: Fallacy and Reality," in *Israel: The First Decade of Independence*, ed. S. Ilan Troen and Noah Lucas (Albany: State University of New York Press, 1995), 78–81 (Appendices A and B). Used with permission.

protests of ill treatment from the Agudah (whose members were overwhelmingly concentrated in Jerusalem) to the international community might be a public relations disaster. Thus, as shown in the second document, the government offered the Agudah key concessions.

Jewish Agency Executive
to the World Federation of Agudat Yisra'el
(1 Tammuz 5707/June 19, 1947)

Gentlemen:

The Jewish Agency Executive has heard from its Chairman your request to guarantee marital affairs, the Sabbath, education, and *kashrut* in the Jewish state to arise in our day.

As the Chairman of the Executive informed you, neither the Jewish Agency Executive nor any other body in the country is authorized to determine the constitution of the Jewish state-in-the-making in advance. The establishment of the state requires the approval of the United Nations, and this will not be possible unless the state guarantees freedom of conscience for all its citizens and makes it clear that we have no intention of establishing a theocratic state. The Jewish state will also have non-Jewish citizens—Christians and Muslims— and full equal rights for all citizens and the absence of coercion or discrimination in religious affairs or other matters clearly must be guaranteed in advance.

We were pleased to hear that you understand that no body is authorized to determine the state constitution retroactively, and that the state will be free in certain spheres to determine the constitution and regime according to the will of its citizens.

Along with this, the Executive appreciates your demands and realizes that they involve issues of concern not only to members of Agudat Yisra'el but also to many defenders of the Jewish faith, both within the Zionist camps and outside party frameworks, who would understand fully your demand that the Jewish Agency Executive inform you of its position on the issues you raised and stipulate what it is prepared to accomplish regarding your demands on said issues, within the limits of its influence and decision-making powers.

The Jewish Agency Executive has appointed the undersigned to formulate its position on the questions you mentioned in the discussions. We hereby inform you of the Jewish Agency Executive's position:

A. The Sabbath: It is clear that the legal day of rest in the Jewish state will be Saturday, obviously permitting Christians and members of other faiths to rest on their weekly holiday.
B. *Kashrut*: One should use all means required to ensure that every state kitchen intended for Jews will have kosher food.
C. Marital Affairs: All members of the Executive recognize the serious nature of the problem and the great difficulties involved. All bodies represented by the Jewish Agency Executive will do all that can be done to satisfy the needs of the religiously observant on this matter and to prevent a rift in the Jewish People.
D. Education: Full autonomy of every stream in education will be guaranteed (incidentally, this rule applies in the Zionist Association and "*Knesset-Israel*"[1] at present); the Government will take no steps that adversely affect the religious awareness and religious conscience of any part of Israel. The state, of course, will determine the minimum obligatory studies—Hebrew language, history, science, and the like—and will supervise the fulfillment of this minimum, but will accord full freedom to each stream to conduct education according to its conscience and will avoid any adverse effects on religious conscience.

Sincerely,
On behalf of the Jewish Agency Executive
D. Ben-Gurion
Rabbi Y. L. Fishman[2]
Y. Greenbaum[3]

David Ben-Gurion to Rabbi Y. M. Levin[4] (25 Nisan 5709/April 24, 1949)

I enclose herein a summary of our clarifications regarding religious affairs, according to which the present Government will operate:

1. The Sabbath and Jewish holidays will be legal days of rest in Israel according to the law of the State. Non-Jews will have the right to observe their holidays and Sabbaths.
2. Every kitchen opened by the Government for Jews will observe *kashrut*.
3. The State will satisfy public religious needs through national

[bodies], municipalities, and local councils, but there will be no state intervention in religious affairs.

4. Freedom of religion and conscience will be guaranteed. This means that every citizen of the state can preserve his way of observing the customs of his faith, with no coercion on the part of the Government. Obviously, everyone will be guaranteed freedom of conscience regarding his own internal conceptions, on condition that they do not contravene the laws of the state and the rights of others.

5. The legal status of women in the State of Israel will be equal to that of men in all civil, social, state, economic, and cultural affairs. This will also obligate the courts that decide questions of personal status, inheritance, support, etc.

6. This Government will not introduce a law of civil marriage and divorce in the State and the existing law on this matter will be retained.

7. The recognized streams in education will continue to benefit from their autonomous status in the state educational system, according to Chapter 7 of the Government Program approved by the Knesset on 9 Adar of this year.

Rabbi Y. M. Levin to Prime Minister D. Ben-Gurion (27 Nisan 5709/April 26, 1949)

Based on your letter of 25 Nisan, in which you summarized our discussions concerning religious affairs during the formation of the Government—and especially section 5 of this letter, regarding the equal status of women in all respects, I also wish to remind you that at the Government meeting to consider the matter, when you recalled the issue of equal rights for women, I announced that if the rabbis find a way for the proposal not to contravene the laws of Torah, I will assent to it. However, if they oppose it and claim that I must draw the appropriate conclusions, I will have to do so without delay.

NOTES

1. Under the British Mandate, the body politic of the Zionist Yishuv, which elected a national council and representative assembly. The ultra-Orthodox did not belong to Knesset Israel.

2. Rabbi Yehuda Leib Fishman Maimon (1875–1962) was a leader of the Mizrahi Party and its representative on the Jewish Agency Executive.

3. Yitzhak Greenbaum (1879–1970) was the first interior minister of the state of Israel.

4. Rabbi Yitzhak Meir Levin (1893–1971) was the leader of Agudat Yisra'el in Palestine from 1940. He served as minister of welfare from 1948 to 1952, when his party left the government in protest over a law mandating national military service for women. Levin remained in the Knesset, however, until his death.

Glossary

Agudat Yisra'el: political organization of ultra-Orthodox Jews, founded 1912
Ahdut Ha-Avodah: Labor Zionist party, 1919–30
aliyah: "ascent," immigration to the Land of Israel
Betar: Revisionist youth movement, founded 1923
Gedud Ha-Avodah: a labor collective, 1920–29
Haganah: Yishuv militia, founded 1920
Ha-Po'el Ha-Tsa'ir: nonsocialist labor party, founded 1906
Ha-Shomer Ha-Tsa'ir: left-socialist youth movement (founded 1913), kibbutz movement (founded 1927), and political party (founded 1946)
Histadrut: Yishuv-wide trade union, founded 1920
Hovevei Tsion: Lovers of Zion, first international Zionist federation, founded 1884
Irgun Tsva'i Le'umi: right-wing Jewish militia, founded 1931
kibbutz: a large collective agricultural settlement, often with industrial branches
kvutzah: a small collective agricultural settlement
Lehi: see Stern Gang
Mapai: Labor Zionist party that merged Ahdut Ha-Avodah and Ha-Po'el Ha-Tsa'ir, founded 1930
Mizrahi: Religious-Zionist political party, founded 1902
moshav: a smallholders' cooperative agricultural settlement
moshava: a plantation colony
Neturei Karta: extreme ultra-Orthodox group, founded 1938
Palmach: standing military force within the Haganah, founded 1941
Po'alei Tsion: Socialist-Zionist political party, founded 1906
Stern Gang: extremist Jewish militia, founded 1940
Yishuv: Jewish community in pre-1948 Palestine

For Further Reading

GENERAL OVERVIEWS OF THE HISTORY OF ZIONISM,
YISHUV, AND ISRAEL

Almog, Shmuel, Jehuda Reinharz, and Anita Shapira, eds. *Zionism and Religion*. Hanover, N.H.: Brandeis University Press, 1998.

Avineri, Shlomo. *The Makings of Modern Zionism: The Intellectual Origins of the Jewish State*. New York: Basic, 1981.

Brenner, Michael. *Zionism: A Brief History*. Princeton, N.J.: M. Wiener, 2003.

Cohen, Mitchel. *Zion and State: Nation, Class, and the Shaping of Modern Israel*. New York: Columbia University Press, 1992.

Dieckhoff, Alain. *The Invention of a Nation*. New York: Columbia University Press, 2002.

Dothan, Shmuel. *A Land in the Balance: The Struggle for Palestine, 1918–1948*. Tel Aviv: MOD Books, 1993.

Engel, David. *Zionism*. New York: Longman, 2009.

Halpern, Ben. *The Idea of the Jewish State*. 2nd ed. Cambridge, Mass.: Harvard University Press, 1969.

Halpern, Ben, and Jehuda Reinharz. *Zionism and the Creation of a New Society*. New York: Oxford University Press, 1998.

Hertzberg, Arthur. *The Zionist Idea*. Philadelphia: Jewish Publication Society, 1997.

Laqueur, Walter. *A History of Zionism*. New York: Schocken, 1972.

Pappé, Ilan. *A History of Modern Palestine: One Land, Two Peoples*. Cambridge: Cambridge University Press, 2004.

Penslar, Derek. *Israel in History: The Jewish State in Comparative Perspective*. London: Routledge, 2006.

Rabinovich, Itamar, and Jehuda Reinharz, eds. *Israel in the Middle East: Documents and Readings on Society, Politics, and Foreign Relations, pre-1948 to the Present*. 2nd ed. Waltham, Mass.: Brandeis University Press, 2008.

Reinharz, Jehuda, and Anita Shapira, eds. *Essential Papers on Zionism*. New York: New York University Press, 1996.

Sachar, Howard. *A History of Israel: From the Rise of Zionism to Our Time*. New York: Knopf, 2000.

Shimoni, Gideon. *The Zionist Ideology*. Hanover, N.H.: Brandeis University Press, 1995.

Stein, Leslie. *The Hope Fulfilled: The Rise of Modern Israel*. Westport, Conn.: Praeger, 2003.

Troen, S. Ilan. *Imagining Zion: Dreams, Designs, and Realities in a Century of Zionist Settlement*. New Haven, Conn.: Yale University Press, 2003.

GENERAL WORKS ON THE ARAB–ISRAELI CONFLICT

Bickerton, Ian J., and Carla L. Klausner. *A Concise History of the Arab–Israeli Conflict*. 4th ed. Upper Saddle River, N.J.: Prentice Hall, 2002.

Dowty, Alan. *Israel/Palestine*. Malden, Mass.: Polity, 2005.

Laqueur, Walter, and Barry Rubin, eds. *The Israel–Arab Reader: A Documentary History of the Middle East Conflict*. New York: Penguin, 2008.

Morris, Benny. *Righteous Victims: A History of the Zionist–Arab Conflict, 1881–1999*. New York: Knopf, 1999.

Shlaim, Avi. *The Iron Wall: Israel and the Arab World*. New York: Norton, 2000.

Smith, Charles D. *Palestine and the Arab–Israeli Conflict*. 4th ed. New York: St. Martin's, 2004.

Tessler, Mark. *A History of the Israeli–Palestinian Conflict*. Bloomington: Indiana University Press, 1994.

BIOGRAPHIES OF MAJOR ZIONIST AND YISHUV FIGURES

Avineri, Shlomo. *Arlosoroff*. New York: Grove, 1989.

Bilski Ben-Hur, Raphaella. *Every Individual a King: The Social and Political Thought of Ze'ev Vladimir Jabotinsky*. Washington, D.C.: B'nai B'rith, 1993.

Katz, Shmuel, *Lone Wolf: A Biography of Vladimir (Ze'ev) Jabotinsky*. Fort Lee, N.J.: Barricade Books, 1996.

Kornberg, Jacques, *Theodor Herzl: From Assimilation to Zionism*. Bloomington: Indiana University Press, 1993.

Pawel, Ernst. *The Labyrinth of Exile: A Life of Theodor Herzl*. New York: Farrar, Straus and Giroux, 1989.

Porat, Dina. *The Fall of a Sparrow: The Life and Times of Abba Kovner*. Stanford, Calif.: Stanford University Press, 2010.

Reinharz, Jehuda. *Chaim Weizmann: The Making of a Zionist Leader*. New York: Oxford University Press, 1985.

———. *Chaim Weizmann: The Making of a Statesman*. New York: Oxford University Press, 1993.

Shapira, Anita. *Berl: The Biography of a Socialist Zionist*. Cambridge: Cambridge University Press, 1984.

———. *Yigal Allon, Native Son: A Biography*. Philadelphia: University of Pennsylvania Press, 2008.

Sheffer, Gabriel. *Moshe Sharett*. New York: Oxford University Press, 1995.

Teveth, Shabtai. *Ben-Gurion: The Burning Ground, 1886–1948*. Boston: Houghton-Mifflin, 1987.

Zipperstein, Steven J. *Elusive Prophet: Ahad Ha-Am and the Origins of Zionism*. Berkeley: University of California Press, 1993.

THE ZIONIST MOVEMENT AND THE YISHUV
UP TO WORLD WAR I

Aaronsohn, Ran. *Rothschild and Early Jewish Colonization*. New York: Rowman and Littlefield, 2000.

Berkowitz, Michael. *Zionism and West European Jewry before the First World War*. Cambridge: Cambridge University Press, 1993.

Karlinsky, Nahum. *California Dreaming: Ideology, Society and Technology in the Citrus Industry of Palestine, 1890–1939*. Albany: State University of New York Press, 2005.

Katz, Yossi. *The Battle for the Land: The History of the Jewish National Fund before the Establishment of the State of Israel*. Jerusalem: Magnes, 2005.

Levine, Mark. *Overthrowing Geography: Jaffa, Tel Aviv, and the Struggle for Palestine, 1880–1948*. Berkeley: University of California Press, 2005.

Luz, Ehud. *Parallels Meet: Religion and Nationalism in the Early Zionist Movement, 1882–1904*. Philadelphia: Jewish Publication Society, 1993.

Penslar, Derek J. *Zionism and Technocracy: The Engineering of Jewish Settlement in Palestine, 1870–1918*. Bloomington: Indiana University Press, 1991.

Salmon, Yosef. *Zionism and Religion: First Encounters*. Jerusalem: Magnes, 2002.

Shafir, Gershon. *Land, Labor and the Origins of the Israeli–Palestinian Conflict, 1882–1914*. Cambridge: Cambridge University Press, 1988.

Shilo, Margalit. *Princess or Prisoner? Jewish Women in Jerusalem, 1840–1914*. Waltham, Mass.: Brandeis University Press, 2003.

Vital, David. *The Origins of Zionism*. Oxford: Clarendon Press, 1975.

———. *Zionism: The Formative Years*. Oxford: Clarendon Press, 1982.

———. *Zionism: The Crucial Phase*. Oxford: Clarendon Press, 1987.

THE YISHUV AND THE ZIONIST MOVEMENT
UNDER THE BRITISH MANDATE

See the books by Nahum Karlinsky, Yossi Katz, and Mark Levine above, as well as:

Berkowitz, Michael. *Western Jewry and the Zionist Project, 1914–1933*. Cambridge: Cambridge University Press, 1997.

Bernstein, Deborah, ed. *Pioneers and Homemakers: Jewish Women in Pre-State Israel*. Albany: State University of New York Press, 1992.

Biger, Gideon. *An Empire in the Holy Land: Historical Geography of the British Administration in Palestine, 1917–1929*. New York: St. Martin's, 1994.

El-Eini, Roza. *Mandated Landscape: British Imperial Rule in Palestine, 1929–1948*. London: Routledge, 2006.

Horowitz, Dan, and Moshe Lissak. *Origins of Israeli Polity in Palestine*. Chicago: University of Chicago Press, 1978.

Kamen, Charles. *Little Common Ground: Arab Agriculture and Zionist Settlement in Palestine, 1920–1948*. Pittsburgh: University of Pittsburg Press, 1991.

Kaplan, Eran. *The Jewish Radical Right: Revisionist Zionism and Its Ideological Legacy*. Madison: University of Wisconsin Press, 2005.

Liskhovsky, Assaf. *Law and Identity in Mandate Palestine*. Chapel Hill: University of North Carolina Press, 2006.

Makovsky, Michael. *Churchill's Promised Land: Zionism and Statecraft*. New Haven, Conn.: Yale University Press, 2007.

Near, Henry. *The Kibbutz Movement: A History*. 2 vols. London: Littman Library, 1992–97.

Segev, Tom. *One Palestine, Complete: Jews and Arabs under the British Mandate*. New York: Metropolitan Books, 2000.

Shavit, Yaakov. *Jabotinsky and the Revisionist Movement, 1925–1948*. London: Frank Cass, 1988.

Stein, Kenneth. *The Land Question in Palestine, 1917–1939*. Chapel Hill: University of North Carolina Press, 1984.

Sternhell, Zeev. *The Founding Myths of Israel: Nationalism, Socialism and the Making of the Jewish State*. Princeton, N.J.: Princeton University Press, 1998.

Wasserstein, Bernard. *The British in Palestine: The Mandatory Government and the Arab–Jewish Conflict, 1917–1929*. London: Royal Historical Society, 1978.

ZIONIST CULTURE

Almog, Oz. *The Sabra: The Creation of a New Jew*. Berkeley: University of California Press, 2000.

Chaver, Yael. *What Must Be Forgotten: The Survival of Yiddish in Zionist Palestine*. Syracuse, N.Y.: Syracuse University Press, 2004.

Diamond, James S. *Homeland or Holy Land? The "Canaanite" Critique of Israel*. Bloomington: Indiana University Press, 1986.

Harshav, Benjamin. *Language in Time of Revolution*. Berkeley: University of California Press, 1993.

Mann, Barbara. *A Place in History: Modernism, Tel Aviv, and the Creation of Jewish Urban Space*. Stanford, Calif.: Stanford University Press, 2006.

Myers, David N. *Re-inventing the Jewish Past: European Jewish Intellectuals and the Zionist Return to History*. New York: Oxford University Press, 1995.

Saposnik, Arieh Bruce. *Becoming Hebrew: The Creation of a Jewish National Culture in Ottoman Palestine*. New York, Oxford University Press, 2008.

Shavit, Yaakov, and Shoshana Sitton. *Staging and Stagers in Modern Jewish Palestine: The Creation of Festive Lore in a New Culture, 1882–1948*. Detroit, Mich.: Wayne State University Press, 2004.

Stanislawski, Michael. *Zionism and the Fin de Siècle: Cosmopolitanism and Nationalism from Nordau to Jabotinsky*. Berkeley: University of California Press, 2001.

Zakim, Eric. *To Build and Be Built: Landscape, Literature, and the Construction of Israeli Identity*. Philadelphia: University of Pennsylvania Press, 2006.

Zerubavel, Yael. *Recovered Roots: Collective Memory and the Making of Israeli National Tradition*. Chicago: University of Chicago Press, 1998.

JEWISH-ARAB CONFLICT AND ZIONIST RESPONSES

Ben-Eliezer, Uri. *The Making of Israeli Militarism*. Bloomington: Indiana University Press, 1998.

Cohen, Hillel. *Army of Shadows: Palestinian Collaboration with Zionism, 1917–1948*. Berkeley: University of California Press, 2008.

Eyal, Gil. *The Disenchantment of the Orient: Expertise in Arab Affairs and the Israeli State*. Stanford, Calif.: Stanford University Press, 2006.

Gelber, Yoav. *Jewish–Transjordanian Relations, 1921–1948*. London: Frank Cass, 1977.

Khalidi, Rashid. *Palestinian Identity: The Construction of Modern National Consciousness*. New York: Columbia University Press, 1997.

———. *The Iron Cage: The Story of the Palestinian Struggle for Statehood*. Boston: Beacon, 2006.

Kimmerling, Baruch, and Joel Migdal. *Palestinians: The Making of a People*. Cambridge, Mass.: Harvard University Press, 1993.

Lockman, Zachary. *Comrades and Enemies: Arab and Jewish Workers in Palestine, 1906–1948*. Berkeley: University of California Press, 1996.

Luz, Ehud. *Wrestling with an Angel: Power, Morality, and Jewish Identity*. New Haven, Conn.: Yale University Press, 2003.

Mattar, Phillip. *The Mufti of Jerusalem: Al-Hajj Amin al-Husayni and the Palestinian National Movement*. New York: Columbia University Press, 1988.

Shapira, Anita. *Land and Power: The Zionist Resort to Force, 1881–1948*. New York: Oxford University Press, 1992.

THE HOLOCAUST, ILLEGAL IMMIGRATION, AND THE YISHUV

Bauer, Yehuda. *From Diplomacy to Resistance: A History of Jewish Palestine, 1939–1945*. Philadelphia: Jewish Publication Society, 1970.

Halamish, Aviva. *The Exodus Affair: Holocaust Survivors and the Struggle for Palestine*. Syracuse, N.Y.: Syracuse University Press, 1998.

Heller, Joseph. *The Stern Gang: Ideology, Politics, and Terror, 1940–1949*. London: Frank Cass, 1995.

Porat, Dina. *The Blue and the Yellow Stars of David: The Zionist Leadership and the Holocaust, 1939–1945*. Cambridge, Mass.: Harvard University Press, 1990.

Segev, Tom. *The Seventh Million: Israel and the Holocaust*. New York: Hill and Wang, 1993.

Teveth, Shabtai. *Ben-Gurion and the Holocaust*. New York: Harcourt, Brace, 1996.

Zertal, Idith. *From Catastrophe to Power: Holocaust Survivors and the Emergence of Israel*. Berkeley: University of California Press, 1998.

THE 1948 WAR

Cohen, Michael J. *Palestine and the Great Powers, 1945–1948*. Princeton, N.J.: Princeton University Press, 1982.

Milstein, Uri. *History of the War of Independence*. 2 vols. Lanham, Md.: University Press of America, 1996–1997.

Morris, Benny. *The Birth of the Palestinian Refugee Problem Revisited*. Cambridge: Cambridge University Press, 2006.

———. *1948: The First Arab–Israeli War*. New Haven, Conn.: Yale University Press, 2008.

Karsh, Efraim. *Palestine Betrayed*. New Haven, Conn.: Yale University Press, 2010.

Pappé, Ilan. *Britain and the Arab–Zionist Conflict, 1948–1951*. New York: St. Martin's Press, 1988.

———. *The Making of the Arab–Israeli Conflict, 1947–1951*. London: I. B. Tauris, 1992.

Rogan, Eugene L., and Avi Shlaim, eds. *The War for Palestine: Rewriting the History of 1948*. Cambridge: Cambridge University Press, 1988, 2001.

Segev, Tom. *1949: The First Israelis*. New York: Free Press, 1985

Tal, David. *War in Palestine, 1948: Strategy and Diplomacy*. London: Routledge, 2004.